northern protestants
an unsettled people

NEW UPDATED EDITION

Susan McKay

THE
BLACKSTAFF
PRESS
BELFAST

Grateful acknowledgement is made to: Alfred A. Knopf for an extract from *The Last September* by Elizabeth Bowen Copyright © 1929, 1952 by Elizabeth Bowen, reprinted by permission of Alfred A. Knopf, a Division of Random House Inc.; Blackstaff Press and the Estate of John Hewitt for permission to reprint 'Coasters' (extract) by John Hewitt from *The Collected Poems of John Hewitt* (ed. Frank Ormsby) (1991); Curtis Brown Limited for an extract from *The Last September* Copyright © 1929 by Elizabeth Bowen, reproduced by permission of Curtis Brown Limited, London; Gallery Press and the author for kind permission to reprint 'Glengormley' (extract) by Derek Mahon from *Collected Poems* (1999); Faber and Faber Limited and the author for permission to reprint 'Desertmartin' (extract) by Tom Paulin from *Liberty Tree* (1983); Jonathan Cape and the author for permission to reprint 'Poppies' (extract) by Michael Longley from *The Ghost Orchid* (1995); Peters, Fraser and Dunlop Group and the author for permission to reprint 'Wounds' (extract) by Michael Longley from *Poems 1963–1983* (1991); Secker and Warburg and the author for permission to reprint 'Wounds' (extract) by Michael Longley from *Poems 1963–1983* (1991); Wake Forest University Press and the author for permission to reprint 'Poppies' (extract) by Michael Longley from *The Ghost Orchid* (1995).

First published in May 2000 by
Blackstaff Press

Reprinted May 2000, June 2000,
July 2000, November 2000 (twice), 2002

This edition published in 2005 by
Blackstaff Press
4c Heron Wharf, Sydenham Business Park
Belfast BT3 9LE, Northern Ireland

Susan McKay has asserted her right under the
Copyright, Designs and Patents Act 1988 to be identified as
the author of this work.

Typeset by Techniset Typesetters, Newton-le-Willows, Merseyside (2000)
and CJWT Solutions, Newton-le-Willows, Merseyside (2005)

Printed in England by Cromwell Press

A CIP catalogue record for this book
is available from the British Library

ISBN 0-85640-771-2

www.blackstaffpress.com

to Mike

CONTENTS

ACKNOWLEDGEMENTS

My thanks to all those who helped me write this book, particularly all the people who agreed to be interviewed, trusting me to represent them fairly. I hope they will feel I have done so. Some interviews did not make it into the book, but I still benefited greatly from talking to those who gave them. For a variety of reasons, some people asked me not to use their real names. In such cases, the interviewee is introduced using a first name only, and details of his or her background have been changed.

I am grateful to Margaret and Laurence Martin, Philomena and Justin Morgan and the late Rosemary Nelson for inspiring me with their bravery in the face of terrible things.

My thanks to those who encouraged and advised me at various stages. Fionnuala O Connor, Póilín Ní Chiaráin, John Gray, Eilis Rooney, David Dunseith and Vinnie McCormack applied their sharp minds to drafts of various chapters, and Brian Feeney was particularly generous with his time and vast historical knowledge. Yvonne Murphy and Ciaran Crossey, keepers of the Linen Hall Library's political collection, Kathleen Bell, librarian at the *Irish News*, and Paul O'Connor of the Pat Finucane Centre were always helpful. Thanks also to Kelvin Boyes and Inez McCormack. Hilary Bell was a most encouraging and insightful editor, and it has been a pleasure to work with the great women at Blackstaff Press.

I could not have written the book without the generous financial support of the Joseph Rowntree Charitable Trust, and Stephen Pittam's enthusiasm for the project was inspiring.

My parents, Joan and Russell McKay, have been unfailingly supportive. My daughters, Madeleine and Caitlin, have kept me happy. Above all, my thanks to Mike Allen for his love and support, and for looking after me.

Border Turtle, 2002
DERMOT SEYMOUR

INTRODUCTION

to the 2005 edition

A small, headless Orangeman holding a band-stick stands on top of a giant, dying turtle, the curved back of the turtle suggesting a small hill. The small hill is that of Drumcree, in fact, which came into the mind of the painter, Dermot Seymour, when he was in Mexico. After visiting a beach that was covered with dead and dying turtles, he went into an Internet café in a nearby town and looked up the Northern Ireland news. It was all about Drumcree, he said. And so 'Border Turtle' was painted, in 2003. A year later, it was shown in the mid-Ulster town of Portadown, as part of a retrospective of Seymour's work entitled 'The Bloated Inability to Eat Flags'.

The exhibition was held in a gallery within sight of St Mark's Church, scene of so many fervent rallies in support of the Orangemen at Drumcree, and just around the corner from the Carlton Street Orange Hall, where journalists used to be briefed about impending doom if the Orangemen didn't get their way. The exhibition also included 'Beyond Bovine Testicular Union', which showed two loyalist bandsmen sitting on a red, white and blue kerb, apparently oblivious to the fact that the Queen's Highway down which they are no doubt planning to walk is about to teeter off into the void.

The gallery, in the Millennium Court Arts Centre, is new and handsome and full of light. It opened in 2003, and runs an eclectic mix of contemporary art exhibitions, creative writing groups, theatre, concerts, readings, and events for children. There was no public outcry about any of the unflattering depictions of loyalist life in Seymour's exhibition. In the 1990s, the unionist-dominated Lisburn Borough Council had decided that his painting 'Arise, O Great Zimbabwe' was not suitable for unsupervised viewing. It was locked in a private room and anyone wishing to see it had to ask permission.

During the heyday of Drumcree, Portadown fairly crackled with paranoia, and offence might well have been taken over Seymour's paintings. True, during the exhibition, someone scrawled UVF [Ulster Volunteer Force] on four of the canvases. True, Democratic Unionist Party members of Craigavon Borough Council objected to an exhibition of another artist's work in 2004 at the Millennium Court Arts Centre. This consisted of a series of large panels on which the Good Friday Agreement (also known as the Belfast Agreement) was printed. However, the Council did agree to continue funding the centre. The mood in Portadown has changed.

Soon after *Northern Protestants* was first published, in 2000, the satirical website *Portadown News* advertised that the author of 'Norn Prods – A Shower of Bastards' would be reading from the book in the town. 'Come early as security is expected to be heavy,' it advised. In 2005, I did read from the book in Portadown, and I read about Drumcree. I was nervous, but the event, at the Millennium Court, was well attended, the discussion civil.

Drumcree has run its course. It isn't resolved, but old Harold Gracey, the Orange Order's district grand master, is dead, and the supporters of the parade no longer defend their cause so fiercely. As far as the wider Protestant population is concerned, the Orange Order went too far. In 2000, loyalist mass murderer Johnny Adair came to the mid-Ulster town of Portadown with a hundred or so of his Ulster Defence Association thugs. Along with their allies in the Loyalist Volunteer Force, they marched up and down the hill at Drumcree with Orangemen in sashes. Lest anyone be in any doubt as to what they represented they wore 'UDA – simply the best' T-shirts. At night, there were gun salutes for the television cameras in the fields.

Orangeism was disgraced. There was no way it could distance itself from this, in the way it had tried to distance itself from the dozen or so murders which were related to events at Drumcree. There have been no huge confrontations at Drumcree since then.

The BBC's Kate Adie no longer attends. Portuguese and Latvian people have come to work in local factories and have been allocated houses on the Garvaghy Road. Breandán Mac Cionnaith, the spokesman for the nationalist residents of the Garvaghy Road, has got a job with Sinn Féin.

Portadown's business community has flourished in the absence of the annual July showdown. The car parks are full at shopping centres packed with the most expensive of international goods. According to David Armstrong, the editor of the local paper, the *Portadown Times*, the town has the largest number of private houses being built anywhere in Northern Ireland. In some parts of town, the paramilitaries still hold sway, but Portadown is no longer always a byword for bad news.

The UK general elections in the spring of 2005 brought evidence of dramatic political change too, when the leader of the Ulster Unionist Party, David Trimble, spectacularly lost his Upper Bann seat in the House of Commons at Westminster to the DUP's David Simpson. Simpson, the wealthy owner of a local meat plant, sings gospel in the style of Willie McCrea (more Daniel O'Donnell than Sam Cooke) and was mayor of Craigavon in the run up to the elections. Plenty of smiling photos in the press – kissing of babies, kissing of pensioners, opening of businesses.

All over the North, the UUP was decimated in the elections. It lost seats in South Belfast, South Antrim, Upper Bann, and East Antrim, the area Roy Beggs, interviewed in this book, had held for the UUP for more than twenty years. It had already lost Lagan Valley when Jeffrey Donaldson defected to the DUP in 2003, and had lost four seats in 2001, three of them to the DUP. Fermanagh–South Tyrone was lost to Sinn Féin in 2001 and they held onto it in 2005. The 2003 Northern Ireland Assembly elections saw the DUP overtake the UUP as the largest unionist party. (At the same time, Sinn Féin surged ahead of the Social and Democratic Labour Party.)

On 6 May 2005 the victorious DUP leader Reverend Ian Paisley came to the count at Banbridge Leisure Centre to celebrate the defeat of his rival for the leadership of unionism. His supporters roared and bashed Lambeg drums while Trimble spoke of his bitter disappointment. Trimble resigned as UUP leader within days. Asked later if he felt sorry for Trimble, Paisley replied, as is his wont, 'No'. He claimed Trimble owed his earlier success to him and had only himself to blame for his downfall. 'I held him by the hand in Portadown. I was the kingmaker,' he said.

This was a reference to the notorious moment of triumphalism the pair shared at Drumcree in 1995 when the Royal Ulster Constabulary changed its ruling and allowed the parade to go ahead. Trimble insisted there had been 'no compromise' with local nationalists. This, according to Paisley, was how to lead unionism. He said it on 12 July 2004, as he'd been saying it for nearly half a century before: 'No compromise, no sell-out and no surrender.' The DUP had defined itself as representing 'traditional unionism', while the UUP represented 'pushover unionism'. Using one of his favourite metaphors, Paisley said 'the spirit of Trimbleism must be buried in a tomb from which there is no resurrection'.

What went wrong with the brave new Northern Ireland of 1998, when the Good Friday Agreement heralded the opening of an assembly at Stormont in which power was to be shared by nationalists and unionists; when Catholics applauded the emergence of the Progressive Unionist Party from a paramilitary army that had carried out hundreds of sectarian murders? Too much went wrong to be covered in this brief introduction. However, among northern Protestants, it is clear that what happened was a gradual but ultimately dramatic decline in support for the Agreement, and perhaps even for the idea of power-sharing.

In 2000, when this book was first published, I wrote that half of Protestant voters appeared to have supported the Agreement, while half opposed it. Three years later, the Assembly collapsed when unionists withdrew over allegations that Sinn Féin was involved in spying. Two years after that, unionists have voted overwhelmingly for the party that vowed to 'smash' the Agreement.

The DUP has played its politics cleverly, though. When the Assembly was set up, the party denounced it but took its seats and its ministries and worked hard in its various committees. Paisley even went on a fact-finding trip to the hardline fishing village of Portavogie with an agriculture committee that included Sinn Féin's Francie Molloy. Local loyalists came out in protest.

The UUP, on the other hand, was split from the start. When Trimble signed up for the Agreement in 1998, Jeffrey Donaldson walked out. Trimble quickly focused on demanding Irish Republican Army decommissioning, under the slogan 'no guns, no government'. There was bare cordiality with the SDLP, none with Sinn Féin. The first handshake with Gerry Adams came late, and behind closed doors. Infamously, Trimble once said of the party with which he shared power, 'these folks ain't house-trained yet'.

Donaldson, backed by David Burnside and others, went on to mount a series of challenges to the pro-Agreement leadership of the party. Although Trimble survived, he did so not by arguing that the Agreement was good for unionism but by trying to seem as hardline as his opponent, claiming after one bitter showdown that the only difference was one of tactics. In his farewell speech of 2005 he said he had 'unambiguously endeavoured' to implement the Agreement. It had not seemed so. It seemed that, like many Protestant voters, Trimble had been at best 'Agreement acquiescent'. Many thousands of unionists who had been motivated to come out and vote in 1998 did not come out again.

It is said that the younger generation in the DUP, meaning the men in their fifties, want to do a deal to restore Stormont. There is much talk, in the media, of their 'pragmatism'. In December 2004, the DUP and Sinn Féin were supposedly on the verge of reaching such a deal. The IRA would decommission all its weapons. The DUP would share power. The deal faltered over demands by the DUP that the IRA's decommissioning be filmed and photographed.

Then Paisley and his son, Ian Junior, appeared at an event in Ballymena at which the party leader declared that 'the IRA needs to be humiliated ... they need to wear their sackcloth and ashes, not in a back room but openly'. No photographs, no deal, said the DUP. Sinn Féin leader Gerry Adams replied that the IRA would not be humiliated, and that the deal was off. 'Dead and gone and buried in Ballymena.' Within weeks, a huge bank robbery in Belfast was attributed to the IRA, and soon after that, IRA men murdered a Catholic man, Robert McCartney, outside a pub in the city. These events led to huge opprobrium for the Republican movement. It was seen to have humiliated itself. Paisley was seen to have been vindicated.

During the 2005 election campaign the UUP attempted to embarrass the DUP by revealing that senior figures in that party had been flown to Dublin in the private plane of a southern businessman to attend a dinner. The revelation did Paisley's party no damage whatsoever. The DUP is happy to be seen to cultivate potentially lucrative links with the Republic, and indeed has enjoyed an increasingly cordial relationship with its government. The Republic's Minister for Justice, Michael McDowell, is so good at fulminating against Sinn Féin and the IRA that Paisley urged the British government to take a leaf from his book. 'You couldn't ask for better,' he said. The Taoiseach, Bertie Ahern, speaks in his matey way of doing business with 'Ian'.

Maverick UK unionist Bob McCartney lost his North Down seat to Lady Sylvia Hermon of the UUP in 2001. In 2005, after talks with the DUP, he agreed not to stand, in order to maximise the chances of Peter Weir taking the seat. He claimed to have been reassured by Peter Robinson that the DUP would not contemplate going into government with Sinn Féin 'for a generation'. It was James Molyneaux, the anti-Agreement former leader of the UUP, who introduced the idea of a lengthy 'decontamination period'. Paisley has said, variously, 'Never', and 'once there are no arms and no crime'. After his first meeting with British Prime Minister Tony Blair following the 2005 elections, Paisley emerged from 10 Downing Street to say that the Good Friday Agreement was 'dead'. It was 'time for a new beginning'. The DUP wants to be seen to have defeated the IRA. In the meantime, direct rule is perfectly fine, with nine MPs in the House of Commons.

Hermon did, in fact, hold her North Down seat in 2005, the sole UUP candidate to do so. She considered standing for the leadership of the party, and spoke of her 'Presbyterian conviction of duty to others and service, of letting one's light shine'. On the other hand, she spoke of her husband's illness, and of marriage vows to care for him 'in sickness and in health'. Party colleagues were dismissive of her success and her ambitions. David McNarry said she was a maverick. David Burnside said she was a 'wishy-washy liberal' and – with no sense of irony, given that he'd lost his own seat – that she lacked 'presence in the House of Commons'. What was not said, but went without saying, was that she was neither a man nor an Orangeman. In the end, she declined to stand.

The fact that McNarry and Burnside were both seen as potential contenders for the UUP leadership was indicative of the ongoing strife within the party. McNarry is meant to be pro-Agreement. Burnside told me that if the price of Stormont was having Sinn Féin in the executive, 'I'd close Stormont. We don't need them about the place.' He favours a merger with the DUP 'post-Trimble and post-Paisley'. One down, but he might need to remember that in 2003, Paisley said after rumours of his ill health, 'They say that I am dying. It takes a long time to die.'

'Temporary borders soon harden into permanence,' said Winston Churchill – and in the twenty-first century Northern Ireland is still erecting temporary borders. Peacelines have been built, heightened and fortified along 'interfaces' in working-class areas of Belfast, while elsewhere, in villages and towns, estates are more and more characterised by being entirely Catholic or entirely Protestant. Much of this is the work of loyalist paramilitaries. Since this book's publication in 2000, John Grugg Gregg, interviewed in the North Belfast chapter, has been murdered, during another bloody loyalist feud. He was one of the UDA's six 'brigadiers'. Johnny Adair's faction was blamed. Some of his key allies fled to England and Adair followed as soon as he was released from prison.

Since then, the UDA has been promising to clean up its act. The notion is that it has lost its way and strayed into gangsterism and criminality; that it needs to get back to its traditional values. (God forbid – a return to the good old days of killing Catholics for Ulster.) Under the 'John Gregg initiative' it 'stood down' another 'brigadier', Jim 'Doris Day' Gray, for allegedly drug dealing. The Assets Recovery Agency, headed by former deputy chief constable Alan McQuillan, has seized various gentlemen's residences, complete with riding paddocks and security lights. The loyalists, too, have overcome their scruples about the grey skies of the Irish Republic – some have acquired property in booming Dublin.

Intimidation against Catholic families in mainly Protestant areas is still rife. In one incident, in 2003, a young Catholic woman living in a tiny mixed enclave in North Belfast, opened her front door one morning to find her daughter's pet cat dead on the step. Its paws and tail had been cut off. 'Taigs out' was written on a wall across the way. She moved out. The loyalists responsible were from Glenbryn, a small estate on the edge of the largely nationalist Ardoyne. In 2001, Glenbryn residents set up a blockade of the Catholic Holy Cross primary school. They hurled sectarian abuse and bags of urine at four-year-old girls and their parents, and a blast bomb at police separating them from the children.

Afterwards, the Office of the First Minister and Deputy First Minister (OFMDFM) launched an initiative to assess the needs of the nationalist and loyalist communities in the area. The lack of community infrastructure made it difficult to work in Glenbryn. James Leslie, then a junior minister in the Assembly, said that what was needed in Glenbryn was 'unskilled jobs'.

The DUP constantly reinforced its followers' sense of grievance. The Agreement had been good for Catholics, it said, bad for Protestants. However, in a New Year's message for 2004, Peter Robinson struck a different note. 'A new spirit exists within unionism,' he said. 'Buoyed up with a confidence and boldness that has been absent for a generation, unionists can get up off their knees and meet their adversaries with self-belief and assurance. We have for years been demonised and wronged. Everything British, unionist, loyalist or Orange has been despised.' But, he concluded, 'The worm has turned.'

It is hard to see how this vision of unionists as a 'risen people' can really change life in Protestant ghettos like Glenbryn or Carnany in Ballymoney. The DUP is socially conservative. It supports the retention of the grammar-school system of education, for example, even though just 3 per cent of working class Protestants pass the notorious 11-plus entrance examination. Peter Weir told me a few years ago that the DUP knew that plenty of people voted for it who wouldn't admit the fact. 'They want to seem more respectable,' he said.

However, the DUP has broken that barrier now. It accommodates bankers and barristers and teachers and architects along with its traditional rural and working-class base. Like the old pre-Troubles

Unionist Party, and the Orange Order, it unites the classes without disrupting the social order. The DUP does not challenge the notion of knowing your place. Like the Orange Order, it is still essentially a defensive organisation based on the idea of ethnic solidarity. Some of its leading advisors are former members of the British Conservative Party. On moral issues, the DUP still favours the biblical approach. Ian Paisley Junior said in 2005 that most people in Northern Ireland rergarded homosexual relationships as 'immoral, offensive and obnoxious'. There will be no revolution.

David Dunseith still presents *Talkback* on BBC Radio Ulster. 'There has been an extraordinary change,' he said. 'Coming out of conflict is difficult, but at last among the Protestant community there is an apparent acceptance that there has to be movement. They think Paisley is reliable, and he's at the helm now. There is a beginning of the green shoots of maturity. I sense it.'

David Ervine, leader of the Progressive Unionist Party, spends an increasing amount of time abroad, in Budapest, Sarajevo, Sri Lanka and Australia, talking about peace processes, ethnic conflicts and terrorism. His party has not done well over the years since the Agreement.

He was sanguine, though. 'The people have gone back to Paisley,' he said, 'but this is a different DUP. Look at the way they stood for the Pope.' With a few exceptions, DUP public representatives had taken part in respectful public gestures on the death of Pope John Paul in 2005. 'Reasonable treatment for the anti-Christ from Big Ian,' said Ervine, laconically. However, the deep sectarian undertow remains, and it is dangerous still. The IRA may give up its guns, but the DUP will not renounce the old sectarian rhetoric, even if it doesn't use it in public so much any longer. Those 'ancestral voices prophesying war' can always be called on when a clamour is needed.

Ervine said northern Protestants still had a vision that was 'never based on what we want but instead on what we don't want'. The 'new beginning' that Paisley craves is not a constructive politics. Still, Ervine said: 'There is less bitterness. This community isn't as afraid of its enemies as it was. We have become a more settled people.'

PROLOGUE

'Intreat me not to leave thee, or to return from
following after thee, for whither thou goest, I will go;
and where thou lodgest, I will lodge; thy people shall be
my people, and thy God my God. Where thou diest, will I die,
and there will I be buried.'

RUTH 1:16–17

Bernadette Martin was a fine young woman, not yet twenty. She
danced in a purple dress, plaited her little sister's hair, worked in a
factory. She was a Catholic. She was going out with a Protestant,
Gordon Green, who played the flute in an Orange band. Religion
didn't matter to her. She liked him. She maybe even loved him. They
met at the Christmas party at the factory where they both worked, in
Lurgan, County Armagh. Bernadette's job was to make sandwiches.
She used to win beauty contests as a child, and had medals for ball-
room dancing. She'd teach her Aunt Bernie disco routines in the back
yard of her home in the Pinebank housing estate in Craigavon. 'She
had a big, broad smile, as if to say, isn't life wonderful?' her aunt said.

'She was gorgeous,' said Gordon. 'She was a good laugh, a brilliant
dancer. When we met at the party we talked all night. I asked her for a
kiss. A few days later she rang and asked me out again. It took off from
there.' That was Christmas 1996. In the months that followed they

were always together. She would put on her crop tops and her mini-skirts and shake out the long blond hair she normally kept scraped back in a ponytail, and out they'd go. 'The glam really suited her,' said her aunt. 'She loved it.'

Gordon had won medals too, for playing the flute in an Orange band. Until 1997 he always paraded on the Twelfth, but he left the band soon after he took up with Bernadette. There was talk that he had been told to leave. No, he said, he hadn't. 'Bernie always said she'd have loved to see me playing.' There was talk that he had been warned to split up with 'the fenian'. No, he said, he hadn't. They used to go dancing, or sit on the lake shore, swigging wine, having a laugh. She became friends with his sisters. She sometimes stayed in his house, and he in hers. Both of their families have framed pictures of them, kissing on the sofa.

Bernadette is dead and buried now. Not with Gordon's people, though, the Protestant people of Aghalee in County Antrim. His father and mother had welcomed her into their home, an old stone house in the village near the shores of grey Lough Neagh. But there were those in the community who saw in the vibrant young stranger not her beauty or the happiness she brought to one of their own, but only that she was a taig, a fenian. On 15 July 1997 Trevor McKeown murdered her as she lay in Gordon's arms. He shot her while she slept, through one of her beautiful eyes, and through her mouth, and twice more, until his full hatred was discharged.

Bernadette was a political innocent. When she was born in 1978 the Troubles had already raged for a decade. She was fourteen when members of Billy Wright's Ulster Volunteer Force (UVF) gang murdered two teenage girls and a man at a mobile shop in a Craigavon estate just a couple of roundabouts away from her home. Her family's church was virtually demolished by an IRA bomb attack on the police station. Yet, as a teenager Bernadette asked, 'Daddy, what's the IRA?' She was Laurence Martin's first-born daughter. 'She was very special to me,' he said. 'I had great plans for her, though she didn't know it.'

Trevor McKeown was a friend of Gordon's, a friend of the family, really. McKeown was older, in his thirties when Gordon was reaching twenty, but he'd been in and out of the house on Soldierstown Road since Gordon was a child. They walked their dogs together in the fields around Aghalee, and McKeown was often in the company of Gordon's father, John. People saw John Green as someone with a calming influence over Trevor McKeown. He'd been good to McKeown's father, and when old McKeown died of cancer, John tried to keep the son on the straight and narrow, a path off which Trevor's older brothers, Clifford and Malcolm, had long since careered. There were five brothers and two sisters. Their parents had separated when Trevor was a child. Their father reared them, cycling off to work in the morning and back in the evening to make their dinner. Their mother lived in Portadown, a few miles from Aghalee. The failed city of Craigavon, built in the sixties, was meant to link Lurgan and Portadown, but they had remained sullen and separate, with Craigavon as a string of housing estates in between. Portadown was a town where a young man inclined to turn hard might find every encouragement.

Clifford was drawn to King Rat, the late Billy Wright, whose much-feared loyalist gang was part of the mid-Ulster UVF until 1995. The gang had carried out perhaps forty sectarian murders. Clifford McKeown had turned supergrass in the early eighties, but had retracted his evidence under pressure from Wright, whom he had incriminated; in late 1997 Clifford McKeown was convicted of armed robbery. His brother Malcolm had served as a British soldier. He too had served time for criminal offences. In September 1999 he was shot and injured in Craigavon.

The main loyalist paramilitary organisations had been on ceasefire since 1994, when they expressed 'abject and true remorse' for the suffering they had caused. Portadown loyalists thought differently. Wright's new Loyalist Volunteer Force (LVF) had abandoned the ceasefire, rejected the peace process, and was threatening just about everybody. It had also dedicated itself to supporting the cause of getting the Orange Order down Portadown's Garvaghy Road for its annual Somme commemoration held on 5 July. Residents of the largely nationalist Garvaghy Road objected to the parade. These were the events known as Drumcree.

Trevor McKeown worked for a builder, a Catholic man who had done well for himself in the prosperous farming community. His boss was good to him. Those who knew McKeown said he was good company most of the time, but had a violent temper which could easily be ignited. Then he might lash out. He was said to have a chip on his shoulder, liable to turn on anyone who came out with anti-loyalist talk, or seemed to be looking down on him. He was a drinker, and his rages were most likely to occur when he was drunk. He hated the Royal Ulster Constabulary (RUC), and claimed he had been beaten up by them while in custody. He had gone to prison for robbery and other anti-social crime, but people had been known to put up with smashed windows, wrecked rooms or a black eye rather than risk provoking him still further by involving the police.

Bernadette knew McKeown. He was one of the crowd with whom she and Gordon would drink. She had no fear of him. The teenage couple had stayed in his house in Coronation Gardens, the little housing estate just up the road from Gordon's home. They stayed there on 3 July 1997, just two nights before Drumcree. McKeown, said Gordon, was perfectly friendly. He was up and down to Portadown, where Orangemen were preparing for confrontation on the hill at Drumcree.

McKeown's circle was deadly serious about Drumcree in 1997. The Reverend Ian Paisley had described the right to this annual parade from the Church of Ireland church back to Portadown as a matter of life or death, freedom or slavery. The previous year paramilitaries acting for Billy Wright had murdered Michael McGoldrick, a Lurgan taxi driver, by way of a warning as to what might happen if the parade was not allowed. The killing followed a pattern so well established it had a name. To summon a victim, the assassins would ring a taxi firm known to have a Catholic work force – 'dial-a-taig', they called it. Easy. Michael McGoldrick was lured to a leafy road near Aghalee and shot in the head. The parade was allowed down the disputed route.

The UVF expelled Wright and his unit, and threatened to kill him. In defiance, he formed the LVF. In June 1997, as marching season tension tightened its grip on the people again, the IRA murdered two community policemen in the centre of Lurgan. There was widespread revulsion. In the fields and lanes around the old church at Drumcree, summer darkened the leaves, though the skies stayed grey. After a confused period when it seemed the parade would be stopped, riot police forced it violently through the Garvaghy Road.

The LVF boasted that this victory was their achievement, a view which appeared to be confirmed by the RUC's chief constable, when he said he had taken his decision because he believed that otherwise, loyalists would kill Catholics.

In the days that followed, the Irish National Liberation Army (INLA) threatened to kill Orangemen, there was widespread rioting in nationalist areas, and it appeared that massive street confrontations were about to occur in Derry and Belfast. Then on 10 July the Orange Order agreed to re-route two of its most contentious parades. There was a profound sense of relief – but not all round. Paisley said the re-routing represented a surrender on the same scale as the Munich Agreement between Chamberlain and Hitler.

Aghalee in early July was a whirl of loyalist activity. Ulster flags, Drumcree flags, Union Jacks, red, white and blue bunting. Every lamppost had its flag. In Coronation Gardens many of the houses had two, a Union Jack and an Ulster flag. There were signs directing people where to leave wood for the Eleventh night bonfire, and young men trailed pallets, broken planks and tyres to the site in a field by the river. Someone had daubed LVF on the gable of a derelict house.

Bernadette wasn't bothered. She came and went with Gordon as usual. She and a few of her girlfriends were going to Turkey for a package holiday in August. She was thinking of getting a dolphin tattoo on her shoulder before she went. She had a thing about dolphins. She told one of her friends that if you got cancer you should make sure you got to ride on the back of a dolphin before you died.

The Twelfth holiday has its routines for loyalist families. The Greens always went to Bangor, County Down, on 13 July to watch the Lurgan Black preceptory parade there. The parade is not held on 'the Sabbath', so in 1997 it actually took place on 14 July. Gordon was working. That morning, his father left him to the factory, where Bernadette was waiting with her big radiant smile. The young couple kissed and went in together. Back in Aghalee, McKeown had breakfast at the Greens' house. John had invited him to join him and his wife, Josie, and their daughter, on the trip to Bangor.

When they arrived the bars weren't open, but they found a hotel on the seafront and the men started to drink pints. Later, they watched the parade, which is known as one of the most respectable and traditional of the Twelfth celebrations, a bowler-hat-and-white-gloves affair. The 'Black men' are the élite of the loyal Orders. The rest of the day was put in with pints, a few trips to the bookies, chips, ice cream and chats with friends and acquaintances. Then Josie drove them back to Lurgan, where the returning Black men paraded again.

Sticking with his annual routine, John Green went to the Institute, a Protestant working-men's club at which McKeown was not particularly welcome. He had arrived one night with an obstreperous acquaintance, a Catholic, who insisted on singing republican songs. On this occasion McKeown went to the Talk of the Town instead. The Institute was busy. There was a good crowd of family and friends, including members of Gordon's old band, the Clougher Flutes. Out on the streets, a Scottish loyalist band played, and men with pints drifted in and out of the bars.

When they finished work, Gordon and Bernadette bought a bottle of Buckfast and headed for the artificial lakes at Craigavon. (Buckfast, a sticky sweet tonic wine, made by Catholic monks in the south of England, is a great favourite with young loyalists around Armagh. It is known as 'Lurgan champagne', bought by the case for loyalist events, and available on tap in some bars. Loyalist shops sell Buckfast clocks and ashtrays.) The lakes lie wanly in the low fields between Craigavon and the M1 motorway, overlooked by the courthouse and the civic centre. In the heady Unionist dream for the new city there was a notion that water taxis would ferry the people to and fro across the man-made lakes to shops that were never built.

Later the young people made their way up the road to Bernadette's house. Bernadette's mother Margaret wanted them to stay in, but they had other plans. Bernadette rang a taxi. When it arrived, she called in to Margaret, who was ironing, 'I'm away.' Then she was away with Gordon, down through the path of white rose bushes in her parents' garden. Never to return.

They got the taxi driver to drop them at the Institute in Lurgan. Gordon went in to look for his father. Bernadette waited outside – it was, after all, a Protestant club. Gordon told his father that Josie was coming to pick up him and Bernadette, but John Green decided to stay. Josie Green was happy to collect her son and his girlfriend – she knew that it wasn't everyone who would be happy to see 'one of the other sort' in their midst in the charged atmosphere of the Orange celebrations. It was the same for the Martins. 'Things can get complicated round here,' said Laurence. Things had been said to Gordon in the shops at Pinebank where Bernadette lived, and one day, when the couple were elsewhere and among loyalists, someone had hit Bernadette. Gordon's mates had taken to calling him Popehead. After Josie brought the young couple out to Aghalee, they went for a drink. It was about half ten.

There had been a lot of drinking going on that day. Paul Camlin and Noel Best had spent the afternoon in a local pub, playing pool and the poker machines, drinking pints of lager. Later, their friend Jonathan Budd had come in. The young men left around six, went to Camlin's house for chips, and then to Trevor McKeown's. He wasn't in. They went back to the pub, but their afternoon winning streak was over. They spent the evening drifting about, mostly drinking Buckfast and beer at McKeown's house, where a couple of other young people joined them, though McKeown himself had still not returned. At about eleven, Camlin and Best took a Union Jack and an Ulster flag from the house and paraded off down the street, drunk, trying to whistle. They saw Gordon and Bernadette across the road, and Gordon called over to them. Joking. 'Up the Provies.'

McKeown was in the Institute by this time. Lynne Green, Gordon's younger sister, was talking to him. She had known him all her life, and had fancied him, growing up. It had become a joke between them. He was drunk. He said something strange to her. He said he was going to get the gun that was used to shoot McGoldrick and shoot himself. She told him to 'stop talking crap'. It wasn't the only strange thing he said that night. He told people he needed someone to drive him to 'do a job'.

When Gordon and Bernadette got home they went upstairs to Gordon's room with his sister, Wendy. Lynne, who came home in a taxi, heard them 'laughing and carrying on' as she passed the door on her way to bed across the landing. They were lying on the two beds in the room, listening to disco music. Later, John Green got a lift home and went to bed. The old house creaked and settled into silence.

At around three in the morning McKeown got out of a taxi at his house in Coronation Gardens. His mates, Camlin and Best, were back inside. Best told him about the encounter with Gordon and Bernadette on the road. McKeown went upstairs. He got the gun that killed Michael McGoldrick. He walked down to the house on Soldierstown Road. He knew the back door would be open, because it always was. He put on a balaclava, climbed the stairs, and entered Gordon's bedroom. Bernadette was asleep in Gordon's arms. He put the pistol to her sleeping head.

The gunshots woke Gordon. He saw the black balaclava of the assassin as McKeown charged out the door, heard the footsteps plunging down the stairs. He pulled down the blanket and saw blood. Bernadette was moaning. He roared for his parents to come and he held her in his arms, cradling her head. 'Don't die, Bernie,' he pleaded. 'Don't die.'

But she did. Bernadette Martin, aged eighteen, died at the Royal Victoria Hospital in Belfast, twelve hours after McKeown had shot her. The parents of the young lovers met formally for the first time in the intensive care unit.

Laurence and Margaret Martin were by their daughter's side when she died. Earlier, they had gone out to a chapel on the Falls Road while the doctors worked intensely to try to save their girl. 'As we walked in I suddenly remembered going into a chapel on the day Bernadette was born,' said Laurence. When they returned to the hospital they were told there was no hope.

While she was dying, her killer hid the gun in a potato field, and went home to bed. In the morning he put his murderer's clothes in the washing machine and was naked, washing his hair under the cold tap in the bath, when the RUC arrived to arrest him.

Laurence Martin and his family were hospitable and gracious to the reporters, neighbours, friends and strangers who streamed through their house in the days after their daughter's murder. Bernadette's Aunt Bernie poured tea and cut cake. 'She was like a second daughter to me,' Bernie said. In the darkened front room her sister Margaret walked up and down the length of the coffin in which Bernadette was laid out. She cried out in pain as she stroked her child's white, cold face and her folded stony fingers.

Bernadette was the same age as her dark-haired cousin, Angela. 'We couldn't live without each other and we couldn't live with each other,' said Angela, her face blue and wet with weeping. 'We missed each other when we were apart and we fought the bit out when we were together.' Angela, a student nurse, called Bernadette 'the Milly', after the loud, cheerful mill girls. Bernadette called Angela 'the Snob'. Angela wrote a song for Bernadette's funeral: 'You are the one that makes me happy. You are the one who makes me cry. You are the one who listens when I'm in need of a friend. All I want is you back again.'

Laura, aged eight, sat on her daddy's knee and talked about her big sister. 'I love Bernadette,' she said. 'She'd do your hair for you in French plaits. She'd always look after you.' Laurence asked her gently if she knew what had happened to her sister. 'She got shot,' Laura answered in a whisper, letting her long blond hair fall in curtains across her little face. 'She's in heaven now. She's an angel in a pink dress. But she is still going to help me with my homework.' At the funeral Laura sobbed uncontrollably. Her family held her tight against the battering waves of grief.

In the church Gordon Green looked no different from the other young men of Bernadette's circle. Dark-haired, in a grey suit, with tears streaming down his face, he carried the coffin, along with her brothers and her father. His girlfriend, murdered by his friend. 'I feel sort of guilty,' he told me. 'It is hard to explain. I loved her to bits.'

Out in Aghalee, behind doors that were not opened to reporters, the Northern Ireland news could be heard: 'Police believe the murder of eighteen-year-old Bernadette Martin at her boyfriend's house in Aghalee, County Antrim, may have been sectarian.' A woman in Coronation Gardens showed me a sympathy card that she and her neighbours were sending to the Martins. 'What has happened is outrageous. The card is from Christian people who do not condone this. We are proud to be Protestant,' she said, indicating the flags and the bunting all around. 'But what has been done is sickening. Decent, hard-working people here haven't time for all that bigotry and hatred.'

On the eve of her funeral Laurence Martin spoke brave, terrible words about his beloved daughter. 'If her death means it is the last death in this country, then maybe it is worth something and we can live in peace,' he said. The day after her funeral the IRA renewed the ceasefire it had broken with the Canary Wharf bomb in 1996. The next day, a Sunday, the village hall was packed for a commemorative service. Catholics and Protestants stood together and wept.

Before the week was out, Orangeman Norman Coopey, full of drink and Ecstasy, was cruising the roads around Newcastle, County Down, in a silver car. He was with another man, and they were hunting for a 'taig'. They picked up sixteen-year-old James Morgan as he hitched along a road near his home in Annsborough. They beat him to death with a claw hammer, set fire to him, and buried him in a pit full of the rotting carcasses of farm animals. The body could only be identified by dental records. Coopey gave himself up the following morning, but subsequently pleaded not guilty to the murder. Shortly after the start of his trial in 1999, he changed his plea. Like McKeown, he was sentenced to life imprisonment. His accomplice was not caught, but his identity is well known locally.

Bernadette Martin and James Morgan were young people full of life and much loved. Their circles included Catholics, Protestants, and others who had allegiance to neither faith. But to the men who murdered them, they were simply taigs, fenians. The enemy.

When Mr Justice McCollum told the criminal court in Belfast in June 1999 that he found McKeown guilty as charged with the murder of Bernadette Martin, McKeown started to roar abuse from the dock. 'You done Billy Wright you bastard ... you're nothing but a peeler in disguise, you fucking scumbag bastard.' He also called the judge a fenian. (McCollum was the judge who jailed Billy Wright for intimidation in 1997, and Wright's followers maintained, inevitably, that he had done so because he was a Catholic.) The judge remarked that McKeown's outburst was an indication of his 'violent and unstable character'.

Margaret Martin said she felt no hatred for her daughter's killer. All she wanted still was for peace to come. Philomena Morgan, James's mother, called for there to be no revenge for her son's murder. She also wanted to know why Coopey had not been expelled from the Orange Order.

This book is about Protestants. I have started it with this description of the sectarian murders of two young Catholics not because such violence is typical – it is not – but because it represents the worst outcome of a type of strong political Protestantism. Both of the killers supported the Orange Order. Trevor McKeown was a Drumcree foot soldier. Norman Coopey was an Orangeman, a member of the brotherhood. Loyalist, unionist, Orange. I wanted to explore the influences which were capable of producing such violent hatred. I also wanted to find out the views of other Protestants exposed to the same influences, who would abhor the actions of Coopey and McKeown. How, in some, did being 'proud to be Protestant' turn pathological?

The sense of place is important in the North of Ireland. The ground beneath our feet has its particular history, and wars which seem over in some parts, still rage in others. I have chosen to look at Protestant people in six places. I have not attempted to present portraits, but have focused instead on certain aspects of life which are in some way typical of each of those places.

North Down is a place where many people live comfortable and affluent lives, relatively untroubled by political strife. Overwhelmingly populated by Protestants, it is a heartland of 'middle unionism'.

North Belfast was one of the North's most heavily industrialised areas, but has suffered acute economic decline. The Protestant population has fallen dramatically. In working-class communities like Rathcoole, loyalist paramilitaries play a significant role.

Portadown has become known as the 'Orange citadel', and is the focal point for those opposed to the Belfast Agreement. Many Protestants see Drumcree as a last stand for loyalist Ulster.

Along the border, which separates Northern Ireland from the Republic, large numbers of Protestant farmers joined the security forces. Many have been murdered by the IRA, leading to claims of 'ethnic cleansing'.

Ballymoney is a small market town in the Bible Belt of County Antrim. It is predominantly Protestant, but mixed, and with a liberal tradition. It was known as a quiet town, but in 1997 loyalists kicked a policeman to death, and in 1998 they petrol-bombed the home of a Catholic woman, Christine Quinn, burning to death her three children.

'I don't think Ulster was ever meant to be a place ... it was just meant to be the Protestant people.' So said one of the young people quoted in Desmond Bell's *Acts of Union*. Northern Protestants have an eloquent artistic and intellectual tradition, though it is often obscured.

This is the terrain of 'Places of the Mind'.

Derry, on the north-western edge of the North, is famous for its siege in 1689, and as the place where the Troubles erupted in 1969. Protestants are in a minority. It has become a place where political compromises may, tentatively, be reached.

The book was started just before the referendum which endorsed the Belfast Agreement in May 1998. Seventy-one per cent of the North's population voted in favour of the agreement, which was intended to pave the way for a democratic powersharing government. Within the unionist community, most pro- and anti- activists claimed they had the support of most Protestants. However, it appears that the Protestant vote was almost equally divided. I have used this result as a guide to try to ensure that the balance of voices here is representative of the broad lines of thinking among northern Protestants.

NORTH DOWN
Gold Coasters

'Now the fever is high and raging;
who would have guessed it, coasting along?'

from 'The Coasters', JOHN HEWITT

'RENT-A-MOB'

'We have a good life. Holywood is a great wee town and I'm very fond of it. We play a lot of golf and the children play rugby and tennis. We like to eat out and there are good restaurants locally. We go to Belfast to the Waterfront, the Opera House and the Lyric theatre. We love musicals, and the Ulster Orchestra is wonderful, superb. I tend to stay away from Irish plays – too depressing. A lot of my friends pay a fortune to send their kids to prep schools – I think we are lucky in the state schools. We holiday on the north coast and once a year we go abroad – skiing or to the sun.'

In the frantic days before the referendum vote in 1998 Tony Blair paid a visit to Holywood, the hub of North Down's gold coast, a pretty little spot packed with places in which large amounts of money could tastefully be spent. Planes, trains and automobiles service it, and Belfast Lough had left its sloblands behind to look blue and picturesque from Main Street. Lesley, a hospital consultant, had been doing a bit of shopping on her way home from work when she spotted television cameras and a crowd, and realised the prime minister was in town. She pushed her way through to Blair and shook his hand. 'I thanked him very much for all the hard work he'd done. He was anything but relaxed. Then Mr McCartney, our local MP, unfortunately, arrived. We felt he had shortened the prime minister's visit and was trying to grab the limelight. People were heckling him, which is very unlike Holywood people, and I heard him say, "This is rent-a-mob." I saw red. I went up to him and said, "Excuse me, I am a local resident and I resent you speaking to me in that way." He said, "I rest my case." Which was a funny thing to say.'

Lesley was certainly not the sort normally associated with the idea of rent-a-mob. As I parked on the tree-lined avenue where she lived, a girl in school uniform was also parking her car. She and her friend walked by, leaving lunch-time shopping bags strewn on the back seat. Lesley gave me tea and sandwiches in the large private gardens behind her spacious house. She was embarrassed because she knew I'd spent the morning talking to people in Rathcoole, the huge north Belfast housing estate which could just be seen, blurred by distance and sea haze, across Belfast Lough. 'This must all seem terribly ...' She shrugged. 'You know.'

'My husband and I were absolutely flabbergasted by the reaction to my little altercation with McCartney. It was on TV and radio and it was reported in all the papers. People were coming up to me in the golf club and saying, "Well done, Lesley, you've changed the face of politics in North Down." They said I was the talk of the Bar library – they even knew my handicap! On the whole, people we know don't talk politics because they know you can't change people anyway.'

Lesley's family had a tradition of involvement with the medical profession. She went to college in England in 1972. 'I wanted to get away from parochialism and see how the other half lives.' She had not seen much of the Troubles, but remembered going on a peace march up the Falls Road. 'It was a wonderful feeling. I haven't been up there since.'

She came back 'to get the roots out of my system', met her husband, and stayed. 'I came back with the decision that I'd make an effort to make the place better. I joined my local Alliance Party branch. There wasn't any other politics which was in any way suitable. The Unionists were still too entrenched. But sadly, Alliance hasn't made any leeway whatsoever. They haven't made enough play of being for the Union with Great Britain. And they are seen as being too middle class. But I think the British government listened to Alliance – so much of what has been implemented in the agreement – a bill of rights and power-sharing – all that is Alliance-speak. I like the Women's Coalition – though I think they took Alliance votes. The two ladies they got in are both marvellous.' The Northern Ireland Women's Coalition had won two seats in the new Assembly. Its leader, university professor Monica McWilliams, won a seat in South Belfast, and Jane Morrice, formerly head of the European Commission in the North, took a seat in North Down.

Lesley had seen the effects of the violence through her work in the hospital. 'I remember a multiple shooting not long after I returned here. I thought, what the hell am I doing here? I must be bats. Sometimes when loyalist paramilitaries were brought in, I wished I had the courage to say to them, you are letting the Protestant people down. I think we had all reached the end of our tethers by 1994 and it was funny, soon after that the ceasefires came about.'

I asked Lesley what she thought of Paisley. She glanced around in a pantomime of anxiety and said in a whisper, 'Oh! Fundamentalists!' She shook her head disapprovingly, then added, 'Don't you dare write that down or they'll be hammering my door down.' I said I thought they would be pleased to be so described. She said she supposed it would be all right. It wasn't a particularly inflammatory remark, but her anxiety about it was indicative of a sensitive instinct for self-protection among 'comfortable' Protestants, who fear incurring the wrath, not so much of the IRA, as of loyalists. One man said he couldn't talk frankly to me because, some years previously, someone had painted 'UVF' on his garden wall. 'I have to think of my family,' he said.

'I've had a very middle-class life in Protestant areas, very much untouched by the Troubles,' said Lesley. 'There definitely is a whole other side of life here that I haven't a notion about. The Catholic population undoubtedly felt put upon – though Iris Robinson of the DUP [Democratic Unionist Party] had a letter in the paper the other night about the wonderful democracy we used to have. The Orange parades definitely caused hassle to people. Sometimes I'm amazed at how strongly Orange Order people feel about it. I remember a friend of mine walked across the road in front of a parade, which evidently you aren't meant to do, and the leader of a band put him up against a wall and said, "Do that again and you are dead." She sighed. 'There are two sides to every story. I just wish people could see that.'

'AS GOOD AS IT GETS'

On the stage of the Good Templar Hall in Bangor, North Down's member of parliament and the leader of the UK Unionist Party (UKUP), Bob McCartney, quoted Lenin and Malcolm X to make the case that the IRA was winning the war. There were just two days left to persuade the electorate to reject the Belfast Agreement. The night before the Bangor meeting, Ulster Unionist leader David Trimble and Social Democratic and Labour Party (SDLP) leader John Hume, presided over by a rapturous Bono, had shaken hands and grinned on stage at the Waterfront Hall in Belfast, during U2's pro-agreement concert. They looked awkward, but it was a winning gesture which had revived a floundering campaign.

Bangor is a few miles out the North Down coast from Holywood, along fine, fast roads. A journalist had described it as a place where it was not a matter of the haves and have nots, but of the haves and the have yachts. It has a big new marina, and the town's facilities include a health club with a pool whose waters are identical to those of the Dead Sea, so that you can float and think of nothing. Bangor also has estates as deprived as any in inner city Belfast. In Bangor West the contrast is particularly sharp, with mansions on one side of the road, and, on the other, an estate in which drug wars between paramilitary factions have led to several murders in recent years.

Out along the coast beyond the town lie big caravan parks known witheringly to the local wealthy as Shankill-sur-Mer, where inner city Protestants from Belfast holiday, bringing their flags with them. There is also a bleak little estate facing the sea, in which prison officers intimidated out of their homes are temporarily housed. Most of Bangor is solidly middle class and Protestant, and the farms out in the rolling hills are rich ones.

McCartney told his Bangor audience that the Belfast Agreement would put armed terrorists in government. 'This agreement shows that violence and crime does pay – it will make you a minister of state.' There was a smattering of applause. The most appreciative of the sixty or so crowd was a cluster of middle-aged women with firm hairstyles, cardigans and flat, peep-toe sandals.

The attack on Sinn Féin and the IRA was standard – but McCartney had supported his argument with the words of the Russian communist revolutionary, and the US black power leader. A wealthy barrister who favoured integration of the North with the United Kingdom, he was expelled from the Ulster Unionist Party (UUP) in a row about the 1985 Anglo-Irish Agreement, and once grabbed a microphone from Ian Paisley to denounce the DUP. He had described the 1995 Framework Document as a 'constitutional conspiracy' against unionists who had 'suffered in silence'. In the same year he had spoken favourably about New Labour's social policies. In 1982 he had said the DUP was fascist and sectarian, relying on 'marching feet, uniformed rallies, the mass hypnosis of organised propaganda' (quoted in the *Irish News*, 21 May 1998). Whatever else might be said about it, the DUP cannot be accused of having changed its tune. Yet at the Bangor meeting, stage right of McCartney, sat the DUP's deputy leader, Peter Robinson. Robinson had achieved notoriety when, in 1986, he led a party of five hundred loyalists across the border. The loyalists beat up two members of the Garda Síochána, then daubed anti-Anglo-Irish Agreement slogans on a wall. A few months later, he headed a colour party for Ulster Resistance, set up to take 'direct action' against the agreement. When Ulster Resistance went on to import arms, the DUP denounced it.

On the left of Robinson and McCartney, old, tight-lipped and bolt upright in his chair, sat Captain Austin Ardill, first elected as an Ulster Unionist MP in 1965, when there appeared to be little to trouble the Protestant rulers of the Protestant state. The IRA was dormant, the DUP a mere glint in a young preacherman's eye. Ardill was staunch.

McCartney jeered at 'phoney Tony', the British prime minister, who had 'all the sincerity of a salesman of *Encyclopaedia Britannica*'. He derided Alliance, 'those touchy-feely whited sepulchres', supporting the Belfast Agreement 'for the children'. Within 'Trimble's camp', it was the lawyers and the accountants, 'the ones with the brains', who opposed the agreement. 'Why would 90 per cent of nationalists be voting for the agreement if it strengthens the Union? The purpose of the cross-border bodies is to bring about a united Ireland.' He held his hands up as if in prayer. 'If ever there was something I felt it was right to say no to it is this agreement.'

The chairman of the meeting said a Sinn Féin spokesman had been on television the previous night claiming that not a single bullet would be handed in 'until the final solution'. The reference to Hitler was undoubtedly his own paraphrase. Unionists opposed to a settlement which included Sinn Féin frequently used emotive vocabulary from the Second World War. Paisley has claimed simply that it was being fought all over again on Northern Irish soil. Gerry Adams has been routinely referred to as Gerry, like 'Jerry', the term used by the British for the Germans. During the 1941 air raids, 14 bombs exploded in Bangor, killing 5 people and injuring 35. Robinson started his speech with the claim that 'never has there been such a bombing and blitzing of pressure and propaganda' as there had been from the pro-agreement forces.

The DUP specialises in sneering at the enemy. Robinson, grim-faced and with none of his leader's jocularity, unsmilingly made a joke about Bill Clinton 'the White House groper', another about Boris Yeltsin being dragged away from his vodka bottle, and several about 'fuzzy Blair'. The audience tittered, hands raised to cover mouths. Aware that the *Irish News* would the following morning quote McCartney's 1982 remarks on the DUP and fascism, Robinson had dug into the archives himself. He quoted UUP leader David Trimble, who said in 1977 that 'it is now clear that London does not see us as part of the United Kingdom. They want to build a structure and tiptoe out.' Robinson said the agreement was carefully crafted. 'It will take you all the way to Dublin.' He asked the audience how they would feel about 'Chief Constable Martin McGuinness'. There was another dutiful ovation.

McCartney gave Captain Ardill an emotional introduction and pushed the old man to his feet. Ardill, who had pressed for the resignation of the reformist Northern prime minister, Terence O'Neill, in 1969, had been deputy leader of the shadowy Vanguard movement in 1972. O'Neill had sacked Vanguard's leader, Bill Craig, who talked of the need to 'liquidate' the enemy. Trimble had cut his political teeth in the organisation. Ardill had been deeply involved in the Ulster Workers' Strike of 1974, which brought down the powersharing Sunningdale Agreement. His star had faded by 1986, when, in the aftermath of the Anglo-Irish Agreement, he and Harry West formed the Charter Group, which had demanded 'a full-blooded devolved legislature for Stormont'.

Ardill's voice as he spoke now was pained. Of those advocating a Yes vote he said, 'Some are green, some are yellow, and there's not a straight one among them.' He said that one of his first jobs had been to fight the IRA, while 'our friends across the border were supplying them'. Opposition to the Belfast Agreement had brought together unionists of all strands. 'I would be proud to hold Paisley's hand rather than hold up the hand of Bono,' he said, pronouncing the alien, foolish name with scorn. As one of the three trustees of the Ulster Unionist Party, he was disgusted. 'They are not worthy of the name they are trading under. The majority of our MPs are against this. It will lead to the ruin of this little country that we have fought for. Good-night and vote no.'

He sat down stiffly, and McCartney, apparently moved almost to tears, held his hand. Another polite ovation and the meeting was over. No questions were asked for, and no questions were asked.

I was back at the Good Templar Hall the following night, the eve of the referendum, to hear David Ervine, the leader of the Progressive Unionist Party (PUP), put the case for the agreement. Knots of men stood outside, smoking. Some of the older ones had sleek, duck's arse hairdos and the sort of suits that Belfast bouncers wore. Some of the younger ones were muscular and with shaved heads. Inside, a crowd of boisterous women in their thirties or forties were passing around a small slide viewer and guffawing.

An hour late, Ervine arrived, swept into the hall by big men. The PUP is the political party which has emerged from the paramilitary UVF. 'Had only unionism been negotiating with unionism, we would have got a better agreement,' said Ervine. 'But that is not how it is. We have 3,500 people dead. Now the Union is safe.' When the Conservatives had said the British had no strategic interest in the North, it had 'wounded the unionist community to its heart'. However, the principle of consent, 'the will of the people of Northern Ireland', was now enshrined in the agreement. 'We have to take responsibility.' Tony Blair had a huge majority – he did not need the Unionists' votes.

'We always believed that nationalism wanted to destroy us. Isn't it amazing that they too have accepted the principle of consent? Danny Morrison said yesterday there is no support for armed struggle. I have spent twenty-five years watching the Provos and I am telling you, the war is over. They may never be defeated, but they will never win.' A debate about the morality of war had been going on since 1988, and now the IRA had torn up its constitution. 'Their recognition of partition is earth shattering. I look forward to being part of the assembly with the Provos. I am not afraid of them.' He said, 'the way Prods work' was to demand – whereas nationalists were strategists. He quoted figures on pass rates for the eleven plus, the competitive exam which Northern Irish children sit at the age of eleven and which determines whether or not they will get a grammar school education. In nationalist areas, he said, the average pass rate was 27 per cent. On the Catholic Falls Road, hardline and working class, it was 12 per cent. 'We think, dear God, that's terrible,' he said, pausing dramatically. 'In loyalist working-class areas the pass rate is 3 per cent. One in a hundred will go on to further and higher education. In twenty years' time nationalists will have the top jobs.'

Left at that, his point could have been made by the DUP. However, Ervine went on. 'They are better than us. They are cleverer. They make an effort. They have someone who looks after them.' He said that after the agreement there would be a greater appreciation of culture. 'Nationalist areas have cultural centres, heritage centres ... they have worked feverishly for their culture. Now you look at the Field at Edenderry. There isn't even a toilet. For thirty-nine years I have walked past a big mausoleum of an Orange hall. What have we done for our culture?' He said that in a 'troubled, evil, brutal society' it was immoral to blame the prisoners. 'I believe in my heart in this agreement. This is as good as it gets.'

There was huge applause, and then something happened which I had seen before only in republican areas. The audience debated. Would Sinn Féiners become government ministers? Why didn't the

PUP 'take the gloves off' over 'DUP hypocrisy'? Would there be a truth commission? Gerry Adams was saying the agreement would lead to a united Ireland – who was right? Ervine said Adams had brought his people 'light years'. There would be no united Ireland. 'It is a case of Ireland approaching again the people in this part of the country, the people it had moved away from when they went for independence.' If you didn't change, you died as a society. You had to transform politics.

Then a man stood up and said he was a Catholic, a socialist and a PUP voter. He was applauded by men who had supported or been involved with a paramilitary organisation which, simply, killed Catholics. It was hard to believe this was for real. Oh brave new Northern Ireland . . .

'ABOVE ALL THAT'

Ellen lived in a beautiful old house full of lovely things, and sur-rounded by spacious gardens planted with flowering trees. Her hus-band was a company director – she looked after their children and their home. They had lived abroad for years, returning to Northern Ireland in 1991. Wealthy people in search of a suitable place to live, they asked around. 'We were warned off Malone,' she said. 'People said it had been taken over. That was a shock to me – that people would say that.' The Malone Road was synonymous with well-established wealth and ease, and was until the seventies almost entirely Protestant. Then large numbers of newly prosperous Catholics started to move there, many of them from alien places like the Falls Road.

'Here in Holywood we work hard at being tolerant – we would like very much to be above all that. But I always remember when I was fifteen and I worked in a guesthouse in Portrush. There was a Catholic girl working there too and we used to argue. I said I had no prejudices and I wasn't sectarian. She said what we were was bred into us and there was no getting away from it. She was right. It is in our psyche. It is deep-rooted. I went through a phase of being almost republican – it was a way of covering up my guilt about how I really felt. It still shocks me to think of how callous we were about Bloody Sunday.' On Bloody Sunday, 30 January 1972, British paratroopers shot dead thirteen people at a banned civil rights march in Derry; another was fatally wounded. All of the dead were unarmed. I asked Ellen what she meant by callous. How had her people reacted? Her response was instant, and shocking: 'Like a football score. But I still haven't got my head around it. I mean, I do feel if something is banned it shouldn't go ahead ...'

Her parents were 'innately decent' people who did not wish harm on anyone. Her father had taken a stand when a Protestant was made a bank manager when the job should have gone to a Catholic. Her father was Church of Ireland, her mother Presbyterian. 'Presbyterianism is definitely more bigoted. I remember a relation on my mother's side coming to have a word with my father after my parents gave my brother a name which this man felt was a Catholic name.

'We are in the Church of Ireland, which is more wishy-washy. It is all left up to yourself. But a lot of people leave it and go to the fundamentalists – they don't want to have to take personal responsibility. Catholicism seems more straightforward – you don't agonise about being saved. They don't have this agonising emotional relationship with God.'

Ellen said that 'middle-of-the-road Protestants' were having an identity crisis. 'When we lived abroad I would have said I was Irish first, and then if someone showed an interest, I'd say, Northern Irish. We were skiing in Switzerland the day the two soldiers were killed in west Belfast – I didn't want to open my mouth at the resort because I was ashamed. I felt shame about the Birmingham bombs as well ...' The two British corporals were dragged by a mob from their car and brutally beaten before being shot during a republican funeral in 1988. The young republican had been one of those murdered by loyalist Michael Stone, who had launched an attack on mourners at the funeral of three IRA volunteers. This was one of those vicious spirals – they had been murdered by British soldiers in Gibraltar while on a bombing mission, but unarmed. The IRA's Birmingham bombs had killed 21 people in 1974 and injured almost 200.

'But then I am *not* Irish,' said Ellen. 'I wonder how many other people feel this gaping hole in their identity. Nothing to be proud of. When you are a Catholic you have all that marvellous culture of music and dancing – I have worked hard to get my children into that. There

is an exceptionally good music department at their school. I feel that
Catholic nationalists have denied us that. If you look at the famine, the
Irish have taken it over as if it was an anti-Irish phenomenon. I come
from a big rugby family – one of the best things that has happened is
that rugby is now being taught at Catholic schools.

'Protestant culture is Orange and I can't identify with that – it is as
alien to me as rabid republicanism. Last year I would have gladly gone
to Harryville to stand beside the Catholics. It was so iniquitous. This
year I had actually mentioned it to people. But I think that it has
stopped now.' Loyalists picketed Harryville chapel in Ballymena for
twenty months in protest over the stopping of a loyalist parade
through Dunloy, a nationalist village fifteen miles away. The
Harryville picket was a violent affair, and Protestants who objected to
it were derided as traitors. Ellen did not, in the end, make the journey.
'I feel very sorry in retrospect.'

'In middle-class communities there is a lot of not owning up to
things. When Drumcree erupted in 1996, people were really shocked.
But when we look at Drumcree, maybe we are looking at some sort of
mirror image.' She shuddered. 'When we lived in Germany we had a
brush with neo-fascists and I was terribly upset. When I spoke to
neighbours, they said, "Oh, that's just a small band of extremists, pay
no attention." I realise now, that is what Holywood people would say
to a foreigner who was frightened about loyalists burning cars over
Drumcree. It is not adequate. It doesn't really explain it.

'Politics is not talked about among the women in the coffee
morning circuit. I have no political involvement myself, but I have a
couple of very close friends with whom I talk about these things. One
of them is an ecumenical Catholic. I was talking to her today about
how hard it is for Protestants to face up to the idea that there are bad
apples in the police. I am amazed at the common sense David Ervine
talks – I find him remarkable.' She paused. Then she added, as though
it was not something she had spoken about often: 'That was a daring
thing I did – I voted for him. My husband would not. He has a
problem with people who have blood on their hands. But where would
we be if we didn't have the former paramilitaries on board?

'We had to come home to Northern Ireland – you don't really
belong anywhere else. But I also have a sense of not quite belonging

here. I identify very much with the poet John Hewitt. I feel slightly disenfranchised. I do charity work. That is my justification. Every Holywood wife has to have her charity.' She laughed, a little self-deprecating, a little uneasy.

Not all Holywood wives shared her misgivings – I spoke to one woman who candidly admitted that her family had done well during the Troubles: her husband ran a glazier business. Others, and this would prove probably one of the most typical remarks from middle-class Protestants all over the North, simply said, 'We don't bother about politics.' There are plenty who regard the latest exotic produce at Tesco's, Sainsbury's or Marks and Spencer's as infinitely more interesting.

Hewitt's fine poem 'The Coasters' is a devastating critique of the transition from the old certainties of sectarian Ulster to the Troubles. It satirises those who 'coasted along/ to larger houses, gadgets, more machines,/ to golf and weekend bungalows', while supporting 'worthy causes', and living 'a good and useful life', which, after all 'did the business no harm'. Those who had one or two friends 'of the other sort' and when they looked in the mirror felt moved by their own broadmindedness. 'Relations were improving.' The parades had begun 'to look rather like folk festivals'. The coasters thought 'that noisy preacher' was 'old fashioned' and rough. 'But you said, admit it, you said in the club,/ "You know, there's something in what he says."' All the while the 'old lies festered', but the coasters kept things going, voted discreetly in elections which were really 'plebiscites for loyalty':

> Now the fever is high and raging;
> who would have guessed it, coasting along?
> The ignorant-sick thresh about in delirium
> and tear at the scabs with dirty fingernails.
> The cloud of infection hangs over the city,
> a quick change of wind and it
> might spill over the leafy suburbs.
> You coasted too long.

Ellen said that in the circles in which she moved she was not challenged much in her thinking. However, she listened regularly to the BBC's *Talkback* programme on the radio, and was surprised by her reactions. 'I find myself bridling and thinking – we have made concession after concession ... we have bent over backwards ... we are being sold down the river. These old reflexes.'

'OPEN MINDS AS OPEN AS A TRAP ...'

Although it attracts callers of all persuasions, it is as a sort of Protestant confessional that *Talkback* is remarkable. According to BBC press office figures, its daily listenership in 1999 was about 120,000, which is almost 39 per cent of the North's radio audience. In the week before Drumcree in 1997, 21,000 people called its switchboard, one in fifty of the population (Coleman, *Public*, no. 2, vol. 5, 1998).

Presented with peculiar grace and humour since 1989 by David Dunseith – sometimes indulgent, sometimes scathing, occasionally, it seems, utterly depressed – the lunch-time programme has a dedicated following among 'Bible-believing Protestants' who often ring to warn of signs that 'the last days' are coming. Callers have proposed apocalyptic solutions to current affairs issues, and berated other participants, and Dunseith, with a zeal which is sometimes ferocious. They are particularly incensed by nationalists, or by Protestants who phone in urging compromise. What Ellen's experience suggested was that wealthy 'Holywood wives' who seldom, if ever, turn their attention to politics, might none the less, listening to the radio in the sleek comfort of their designer kitchens, have gut reactions which are surprisingly extreme. Such reactions were, she believed, largely unexplored. Sometimes they were simply self-interested. One caller phoned in to say she was a middle-class citizen of North Down who, because the political situation had not been sorted out, had to spend thousands of pounds sending her children to public schools in England. 'I'm fed up with the unarticulated people of Northern Ireland attacking Mo Mowlam,' she said.

I met Dunseith in the coffee bar of the Europa Hotel, where, on a workday midweek afternoon, a pianist was tinkling out highly ornamented versions of 'As Time Goes By' and other romantic favourites. Dunseith looked a bit like a ruffled owl, serious, quizzical, with furrowed brows. A man who is recognised everywhere – he also presents a late night television debate with a large studio audience – he headed for a table in the corner, overlooking Great Victoria Street.

The Europa is famous as one of the world's most frequently bombed hotels. Its owner, Billy Hastings, is one of the North's wealthiest men, and a citizen of North Down. He had supported the agreement on the grounds that it would be good for business re-generation. Asked how he'd feel about the early release of the sort of men who had bombed his hotel, he said he'd rather they came into his hotel as customers than as bombers.

Dunseith showed me some transcripts of calls to the *Talkback* studio during discussions. One was from a caller who identified himself as a Londonderry unionist. His comment was: 'Most beef farmers in Ulster are from the Protestant/Unionist community. Mr Dunseith's own vegetarian beliefs are being broadcast frequently to downgrade us. It's another way for him to get at the Protestant people.' A woman had faxed in a handwritten letter, asking him if he did not realise that 'all you say and think is recorded in heaven', and warning him that he was facing 'a lost eternity'. Another caller had simply stated that he was 'a fucking fenian bastard'.

These were from the extreme edge. There is much good-humoured banter on the show too. *Talkback*, Dunseith felt, took a representative sounding from 'the silent majority'. He quoted Thackeray's claim that there were two truths in Ireland, 'a Protestant truth and a Catholic truth'.

'Protestants are an embattled minority,' said Dunseith. 'They see that Britain was willing to send a task force to defend the concept of Britishness in the Falkland Islands away off near Argentina. They see the way Britain fights to keep Gibraltar from Spain. And then they listen to the British political leadership saying that Britain has no selfish or strategic interest in remaining in Northern Ireland. They ask, "What do they care about their kith and kin here a few miles from them?" They fear the imperial power of Rome. They dread the Re-public. They feel they are losing everything. It almost reaches the level of hysteria. The sense of identity among Catholics is much stronger.'

He said many Protestants were suspicious of exploring new ideas. 'It is a fear of what is out there, a fear of leaving base camp. The Protestant heritage here is defensive. There is a dangerous, grey area. We find on *Talkback* that when there is a loyalist atrocity, you don't tend to get a barrage of condemnation. They wait to see what way the wind blows. You'll find people in golf clubs and other such places and they'll say, "That's terrible ..." Then there is a pregnant pause and you know that there is a "but" coming. There is this need always to find some atrocity carried out by "the other side" to balance it. And then, of course, for some Protestants, there are good terrorists and there are bad terrorists. Good ones are loyalist.' He had asked callers who complained about him having nationalists or republicans on the air whether they would rather that the BBC renamed itself Protestant Radio.

Dunseith recalled his days as a reporter out on the streets of Belfast. 'There was a riot going on on the Newtownards Road and some boy was shouting at us, "Tell the truth, why don't you tell the truth, for a change?" So I offered to interview him. The cameras were there. We were ready. But he and his friends started roaring at us to get out. There is this fear about trying to express yourself, and that can become aggression ...' There was, he observed, a kind of 'Scots canniness', which combined with a fundamental suspicion about the act of expression. He told me about a man he had met. 'Here, in this very hotel, in fact.' A well-to-do Protestant farmer who had approached him to say that he 'knew a thing or two' about some subject which had been debated on the programme. The man had repeated his claim several times. 'I said, "Well, in that case, why don't you give me a ring at *Talkback* and tell me about it?" The man stepped back. "Ah no," he said, "you wouldn't catch me like that." ' The story made me think of the Derek Mahon poem 'In Belfast', with its line about 'The spurious mystery in the knowing nod', its 'sullen silence' and its 'astute salvations'. It evoked another poem for Dunseith. He quoted Seamus Heaney, from the poem 'Whatever You Say, Say Nothing': 'O land of password, handgrip, wink and nod,/ Of open minds as open as a trap...' 'The more I sit in the *Talkback* chair, the more I feel Seamus Heaney cracked it.' Dunseith laughed – in the way described by Samuel Beckett, mirthlessly.

'STRAIT IS THE GATE'

'Bangor is a nice town,' said Richard McIntosh, who lived there with his grandmother and studied at Queen's University in Belfast. He was nice too, a pleasant and cheerful young man. His parents were Salvation Army officers who had gone to run a corps in England, and he himself was a 'senior soldier'. The army combined social work with the saving of souls. 'The army's ethic is, "With heart to God and hand to man". I have always been involved. At sixteen, I signed the articles of war.'

Militaristic language aside, the Sally Army is held in affection by many who dread the baleful approach of other evangelists. There is its social service work, its music – the brass bands at Christmas, the quaint bonnets the women wear. 'It is evangelical, very much so, but we try to draw people in, not snatch them. But it has become harder and harder. There is so much else going on now, and religion is frowned upon. Islam is growing at an alarming rate and that is worrying. What is the Christian Church doing? Not spreading the gospel anyway.'

He had lived in England until he was thirteen. 'I didn't know the terms Catholic and Protestant till we came here. I went to a Protestant school in Portadown and I felt there was an awful lot of prejudice there towards Catholics. They called them fenians and said bad things. Violent things.'

A tenor in the army's youth chorus, he had sung in a cross-community choir in Portadown and loved it. He could not see himself ever having a relationship with a Catholic girl, but felt his religious involvement meant that he would be just as incompatible with other Protestants. He had recently met a girl who was also in the Salvation Army. 'I don't agree with evangelicals who say that Catholicism isn't a Christian religion, though I don't agree with aspects of its teaching. As a Catholic, you can become a born-again Christian, just the same as a Protestant can.'

In his poem 'In Belfast' Derek Mahon had written about 'the cold gaze of a sanctimonious God'. Lorna came from a sect which, she said, did not preach discrimination against Catholics, because it was just as removed from mainstream Protestantism. I met her through a friend, who told me she had been thrown out of her Plymouth Brethren community for some apparently trifling offence. She agreed to talk to me, provided I concealed her identity. She did not want to cause offence to her parents, neither of whom have spoken to her for twenty years.

We met at her suburban home, in a living room cluttered with family photographs. Some were of stern-faced ancestors fading into sepia in their silver frames. She was in her early forties, I guessed. She had an intense stillness to her, and it seemed as if a crack of silence opened between anything I said and her response to it, even if her response was a lovely, frank smile.

'We weren't allowed to mix with other children. We had meetings seven days a week, in a big hall with no windows. All day on Sunday you were at a meeting. There was nothing separate for children. You weren't allowed comics or magazines, and there were no books to read and no recorded music. You weren't allowed to watch television or listen to the radio. At school we weren't allowed to go to assembly or religious education. They have their own Bible, and their own hymn book. Girls had to have long hair, keep their heads covered, and you weren't allowed to wear trousers. As a child, I used to look over the fence and long to go out and play.

'You were brought up to believe that anyone outside of the Brethren was unclean. My family would not live in a semi-detached house, or share a septic tank with another household. Everything worldly was wrong and forbidden. At school you felt very much alone. The teachers didn't bother much about us because they knew we would be leaving anyway. You left when you were fifteen. Computers were banned and you couldn't go into the civil service or have a building society account. You had to go into the family business. It was a mortal sin to set foot in another church.

'If you went out with a boy, you had to marry him. I got married when I was seventeen. After that you weren't allowed to work – you had to be subject to your husband. There was no contraception, so before I was twenty-one I had three children.' Although it had been very restrictive, her childhood was not unhappy. As a teenager, though, she started to rebel. She went to the cinema, and to pubs. 'There was hell to pay.'

It all ended abruptly. 'My husband and I had left our car into a garage to be serviced, and a member of the community, who happened to be in the garage, noticed that there was a radio in the car. I loved the radio. We had kept a television hidden in the wardrobe for the previous two years. But once the radio was found, that was it. My husband was summoned to a meeting and denounced. My parents haven't spoken to me since.'

She knew the story was extraordinary and tried her best to exonerate her parents. 'They do no harm. They are just blinkered.' She loved 'the world', but said she still had a legacy of shyness. It was hard for her to be spontaneous. She had been shocked by the 'ingrained bitterness' of some Protestants she has met since leaving the Brethren. 'I say "leaving", even though I was really thrown out,' she said, laughing. 'Children who aren't even old enough to go to primary school yet know what religion they are and bitterness and hatred are still being bred into them. Although I guess most Plymouth Brethren would be loyalist, we never heard talk of fenians in our house.

'My children are Protestants, but without that bitterness. One of them is going with a Catholic. They have made choices in their lives which they couldn't have made in the Brethren, and I cannot regret that.' Still, when she saw her mother across a downtown supermarket and her mother looked away, Lorna was sad.

The Brethren lost another soul to the world in the person of Max Wright, the author of the wonderful memoir *Told in Gath*. Wright was born in Bangor in 1932, and was 'saved' during an evangelical service on the beach at Ballyholme when he was seven. During the 1941 German air raids, a bomb hit Wright's home, killing his father and blowing off one of his mother's legs. From then on, he was bound to her by guilt.

'There were bibles everywhere in those days ...' he wrote (Wright, p. 79). His mother read the Bible from beginning to end every year, and after his baptism as a boy, he too embarked upon this project. During his second year at school, he noted an 'increasing langour' about the daily passage, an increasing liking for blockbusters and Graham Greene. None the less, he spent his childhood immersed in hymns and services and Bible readings. Fiction was immoral and dangerous.

He noted the preoccupation with reward – 'the temporally disadvantaged who will be eternally compensated', 'the last laugher'

(Wright, p. 34), and the use of monetary metaphors in the songs favoured by the missionary preachers. 'Portrait of the young Christian as a small investor', as he characterised them. The emphasis of the Brethren, according to Wright, was on Jesus as the master, rather than the friend. There was a suspicion of love of one's fellow man, and of philanthropy: 'Salvation is of the Lord and not of works.' Medical missionaries to the so-called Copper Belt of Africa administered drugs and carried out operations, but their main business was saving souls. 'Many were the stories of the black man who had been led to Christ after a successful appendectomy' (Wright, p. 98).

He recalled his instruction in the Book of Revelation. 'The Roman Catholic Church [was] "the great whore that sitteth upon many waters, a golden cup in her hand, full of abominations and filthiness of her fornication", a woman "drunken with the blood of the saints and with the blood of the martyrs of Jesus", upon whose forehead is written, in capital letters, no less, "MYSTERY, BABYLON THE GREAT, THE MOTHER OF HARLOTS AND ABOMINATIONS OF THE EARTH" . . .' (Wright, p. 91).

The Book of Revelation is a favourite source for anti-Catholic rhetoric. In January 1999, just months before standing again for the European Parliamentary elections, Paisley preached an 'old time gospel hour' at his huge Martyrs Memorial church in Belfast. The subject was 'The restoration of the money of Babel, part 2. The woman riding on the beast depicted on the coin – the special permission granted to the Pope to be superscribed on the coin – the aim to make the Euro one world coinage.' The advertisement for the service, carried in the *News Letter* on 15 January, went on to quote Revelation 13:16–17: 'And he causeth all, both small and great, rich and poor, free and bond, to receive a mark in their right hand, or in their foreheads: And that no man might buy or sell, save he that had the mark, or the name of the beast, or the number of his name.' In June, 192,762 northern voters elected Paisley to represent them in the parliament responsible for this Romanist plot.

Wright was sent as a boarder to the exclusive Campbell College, where he was decidedly out of place. The housemaster's lip would curl when he asked to go on Sundays 'not with the *bien élevés* to either the parish church of St Mark at Dundela or to the Presbyterian church at Belmont, but to the Ballyhackamore Gospel Hall', lower-class, mission hall Protestantism, at which the other boys also sneered. Subject to doubts and backsliding, Wright had stopped believing in his faith long before he stopped preaching it. He counted his knowledge of the Bible as a happy outcome of having been brought up among the Brethren. The only other such outcome he noted was 'an equally deep-rooted pessimism about worldly endeavour' (Wright, p. 95). Now retired, Wright had gone on to teach philosophy at Queen's University Belfast.

There are several branches of the Brethren in the North, not all of them as rigid as the community which had rejected Lorna. There are dozens of small evangelical congregations. The 1999 census included fifty-seven choices of denomination, most of them Protestant.

'I WAS THAT NODDING DOG ...'

North Down people are not great voters. The constituency is solidly unionist, so there has never been any need to vote for one's own in order to keep 'the other side' out. Because many of the people who live there commute to work in Belfast, there is no strong sense of community and, for middle-class people at least, issues to do with provision of local public services are of little relevance. They are, however, representative of a crucial bloc, which had been identified by the Yes campaign during the 1998 referendum as the key to its outcome. 'Everyone agreed that the key floating constituency was middle unionism – middle class, middle of the road, and middle ground. No one could afford to alienate them' (Oliver, 1998).

The late James Kilfedder had kept his Westminster seat from 1970 until his death in 1995. He had a heart attack, apparently after British gay rights militant Peter Tatchell threatened to 'out' a number of MPs. Kilfedder regularly took around 70 per cent of the vote, on turnouts of only around one-third of the electorate. Like Bob McCartney, he had been a barrister, was outside the Unionist mainstream and had a large personal following. According to Lynne Sheridan, who works in McCartney's constituency office, those who voted United Kingdom Unionist Party (UKUP) were predominantly retired people, and those who voted UUP were even older. The young, she said, had no interest.

'I was reared in a Unionist home, and I was brought along to meetings from I was a child,' she said. 'You just sat there like clones taking it all in. You didn't ask questions. I admit it – I was that nodding dog.' She said McCartney's party was 'more democratic' – not the view taken by Cedric Wilson and the others who were elected to the Assembly as UKUs but dramatically split with their former leader within months, leaving him the leader of a party with no other members in the Assembly. There was a trading of insults.

I interviewed Lynne just before the European elections of June 1999. McCartney was pitching for 70,000 votes. He was confident that Paisley's attempt to run the election as a new referendum on the Belfast Agreement would see the DUP leader's second-preference votes heaped upon him. In the event, that did not happen. Paisley topped the poll, but according to the UUP's Chris McGimpsey, tally figures showed that more than 90 per cent of his surplus transferred to the UUP's Jim Nicholson. The UUP did not publicise this. McCartney suffered the indignity of getting just over 20,000 votes, less than David Ervine, whose party he despised.

Ms Sheridan said that there were a lot of skeletons in the UUP closet, and predicted that they were about to come out. She rhymed off a list of incipient scandals involving leading Unionists. 'Bob has never had so much as a parking ticket,' she said. It was odd that she should talk like this. The previous Sunday, the *Sunday Life* tabloid had published an article about the nursing home she used to run in North Down. She had been struck off the nursing register in 1996 after she was found guilty of eleven charges of professional misconduct. In 1999 she was declared bankrupt.

She had just been awarded a degree in politics at Queen's University, and said she had a lot of admiration for the republican ethos. 'It mightn't be what I believe, but they have a goal,' she said. 'On the loyalist side, it has been reactionary. Paramilitaries I've spoken to, their attitude is, "Fenians have done this or that to us, and we are paying them back." My brother is a historian. He has written a book about the United Irishmen, showing that both sides were involved. But that has been captured . . .' This was to be a constant theme – the Protestant quest to capture, or to recapture from republicans, the roles of the hero, and of the victim, in history.

'BABY BARRISTER'

Good orators are rare among Unionist politicians, and there is no sign that the younger generation is breaking the mould. They are conservatives, harking back to old values, scolding those among the older generation for stepping out of line. UUP Assembly member for North Down, Peter Weir is one of the so-called 'baby barristers'. He formed the Union First group to oppose the Belfast Agreement from within his party. The group claims a membership of five hundred. On a frosty January night in 1999 he was the key speaker at a meeting in Craigavon. He had just lost the party whip for going against the leadership in a crucial vote on the implementation of the agreement.

The meeting was opened by Jonathan Bell, a young local Unionist councillor. He started with a joke. There was this little boy who was asked to give grace before a meal, and having never done it before, he asks the boy beside him what he should say. The boy advises him to say what his father says. So the boy says, 'Easy on the butter boys, it's half a crown a pound.'

Weir was flanked by all of the party's overtly anti-agreement MPs, six out of ten – Roy Beggs, Clifford Forsythe, Willie Ross, Willie Thompson, Martin Smyth, and Jeffrey Donaldson. 'The battle for democracy begins here tonight,' he said. 'What kind of society will we have if we allow gangsters into government?' He called for a suspension of prisoner releases, a defence of 'the gallant men and women of the RUC', and exclusion of Sinn Féin from government. Donaldson accused the Secretary of State Mo Mowlam of turning a blind eye to ongoing terrorism, and called for 'total decommissioning'. Ross said that it was 'always nice to listen to the young folk having a word to say'. Then he made a dismissive remark about Mowlam. In response, more than a few middle-aged women in the audience hissed, 'Jezebel'.

It was years since I'd heard that biblical name. In the Old Testament Book of Kings, Jezebel 'stirred up' her husband to defy the Lord, who had forbidden him to give up 'the inheritance of my fathers'. Her punishment, devised by the Lord, was to be eaten by dogs at the wall of Jezreel. A Jezebel was a no-good woman. The UUP's distaste for Mowlam crossed the divide between the pro- and anti-agreement camps. She was an unsuitable woman. Unsuitable, not least, because she was a woman.

Thompson opened with the statement, 'I was completely against this agreement' and went on to say that if the UUP gave in on arms 'it's the end of this party'. I had heard Thompson boast on the radio that once he'd made his mind up, that was it. Inflexibility is one of the traditional Unionist virtues. Forsythe, who is rarely heard to speak, mumbled about standing by our principles or hanging our head in shame. Smyth paid tribute to 'the steadfastness of Peter Weir'. Beggs said that where he came from in Antrim there was an old saying: '"When the oul cock crows the young ones will learn." The young ones have well learned. For Ulster. The future of our province will through Union First be delivered.' This rattle of the old guns was the closest the dull, sullen and poorly attended meeting came to drama. Reporters were asked to leave before questions were allowed from the audience.

I met Weir at his office in Bangor. He shared the building, a small terrace house, with Sir John Gorman, the UUP's uppercrust Catholic. I asked him how he felt about being known as a baby barrister. 'It's an improvement on the C team,' he replied affably. The latter term had come from a furious Dick Spring, who, when he was the Republic's tánaiste and minister for foreign affairs, had turned up to a meeting expecting to meet the UUP leader and had instead been faced with, among others, young Weir.

The benign way Weir presented it, Union First had been conceived as a sort of safety valve for the UUP, almost, if not quite, officially sanctioned. 'Once the agreement was signed, a large section of the party was hostile to it. They felt we had given away too much, both on the North–South bodies and on decommissioning. The party as a whole would have had difficulty expressing these views. After all, it had signed up to the deal. There was also the feeling that people in the party who were against the agreement were pariahs. There was a risk of people leaving. We needed a focus, a device to hold people in the party.'

It is not a view shared by those loyal to David Trimble. The party leader came to Bangor to perform the official opening of Weir's constituency office in May 1999, and Weir admitted that they did not exchange a single word. Weir's vote against the party line on implementation of the Agreement could, had even one other dissident joined him, have cost the pro-agreement unionist lobby its majority in the Assembly. The anti-agreement MPs and Assembly members were seen to have their knives poised behind Trimble's back. 'Things are fairly frosty,' said Weir pleasantly.

'SO LONG AS EVERYONE IS HAPPY'

North Down is by no means the only place in the North where wealth and ease are to be found. Almost every town has its fringe of gold. But most places have boundaries where other, less comfortable, realities intrude. In large parts of North Down it has been possible to live in such a way that the Troubles impinged only on the television evening news. Something nasty, distant, incomprehensible. It had drawn near with IRA attacks on the homes of prominent citizens, judges and civil servants, but it had always retreated again.

The Troubles have not, in fact, disadvantaged everybody. Since the introduction of direct rule in 1972, it has been the policy of successive British governments to ladle money into 'the province'. In 1994 a third of the North's GDP came from Westminster's financial subventions. Four out of ten workers were employed directly by the British state, another three indirectly. Whereas the excesses of Thatcherism were, belatedly, visited upon the poor, the middle classes had enjoyed uninterrupted prosperity by virtue of the 'temporary' nature of the state. They were well paid, and benefited from house prices which were relatively low.

The beneficiaries of this ease have been mainly Protestants. The absence of a local parliament means that their business and professional contacts are largely with 'the mainland', so that they have become more intensely assimilated into the United Kingdom. In North Down this has been facilitated by the conveniently located Belfast City Airport, with its frequent daily flights to London. Belfast can be bypassed altogether. As Colin Coulter pointed out in an interesting essay on these, the contented classes: 'the era of direct rule has ... ensured that the United Kingdom has come to constitute a community that is not only imagined but real' (Coulter in Shirlow and McGovern, p. 123). The least vehement in their loyalism were the most obvious in their Britishness.

The fact that the middle classes have largely withdrawn from politics reflects an ambivalence about this situation. The Unionist demand for a Belfast-based parliament has its drawbacks for those benefited by direct rule. Full integration is not favoured either. The British Conservative Party made a brief attempt to organise in North Down in the early nineties. It undoubtedly represented the interests of the local business and professional classes, but the project was a dismal failure.

While there is no local parliament, there is little to be gained from involvement in politics. Protestants seeking prominence have involved themselves in professional bodies and in high-profile voluntary works of the kind which 'attract civic honours and invitations to those social occasions orchestrated by the Northern Ireland Office which offer a pastiche of . . . baroque Home Counties gentility' (Coulter in Shirlow and McGovern, p. 131). The Yes campaign in the referendum pitched itself towards middle unionism by stressing things like the benefits of peace for investment, and of cross-border co-operation in the era of the Celtic Tiger. Self-interest was the key.

Interior designer Lindy Clarke was one of the bright, affluent young set who commutes to Belfast from the gold coast, their jeeps and sleek cars edging out from leafy lanes to the dual carriageway. She had no interest whatsoever in politics. 'I don't care if it's a united Ireland or British rule, so long as everyone is happy,' she said. 'When things are good politically, people are happy and they spend. When things are going on like the Drumcree waffle, nobody goes out and they don't spend money. When there was a ceasefire a few years ago, people spent.' She paused. 'I think there is a ceasefire at the moment, but I don't really know.' She had grown up in a happy, comfortable home in the suburbs. 'There were bomb scares, and sometimes you would hear of something happening and it would upset you. You get fed up with the whole thing. To me, nobody knows what they are fighting about.'

Young, beautiful and obviously talented, Clarke was ambitious and successful. She ran her business from a studio in the ground floor of an east Belfast building owned by her architect father, who worked upstairs. She hoped to work on joint projects with him in the future, designing a hotel, maybe. She liked the best of materials – silks and brocades, hand-painted terracotta tiles. 'I set my goals high. I had a shop in Carrickfergus, but we weren't attracting the right kind of clients. The good customers had to come from Belfast. Not everyone could afford our materials.' She did a lot of business in London, and she said a lot of Northern Irish designers were 'trying to nab' the influx of famous young wealthy people who had been settling in Dalkey, County Dublin. She said Dublin was more stylish and cosmopolitan than Belfast.

She lived with her husband in Crawfordsburn, on the coast between Bangor and Holywood. 'He is in coal. He's a coal consultant.' When they moved there seven years ago, they felt there were a lot of old people around. 'We thought – nightmare – we are the youngest people round here. But a lot of young people have moved back there since. People are coming back. There are good restaurants. We both work hard and we like to relax.'

She blamed the media for making people think that Northern Irish people hated each other. 'The fact is, we don't.' She said a lot of her friends were Catholics or in mixed marriages, and her clientele was about fifty-fifty Catholics and Protestants. 'It doesn't bother me in the slightest. I suppose I have lived a sheltered life. It might seem snobbish, but maybe it's if people are slightly more educated, you learn to accept people for what they are.'

'CATHOLICS ARE UP AND RUNNING'

Mervyn Long thought that middle-class Protestants had problems about accepting people for what they are – especially people in their own community. He lived in a neat redbrick house on a pleasant private estate on the outskirts of Holywood, between Palace Barracks, the big Royal Irish Regiment (RIR) base, and the controversial Maryfield secretariat, set up under the Anglo-Irish Agreement. But he was 'born and bred' on Dee Street off the bottom of the Newtownards Road in east Belfast, the tiny redbrick terraces dwarfed by the cranes of Harland and Wolff. 'You walked out of school and into the shipyard. The gates just open and in you go. No question you might want to do something else – politics didn't allow me an education.' He didn't like that, so he joined the British army, and, a few years later, the Ulster Defence Regiment (UDR).

'I remember a winter's night in January 1975. Intelligence had told us that the PIRA was going to attack the RUC headquarters at Knock.' He pronounced the initials for the Provisional IRA as one word, *py-ra*. 'We were doing vehicle checkpoints. This big Rover came along, a man in front with his gloves and his coat. His wife in a fur coat and two boys like dolls in the back. I asked for his ID and he showed me a card from Shorts – he must have been a manager there or something. His wife leaned over and said, "You people are doing a marvellous job." I said, "There's two boys in the back – in a few years they'll maybe be here with us." "Oh no, I'm afraid not," she said. "That's for the ones from the Newtownards Road."

'That incident has never left me. That woman meant that. I could stand out in the freezing cold or lie in Brown's funeral parlour with a Union Jack over me, because that was all I was fit for. But it wasn't for her boys. They were born for better things.' I asked him about the RUC, an altogether more middle-class force than the UDR, or its successor the RIR. 'The only reason there are working men in the RUC is because when things got hot the middle classes didn't want to be there.'

'There's people up the road from here,' he said, gesturing towards leafy Holywood, 'who wouldn't give daylight to the people on the Newtownards Road. I am allegedly a Presbyterian, but I don't like it. I have become very anti the Protestant establishment, especially Presbyterianism. You know there was a Presbyterian church near where I grew up, but did the minister live among his flock? He did not indeed – he was away in Knock.' Belfast's Knock Road is also leafy, well-established and moneyed. 'I heard a Presbyterian minister on *Sunday Sequence* on the radio calling his own Church cold, old and becoming superficial. I concur. The hypocrisy is colossal – it is all about class snobbery – who you know and who you don't know. It is almost like a religious mafia – that is the American influence, you know. It is not about praying to God or anything like that.'

Although the Church of Ireland is traditionally the church of the Ascendancy, I had heard other people talk in similar terms about the Presbyterian Church. It was the North's largest Protestant denomination, with around 337,000 members. They spoke about the overt social climbing which was actively encouraged, and the rewards – becoming an elder, getting positions of responsibility, and the like. One woman told me she was taken aside and advised that she was far too honest, that she ought to make overtures towards certain wealthy people in the congregation, and that it would befit her to dress more expensively, given the social standing attaching to her husband's profession. Long said it wasn't just Presbyterians and it wasn't just the middle classes. 'Being a Protestant gives you a feeling of superiority. They look down on other people. It is inbuilt.'

He met the woman he went on to marry in Robinson's bar in Belfast. 'Before it was blown up,' he remarked. She was a Catholic from the Republic. 'I dwelt on it and dwelt on it. No way would I become a Catholic. In the end we both joined the Church of Ireland. It's not a kick in the arse away from Catholicism anyway.' The next thing was to find a place to live. 'We wanted somewhere that doesn't dwell too much on what you are and who you are.' They chose Holywood. He left the security forces and was now in charge of security at a Belfast college of further education.

'Sectarianism is destroying Protestantism. We never were a sectarian-minded family. I think one of my relations might have been in the Orange Order briefly, and it is as sectarian as you'll get.' He laughed. 'I'd be barred now anyway – I'm no longer suitable material.' The 'Qualifications of an Orangeman' includes an obligation on a prospective Orangeman to swear that he was born of Protestant parents, educated in the Protestant faith, and has 'never been in any way connected with the Church of Rome' and, just to be certain, that 'My wife is a Protestant/I am unmarried' (Kennedy, frontispiece).

These regulations are not anachronisms – after David Trimble, a member of Bangor's Orange Lodge, and the UUP's chairman, Dennis Rogan, attended a Catholic mass, a complaint was lodged within Rogan's lodge. The men had gone to the funerals of two of the Buncrana children murdered by the Real IRA in the Omagh bomb of August 1998. The matter was later resolved.

Long described himself as a typical Ulsterman. 'I think he's a type that is disappearing fast, the wee working-class Ulsterman. He'd be honest, a pint man, says what's on his mind, likes a wee bet ...'

Hardly typical was his love of Dublin. 'It is so unsectarian. It is not anti anybody. I love walking up and down Grafton Street smoking a few cigars and then go into Neary's and drink as much Guinness as I can . . .' On a recent visit he got the barman in McDaid's to show him the room in which Brendan Behan joined the IRA in 1923. 'I love Killycolmain jail too,' he said, inadvertently renaming Kilmainham after a loyalist housing estate in Portadown. 'We were in the chapel where one of the 1916 men married his girlfriend. It is so sad. A lot of Church of Ireland people were in there too, you know.

'I am very, very much Irish. It is crap to say you have to be Catholic to be Irish. I am a unionist too. I won't hear a word said against the UDR. There's UDR men lying in graveyards all over Northern Ireland. But I regret that it was ever formed. It was a waste of time. You can't fight terrorism through law and order. That is why the United States was put out of Vietnam.' What was his alternative? I asked. So many Protestants advocated 'gloves off' security solutions. Not Long. 'You seek to talk,' he said.

The IRA's Oxford Street bomb in July 1972 was a turning point for Long. It was one of the Bloody Friday bombs. Placed in a crowded bus station in central Belfast, it killed six people, including two teenagers, and injured more than a hundred. I saw the television images of it in colour for the first time during Peter Taylor's BBC programme *Loyalists* in 1999. The sight of the pieces of bloody flesh that littered the street after the blast was horrifying. In Taylor's *Provos* (p. 149), an RUC man described the scene:

> The first thing that caught my eye was the torso of a human being . . . it was recognisable as a human torso because the clothes had been blown off and you could actually see parts of the human anatomy. One of the victims was a soldier I'd known personally. He'd had his arms and legs blown off and some of his body had been blown through the railings. One of the most horrendous memories for me was seeing a head stuck to a wall . . .

'After the bomb I was asked to join the UVF – well, not asked, in-timidated,' said Long. 'I was in the UDR at the time. I didn't want to join the paramilitaries. I didn't think the way to fight the IRA was to be like them. I had to move and live in Palace Barracks.' So Long was another Protestant terrified of retribution from his own kind.

He voted for the Belfast Agreement, but when I asked him if he thought it was a good deal for Protestants, he surprised me. 'No,' he said. 'If the agreement works, the nationalist community will have a grip. Sinn Féin is on a high – you have to admire them for it. Adams and McGuinness have played a tremendous hand. Republicanism is one tree, with one set of rules. Unionism is too many branches.'

This belief is widely held, that unionism, like the Protestant Churches, were too badly split to function, whereas the 'pan-nationalist front' of Sinn Féin and the SDLP, backed by the Catholic Church, is a gleaming and powerful machine, zooming ahead. 'The DUP is the biggest obstacle to peace in Ulster,' said Long. 'They still think Catholics are an irrelevance. But Catholics are up and running. The difference is that Catholics are running forward and Protestants are running backwards.' He said that if the agreement failed, there would be civil war.

He was profoundly pessimistic about the future of the Protestant people. 'Northern Prods have got through the last thirty years on numbers only. If there wasn't a million of us we would have become an irrelevant ethnic minority by now. Working-class Protestants have become so dull – they live in these sprawling housing estates and they are not involved in anything. They sit in their houses smoking or they go to the pub. Their lives are a waste of time. The whole community is fading away. I see it at the college. The Catholics are out and about, getting educated, getting on.'

I asked him what he thought about Bob McCartney's remark at the Belfast Forum to the PUP's Hugh Smyth. McCartney said that, like Smyth, he came from the Shankill. The difference was, he had got out. 'Well, I wouldn't fault him for that,' he said. 'I reckon I've done well. My mother had to scrub floors. I could never contemplate going back to that.'

'PERISH THE THOUGHT'

While Irene Cree was making her way to the podium during the UUP's annual conference, there was a noticeable drift towards the exit doors.

A former mayor of North Down, and leading member of the Ulster Women's Unionist Council, she was to speak about women. The motion included the assertion: 'The party is perceived as a male bastion.' Mrs Cree said she would start with a short history lesson. 'Eve, Boadicea, Abigail Adams, Florence Nightingale, Marilyn Monroe. This list could be endless. Women have made their mark – but not many were Ulster Unionists.' She praised 'our first lady' Daphne Trimble, but complained that while 55 per cent of the North's population is female, all four people on the UUP platform, as well as the chair, were men. She said that the previous year she had raised the same issue. 'You nodded, patted my arm, agreed.' She said the men had no choice but to take this seriously. 'Otherwise you'll have no clean shirts next week.' She reassured them that she was not looking for positive discrimination: 'Perish the thought.'

She was followed by a middle-aged man from Antrim, who extolled his mother. 'I had ownership of her for fifty years. She was a loyal woman who religiously followed the Ulster way,' he said in a maudlin voice. 'The unionist way in her mind was a Calvinistic attitude to ideals and integrity in maintaining the Union. Women are important. They can influence the children to grow up the Ulster way.' He said he was a salesman and often in Andersonstown, where 'the roads are black with the citizens of the future'. The future was not unionist, he implied. Andersonstown is a strongly nationalist part of west Belfast. The man demanded an end to the early release of prisoners, and for the party to hold out for decommissioning. These were all, he said, part of the Ulster way.

I went to see Mrs Cree at her home in the lush North Down countryside, not far from Bangor. When I arrived at her electronic security gates it became obvious she had forgotten I was coming. She was busy, eating sponge and custard, the end of her dinner. She was just back from a few days away at a relative's wedding in South Africa; there was washing to do, gardening, sandwiches to make for her son, a UUP meeting that night. But she agreed to talk anyway. We sat in the early summer sun at a picnic table in her large, busy vegetable garden. Several big old cats and dogs wandered stiffly by. She fussed over them.

She was very annoyed that day because Jim Nicholson had just launched his campaign to be re-elected to the European parliament, and had done so in front of the media, surrounded by men. 'Not a woman in sight,' she said, crossly. 'You'd think in the circumstances ...' The circumstances were the revelations about his extra-marital affair which had surfaced some months earlier. The normally reticent *News Letter* had descended to the use of words like 'scantily clad' and 'love nest'. The *Sunday Life* published a photograph of the, inevitably, younger woman, and another, unkind, of Elizabeth Nicholson, wearing an apron, doing the ironing, and smiling. Every inch the traditional wife and following the Ulster way. Mrs Cree was disappointed in Jim, her friend, but accepted his apologies and was backing his campaign. If God could forgive, then we must do likewise. She said she had warned her boys that if they wanted to go into politics, they would have to make sure there were no skeletons in their cupboards.

'These lesser unionists, like McCartney and Ervine, are breaking up the unionist family,' she said. 'They are doing the enemy's work for it.' She felt the same about Drumcree. 'The Orangemen should have turned the other cheek and walked away. Once they hadn't done that, they should have stood between the police and the hooligans. I have family in the RUC. You get the bad boy in all barrels. But you can't have the police fighting with the Protestants.'

She had supported the agreement, but felt the Ulster Unionists could have done 'far better' if the DUP and the UKUP had come on board. 'The prisoners deal should have been tit for tat – guns for releases,' she said. She was unhappy about the way US President Bill Clinton, who had left no stone unturned to catch the Oklahoma bombers, had welcomed 'a terrorist like Gerry Adams' into the White House. 'But then, look at the kind of man Clinton turned out to be,' she said. A year on, with the executive still not formed and the UUP and Sinn Féin deadlocked over what the agreement meant about decommissioning, she still thought the deal could work. She said the government had to back 'David and Seamus – provided Seamus will come in and leave Sinn Féin out'. It sounded odd, the familiar way she spoke about the deputy first minister, the SDLP's Seamus Mallon. If people did not realise they had to make the deal work, then it showed, she said, that 'we haven't suffered enough'.

Her father had been a farmer, and the family tradition included involvement in the UUP, the Presbyterian Church and the Orange Order. She had spent eight years in local government, was a Sunday school teacher and a past Worshipful Mistress in her local lodge. *'Can't* and *won't* are two words which are not in my vocabulary. My father encouraged me from I was knee high that anything a man could do, I could do and do maybe better. I'd tackle anything.' She stroked the wall beside us with a work-hardened hand. 'I built that myself. We built two houses.'

She had been a teacher, but gave it up to care for her ageing parents. She and her husband had lived for three years in the South. 'I was born in Northern Ireland. I am Irish, Ulster Irish. I have an allegiance to the UK while they want us, but I've a feeling they don't. I'd go independent – unless the south of Ireland became a more pluralist society. If we got our fair share there, it could work. We are all Europeans, but individuality is important.' She said she was a great royalist.

She was disgusted by the attitude of Ulster Unionists to women in the party, pointing to prominent women in all the other parties, Alliance, Sinn Féin, the SDLP. 'Even the DUP – but our ladies don't get a look in.' There were no female MPs, 2 female Assembly members out of 27, 23 female councillors out of 171, and 2 female party officers out of 14. 'A lot has to do with the traditional Ulsterman of the older generation. They feel a woman's place is in the home. And then a lot of women don't want to be centre stage – they are happy behind the footlights.'

Then, surprisingly, Mrs Cree revealed that she had herself wanted to be centre stage, in a different sort of life altogether. 'If I had my life over, I'd be an actress. But my father didn't agree with it. I sang with a dance band in Ballynahinch when I was twenty-one. We played at Young Farmers' Club dos and the like. Then my father heard about it and put a stop to it. He wouldn't let me have the car. It's that old Protestant thing of respectability. It is all right to sing in church, but not to make a living from it. You could go to the Women's Institute or the Presbyterian Women's Association, or there's young wives' groups. I was captain of the Girls' Brigade for years. All that was all right . . .'

It was what the man at the conference had praised as the 'Ulster way'. Unionist ideas of politics and power were male – when the Patten Commission on policing reported in September 1999, David Trimble reacted angrily. He said if Patten was implemented, the RUC would be 'emasculated'.

The week I met Irene Cree the local papers were full of horrific reports about the conviction of a Bangor man for the brutal rape and beating of his young partner and the killing of their unborn child. Mrs Cree said that a man who hit a woman should have his hand cut off. She said she was ambivalent about abortion, but that in certain cases it should be left to the woman 'to quietly decide'. But she was most definitely not a feminist. 'A Christian can't be a feminist – her husband is the head of the house. Mind you,' she added coyly, 'the woman is the neck – which turns the head.' Women had more independence now. 'That's what's wrong. There's no stickability any more. Women can get their rights in their own little ways. They can do it nicely, without putting the men down. A man's ego is very easily bruised. I know quietly we are far better than them, but there's no need to shout it from the mountain tops.'

She was running out of time – her son had to leave soon and needed his sandwiches. We returned to the house, where a young man was pacing about in motorbike gear, looking at his watch. Her son, aged twenty-seven. She took two slices from a sliced pan loaf, spread them with butter, placed pieces of cooked chicken on one, and made a lid with the other. Then she cut the sandwich in two, and put it in a plastic supermarket bag. He put them into his carrier and zoomed off into the world.

When he'd gone, Mrs Cree became agitated about moral issues and declining standards. Sex on television; young women going into pubs. 'Where will it all end?' she said, with a very heavy sigh.

'THIS THING OF NOT MAKING A FUSS'

'Respectability' was a word used by northern Protestants as frequently as Orangemen speak of dignity. It had many definitions, but fundamentally, to be respectable was to be seen to be virtuous. Lindsay Brown, who had been deputy head of the prestigious Bangor

Grammar School, a leading light in the Scripture Union, and the brother of a former moderator of the Presbyterian Church, appeared to epitomise it. Paul, one of the many boys he sexually abused over a period of several decades, believed that respectability was what protected Brown and made it safe for him to continue his assaults long after they were first reported to people in authority.

'Brown nearly got away with it,' he said. 'He was part of a golden circle. It took years to get him to trial. He was promoted to have responsibility for child welfare in the school two years after allegations had been made. It's collusion – it's not just those who abuse who are culpable but those who protect them. Why do people blinker themselves to these assaults? Probably because Brown had moral and spiritual authority, and he also had power.' Brown was head of the junior school, and of the religious education department. He was also, since 1993, two years after a complaint had been made about his activities, vice-principal and the designated teacher for child abuse cases. 'All that inculcates at a deep level a sense of shame in those he abused,' said Paul. 'As for those who protected him ... Northern Ireland is so old fashioned. It has its respectability, its conformity, this thing of not making a fuss.'

The 1998 report of the independent inquiry into Bangor Grammar School's handling of the case found that the school had been 'seriously at fault' in a number of ways. 'The impression given by the headmaster's and the chairman's attitudes to the 1991 complaint was that the school's reputation had to be protected from what was seen by them as an exaggeration or overdramatisation by the boy and his parents,' the report concluded.

'Brown's supporters wrote to the papers saying he was a saintlike character who just had a little weakness,' said Paul. He mimicked a nice North Down accent: ' "Let us not cast stones – who knows what temptations he faced ..." ' These people don't seem to take it in that this man seriously assaulted boys. His religion was his veneer of respectability. He used to bring us on summer camp to Guysmere in Castlerock and in the morning he'd come in when he was aroused, sit boys on his knee and get them to recite prayers. He turned spiritual conversation into explicitly sexual conversation. But even in court, when he was being sentenced, there was a big crowd of clerics there supporting him. I just thought, God almighty.'

Once the case was off the ground, Paul said he was aware that being middle class helped Brown's victims – they were able to use their contacts and connections to push the issue. They fought for the inquiry – which was resisted by the board of governors on the grounds that it 'would not serve in the best interests of the school' (*County Down Spectator*, 18 June 1998). Then Brown's golden handshake redundancy deal was revoked after lobbying at the highest levels. The headmaster of the school took early retirement.

The then minister of education, John McFall, criticised the decision by the board of governors at Bangor Grammar to give Brown early retirement 'while facing charges of which he would only a short time later be convicted'. McFall said that the board had provided Brown with 'substantial financial benefits' (*Irish News*, 4 December 1998). 'If you are literate and can speak in the same way as government ministers and BBC editors, there is a reciprocal thing,' said Paul. 'They understand you. I'm no class warrior, but I'm not sure you'd be taken so seriously if you were from a poor background.'

'A TRIBE OF WARRIORS'

Jeff Dudgeon had worked as Bob McCartney's constituency office manager during the period when Brown was tried and convicted. He told me that there was a lot of paedophilia in North Down. He had dealt with matters connected with about twenty cases in the course of three years. The cover of evangelical religion was not uncommon, and had featured strongly in the Kincora scandal too. William McGrath, Orangeman, Free Presbyterian and leader of a bizarre paramilitary organisation called Tara, ran Kincora Boys' Home in Belfast. McGrath and a number of other staff members systematically abused boys there during the sixties and seventies. The British security service, MI5, knew about this, but allowed it to continue – McGrath was an agent. Another paramilitary leader of the time, John McKeague, was a regular visitor, and also had a liking for sex with boys. It all tended to undermine somewhat the scathing references made by loyalist evangelicals, including Paisley, to the paedophile priests of Rome.

Loyalist paramilitary organisations frequently put it about that people they had beaten up or kneecapped were child abusers, and made no distinction between child abuse and homosexuality. Dudgeon had given advice to David Templeton, a young Presbyterian minister who had been stopped at customs with a homosexual video and was later investigated by the RUC. Disgraced, he had moved from North Down to a hardline estate in north Belfast. There he was brutally beaten by a UVF gang and died six weeks later. The UVF went on to claim, without any evidence, that he had been a child abuser. Dudgeon blamed the tabloid newspapers. 'The tabloids are the new religion. They provide the morality. Confessors who don't forgive.'

Homosexuality was certainly not respectable. When Eoin McNamee's novel *Resurrection Man* was made into a film, much was made of its similarity to the activities of the murder gang which became known as the Shankill Butchers. These men had committed mass murder, and terrorised the Catholic community during the 1970s. Several commentators on the film pointed out that there was an element of homo-eroticism in the relationships between members of the gang. The Reverend Roy Magee, a Presbyterian minister who had been instrumental in bringing about the 1994 loyalist ceasefire, reacted indignantly to these claims. They amounted to 'a slur' on 'family men'. A relative of one of the Butchers' victims retorted that the claims were a slur on homosexuals.

Dudgeon said that there was a 'prominent homo-sensibility in unionism', dating back to the days of 'big house' unionism. He included among those he believed to have been gay James Stronge, son of Sir Norman Stronge. Father and son were murdered by the IRA at Tynan Abbey in 1981. 'Protestantism is a community in decline, and there tends to be a decrease in heterosexuality in such communities. The breeding instinct dies out.'

Dudgeon had been probably the North's most prominent gay spokesman. He had been to the fore during the fight-back against Paisley's Save Ulster from Sodomy campaign in 1977, when a Labour government proposed to decriminalise homosexuality in Northern Ireland, bringing it into line with the rest of the United Kingdom. Gay rights activists had countered the evangelicals with placards and T-shirts emblazoned with: 'Save Sodomy from Ulster'. In the end

Dudgeon had brought the British government to the European Court at Strasbourg, and the law was changed in 1982. He had been involved in the Campaign for Equal Citizenship after the Anglo-Irish Agreement, where the unlikely alliance of the late Limerick socialist Jim Kemmy and Bob McCartney fell apart after political feuding. The campaign had its roots in the British and Irish Communist Organisation (BICO), then in a unionist phase, later to turn nationalist.

Dudgeon described a party in 1987 after McCartney failed to get elected as MP, at which 'Glad to be Gay' was played on the piano. 'Bob is a sixties liberal on gay matters,' he said. When McCartney was elected in 1995, Dudgeon started to work for him. The participation by a radical homosexual in the anti-agreement alliance between McCartney and the DUP seemed bizarre, particularly since one of the grounds on which the DUP opposed the agreement was its tolerance of homosexuality. 'It was a tactical alliance, so I could live with that,' Dudgeon said. 'I'd been on TV with Robinson the time homosexual law was being debated. The first time I met Paisley, he introduced me to Robinson who said, "I think we've already met". Bob had warned Robinson just in case it would ever cross his mind, that he was never to try to use me as Bob's Achilles' heel. He said I was a hero of sorts who had taken on the British government at Strasbourg. There are gays in the DUP, of course. The party has stopped picketing the gay pride march, which is a pity. It reduces the numbers.'

When the referendum was passed in May 1998, Dudgeon resigned. By this time he had changed his tune on his former leader. 'McCartney has returned to the heartland of unionism. He is being applauded by unreconstructed unionists of the old school. He is becoming one of them. The waifs and strays and fundamentalists are looking to him. After the Good Friday Agreement was signed, I felt that just being negative was no longer appropriate.'

Dudgeon was involved in the Irish Association, which, he said, existed 'to maintain contact across the partitioned island in an atmosphere of mutual respect for difference'. He introduced me to a term I hadn't heard before. 'A lot of Women's Coalition types are guilties,' he said. A 'guilty', he explained, is a Protestant who is ashamed of his or her background and constantly apologises for it, or supports those who radically oppose unionism. He had no doubt himself that Catholics were every bit as sectarian as Protestants. Not that he looked at Protestants through rose-tinted glasses. 'There is more aggression in Protestants than Catholics – it's the frontiersman mentality. God and a rifle. A chunk of them went off to the States in the eighteenth century and were ruthless scalpers of Indians. A friend of mine who is an Ulster ethnic buff in New York brought me to these farms in Virginia where the Ulster farmers had gone. They had worn out the land and then moved on. Northern Irish Protestants are under perpetual threat. Half the people under-react dangerously, and half over-react.'

'In 1912 everyone knew the threat was there. Now half of them have forgotten. If the frontiersmen hadn't been there, the others would have been driven out. Eddie McGrady of the SDLP said in 1989 that the border was now on the edge of Belfast. The fighting on the edge of the Garvaghy Road is about getting the Prods out. Look at the burnings of Protestant businesses on the Ormeau Road last year. The Catholic mob knows what it has to do.

'Because this is a society in perpetual crisis, bad Protestants are allowed their head. Once they have become socially degraded, nothing, including religion and respectability, holds them back. In an odd way, maybe the saving of Ulster will be the single mums, breeding without family planning. A tribe of warriors who will hold the frontier. Uncivilised and unscrupulous. It is a feature of the withdrawal of the unionist middle classes from politics. The paramilitaries are an army without an officer class. They are lawless. There is no control mechanism – they'd cut a person's arm off with a garden shears.'

NORTH BELFAST
Frankenstein, Fiends and Fallen Angels

'Be calm! I intreat you to hear me before you give vent to your hatred on my devoted head ... Remember that I am thy creature; I ought to be thy Adam, but I am rather the fallen angel.'

from Frankenstein, MARY SHELLEY

'MARY SHELLEY COULD HAVE WRITTEN *FRANKENSTEIN* ABOUT US'

Jeff Dudgeon's monstrous vision of the warrior classes might, I suspected, have been camped up for effect. But Billy Mitchell, who had two paramilitary murders behind him and had spent fourteen years in prison, shared his notion of an army without an officer class. 'When you incite people to form armies and then walk away, you create a monster and the monster does what it wants,' he said. 'Basically, I think Mary Shelley could have written *Frankenstein* about us.'

North Belfast lies between the Cave Hill, with its distinctive Napoleon's-nose skyline, and the docks. It includes old redbrick terraces which used to house the workers in the shipyards, in numerous factories, including Gallaher's huge tobacco business, and in the linen mills. In fact, the area was originally a series of mill villages, and still has the remnants of that structure. There are sad streets with an air of faded grandeur, villas declined to bedsits, a pervasive smell of damp. There are tree-lined enclaves of wealthy ease. North Belfast also takes in the huge Rathcoole housing estate, and great swathes of suburban bungalows.

It was on the Cave Hill in 1795 that the United Irishmen swore their oath 'never to desist in our efforts until we have subverted the authority of England over our country and asserted her independence (quoted in Bardon, p. 223). However, by 1912 the area was established as a unionist stronghold, and largely remained so until the beginning of the Troubles, when huge population movements occurred across Belfast. Today it is characterised by its small, tight, segregated communities, many of them poor. Some of these are physically separated by peacelines, high walls and fences topped with barbed wire, and with gates which might be closed at night, or for days during times of high tension.

Boundaries have been constantly shifting, house by house, street by street, identified by flags and painted kerbstones. The constant was that Protestants were losing territory, and Catholics were gaining it. Unionists lobbied for peacelines, only to find Catholics moving into streets on the Protestant side of the lines. These borders were dangerous places, and had continued to be volatile after the 1994 ceasefires had brought their 'imperfect peace', as it became known. Flashpoints.

North Belfast has seen some of the worst violence of the Troubles – almost 550 people were murdered there, out of a total of more than 3,600 dead. Loyalist paramilitaries have mounted a particularly intense murder campaign against Catholic civilians in the area. Within the Protestant enclaves, the territories controlled by different paramilitary factions are clearly delineated.

Born in 1940 to a Baptist mother, and a father who died when he was two, Mitchell was reared in poverty at the end of the tramlines, in what became the big suburb of Glengormley on the outer edge of north Belfast. He was saved when he was eight, and saved again every time a mission came to the area. The white tents of the missions are still a familiar sight around the North in summertime – the harvesting of souls. 'Every time you had a bad conscience you went to the mission,' he said. He forgot about religion when he left school. He started as a copy boy at the *Belfast Telegraph*, intending to become a reporter. But it was too slow a ladder. He left and took work as a lorry driver. 'Life was good. It was the fifties, the birth of rock-and-roll. If you left one job you got another. I was in a wee flute band and we started to take part in the Paisley rallies – that was the first time the Protestant–Catholic thing came up. We got carried away with the rhetoric. We were told we needed to prepare for a doomsday situation. As time went on, the rhetoric got stronger, about the need to fight and the need to arm ... Of course the preachers and the politicians say they were speaking in spiritual terms, and we do have to take responsibility ourselves for what we did. But for us it was reality. We took them literally. It got out of control.'

In his essay on 'Paisley's Progress', the poet Tom Paulin quotes the preacher: 'Good preaching is charged with the dynamite of heaven. When the fuse of true prayer is set alight with the fire of the Holy Ghost, and thus the gospel dynamite is exploded, what tremendous results occur.' As Paulin comments drily, 'Puritan metaphor is a form of irony which has a habit of becoming literal' (Paulin, 1996, p. 36).

'We weren't like the Provos or the Stickies or the IPLO or the INLA,' said Mitchell. The Provos are the Provisional IRA, which broke away from the Official IRA in 1969 to become the dominant republican body, with Sinn Féin as its political wing. The OIRA became known as the Stickies, with the Workers' Party as its political wing. The IPLO is the Irish People's Liberation Organisation, a 1986 breakaway faction of the INLA, the Irish National Liberation Army, which was set up in 1975 by disaffected members of the OIRA. All these republican groups engaged in fierce ideological battles, as well as in feuding.

'We didn't have a coherent ideology,' Mitchell continued. 'Our political analysis was that Ulster was being sold out. Our philosophy was, Not an inch. We knew what we were against, but we didn't know what we were for. Sometimes you did try to justify things – you'd say, look what the British did in Dresden, there was civilians killed there, so it must be all right. If I don't know the difference between a Ra [IRA] man and a taig, look what Bomber Harris did. But mostly we didn't rationalise. We were just caught up in the hurly-burly. You didn't think of a target as a person with a family and feelings. A target was an enemy of Ulster. A thing.'

What Mitchell said reminded me of something another former paramilitary murderer had said to me. We had been talking about the phenomenon of loyalist killers becoming born-again Christians in prison. He told me that it had taken him years of reflection, and his prison conversion, to realise that Catholics were human beings. Such religion was like a heavy drug, effective, but unreliable.

Mitchell had been in the UVF. The men he murdered were in the Ulster Defence Association (UDA). 'It was an internecine feud. About territory, personalities.' Jailed in 1976, he was of the prison generation that went on to provide the leadership of the PUP. They came under the influence of Gusty Spence, who had carried out one of the first sectarian murders of the Troubles, but had started to think differently in jail. 'We would go into prison as macho men, talking militant. Gusty would ask us, "What are you here for?" and we'd say, someone squealed on us or we got caught, and he'd ask again. He was looking for an ideological answer and we didn't have one. We began to interact with the republican prisoners, and through reading and debating, especially with the Stickies, we began to learn about the history we hadn't been taught in school. A lot of us were educated in Long Kesh who never would have been otherwise.'

Spence's father had been in the UVF when it was formed by Edward Carson in 1912, the military muscle to back the Unionist rebellion against home rule. The UVF was led by the local unionist aristocracy and business community, and encouraged by the Protestant clergy. They imported a large shipment of German arms through Larne. The Reverend F.J. MacNeice, father of the poet Louis MacNeice, spoke of an 'unparalleled betrayal' which had united unionists of all classes; he suggested that no predominantly Roman Catholic parliament had ever done justice to Protestants. During a 1989 commemoration of the gunrunning, the Ulster Society used the motto: 'God give us men ... for Ulster and her freedom'.

In 1914 the Unionists, united in the Ulster Unionist Council, saw their action as being in the tradition of the Scottish Covenanters. One Presbyterian preached that 'You and I ... have what we have today because of those who, in other days, refused to be bound by enactments of state which were antagonistic to their religion and their liberty ... It was said to them as it was said to Athanasius – All the world is against you, and they replied as he did, Then we are against the world.' This was the argument of the Orangemen at Drumcree, and David Trimble echoed the sentiments after the UUP refused to accept the Way Forward deal to introduce multiparty devolved government in July 1999. The UUP said then that the holding of illegal weapons was incompatible with democracy. Four months later, Trimble got the support of 58 per cent of his party's ruling council, to enter a devolved administration which included Sinn Féin. He revealed that he had written a letter of resignation which would take effect if by 12 February 2000 the IRA had not decommissioned. He placed the letter in the hands of Sir Josias Cunningham, president of the council. It was Sir Josias's grandfather who signed the cheque that paid for the UVF's guns in 1912. One of the 1912 guns turned up again in 1998 when it was among the weapons 'decommissioned' by the LVF.

Four months after the UVF's guns were landed, the First World War broke out. Carson ordered his 35,000-strong Ulster Volunteers to fight for the king, in the 36th (Ulster) Division. In his poem 'Wounds', Michael Longley describes 'pictures from my father's head'. His father had survived the Somme.

> First, the Ulster Division at the Somme
> Going over the top with 'Fuck the Pope!'
> 'No surrender!': a boy about to die,
> Screaming 'Give 'em one for the Shankill!'
> 'Wilder than Gurkhas' were my father's words
> Of admiration and bewilderment.

Between 1 and 2 July 1916, 5,500 Ulster soldiers were killed.

The 'sacrifice at the Somme' was seen as a crucial part of the unionist contract with Britain, the part for which unionists feel they are still owed something in return. The bulk of the UVF was assimilated into the new Ulster Special Constabulary in 1920. The Specials took part in the forcing out of Catholics by loyalists and Orangemen in north Belfast and other areas in the twenties and thirties.

In the early sixties the UVF attempted to step up sectarian conflict, and in 1966 an elderly Protestant woman, Matilda Gould, was murdered when her house in the Shankill Road area was petrol-bombed in an attack on a Catholic-owned off-licence next door. 'This house belongs to a taig' had been daubed on the wall. Later that year the UVF declared war on the IRA. Responding to Prime Minister Terence O'Neill's efforts at reforming the Protestant state to deal with the rising civil rights movement, the UVF warned that there should be 'no more speeches of appeasement. We are heavily armed Protestants dedicated to the cause.'

On 16 June 1966 Ian Paisley addressed a rally at the Ulster Hall, where he claimed he had the support of ex-servicemen from both world wars, 'defenders of the flag of Ulster' and 'now comprising four divisions of the UVF'. Just over a week later, Spence attended a Paisley rally. The next day he and others attacked four Catholic barmen, killing young Peter Ward. One of those convicted of the murder, Hugh McClean from Carrickfergus, said that when he was in the process of joining the UVF he was asked if he agreed with Paisley and was prepared to follow him. Paisley, however, said he knew nothing about the UVF, and was only connected with legal organisations. He has always insisted that he could not be responsible for the activities of those who supported him. O'Neill proscribed the UVF within days of the killing, calling it an 'evil thing'. Referring to the role of the UVF at the Somme, he said there was no connection between that body and 'a sordid conspiracy of criminals prepared to take up arms against un-protected fellow citizens' (McDonald and Cusack, p. 10).

However, the modern version of the UVF boasted of its lineage, which allowed it to consider itself a cut above the other loyalist paramilitary army, the UDA. On parade it carried banners and drums emblazoned with 'UVF 1912', and the organisation had numerous songs linking the two periods of UVF activity, and particularly boasting of its role at the Somme. (The fact that thousands of nationalist Irishmen also took part was conveniently forgotten, and the disastrous slaughter at the Somme was treated as a loyalist victory.) 'Suicide Battalion' is typical, with its reference to John Major, the former Conservative prime minister:

> They fought and they won the battle of the Somme
> But for Major and Dublin the fight will still go on
> For God and for Ulster is cast on every breath
> Of the suicide battalion of the UVF.

When, in late 1969, Lord Hunt recommended the disbandment of the B Specials and the disarming of the RUC, the UVF, during rioting, shot dead the first policeman to be killed in the Troubles, Constable Victor Arbuckle. The organisation hastened the political demise of O'Neill when it began a bombing campaign which was attributed to the IRA, hardening Protestant attitudes against reform.

The UVF had two particularly militant and violent units. Its Portadown unit terrorised mid-Ulster from the seventies to the nineties. The Shankill Butchers were so called because they used butcher's knives to torture and kill their victims, mostly Catholics picked up at random on the city-centre edges of west and north Belfast in the seventies. The UVF included former British soldiers, and some still serving in the UDR, one of these a Shankill Butcher. In 1974 it bombed Dublin and Monaghan, killing thirty-three people. To date it is believed to have murdered about 534 people. Its 1994 ceasefire was announced by Gusty Spence at Fernhill House, ancestral home of the Cunninghams, now a museum of loyalist history.

Released on licence in 1990, Mitchell had been working since then on 'conflict transformation' in north Belfast, particularly along the interfaces between the communities. He works with republicans, including a brother of the prominent Sinn Féin spokesman Alex Maskey. 'The idea is to bring people from loyalist and nationalist backgrounds together to talk about the hurt of the past years and start laying myths. To understand what we had in common – the bad housing, unemployment, dereliction – to unpack those issues and to work together.'

The peacelines were surrounded by streets so dangerous that many of them had been abandoned. After the ceasefires, many of these houses were bought up by property speculators, north and south of the border. Glossy property supplements in newspapers in the Republic featured full-page advertisements, row upon row of photographs of these run-down terrace dwellings, montages of deprivation turning into investment potential. Mitchell and others got funding to buy some of the houses, which were then rebuilt, by loyalists on the loyalist side of the lines, by republicans on the other.

Small traditional communities did cling on in these desolate-looking places. I visited Torrens one night, in the company of Billy Hutchinson, who, as a local councillor, had been called in because republican youths had crossed the peaceline and attacked a house. We sat in the tiny living room of a man who was obviously an old paramilitary. He was rearing to go, to sort things out in the old style. But he knew it was not an option. He shook his fist. 'See this fucking ceasefire?' he said.

'The idea is to transform the idea of patriotism, so that it can include things like rebuilding your community after years of war,' said Mitchell. 'It is not the old community relations idea of tea and buns. We recruit mainly ex-prisoners, people with a bit of credibility, a bit of respect, who have seen that violence is counter-productive and that we need to build bridges. Peace will be brought from the ground up. We work on a cascade system – key players are trained and they go out and talk and debate and they bring in others.'

Mitchell co-ordinated a community forum, believing that 'participative democracy and representative democracy have to go hand in hand'. He described himself as a Christian socialist, an evangelical but not a fundamentalist. 'Paisleyism is really Protestant nationalism with Ulster as the sacral state. The danger is that you can end up down the road of theocracy, people getting messages from God . . .' This indeed was the road taken by some of the new loyalist paramilitary organisations of the late nineties. Led by self-styled pastors, they quoted the Bible to justify their violence against Catholics.

Mitchell had debated the 1798 rebellion, and shared platforms with republicans in hardline republican areas. Although as an evangelical Christian he opposed homosexuality and abortion, he supported a woman's right to choose, and equality of opportunity for gays. He writes a column in the *North Belfast News*, a nationalist newspaper, to show readers that unionism is a valid philosophy which can embrace democratic socialism and pluralism. He questioned whether Sinn Féin was really a socialist party. 'Some would say they are the social conscience wing of Fianna Fáil.' The populist Fianna Fáil, founded by Eamon de Valera, is the largest political party in the Republic.

There are also 'restorative justice' schemes, controversial programmes through which people, some of them with links to the paramilitary organisations, attempt to work with those, mostly young men, who have been accused of 'anti-social behaviour', like joyriding or stealing. The idea is to encourage the offender to mend his ways, without recourse to so-called punishment beatings and shootings.

The punishment beatings have gone on, however – testimony to the multiple feuds which have raged between loyalist gangs in the post-ceasefire period. North Belfast has been particularly badly affected. Mitchell said it was a problem, but that in many ways it was similar to the type of gang warfare which characterised other big cities. The 'turf wars' between the UDA and the UVF are complicated by faction fighting within the two groups, and new groupings involving gangsters who have defected to ally themselves with the LVF and with newer anti-ceasefire elements. The feuds are about the right to control territory, largely meaning the right to extort 'protection money', or to run moneylending rackets or to sell drugs within a particular patch.

Mount Vernon is one of the estates in which the paramilitary presence is most obvious. It is like a broken-down fortress. Built on a steep hill, the estate of redbrick houses, maisonettes and blocks of bricked-up flats looms over the Shore Road, its entrance marked by a huge, crudely painted mural of armed and masked men. 'Prepared for peace, ready for war', its equivocal message. Almost every lamppost had a purple UVF flag. The area was the centre of several ongoing feuds in 1999. A local UVF leader was shot in the legs, reportedly because he was pocketing money raised by running a brothel in a flat in the estate. He was believed to have ordered the murder of the Reverend David Templeton in 1997, amongst others. He was also in trouble with the UDA, and had been 'stood down' by the UVF's Shankill Road leadership. In 1997 Mount Vernon UVF also murdered Raymond McCord, a young former RAF man who had tangled with the paramilitaries over drug dealing. His father dubbed the estate 'Mount Vermin'. The UVF in Mount Vernon was said to be well armed but paralysed by fears that some of its members were informers.

The hardest objective to realise, Mitchell said, was the building of a 'vertical bridge' to reach middle unionism and civil society. 'The trouble is that on our side, whenever someone gets on, becomes a lawyer or a teacher or a journalist, they forsake their roots. Once they get a wee bit respectable, they don't want to be reminded that they came from among the riffraff in Tiger's Bay or Mount Vernon. They go off to north Down and distance themselves. On the other side, in the nationalist community, there is more solidarity. Their professional people haven't left them. They give something back . . .'

According to Mitchell, this went to the heart of the problem with unionism. 'There is this thing about knowing your place. There is a dichotomy between middle unionism and loyalism. Middle unionism disapproves of loyalists getting above themselves. All this talk about the independence and individuality of Protestants is a nonsense. Those of us born into the 'lower orders' felt we were born to follow, and our betters, the people you touched the forelock to, were born to lead. You look at the way mainstream unionists hate us now. They sneer at our political representatives when they wear suits.' This was a reference to the DUP designation of the fringe loyalists as 'gangsters in suits'. 'They hate community development. Nationalists had a head start on us in this. They had to stand up for themselves, fight for all they got. We sat back, subservient, waiting to be looked after.'

As for the attitudes of mainstream unionists to the paramilitaries: 'They hate us because they can no longer use us as a threat. I'm being honest. The DUP had no trouble sitting down with UVF men when we were killing taigs and that is being blunt about it. The UUP had no problem organising the Ulster Workers' Strike with us. When we stopped, the venom was really aimed at people like Davey [Ervine] and Hutchie [Billy Hutchinson], the ones who brokered the ceasefire, the ones providing the analysis. We've sheathed the sabre, and they can't rattle it any more.

'It is easy to say, "I have nothing against Catholics, some of my best friends are Catholics, we drink with them in the golf club." There is still a them and us. I can take people saying they detest what the loyalist paramilitaries have done, and that they are ashamed of it. I am ashamed of it myself. But a lot of people who say that are in right-wing unionism, which put the boot in the other way – discrimination, keeping them out of parliament, making sure they don't enjoy their culture.

'It was not us who set up and maintained the sectarian state. We have changed and we have a right to expect you to validate that change. There is no one in Northern Ireland has clean hands. You may not have shot someone or bombed, but in many ways we were the social manifestation of your bigotry, even if you say you didn't have it.'

'SHARING NOTHING BECAUSE THERE IS NOTHING TO SHARE'

York Road, where Mitchell was based, and, further out, the Shore Road, used to be the heartland of working-class Protestantism in north Belfast. It had been the scene of fierce sectarian confrontations since the middle of the nineteenth century when people were crowding into Belfast to work in its industries. Streets were literally secured by means of riots. The area was devastated when the Germans bombed the docks and shipyards in 1941. The writer Sam McAughtry told me he remembered seeing a man, a soldier, sobbing on his knees outside a broken house in Tiger's Bay after his wife and children had been killed.

Later, much of the area was redeveloped, and the warrens of little redbrick terraces which characterised it were demolished. Tiger's Bay was partly rebuilt, but most people were rehoused in new estates like the huge Rathcoole and the smaller Mount Vernon. Sectarian violence and the surge of better-off Protestants out to the suburbs left room for the Catholic population of areas like New Lodge to expand. Houses in streets now entirely occupied by Catholics still had the metal brackets on their front walls from which Union Jacks would have hung every July in the Protestant past.

Frontiers, like the once elegant Duncairn Gardens, are still the scene of violent clashes particularly in the volatile summer marching season. Duncairn's Protestant population had declined by almost a quarter in the decade between 1982 and 1991. McAughtry had made a television programme to show the Protestants how the Catholics really lived across the peaceline. He described this as an epicentre. It had its own class structure: 'Shipyard workers might have lived in Duncairn Gardens, but down in Tiger's Bay it would have been un-skilled labourers.' In the film he told a young man from Tiger's Bay that Catholics had crowded into the New Lodge because they had been put out of other places by Protestants. The young man was not impressed. 'You wouldn't trust one of them ones,' he said. 'One minute they'd be talking to you and the next they'd stab you in the back.'

McAughtry had worked for a time in the labour exchange in Cor-poration Street, Britain's largest, he said. 'The exchanges had a way of conveying that the candidate kicked with the right foot,' he said. 'Orange connections weren't as much use as the Masonic. In Short and Harland's, when there were going to be payoffs, people would go out and join the Masonic. It was regarded as being next to the Black preceptory. You'd find a lot of Orangemen would join the Orange Order, take the Arch Purple, go on into the Black and then join the Masonic.'

Despite initiatives like the Belfast Action Teams, there is still high unemployment and low expectations among both communities. McAughtry has used the phrase, 'sharing nothing because there is nothing to share'. However, he commented that Catholic unemployment was consistently higher than Protestant unemployment. Research carried out at the University of Ulster showed a considerable difference in 1995. *A Study of Belfast's Peacelines* by B. Murtagh indicated that peaceline areas of Belfast experienced 'significantly higher' levels of poverty than other parts of the North. On north Belfast's peaceline, 23 per cent of heads of household on the Protestant side were unemployed, compared with 38 per cent on the Catholic side (cited in *Belfast Telegraph*, 6 January 1995). As trade unionist Inez McCormack commented, the Protestant level was appalling, the Catholic level catastrophic.

McAughtry's efforts to represent both communities by standing as a Labour candidate in the 1998 Assembly elections led to him being, in his own word, 'slaughtered'. He got 250 votes. 'Even in the heady days of Terence O'Neill, all he had to do was say on the doorsteps that the Northern Ireland Labour Party (NILP) wanted the border done away with, and it blitzed us. Catholics vote green because it works for them. Protestants vote Orange to try to resist the advance of the Catholics. They feel that every yard the Catholics get is a yard closer to absorption into a hostile united Ireland. The DUP and Sinn Féin can get the people out in hordes. Northern Ireland isn't ready yet for non-sectarian politics.'

Sectarianism was powerfully demonstrated in the thirties when Protestants who tried to stop loyalists from expelling Catholics were themselves dubbed 'rotten Prods' and put out. In 1949 when the Ireland Act was passed, securing the North's union with Britain, the NILP supported partition. It remained unionist, and had at a time four MPs at Stormont, three of them lay preachers.

Lord Brookeborough dubbed unemployment 'a socialist bandwagon'. The NILP attempted to represent unemployed nationalists and unionists – but firmly in the context of the Stormont government. However, internal pressures were building. In 1964 it proposed a bill to outlaw religious discrimination. By this stage, former republican Paddy Devlin had joined its executive. According to historian Frank Wright, it was the unlikely issue of 'Sabbatarianism versus swing parks' which fatally damaged the party, when it split over a vote in 1964 as to whether playgrounds in Belfast should be opened on Sundays.

'NOTHING GOES ON IN NORTH BELFAST THAT THE PARAMILITARIES DON'T HAVE A HAND IN'

'I laugh at these ones in north Down, the ones that think it's all over,' said David Browne. 'They want to come over here during Drumcree.' Browne is an Ulster Unionist councillor who lives in Skegoniel, one of the front lines of inner north Belfast. He sat in the Forum but failed to win a seat in the Assembly. Too many unionists had stood and some had appeared to be in the UUP who were not, he said. He told me that five people had been shot dead within a hundred yards of his door.

There was ample evidence in the area of Protestant rage. On one gable wall someone had written, 'Landlords who rent to taigs will be shot'. One of the first prisoners to be released under the terms of the Belfast Agreement was a young Protestant man who had beaten a Catholic to death in the Waterworks park. The murderer was not acting for a paramilitary organisation – it was a gesture of private, sectarian hatred. This area used to be largely Protestant, but has become almost exclusively Catholic. The Waterworks, a place where street drinkers loiter now, was once a private area open only to keyholders.

I asked Browne about the role of loyalist paramilitaries in the area. 'There is nothing goes on in north Belfast that the paramilitaries don't have a hand in. Business, building, you name it. As soon as a building site is bought, they are in looking for protection money. Businesses are still having money extorted from them. The Provos have never been as bad as our side in this regard – they have their fingers in all sorts of other pies. Our side hasn't the brains for that. On the Shore Road and the York Road you hear Protestants complaining about depopulation. But it's not Catholics moving in that's causing it. It's the paramilitaries.'

In search of a home in Belfast in the eighties, I viewed a flat in one of the big old houses around the Waterworks. The agent led me up a stairway with no banisters. When I asked about this, he explained that the banisters had been torn out and burned in a fire in the hallway. He said this in a nonchalant way, as if it was normal information, like what day the bins were collected, or where the hall light was. (There wasn't one.)

Browne said the paramilitaries had got a firm grip on north Belfast right at the start of the Troubles. He went to school in Tiger's Bay in the sixties and said he remembered boys with guns at school. 'One day a guy called to school and asked me would I drive a car for him at lunch time. I said, "Why?" He said, "We're going to go and kill a couple of taigs." My mother would have broke my two legs if I'd brought the police to our door by getting involved in the like of that. I was never afraid of anyone and I could fight like the best of them. I remember boys beating up a Catholic on the bus one day and I stopped them, and we are as good Protestants as anyone else.'

He agreed with the view that the IRA would never have gone on ceasefire if it hadn't been for the activities of the loyalists. 'There is no question. If it hadn't have been for the Johnny Adairs . . . thon boy was a headbanger.' Adair, who had killed up to twenty Catholics and had been described by the judge who tried him as 'nakedly sectarian', was released from prison in September 1999. Browne said a lot of his friends had gone that way, and ended up in prison. 'See people that voted no in the agreement? I said to them, look at Kosovo. That's what could happen here. I see young lads and the hatred in them is shocking. And the bravado. They could be out killing and it wouldn't bother them.'

He had voted for the agreement, but reluctantly. 'I wasn't happy about the prisoners getting out, for a start.' He felt Unionists had not caught on to the changes that have taken place around them. 'The days when Big Paisley and them could bring this country to its knees are over. You could be sitting in a Protestant area and fifty yards down the road is a Catholic area and it is growing.'

His party had made a mistake in hanging so much on the decommissioning issue, he believed. 'At the end of the day it is not the guns you have to decommission, it's the minds. But we've got ourselves on the hook now and we can't give in. The DUP would make mincemeat of us.' He sympathised with the party leader. 'Trimble had a hard time. He has eejits like Willie Ross and Willie Thompson on his back. But I'm a great one for loyalty. I'd have split the party and taken the ones with me who were loyal. By the time we got to the Way Forward it was too late. He couldn't accept it.'

During the 1998 Assembly elections I had walked through this part of north Belfast with Billy Hutchinson and his team of canvassers. We met at the PUP's Shore Road office, where a faded photograph of the Queen as a young woman looked down on leaflets about welfare benefits. This image, at least thirty-five years old, was far more common in loyalist venues than contemporary photographs of the cross old Elizabeth Windsor of the end of the century. In the window an ad for workers in a Dutch factory specified that knowledge of circuit boards would be an advantage. Suitable work for ex-bombers, I thought, but didn't say. In Tiger's Bay a drunk man came to the door and tore up the PUP leaflet, roaring angrily about dirtbirds and murderers. One of Hutchinson's canvassers jeered at him, 'At least we can read and write.' Hutchinson told his man off. There were the big white vans of market traders parked on one street, and one of the canvassers told me, as though it was the definition of decline, 'The Prods have gone now and the Pakis have moved in.'

'EVERYTHING WAS AT THE SHARP END'

'The Protestant cry in north Belfast is, "They are trying to get rid of us",' said the Reverend Lesley Carroll. An enthusiastic young Tyrone woman, she had spent the ten years since she was ordained in the Presbyterian churches of north Belfast. When I met her she had just started a five-year ministry at Fortwilliam Park. Her church is on the Antrim Road, among houses built in Belfast's Victorian heyday for bankers, merchants, judges, and the like. Wealthy, powerful people. There are still bits of her parish which are, as she put it slightly disparagingly, 'nice', meaning middle class, comfortable. Her manse is on a nice road in a wealthy enclave. The peak of Cave Hill could be seen through the trees that lined the road. But the profile of her congregation had changed radically, and Reverend Carroll said its future was uncertain. 'There used to be seven or eight hundred families in this congregation – now it's down to two hundred,' she said. 'Because it was part of what was known as the murder triangle, the wealthier people just didn't want to live here. They moved out to the suburbs. A lot of houses became businesses, or flats. There would be a lot of retired people. Catholics have bought houses here.' These parts of north Belfast had attracted middle-class Catholics who were not wealthy enough to buy similar-sized houses in 'better' areas, like south Belfast or north Down. Prices were lower here because of the murder risk, and because of the risk of unrest in the surrounding ghettos.

'My congregation would be 70 per cent working class,' said Reverend Carroll, who preferred it that way. She described her previous contract, in Duncairn Gardens, as brilliant. 'Everything was at the sharp end. The church building actually straddles the peaceline between Tiger's Bay and the New Lodge. At a time, its congregation would have lived in New Lodge. That is all Catholic now, but there was still a door from the church out into it, into Hillman Street. It was never opened. One night the Girls' Brigade got locked into the church and we had to open that door to get out. The Girls' Brigade officers were terrified. The children in Hillman Street probably didn't even know it was a church. INLA was delicately sprayed on the back of the door.

'I tried to make a point of going round there to chat. We had a summer scheme and the natural end of things was for the children to stone each other across the peaceline. We tried to negotiate. We drove round there one day, but the Catholic children started shouting, "It's the peelers", and ran away.'

Reverend Carroll grew up in a republican village in Tyrone, but her background was, she said, 'totally Presbyterian', and very sheltered. Mixing was considered dangerous. She knew from an early age that she wanted to be a minister. 'I particularly went over the water because I knew I was coming back. This is where I was meant to be. The Northern Ireland context was very much part of the call.' She liked the freedom of thought she encountered in England, and was dismayed by the difference she found when she returned to complete her studies at the Presbyterian College in Belfast. 'Instead of seminars, you had classes – you were the pupil and someone else was the teacher. You had to watch what you said. People were always judging you, deciding if you were theologically sound. I was unacceptable in the first place because I was a woman. In my first year I was the only woman, and I was one of two in the second. A lot of the men felt we were going against the Bible.'

The Church needed to recognise that it was no longer at the centre of society, she said. It had to work hard now to be relevant. 'I don't think the Church is simply the moral conscience of society. I have to get out on my feet and encounter people and in that encounter expect to meet Christ. I think of Matthew, chapter 25, where Christ talks about the judgment. He praised those of whom he said, "I was a stranger and ye took me in", and when they questioned him he said, "inasmuch as ye have done it unto the least of these my brethren, ye have done it unto me". To me that means that Christ is the hungry, the thirsty, the paramilitary, as well as the well-heeled. North Belfast has a strong paramilitary presence. It is a patchwork of paramilitary control. And when you meet these people they greet you. I find that humbling and deeply moving. I remember a senior Sinn Féin person saying that the difference between Protestants and Catholics is that Catholics love sinners. In Catholicism, everyone is in. In Protestantism, you have to get in.'

Reverend Carroll said she was an evangelical Christian, but that she would not be regarded as such by other Presbyterian evangelicals. 'They are the right wing of the Church – in their eyes I would be a loose liberal.' She laughed. Being unorthodox in such a church could be perilous. In 1985 the Reverend David Armstrong had to leave the North after members of his congregation at Limavady, County Derry, branded him a heretic. He had attended mass after loyalists burned a local Catholic church and had also visited a Catholic church to extend Christmas greetings to his neighbours. He has since joined the Church of England as a minister.

At the 1999 General Assembly of the Presbyterian Church the right wing prevailed. It was decided not to establish a new formal structure with the Irish Council of Churches. 'It was because they didn't want formal links with Catholicism,' said Reverend Carroll, who was disappointed by the decision. 'The Protestant Churches have an anti-Catholic strain because of the way we were formed in the days of the Reformation. I think we need to be more explicit about recognising this in the Westminster Confession. We avoid debating it because we are afraid of stirring up bad feeling among our own, but we need to face up to how Catholics feel about it. They feel the sharp end of it.' The Westminster Confession is the Presbyterian statement of faith. It implies that the Pope is the Antichrist.

The collapse of the Northern Ireland Assembly on the day of its formation in July 1999 left Reverend Carroll in despair. 'I sometimes fear that unionism is just incapable of change.' But she also felt that the peace process had encouraged an alternative sort of politics. 'There are people in the process now who might not agree, but who are developing new ways of sharing opinion and making agreements. Parties like Sinn Féin, the Women's Coalition and the PUP. They are able to operate in ways that neither the UUP nor the SDLP ever managed.'

She was a member of a several ecumenical groups and of the Evangelical Contribution on Northern Ireland. ECONI is based on the question, 'What does the Lord require of us?' and on 'resourcing Christians for a biblical response'. It publishes books, including one on how nationalists see unionists, and runs courses. Some of its members campaigned for the Belfast Agreement. An article in its June 1999 newsletter, ECONI News, reflected on the impasse in the peace process, warning, 'We are in danger of reaping a harvest of bitterness on the streets while those who should know better the power of the tongue (James 3:1–12) continue to disclaim any responsibility for the consequences of their fiery language.' The author, David Porter, said it was time 'for Christians to cry out to God for mercy, lest in his economy time is running out and we will be left to reap the judgement we have sown by our failure to demolish the idols of land and nation that have poisoned our relationships with each other and our worship of the living God'. The reaping of bitter harvests, I was to find, was a Protestant preoccupation.

'ON THE MARGIN OF THE GHETTOS'

According to John Gray, the fracturing of communities within north Belfast had left room between the cracks for at least one little enclave of 'people who have opted out of the imperatives of tribe'. They formed a 'hidden 10 per cent minority of mixed marriage, or no faith, or Bohemian, or alternative'. He lived in Glandore Avenue off the Antrim Road and defined his area as ten streets or so 'on the margin of the ghettos'. The librarian at Belfast's excellent Linen Hall Library, Gray stressed that he was speaking to me in a personal capacity.

He agreed with the idea that Protestants were less forgiving than Catholics. 'In the Catholic community there is more latitude, a presumption that eventually you will return to the fold. Whereas, in the Protestant community you are more likely to be disowned if you stray. It is seen as a manifestation of original sin. You have to remember that apart from the religious division, Belfast is the most socially divided city in the British Isles. Before the First World War the gap between skilled pay rates and unskilled was the widest in the British Isles by a long chalk. Before the end of the nineteenth century you had the process by which in strong Protestant areas the skilled workers were moving out. They established their own areas, leaving the unskilled in the inner city.

'Whereas, in the Catholic community that option was not, until recently, open, so you got an extension of the ghetto. Catholic teachers, doctors, solicitors lived near the community they came from, and serviced that community.' However, Gray believed that middle-class Protestant snobbery was more pronounced in people who had been born into that class than in those who had worked their way up.

Gray described the class structure of north Belfast's geography in terms of social precipices. 'Above us there is a small affluent ghetto under the Cave Hill. Below us is New Lodge.' He was born in south Belfast, on the Malone Road, to English parents who felt they had been exiled to Northern Ireland. His father was a university lecturer. 'The most effective way I ever saw that described was as the "legation quarter" of Belfast, the reference being to imperial Peking, where the embassies had a walled section of the city to themselves. We inhabited a little world between the Malone Road and the Lisburn Road, and below the Lisburn Road you fell into the working classes, supplying the cleaning ladies and maids for the big houses. It was an expatriate structure – the sun had never set on the empire.'

He went to a prep school where the headmaster encouraged the boys to make bombs out of weedkiller and sugar, and watched from his study window while they exploded them. 'This was adventure play for children who would go on to maintain the frontiers of those bits of the map that were painted red.' He went on to Campbell College, a public school, but dropped into a lower caste because he was sent as a day boy rather than as a boarder. He spoke about himself and his schoolboy peers as if they were already men. 'I joined the Ulster Liberal Party. My peers, almost to a man, were Unionists.' One of his friends was Jeff Dudgeon, then sympathetic to the Northern Ireland Labour Party. 'Then, on automatic pilot, I went to Oxford, to the same college my father went to. I was quite sure I was launching forth into the rest of my life away from here.'

Instead, in London in 1968, he became gripped by events back in the North. He got involved with People's Democracy and, in 1972, organised the anti-internment movement in Britain. He married a Catholic from Lurgan, County Armagh. 'One was then talking about campaigning in a situation of the gross injustice that had been done and the wholly asinine nature of government policy.' Things were not to remain so straightforward, however. After a demonstration in London he was charged with riotous assembly. During the trial, he said, the situation changed. 'Direct rule was introduced, but the republican movement decided that nothing had changed and that a purely military offensive would have to go on. I couldn't support that and I resigned.'

Gray said that during this time he had some understanding of the unionist élite but none of its grassroots. He did not meet a Catholic until he was sixteen. 'It is an extraordinary reflection on the social structures of Northern Ireland that I didn't meet most types of people in the community until I was an adult. As a child, if I came home with a slight Northern Irish twang, my parents would pull me up on it every time. They thought such an accent would maim any chance of advancement I might have. Now, when I go to England it is not exactly a foreign country, but it is not my country. My imagined identity is

Irish, and my desired identity is Irish, but I am very specifically Northern Irish.'

He had not found a political party to which he could commit himself. He had leanings towards Sinn Féin in its post-IRA ceasefire form, but felt it hadn't much to offer the Protestant voter. 'I'd agree with Connolly that partition was a disaster. Sinn Féin has staggered out of the cul-de-sac of perpetual war, and they appear to have the ability to persuade the toughest and most irreconcilable elements of the Catholic community that this is the way to go. But it still lacks mechanisms by which they may actually achieve meaningful engagement with the other community.

'Labour politics has failed – like it or not, we have a bitterly divided community and we require – alas – a political agreement which responds to the reality of that and not some pie-in-the-sky idea of a better revolution tomorrow.' He supported the Belfast Agreement. 'However, whereas UUP people do regard North–South links as sensible, Trimble seems to listen to some total loopers who are of the view that everybody in the Irish Republic would still be riding round on donkeys if they hadn't had their Mercs paid for by the EEC. In reality, of course, the Irish economy has surged ahead, while the North's is virtually at a standstill.' As a historian, he admired the United Irishmen. 'As a people, they accepted no frontiers.'

'I'LL GIVE YOU BUNS NOT GUNS'

Pearl's estate could have been exactly the sort of place Derek Mahon had in mind when he wrote 'Glengormley':

'Wonders are many and none is more wonderful than man'
Who has tamed the terrier, trimmed the hedge
And grasped the principle of the watering-can.

Cul-de-sac upon cul-de-sac of neat bungalows, with small, well-tended gardens, sitting quietly on the slopes above Belfast Lough. A place where people said, 'Oh, we don't bother about politics', but turned out to have strong views. A lot of police lived in these estates, and prison officers. Loyalist paramilitaries were spoken of with disgust.

Pearl, who was in her fifties, said she was a very traditional Protestant in many ways – she said her daughters-in-law laughed at the way she 'waited hand and foot' on her sons. She was a liberal unionist, with time for the Women's Coalition. Her sons and daughters would be more mainstream unionist, she said. 'The difference between me and my children is that I am working class and they are middle class. I find the UUP a bit too Tory. But I could never stomach Alliance – they are far too middle class.'

Trimble, she said, had brought the party further than she could ever have imagined when he signed up to the Belfast Agreement. However, she thought he had 'boxed himself into a corner' by his insistence on decommissioning, when it wasn't in the agreement. 'He shouldn't have let anti-agreement people stand in the elections. And he shouldn't have let that wee puke Jeffrey Donaldson back into his negotiating team.' Donaldson had walked out when the Belfast Agreement was reached, and had been a scathing critic of the deal. Trimble had included him in the UUP team for the negotiations which led to the Way Forward proposals of July 1999, when the British and Irish governments urged unionists to accept that there had been a 'seismic shift' on the part of republicans and to go into government. Donaldson immediately rejected the proposals. On the day the secretary of state had ordered the executive to be set up, which would be the devolved government of Northern Ireland, Trimble kept his Assembly party away. The DUP had tabled a motion to exclude Sinn Féin as the first debate. Paisley needed thirty votes, and could count on twenty-eight. Trimble was unable to guarantee that UUP Assembly members might not cross over and give Paisley the votes he needed. 'People have no idea the trouble unionism is in,' said Pearl.

Her mother had been a mill worker, and organised the weekly neighbourhood collection to pay off the local moneylender. She brought her daughters up to serve the men of the family. Pearl's father, whom she adored, worked in the shipyard. Her mother was anti-Catholic, her father more interested in international politics. He had socialist leanings. However, sectarianism was part of the social fabric. 'I remember as a wee girl hating Catholics. The grown-ups used to tell us all sorts of stories that nuns had babies to priests and the wee babies were killed and buried under the foundations of the Mater Hospital. I used to dance to the kick-the-Pope bands all the way to the Field.

'Later on, when I started work, I was with a firm that didn't employ Catholics. It was a very patriarchal family firm – but they looked after their workers. You want to have heard my husband – the way he talked you would have thought Catholics were zombies who couldn't think for themselves and just obeyed the priest.' Her husband was 'very much an Orangeman', the master of his local lodge and founder of a flute band. 'Jimmy had never spoken to a Catholic. He met a girl at a dance once and had arranged to call for her again. When he arrived at the house her sister asked him in. He saw all the religious paraphernalia, made his excuses and left. Mind you, I wouldn't have been allowed to marry a Catholic myself.'

Pearl had been brought up as a Methodist, and had been devout for many years. She had recently lost her faith. 'I just woke up one morning and realised it was all too fantastical.' Her marriage had been happy. She was a factory worker until her first child was born, and then she stayed at home. 'I was privileged enough to be able to be a housewife. People don't realise the pride you can take in having perfectly polished windows and dinner in the oven for your husband when he comes home. There is a freedom in that. It shouldn't be downgraded.'

Her husband joined the vigilantes when they started in 1969. His talk became more and more militant, particularly after he witnessed the aftermath of an IRA bomb on the Shankill Road in 1971. The bomb, on a Saturday afternoon in December when the street was packed with shoppers, was placed in the Balmoral Furnishing Company. Two adults were killed – and two small children, a two-year-old girl and a one-year-old boy. The bomb was seen as a revenge attack. The UVF had bombed McGurk's Bar in Belfast a week previously, killing fifteen. 'My husband would say the war should be taken to the Free State where the succour for the enemy was. He felt the Free State government should get a taste of its own medicine for supporting the IRA, which they did, when you look at Charlie Haughey.' In 1970 Haughey had been tried but not convicted of importing arms for the IRA.

What she did not know was that her husband had become deeply involved in the UDA. She was puzzled when one of her children told her that when they went through barricades with him, masked men saluted. Pearl was vehemently opposed to the paramilitaries, believing them to be fascists. She felt that if a man wanted to be a patriot, he should join the UDR. 'We used to go to the Blues Club on the Shankill Road and my husband used to say to me, "Keep your mouth shut – you'll get us shot." The Blues Club was a supporters' club for Linfield, the loyalist team some of whose supporters used to link the N and the F in 'Linfield' in the National Front sign. It went on to sign Catholic players, and took part in initiatives to combat sectarianism in sport.

When her husband died, the UDA came around wanting to organise the funeral. Paisley, who had visited her husband in hospital, came too and said a prayer. The coffin had a wreath of white carnations with a polystyrene red hand in the middle. 'Paisley never came near me since. I have no time for him. He stirs up people who have hatred in them.' Afterwards she found uniforms and loyalist paraphernalia hidden in her attic. 'I was horrified. I had no idea.' Pearl said she became very strict with her sons, worried that they might be tempted to go their father's way. 'I realise looking back I was very cruel and I will regret it till the day I die.'

She took up an adult education course at Jordanstown, then a polytechnic, later part of the New University of Ulster. There was a drive to get mature students who were highly motivated. She loved it. 'It opened my eyes.'

She went on the peace marches which followed the deaths of the Maguire children in Belfast in 1976, mown down by a stolen car, whose driver, an IRA man, had been shot dead by the British army. 'Even my father-in-law went. He was a terrible bigot. After I started studying he used to say to me, "That bloody poly is making a good fenian out of you." But there was a picture in the paper of him shaking hands with a nun on the Falls Road.' However, she opposed the Sunningdale powersharing agreement of 1974. 'O'Neill was undemocratic. He hadn't even told his cabinet he went to see Lemass. I thought that was too aristocratic. Don't tell the plebs.' Captain Terence O'Neill's meeting with the Irish taoiseach in 1965 had long predated the Sunningdale Agreement. It was interesting that Pearl remembered it as the source of her anger. 'I supported the Ulster

Workers' Strike. I didn't go to college, and I wore a wee sponge.'

A violent year after the collapse of the Stormont government, British Secretary of State Willie Whitelaw presided over the negotiations leading to the establishment of the North's first powersharing executive, headed by Ulster Unionist Brian Faulkner. Central to the agreement was the setting up of a Council of Ireland. Faulkner had been known as a hardliner – he helped bring down O'Neill, took part in controversial Orange parades, and introduced internment. However, the Unionist Party monolith was crumbling. Some of those who were for compromise joined the Alliance Party, which had been formed in 1970. Some who were against it broke away to join Vanguard – they would later join forces with the DUP on the United Ulster Unionist Council. Campaigning under the slogan 'Dublin is just a Sunningdale away', the UUUC won eleven of the North's twelve Westminster seats in the 1974 general election.

The Ulster Workers' Strike was called in the triumphant aftermath of that election, initially by a combination of Protestant workers and loyalist paramilitaries, later by a coalition of these forces with the UUUC and the Orange Order. It was during this strike that loyalists bombed Dublin and Monaghan. But it was probably Prime Minister Harold Wilson's 'spongers' speech which ensured that the strike would succeed in bringing down the executive, not least because it galvanised people like Pearl. He described the strike as 'a deliberate and calculated attempt to use every undemocratic and un-parliamentary means for the purpose of bringing down the whole constitution of Northern Ireland so as to set up there a sectarian and undemocratic state, from which one third of the people of Northern Ireland will be excluded' (Anderson, p. 129). He went on to speak of the murder of British soldiers and destruction of property by 'people who spend their lives sponging on Westminster'. He had already described the strike as sectarian and belonging to the seventeenth century.

Protestants were incensed. The leaders of the strike characterised it as 'not an act of rebellion against a lawful authority but a protest within the law against the denial of the democratic rights of the majority of the Ulster people' (Anderson, p. 126). Pearl and thousands of others wore sponges on their lapels after Wilson's speech, ten days into the strike. There had been widespread intimidation and violence, and four people had been killed the previous night. The North was almost at a standstill and even essential services were on the point of breaking down.

Pearl, while studying to 'better herself', was largely supporting her family on a widow's pension. 'I kept my money because I assumed we'd be asked to send it back to show him we were not spongers but were interested in democracy. I later learned that a lot of the ones running the strike had gone out on the sick, so they were getting paid to be on strike. That taught me to be more discerning. I also didn't like getting stopped at roadblocks by wee thugs who were only children. War is for adults. By the time the strike was over I bitterly regretted taking any part in it.'

Despite major changes to effectively nullify the powers originally intended for the Council of Ireland, loyalists were not to be appeased. The strike went on until the executive collapsed. It had taken just fourteen days. Powersharing had lasted just five months.

Pearl used to encourage young people on the fringes of the paramilitaries to come to her house to talk. 'I used to bake for them. I'd say to them, I'll give you buns not guns.' At college she said she learned about the gerrymandering and discrimination which had been practised by the unionists to establish their control over Northern Ireland. 'I found out things. Like, when the UK brought in children's allowance, the Stormont government voted against it because it would mean Catholics would get more because they had more children. To me, if people are citizens of the land, they are entitled to get benefits.'

She graduated in 1978 at the age of forty. Politically, she was inclined to support the SDLP, but drew back from nationalism because of the rise of Sinn Féin. 'I believed John Hume when he said there was room for both traditions, but I don't think Sinn Féin recognises that. I didn't want to live in a nation dominated by people who thought the way to do it was by bombing and shooting you into submission.' However, she felt that unionists needed to acknowledge the wrongs in their past. 'We should apologise for seventy years' misrule.'

She struggled to see things from a nationalist point of view. 'I find it hard to take their attitude to the RUC. I feel my hackles rising when I hear the police criticised. But I have to accept that although I have never seen the RUC behaving badly, it is not like that for nationalists. They have a different experience. I find what happens is, when I'm with Protestants I'm saying, "Youse are bigots." But when I'm with nationalists I'd be standing up for the unionist position.'

Pearl's attitude to the Orange Order was one I heard often. All her life she had watched the parades. However, she had been horrified by the disorder at Drumcree, and was repelled particularly by the sight of Orangemen attacking the RUC. When I spoke to her in 1998, she was writing the Order off as 'triumphalist bullies'. She recalled bands banging Lambeg drums outside Catholic churches and hospitals, all the signs of paramilitarism, and that her son's pal had been beaten up for no reason, other than the fact that he was a Catholic. She did not think the Order should insist on walking through nationalist areas. On the other hand, she regarded nationalist residents' groups as a concerted campaign against Protestants by Sinn Féin. 'That makes my blood boil,' she said.

However, after the marching season of 1999 had passed off reasonably peacefully, she was more forgiving of the Order. 'The parades have gone back to being more like a carnival.' She was thinking of starting to go and watch them again. 'I think they have reinstated themselves as part of Protestant culture. It's only when things are bad that they get triumphalist and provocative.' Pearl said she was proud to be Irish, and, as a unionist, proud to be British. 'I feel I can be both. We are going into a more federal sort of United Kingdom anyway.'

What happened to Pearl's best friend showed how difficult it was for working-class people to stay out of the ghetto. 'She is a Catholic, and in fact she was very much a unionist. Until she was burned out of her house by loyalists.' Her friend was a Housing Executive tenant, and found that all of the estates around where she lived in north Belfast had become almost totally segregated. She couldn't move to another Protestant estate, after what had happened, but she didn't want to be in a hardline nationalist one either. She moved into emergency accommodation, and eventually managed to buy a house in a mixed area.

Housing Executive figures show that Belfast housing estates were almost totally segregated by 1998. In the rest of Northern Ireland 70 per cent of public housing was segregated, and that figure was rising.

Journalist David McKittrick drew up a series of maps which showed that whereas the figures for each electoral ward might suggest that areas were mixed, a more detailed breakdown revealed a jigsaw of segregation.

Although Pearl had become a teacher and was glad to be out of 'the trough of low pay', she said her friends were mostly working class and she felt uncomfortable about telling people she was a professional person. 'I feel I'm boasting. I feel safer with working-class people. My children are awfully middle class – golf, skiing holidays, timeshares . . . one of them has a BMW and another has a boat. They all have lovely homes. I'm dead proud of them.' She was not one of those who, having moved up the ladder, would forsake her roots. 'Once I retire I know I'll do voluntary work. I feel it's right to give something back to your community.'

'BY THEIR DEEDS YE SHALL KNOW THEM'

Sheila Bradshaw lived a quiet Glengormley life until May 1977, when UDA gunman Kenny McClinton flagged down the Citybus her husband, Harry, was driving, and shot him in the face. It was during 'Paisley's strike', an attempt to repeat the political success of the Ulster Workers' Strike in 1974. In March 1977 McClinton had also murdered a Catholic man, Daniel Carville, in front of Mr Carville's child. Harry Bradshaw was a Protestant whose family was originally from County Wicklow. He had been working an extra shift so as to get a day off for his daughter's wedding. After the murder the UDA wrote to Sheila to apologise – they said they had thought her husband was a Catholic. They enclosed a ten pound note.

McClinton turned out to be a showman. He presented himself naked in court, got life, got saved, got out of prison, said he had left violence behind him. He began to make regular appearances in the media, talking about himself. He revealed that he had been a 'wild man' who had wanted to behead Catholics and put their heads on stakes along the peaceline. He said he and Basher Bates, one of the Shankill Butchers, had performed a baptism ceremony in a prison bath tub. (Robert Bates was murdered in June 1997 by a relative of one of his victims after his release from prison the previous year.) As a pastor, McClinton worked for the Stadium, a youth project on the Shankill Road, before moving to Portadown. He wrote heroic poems about LVF leader Billy Wright, particularly extolling his role at Drumcree. He became the link person between the LVF and General John de Chastelain's decommissioning body, and invited selected journalists to watch the destruction of some of its weapons. Many were not chosen – McClinton was frequently unhappy with the way his story was told in the press.

Sheila was unhappy with the frequency with which he seemed to want to tell it. 'Every time he appears on TV, the man who murdered my husband is in the sitting room. It is like a mental rape. You feel violated. Sometimes Harry's photograph is used to illustrate news-paper articles about McClinton. He lives off those two deaths. He thinks he is a celebrity. My husband was a working man, out serving the public. McClinton was unemployed and going to hold the or-dinary people to ransom. I could have understood it in a way if he had shot an IRA man that they thought they were at war with.

'There are plenty of other lifers out there who served their sen-tences, but now they are out, they go about their lives quietly. The man who was with McClinton – he took his punishment like a man. Since McClinton became born-again, he has piled on the hurt which began in another lifetime. He shows no compassion for his victims' families, who are also his victims. I believe in what the Bible says – "By their deeds ye shall know them."' Sheila said her brother-in-law, who had to identify her husband's body, had nightmares for fourteen years afterwards. She said McClinton's much-vaunted conversion to Christianity should be seen in context. 'He turned five members of this family away from the Church. The only day I can get them to go to church is on Remembrance Sunday.

'I didn't think it was in my psyche to hate, but I hate that man. To me Gordon Wilson's Christian forgiveness of the men who murdered his daughter is sick. I remember there was a policeman shot by the IRA, and his wife was on TV. Harry and I watched her on the news. She said, as a born-again Christian, she forgave her husband's killers. I prefer the old Bible in my Christianity. I'm a great believer in an eye for an eye.'

Sheila was a civil servant until she took early retirement in 1988 because of health problems. She had married again, and said of her husband, 'It takes a very special sort of person to see you through all this.' She was born in north Belfast, and has lived there all her life. 'We were born during the war, and brought up in the fifties, the best time, all the labour-saving gadgets ...' Her father was a Scottish Presbyterian, a sea captain. She remembered being presented in a sailor's dress to Lord Louis Mountbatten. Mountbatten was assassinated by the IRA in 1979. 'I'm part of a large, close, extended family. We used to go to my aunt in Portadown for the summers. I learnt to dance there, but I hated going up the town on a Saturday night because there'd be fellows on the corners blattering away on Lambeg drums and all the drunks would gather around them.' She said she had her first drink when she was twenty-one and didn't have another until she was in her thirties.

The church was the family's social and spiritual life, between services, Sunday school, square dances and socials. She was recently at a funeral party in the Moravian church hall where she went dancing as a girl. 'It hadn't changed at all.' Harry had been her second husband. She was first married to a prison officer in 1959. 'My first husband didn't dance. He was a Methodist. He was a choirmaster, but he was also a bad rip. I had two children to him, and his girlfriend had three.' Sheila had been working as a clerical assistant in the civil service since she was sixteen, but had to leave because of a marriage bar. After her marriage broke up she worked in a shop. 'My life revolved around my home, my sister's home, my mother's home and the Mothers' Circle, a Methodist church group. We had a hymn, a chat, a cup of coffee, and a prayer. It sort of died off a lot after the Troubles started, when people liked to stay at home.'

She went back to the civil service in 1969. 'I have two abiding memories. I remember the Friday the Troubles started. Two Roman Catholic girls came over to me at 4.30 and said they were scared to leave. I asked why, and they said, "They'll know to look at us we're Catholics." There was total silence in the town. I got them home, and then I collected my boys and went home to our flat. We watched the Catholics fleeing with mattresses on the roofs of cars. Then on the Monday morning, I went to work and there was an old lady sitting in tears on the bench. On the Friday night people had come to her house on the Ravenhill Road in east Belfast and told her to get out. They had laid the body of a man at the foot of her stairs. Really, it was ethnic cleansing.' The Scarman Tribunal found that in the summer of 1969 some 1,820 families fled their homes in Belfast. Of these, 1,505 were Catholic. In all, 30 per cent of the city's Catholic population was displaced. Whole streets were burned out.

Sheila said she grew up without knowing what squalor was. When she saw film footage of Derry in the 1940s, she thought it was from another century. 'I can understand the civil rights movement starting. It was the way it went on I didn't like.

'My father would never have let me go out with a Catholic. Our next door neighbour, when I was growing up, was a Catholic, a police inspector. On the Twelfth of July, when my father was district master of the Orange Lodge, Mrs Murphy would bake and send in sandwiches. I always watch the parades. I don't see how they could intimidate anyone. It's a whole big community thing really. You always freshened up your house for the Twelfth.' She said she felt let down when she saw that Orange Order leaders were talking with McClinton. 'If they talk to him, they should definitely talk to that other one, McKenna.' Orange leaders in Portadown refused to talk to the spokesman for the nationalist residents of the Garvaghy Road, Breandán Mac Cionnaith, because he had a terrorist record.

'I remember being in the South with a group of union colleagues. There was this fellow told a whole lot of Paisley jokes. Right enough, some of them were very funny. Then he told this one about the Orange widows' fund. He said, "I'll always give to that because there can never be enough Orange widows." I kept him going about that when we were back at work. He said to me, "Youse are all bastards anyway, the only true marriage is in the Catholic Church."

'My eldest son married a Catholic. That didn't please some of the very serious born-again Christians in the family. As far as I'm concerned, all religions are man-made.' She looked out the living room window at the neat flower beds and borders of her garden. 'I can lose myself in my garden – there is so much resurrection there. You have to have faith when you plant. It is really a memorial garden. I have slips from different gardens – there are some from a manse in County

Antrim, my brother's house. He's a Presbyterian minister who is a nationalist.'

In the early seventies she met Harry, then working as a security man in Belfast. He had been living in Scotland and had three daughters from a previous marriage. The girls had been brought up as Catholics, and, after the two families moved in together, they continued to go to mass. 'One weekend three soldiers were murdered on the Ligoniel Road. The girls felt it deeply, three young Scottish people. The priest the next day gave a stirring sermon against the Brits and said no one was to leave the chapel without signing a petition against them. The girls refused to sign it, and when they came home they said they were going to join my Church the next week. They never went back.

'We had a very happy life. We didn't marry, which made us the talk of the road, as you can imagine. We planned to. Harry used to be like the Pied Piper up on the Cave Hill. We'd go walking and all the children would follow us. It was me got him the job in Citybus. I knew all the councillors. The day he died he came home at lunch time. "Hello hen," he said. And he made me a wee fry. I was worried about him. There had been several attempts to shoot bus drivers on that road. Everyone felt that someone was going to die. But Harry said, "I'm a bus driver and I'm proud to bring people to work."

'He had supported the 1974 strike. But not this one. He kissed me goodbye. For the ten days of the strike, I'd been listening to Downtown Radio. I switched it off, washed my hair and set it in rollers. Then I went and sat by the living-room window. A police car drove in next door. My neighbour was out washing her windows. I went out, and I said to her, "I have an awful feeling I've bad news." They told me Harry had been shot, but it wasn't until I was in the car that they said, "You know he's dead, don't you?" They wouldn't let me see him. They were wrong in that. I didn't need to see his face. I would have known his hands and his feet.' Looking out at her garden, Sheila's eyes filled with tears.

'NOBODY CARES ABOUT US'

Gwen's story was an unspeakably harsh one. She lived in New Mossley, near Glengormley but utterly different in character. A big

1970s estate, it is just settling, after years of being regarded as a place where a disproportionate number of 'problem families' were housed.

It seemed as though Gwen had never, until very recent years, had any real control over her life. 'I'm not really into religion. My husband is a bigot.' She said this cheerfully. 'It's the way he was brought up. His family are all bigots too. He's in the Orange Order, so all Catholics are second-class citizens to him. He works in a factory. I'm a waitress. I'm from the York Road, a poky wee house with no bathroom. It's hard to believe that, and that was in the seventies. There were seven of us.'

Gwen grew up during the worst of the Troubles. She remembered boys making petrol bombs in the living room, vigilantes in huts on the street corners, being evacuated to the church hall, someone up the street getting shot. When she was still a child, her parents were killed in a car crash. Her oldest sister, who was seventeen, took over caring for the family. Two years later, Gwen found her sister unconscious in her bed one morning. She died later that day from a mix of alcohol and pills. Gwen and her siblings were left to fend for themselves, until people noticed that they couldn't. Then they were fostered out to various relations, some of whom were kind, while others were cruel or alcoholic or both.

'When I was sixteen, I got married to a pig who murdered me. I had just left school. He knocked my tooth out, broke another one, sunk his teeth in my leg, trailed me round the living room, wrecked the place. I had no money, no coal, no food. The wee kitchen house we had was condemned. I had a little boy and he saw all the hammerings I was getting, and it was disturbing him. That man was a head-the-ball. One time he brought home a butcher's knife from his work. I used to just curl up in a ball. He went with other girls too and used to come home with lovebites. I'd leave and then he'd come crying crocodile tears and I'd go back. I was in hospital twice. He was in a flute band. I was an orphan with no older brothers. I didn't have anyone who could sort of scare him.'

Her husband's mother used to come around after he had smashed the house up. 'She blamed me. She'd say, "My son is not used to living in a mess like this." It was easy to see why – her sons are all wife-beaters and her daughters are trollops,' Gwen said. The picture she painted was of a macho society where male violence was a defining characteristic. Domestic violence was rife, and if a woman could not call upon a more powerful man to curb her husband, she had to put up with it. Female solidarity could not be assumed, and interventions by social services were intermittent and inept.

Eventually, she got out of the marriage. She moved to New Mossley. Then she met someone else in a bar outside the area. 'He swept me off my feet.' She knew he was a Catholic. What she didn't know was that he was a petty criminal with republican connections. She was pregnant when he was arrested and jailed. There was talk that she would be petrol-bombed for bringing a Catholic into New Mossley.

She married her present husband after her son was born. 'Imagine, him taking on the child of a Catholic. This is a real hardline area. The funny thing is, my son is really into all that. I remember away back at the height of the Troubles, my brother said he was going to join the paramilitaries. My mother was crying and begging him not to.'

Gwen knew plenty of people who had been killed or injured, others who had inflicted death and injury. She wanted peace. She supported the Belfast Agreement, thought it was time politics was directed towards poverty and social issues. As for identity: 'As far as I'm concerned, I'm Irish. My husband says we're British. Nobody cares about us anyway.'

'DOORS BARRED, CHILDREN IN, CATS FED'

Christine had also been subjected to violence in her marriage, and her husband had also been a drinking man. When I met her in Ballyduff she had been divorced for five years. She had stayed in her marriage, keeping up appearances, and also looked after her mother, who lived with them, long after she knew she should leave it. She said her mother would have taken the view that she had made her bed and would have to lie in it. When her mother died Christine ended her marriage. She had remained friends with her former husband, and said he was 'not a bad man in his way'.

Living now with her four children, Christine said that what she liked was, 'I can come in and shut the door.' She did not care much for a lot of what went on outside the door. She had lived for a time on another estate where there was a women's centre, and she missed her involvement in it. The development of a network of such centres in some of the most deprived and war-torn working-class areas in Belfast and elsewhere is a remarkable phenomenon which started in the eighties. In 1999 there were about fifteen such centres, up to a thousand local women's groups, and a range of services for women, provided by women, within the voluntary sector. More remarkable still, the centres, which provide education, training and childcare, manage to find a way of working together which crosses the bitter community divide. 'What I liked about the centre is, you got a lot of support from each other and you could say what you liked,' said Christine. The former Irish president, Mary Robinson, had supported this burgeoning of the women's movement, and had made several visits to northern centres, where she was warmly received. After she visited one centre in a loyalist area, it was firebombed by local loyalist men.

Christine had no time for Orangeism, and none for paramilitarism either. 'There is that much bitterness in this place, I don't see how they'll ever get peace. My mother now – I loved her with all my heart, I really did, but she was such a bitter, bitter person, she really was. When I was growing up our next door neighbour was a Catholic, and my mother would be going on about fenian this and fenian that, and everything was them and us. She was shocking, like. Dear sake. Yet and all, Mrs O'Neill was in and out of our house for a cup of tea and we were in and out of hers. I couldn't figure it out. How was it we were to like Mrs O'Neill and not like Catholics? It's only when you get older you realise it's just so silly.

'I swore I wouldn't be like that for my children. You see these young ones that got involved and their lives are wasted. My children are dead laid back. The children round here, a lot of them are raised thinking that because they are Protestant, they are better than Catholics. There are a few Catholics on the estate. There was actually a Catholic man murdered just a couple of streets away from us here. I've a wee friend lives near me here and she's a Catholic. I've known her twenty years and religion doesn't come into it.

'When those wee Quinn children were murdered in Ballymoney last summer, she was afraid. She is married to a Protestant fellow, but she was afraid. She asked me could her wee boy stay with us for a few days. I felt terrible for her that she was afraid in her own home and her born on this estate. Those Orangemen at Drumcree should have a bit of sense. Tradition can change. You can't always have things your own way. Life doesn't work like that.

'I don't even vote, to tell you the truth. Sometimes I feel it is just hard enough getting from one week to the next, never mind Troubles and all that. In July and August here you would think the place is going to explode sometimes, it is that tense. I know a girl, and her children go out rioting. I don't know how people can let their children do that. I mean they are fifteen, but you are still in charge of them. I was in, doors barred, children in, cats fed. I want no part in any of that. No, no.'

She was sickened by the level of paramilitarism in the estate. 'My neighbours are right and good but I wouldn't talk politics with them. Nobody really runs in and out of houses. I've one neighbour who has been a bad boy, put it like that. You would know not to say anything in front of him. You'd have no kneecaps. He has never done a day's work in his life and yet his house is well stocked up with everything. He has the best of everything, new suite for the living room every couple of years, new carpets. That sickens and annoys me.

'My sons now, they'd have no time for that carry-on. They are doing really well. That's another thing annoys me, the way people says that the children of single parents do badly at school and all that. My eldest boy got every qualification going and walked straight into a good job. He's actually in Dublin now. I'm sure my mother is tossing and turning in her grave. She'd have supported the paramilitaries. "They are ours," she'd have said. "They are helping us." Helping us? Shooting people? I don't think so.'

'JUST TO BLOOD YOU'

The Eastway Social Club was packed. Men with pints of beer, men with pint bottles of beer, men ordering more pints. 'You want to have seen me trying to get home last night,' joked one man. 'Aye, well ah seen ye at four in the afternoon, so ah can well imagine,' laughed another. Men in bandsmen's uniforms, men with drums, men in black suits. Jovial, and in a condition best described by the northern word: 'rightly'. Meaning, more drunk than sober. It was 11 a.m. on Remembrance Sunday, 8 November 1998. Rathcoole was preparing to remember.

All over Northern Ireland the solemn annual ceremonies in memory of the fallen of two world wars, and of the Troubles, were taking place at cenotaphs and war memorials. In Omagh the president of the local branch of the British Legion read out the names of the twenty-nine people who had died in the Real IRA's bombing of the town three months previously. In Enniskillen, the eleven victims of the IRA's 1987 Remembrance Day bomb were remembered. In Downpatrick they remembered members of the UDR murdered by the IRA, in Killyleagh an Ulster soldier killed in the Falklands war. In Portadown they finished their ceremony in the by-this-time traditional manner – attempting to walk down the Garvaghy Road, and being turned back by the security forces.

Watched on television by millions, David Trimble was in London, where he followed the Queen, the prime minister, the leaders of the Conservatives and the Liberal Democrats, in laying a wreath at the Cenotaph. The foreign secretary laid a wreath on behalf of 'the dependent territories' and was followed by a line of high commissioners representing the Commonwealth countries.

Poppy Day, when the Royal British Legion raises funds for ex-servicemen and their dependants, is controversial in the North. Michael Longley's poem 'Poppies' describes how:

Some people tried to stop other people wearing poppies
And ripped them from lapels as though uprooting poppies
From Flanders fields, but the others hid inside their poppies
Razor blades and added to their poppies more red poppies.

I rang the Royal British Legion in Belfast to get some information from its regional organiser, Bill Craig. ('No relation to Vanguard,' he said.) I told him my book was about Protestants. 'That has nothing to do with the poppy,' he said. 'There's no P in poppy for Protestants or politics. Catholics wear poppies too.' I said that, largely, Catholics didn't. 'I suppose in 100 per cent nationalist or republican areas they don't because their political dictators don't let them,' he said. 'It's this political correctness thing. There are places you have to take pictures of the Queen down, and you can't fly the Union flag. It is ridiculous.' BBC newscasters across the United Kingdom wore the poppy, although it was a tradition, not a rule. In 1995 a Belfast presenter declined to do so, arguing that the poppy, like the shamrock on St Patrick's Day, was a symbol of division. She received hate mail, the local press made it a front page story, and the BBC was inundated with protests. The following year the corporation made a rule that newsreaders would wear poppies – those who did not want to do so would be given off-screen duties during the week leading up to Remembrance Day.

I had seen poppies on the lapels of coats and dresses in a shop window on the Ormeau Road. It was near Ballynafeigh Orange hall, the lodge members of which were frequently refused permission to march down the road through a nationalist area. The poppies in the window seemed like a sign of sorrowful pride and defiance. 'After all that we have given, look at how we are repaid.'

'Right boys, let's go.' Grug, one of north Belfast's leading loyalists, rallied the beer-drinking foot soldiers in the Eastway. They shuffled out of the bar into the watery sunlight of the November morning, strapping on drums and hoisting banners. It was time to commemorate their dead. Grug was known as a hero among loyalists because he led the Ulster Freedom Fighters (UFF) 'team' which shot and injured the Sinn Féin leader Gerry Adams. For Remembrance Day he was wearing a dark suit and fashionable square glasses. He cut a very different figure to the huge, swaggering skinhead I'd first seen, big belly and bass drum in front of him, lunging across the barricades in Derry. That was during an Apprentice Boys parade in 1996. He and his men in the Cloughfern Young Conquerors band had broken ranks with the parade. They pointed their flutes like guns and charged at the jeering young republicans behind the police barriers. Several of them, including Grug, were prosecuted for riotous behaviour.

The men formed ranks in the car park outside the Eastway, which, as well as housing the club, also had a fitness centre, run by Grug, with state support, and a loyalist prisoners' welfare office. It had been the Alpha, Rathcoole's cinema until the seventies. The UDA wanted to buy it, but the owner instead sold it to a publican who extensively re-novated it. Just before it was due to open, it was burnt out. Then it was sold to a consortium of loyalists.

The dead who were remembered at ceremonies all over the North included the 1,012 members of the security forces and RUC who were murdered during the Troubles. In keeping with their view that the loyalist paramilitaries were an extension of the security forces, Grug and 'the boys' had gathered to put up a memorial plaque to their own soldiers. First they paraded around the estate, several hundred men and a handful of young women. A few people could be seen watching with worried faces from the windows of the flats. The Eastway is on one side of the Diamond, facing the area's few shops and offices. The Diamond is dominated by huge UDA murals. Above them, a wan metal sculpture dangled. Nobody locally could tell me who made it or what it represented. Someone had put a rope around its neck.

Back at the car park it was time for the unveiling of the memorial. The honour fell to Harry Speirs. 'He'll be our candidate in the next local elections,' Grug told me. 'Normally Tommy Kirkham does this, but he's away in Belgium.' Kirkham, an Ulster Democratic Party (UDP) councillor, ran the Fernhill House museum. When I visited him there, his office was stacked with the plastic lion collection jars of the British Legion. The ceremony he was at in Belgium was to open a peace park made by young people from both communities in the North, and commemorating the war dead of those communities. It was to be attended by Queen Elizabeth and Mary McAleese, the Irish president. The Republic of Ireland was belatedly acknowledging those of its citizens who had fought and died under the British flag.

Speirs unveiled the plaque. At the top it said, in big, blue plastic letters, 'South East Antrim Brigade'. Underneath, gold letters on black, it said, 'This memorial is dedicated to the memory of the of-ficers and members of our organisation who were murdered by the enemies of Ulster and to those who paid the supreme sacrifice whilst on active service during the present conflict. Quis separabit. Loyalist Prisoners' Association.' In his speech Speirs praised the UDA for its role in a war which was, he feared, far from over. He said the orga-nisation would be prepared to fight again, if that became necessary.

Grug was convinced it would. We met a few days later in an office inside the cavernous Eastway, all red carpets and long sloping corridors. The windowless room had a plaque to the Ulster Freedom Fighters, and, on a table, a couple of large bottles of vivid blue liquid which Grug said was aftershave. In a T-shirt and jeans he looked more like the big skinhead of old, but fit rather than fat. 'See the agreement? I voted yes and walking down the road from Rathcoole Primary School, I knew I'd done the wrong thing. I feel a bit ashamed to say it. I sold my principles to see my friends getting out of jail. That was the only reason. I would say 80 per cent of the UDA voted yes for the same reason.

'People ask me what is happening with the UFF – that's the operators. My answer is, they haven't gone away you know. The UFF is ready and waiting. That's what I would imagine, anyway. I honestly don't think they'll get over the impasse of decommissioning. Trimble would sell us out tomorrow if he could get away with it, but his own people would turn on him if he did. We have nothing to lose, because the UDP isn't in Stormont anyway.'

The lampposts of Rathcoole bore posters of John White, the UDP's local candidate in the Assembly elections. Although this is the UDA's heartland, he did badly. White was an unattractive candidate. A double murderer, he had slit the throats of an SDLP politician and his woman friend in the seventies. Although he was on the UDP's talks team, with his grim face and dour manner he had not managed to shake off the sinister aura of his horrific past. White was not the only candidate to perform disappointingly – the UDP failed to get a single seat in the Assembly. Grug said the reason was simple. 'A lot of our boys would still vote DUP. They know what line Paisley is going to take and that he'll stick to that, whereas with the UDP they can't be so sure.'

Grug's admission reminded me of a painted sign I'd seen on one of the many tattered evangelical churches on the Shore Road. I'd passed it on the way out to Rathcoole. 'We preach the one true God,' it said. 'The same yesterday, today and tomorrow.' Paisley was like that. No surprises. Just perpetual apocalypse.

Billy Hutchinson of the PUP had got a seat, and represented Rathcoole in the Assembly. Grug couldn't stand him. 'Everything he stands for is near enough against everything I believe. He thinks like a republican.' Grug's people, loyalists from Rathcoole out to Antrim, would be more 'Billy Wright minded,' he said. Holding fast to traditional Protestant values.

Anything 'lefty' was anathema to Grug. During his nine years in prison he'd done O levels and A levels and started a degree in social sciences. However, he'd thrown in the degree after two years when a design he submitted for a memorial for loyalist prisoners was criticised. 'I just threw the head up. Maybe it was just the way I was reared – the whole social science thing just seemed too lefty, too sort of republican.

'I grew up in the Troubles. A lot of it you saw on TV. The earliest memory I have of it was Londonderry – you know, the civil rights march, troops coming onto the streets. I remember my parents and grandparents saying, these boys will fix them, they'll put an end to the trouble. They had a lot of respect for the British army but obviously it didn't sort it out.' His family was from Tiger's Bay, 'poor as any Catholic that was out demonstrating' – but they saw civil rights as 'a republican sort of thing', and wanted nothing to do with it.

Grug said that his father, despite being a quiet man who trusted the police and the army, joined the vigilantes in the early days. 'You felt there was a real threat coming from republicans. That they would come in from places like Bawnmore and Newtownabbey and burn people out and kill people.' The vigilantes used to patrol the estate wearing masks and carrying cudgels. Similar groups of local men had formed in urban Protestant areas all over the North, and in 1971, they formed an umbrella group – the UDA. Its members saw it as a replacement for the B Specials, subscribing to Paisley's consistent view that a Third Force was a necessary part of the security apparatus of the state. Assisted by former British soldiers, the UDA quickly armed itself, convinced that unarmed vigilantes were 'sitting ducks' and pledging to 'defend my area and my country with all and every means possible' (Bruce, p. 49). The UDA claimed it had up to 40,000 members in 1972, when it took part in political protests against direct rule, and bought large amounts of arms.

The organisation supported Bill Craig's Vanguard movement, and was the muscle behind the Ulster Workers' Strike in 1974. It backed Paisley's strike in 1977, when it murdered Sheila Bradshaw's husband. Grug was working in the shipyard at that time. He hadn't wanted to join the union. He saw it as another 'republican sort of thing'. He joined because he had to – it was a closed shop – and because a shop steward told him it would be to his advantage: 'He took me aside and he said, "Look, in the shipyard we look after our own." He explained that if you did time, your job was held for you. Obviously, if you got life, that would be different, but at that time there was a lot of people getting, say, eighteen months for having a gun. So I joined. Then in 1977 during Paisley's strike, the one that didn't work, I got six months for rioting and my job was held for me.'

Protestants had always been favoured in the shipyards. When Edward J. Harland and Gustav Wolff began their enterprise in the 1850s many workers were Scottish and English Protestants. During sectarian rioting in 1857 the shipyard workers were prominent on the Protestant side. They established an ethos which became self-sustaining. Apprenticeships were given out through family connections and through the Orange Order. Historian A.C. Hepburn quoted the Riots Commission findings of 1864: 'without any direct exclusion of Roman Catholics as such, they were virtually shut out, almost as if there was a positive rule against their admission' (quoted in Hepburn, p. 126). Hepburn added that this 'passive discrimination' was supported by the practice of expelling Catholics at times of civil disorder. There was no shortage of Protestant workers, and Harland and Wolff were both Unionist MPs. In 1912, and again in the twenties and thirties, thousands of Catholics, socialists and 'rotten Prods' were expelled. Hepburn commented that 'violence, the threat of violence or consequently the fear of possible violence, played a key role in maintaining the ethnic boundary in many areas of employment. This was as true in the 1930s as in the 1850s' (Hepburn, p. 127). And indeed in the 1970s to 1990s.

The paramilitaries had a strong presence in the yards, as in other major industrial bases. British trade union leaders were humiliated during the loyalist strike in 1974 when their attempt to stage a return to work at the shipyards failed abysmally. However, in 1994, after loyalists murdered fifty-year-old Catholic Maurice O'Kane in a tanker at Harland and Wolff, shipyard workers downed tools in protest and staged a walkout. That was the year when a horrific accumulation of atrocities was followed by ceasefires.

Sometimes using the *nom de guerre* Ulster Freedom Fighters, the UDA had carried out hundreds of murders of ordinary Catholics, and recruiting posters featured armed men. Steve Bruce quoted a north Belfast vigilante leader who told him: 'We never planned to go on the kill. There was no time that we sat down and said "That's it. Stiff a Taig." ... No, it was ground up. One or two volunteers just started doing it' (Bruce, p. 54). The effect of such random killings was, however, well calculated, and many killings were more strategic. The UDA's efforts to prove that the murder in 1989 of County Down man Loughlin Maginn was not sectarian, and that he was an IRA man, led to the Stevens inquiry. It found that there was collusion between the paramilitaries and the UDR, though it was 'neither widespread nor institutionalised'.

On trial for conspiracy to murder five Catholics in 1992, UDA double agent Brian Nelson claimed that in 1989 he had repeatedly warned his British army handlers about an impending murder, and that no action was taken. Solicitor Pat Finucane was subsequently murdered by the UDA at his north Belfast home. In 1999 journalist Ed Moloney revealed that a UDA man, who had been acting as a police informer, had provided similar information.

The UDA murdered several leading republicans, attempted to murder the former civil rights leader Bernadette McAliskey, and attempted to murder Sinn Féin leader Gerry Adams – Grug's moment of botched glory. The UFF had been proscribed in 1973 after a series of car bombings of Catholic pubs. The UDA was legal until 1992 when it too was proscribed. Its political wing, which became the UDP, was rooted in ideas promoted by its former leader, John McMichael, murdered by the IRA in 1987. In the angry aftermath of the signing of the Anglo-Irish Agreement in 1985, McMichael had been on the steering committee of the Ulster Clubs, set up to co-ordinate opposition to the 'diktat'. The body was founded by Paisley's DUP, and included David Trimble in its membership. In 1987 McMichael published his 'Common Sense' document, which spoke of power-sharing for Catholics within Northern Ireland. McMichael continued, however, to preside over sectarian killings and a massive racketeering system.

The UDA stepped up its campaign of killings in the nineties. In 1992 it was responsible for twenty-one out of a total of thirty-nine sectarian loyalist murders. In 1993 it threatened the entire 'pan-nationalist front of the SDLP, Sinn Féin, the Irish government and the IRA'. That year it killed thirty-one people, including eight in a gun attack on the Rising Sun bar in Greysteel, County Derry, a week after the IRA's Shankill bomb.

In 1994 the Combined Loyalist Military Command, consisting mainly of the UVF and the UDA, called its ceasefire. After the murder of Billy Wright in 1998, elements of the UDA colluded with the LVF in several murders, including two in north Belfast. A UDA bomb-maker was widely believed to have made the device which killed solicitor Rosemary Nelson in 1999. Rosemary Nelson had repeatedly complained of death threats from the RUC. The UDA was also responsible for the campaign of pipe bombings and petrol-bomb attacks on the homes of Catholics in the east Antrim area.

Grug's involvement with paramilitarism had begun when he was a child. He couldn't wait. 'I joined the Young Militants – the junior wing of the UDA – when I was fourteen. You weren't supposed to join till you were fifteen but I told them lies and I got in. At that time, the YMs took part in all the operations, shootings and everything. They used to bring us over to Tiger's Bay when there was riots on and they'd allow us to shoot over into New Lodge. Just to blood you, get you used to killing and being killed. Like the way you see them out on a fox hunt and they rub the blood of the fox on the cheeks of the kids to get them used to it. It's the same principle.'

The Scottish connection was very important to loyalists, Grug said. Coachloads of men and boys went by bus and boat to Glasgow every time Rangers played football there. Grug had been going to matches since he was fourteen. Now he took his own son. His grandmother was from Paisley. 'Loyalists has a lot of good Scottish friends. In Scotland people has offered me money to get photos signed by Stoner, maybe a bit of his hair or something. It's unbelievable.'

'Stoner' was Michael Stone, the Milltown cemetery murderer who was, according to author Martin Dillon, a sort of protégé of John McMichael. He is a cult figure. Loyalist shops sell tapes of 'The Ballad of Michael Stone', praising his prowess. In January 1998, when Mo Mowlam made her controversial visit to loyalist prisoners in the Maze to try to secure their ceasefire, he was centre stage, with his manic eyes and long grey-black ponytail. His appearance at a rally in the Ulster Hall damaged the Yes campaign in the 1998 referendum. However, the UDP organisers did not give him the kind of welcome extended to the Balcombe Street gang by Gerry Adams at the Sinn Féin Ard Fheis around the same time. A few months later, in September 1998, the tabloid *Sunday Life* ran a feature about the 'luxury country love-nest' to which it claimed Stone would be moving on his release.

Back in the early days Grug said loyalists took friends where they could find them. Including the British National Front. 'There's people comes to the club here from Birmingham, say, and they are in the West Midlands UDA and they would also be National Front or-ientated. The National Front was totally behind us when everyone else was against us. Everyone else was condemning us and these people came along carrying Ulster flags and Union flags and they loved us. You sort of latched on to it. I used to have a National Front tattoo but I got rid of it.'

Suddenly, Grug pulled up his T-shirt and displayed his muscular torso. He was heavily tattooed. His shoulder had UFF on it. His back had the entire, full-colour version of a painting which started off as the cover of a heavy metal album and was reproduced as a loyalist wall mural, in prison and outside. It showed a huge, terrifying male figure pounding out of a desolate, shattered urban landscape. His expression was vengeful. Frankenstein's monster in action.

Loyalist men loved tattoos, and heavy gold jewellery. I went to interview someone in a bar in Belfast once and a group of UDA men were sitting around a table showing their gold off to one another, like pirates. Grug told me some loyalist nicknames: Winkie, Dogs, Hacksaw, Ozo, Nipper, Spongie, Basher, Spacer. Like sinister cartoon characters.

Grug changed his mind about the National Front because their hatred of Jews conflicted with a new respect he had developed for the Israelis. 'The Israelis and the white South Africans are in a very similar situation to us. It's not that I have anything against black people. I had an aunt lived out in South Africa and she had to come home to Rathcoole. She and her husband worked hard and they built their farm up. They actually went to Rhodesia first but then the blacks took over there and took over the farm and ruined it. Then in South Africa the blacks kept on attacking them. Like, my auntie would look out the window and there'd be a whole mob of them with machetes.'

The UDP had ordered an Israeli flag for Grug's band to carry in Derry. 'Most of the band wanted it just for a wind-up, to annoy the Bogsiders. But my thing is, there's the IRA, the Palestine Liberation Organisation and the African National Congress, and I detest all three of them.'

Grug was happy to talk about the attempted murder of Gerry Adams, although the story actually seemed to confirm the view of loyalist terrorists expressed in Colin Bateman's comic novel *Divorcing Jack*. Two journalists are fleeing a carload of muscular, tattooed gunmen, who are firing wildly all around them. The American journalist asks the Northern Irish one how he knows the pursuers are loyalists. 'Two ways, really,' he replies. 'One: they fucked up. Proddies have a habit of fucking up operations like this. They outnumber the IRA ten to one but couldn't organise a piss-up in a brewery. Correction. They usually do organise a piss-up in a brewery before they try anything and that's why they fuck it up' (Bateman, p. 98). The second clue was the fact that one of the gunmen had FTP written in felt-tip pen on his forehead. Standing for Fuck the Pope.

According to Chris Ryder, former member of the Northern Ireland Police Authority, the RUC was similarly unimpressed by loyalist skills. 'For years, RUC detectives had talked disparagingly of "Prod jobs": jammed guns, missed victims, getaway cars that failed to start, drunken escapades and petty robberies which enabled the perpetrators to be easily rounded up' (Ryder, 1997, p. 411). However, by the early nineties the UDA was no joke. The death toll inflicted by loyalists had overtaken that of the IRA.

Grug said that in 1984 the decision was taken that republicans were hitting loyalists both politically and militarily, and that Adams was the key. 'He had to be shot. The decision was made and our team was selected to do it. We watched him. Then word came down from a military commander that he was to be in court. We dressed up as solicitors and we waited in the car park. He didn't show when we expected him and we should've abandoned it there and then, but we were excited. What had happened was, the police had let him out the back. A car screeched up eventually and we saw him get in.

'We intended to follow him to the Falls Road and stop the car as if we were detectives, because we were suited up, and, you know, do him in the car. But then we got level with him and one of the team said to me, can you get a crack at him? I was in the back and the other gunman was in the front. I rolled down the window and he turned round and seen me. I could see him yelping. I emptied the gun at him. The other gunman opened fire through my window. I said to my mate, you are going to hit me, and he did, he shot me in the shoulder. All five in Adams's car was hit. One of them had his nose shot off.

'We got lifted straightaway. There was a car following us, and they stopped us. There was a UDR man and a policeman who both went to school with myself and my co-accused, and that was too much of a coincidence. I think we were set up. They weren't worried about Adams – it would have suited them for him to be shot, but they wanted to kill two birds with one stone and lift us afterwards. Exactly the same as the Bernadette case. I was in jail with the fellows that done that and we talked a lot about the two cases and they were very, very similar.' A British army patrol had arrived at the McAliskeys' remote home shortly after the murder attempt in 1981, and gave first aid to the couple, who were seriously wounded. The UDA men who shot them were arrested.

'The doctor said two flattened bullet heads fell out when Adams was lifted out of the car. He was hit in the heart, but he was wearing a flak jacket and that saved him,' said Grug, regretfully. He got eighteen years. Prison, he said, was boring. You listened to news, especially *Talkback*, read the papers, and got into fitness training. He did, however, write to penpals, including a white South African who was in jail too, on death row. 'He went under the name White Wolf, that was the name the press over there gave him. Basically, he just murdered blacks. Someone was murdered in his family and he went on a full revenge mission. I could put it in the context of, if he was a Protestant, he would be like me, or like us.'

The loyal Orders were, according to Grug, 'spineless', though he was in full support of the Drumcree men. As for the Apprentice Boys, at whose parade Grug and the Cloughfern Young Conquerors had disgraced themselves: 'We seen Alistair Simpson that day, the governor of the Apprentice Boys, and his back was covered in spit. Now, if he's going to let the Bogsiders spit all over him, we aren't.'

I went to meet the Young Conquerors at their band practice in the Eastway shortly before they intended to make a return appearance in Derry at the December Apprentice Boys parade. It was night time, and young people were hanging around the stairwells of the old flats at the Diamond, drinking cans of beer, carrying on in a desultory way. It was freezing cold. As always, when I called at the club, I was met with stifled laughter from the young men who directed me through its dark, red corridors.

A lot of young loyalist men have difficulty taking women seriously. Once I went to interview Billy Hutchinson at the Shankill Road offices of the PUP. It was at the peak of the revelations about US President Clinton's dalliance with Monica Lewinsky. A gaggle of youths sprawled behind the reception desk, feet on chairs, smoking and telling jokes. When Hutchinson appeared, he asked someone which office he was to bring me to, and one of the youths said, 'What about the Oval Office?' His mates fell about laughing.

I was shown through the Eastway's bar into a large room in which about forty bandsmen, from young boys in their early teens to middle-aged men, were sitting about, drinking pints. It was meant to be a band practice but the practice room was being used for something else. The barman brought me in a cup of tea in a tall, old-fashioned china cup, perched on a saucer. The men felt aggrieved about the ban the Apprentice Boys had imposed on them. 'They'll use us cos they know we're headers. But then they'll wash their hands of us,' complained one. 'There was talk one time of sending us down the Ormeau Road in front of the parade that was banned in 1996. They'd be quite happy to use us as a battering ram but then they'd be very quick to bar us when we do what they knew we'd do.'

Someone went home and brought back photos of that day in Derry. They looked at them admiringly. 'We just ripped into them,' said one man. 'They started it, but,' said another. 'The RUC told us there was to be a buffer zone but in the end there was tricolours hanging over where we had to walk.' They complained that the Catholic magistrate who dealt with some of them handed out bigger penalties than the Protestant who dealt with others. Fourteen of them got fines and suspended sentences.

They complained that their UFF banner had been seized by the police, and that they'd been stopped for wearing camouflage gear and other paramilitary uniforms. 'Sure, we weren't wearing ski masks.' They said that the UVF got away with carrying banners at parades if they put 1912 on them. 'We were founded in 1973. Same year as the UFF – by complete coincidence,' sniggered one bandsman. 'Our band can hold its head up,' said another. 'We have never bowed to anyone. If everyone had behaved like us, we'd maybe have got somewhere.' The men talked as if they were an uncontrollable force. 'They knew what we're like. What did they expect?' They regaled me with stories of past exploits, like the time they stampeded the cows at the police in the fields around Dunloy in County Antrim, during another parades standoff. 'We're a blood-and-thunder band, kick-the-Pope music. There's other bands go for melody. We're not into that. Others play diddle dee dee wee Irish tunes. We're just your old-fashioned traditional no messing band.'

Grug hated the security forces. He hated prison officers because, he said, they stole his food parcels in prison and because they were Protestants, the same as him, who had got above themselves. 'You'd get a prison officer who had been a binman three weeks previously saying whether you were fit to be released. Big money, easy money. I seen screws poleaxed from drink at two in the afternoon.' He hated the police, for turning on their own and then expecting to live in Protestant areas. 'They have all turned against the Protestants. But – if we get hammered, we get hammered. It's like Martin Luther said, "Here I stand, I can do no other."' This was the line adopted by the Portadown Orangemen too.

Under condition that I would not reveal his identity, a meeting was arranged with the local UDA brigadier. This was the man responsible for a campaign of intimidation of Catholics, people in mixed marriages and members of other paramilitary factions in Carrickfergus and parts of north Belfast. He started by recalling his early days as a vigilante in Rathcoole. 'In those days the RUC turned a blind eye. I remember patrolling streets around here in a stolen Land Rover with the roof cut out, with a rifle. I remember doing foot patrols, armed to the teeth, and nobody covered their faces.

'Nowadays, if anyone does anything, once they do it, they go back to a safe house, they get all their clothes burnt, and they get showered and scrubbed down and then they are away off to a pub where everyone sees you. But then, people would do something, put the gun away and come out without even changing. They'd be out, and the soldiers would say, "Someone's been shot, did you see anything?" and they'd say "No, no."

'The soldiers were new then too. They sort of looked on us as allies. The security forces can't defend us without us helping. It's as simple as that. You take an estate like Bawnmore across the way from here. They have a big Official IRA following, a brave sized INLA following and a good-sized Provo following. Now it's a small estate, so there's very few people down there is not involved in one way or another.

'Before the ceasefires there was a UFF team operating out of Rath-coole. Things were hot and heavy – them ones in Bawnmore couldn't walk out onto the Shore Road. Their bars were like fortresses. They were terrified. That put pressure on the Provies to get things sorted, because the people couldn't stick it. We terrorised the terrorist and the terrorist's people. That brought the ceasefire about.' This was the view which was guardedly shared by many respectable unionists.

The brigadier believed that creating the maximum amount of disruption was the right way to win the marching battle. Burning buses, blocking roads, fighting with the police. 'There's some areas ordered their men not to take any violent actions over Drumcree. We wouldn't do that.' His own men, he acknowledged, continued to police their own areas. 'There's a lot of punishment beatings for anti-social behaviour, torturing neighbours, doing homers ...'

He did not accept that there was feuding, racketeering, money-lending, drug dealing and intimidation. I had been told about a recent incident in which a top UDA man had arrived at a woman's house to threaten her because she was in default on loans. By chance, I had heard about the same incident from another person also connected to it. 'I know some of our boys are not lily white,' he said affably. 'In fact, they are rough. But there's a lot put down to paramilitaries has nothing to do with them.'

Carrickfergus. A rough town and an odd one. It was predominantly Protestant. An RUC man who knew it said there were UVF men there married to Catholic women. An early loyalist supergrass had escaped a courtmartial in the British Legion hall there. The town was famous for its Norman castle. Dean Swift was curate there, and poets like Louis McNeice and Derek Mahon had written about it. In the late 1990s it became one of the most violent places in the North. A teacher told me that around the time of Drumcree, local estates were 'like Beirut'.

Signs abounded, declaring the town a 'Taig Free Zone'. Graffiti included KAT (Kill All Taigs) and ATAT (All Taigs Are Targets). In May 1999 a Catholic workman was shot and critically injured in the town. The Glenfield estate sat on a hill above Carrick, with a pleasant view across Belfast Lough to salubrious north Down. UDA men living on the estate had intimidated Catholic families out of their homes, as well as families connected with rival loyalist paramilitaries; even one single-parent family in which a child had a 'Catholic' name. (The child's mother was, as it happened, a Protestant.)

Not long after I'd written an article about intimidation in Glenfield, I heard there had been a shooting there. I rang someone to find out what it was about. It turned out that a man had called to the house of the local UDA leader to see about his unpaid television licence. The UDA man had seen him off like any gangster – with shots in the air. The brigadier said there was a lot of exaggeration. However, the Catholic population was taking no chances. Catholics were in a tiny minority of under 7 per cent and falling. They were moving out of the Housing Executive estates and out of private houses. In nearby Larne, a similar situation was developing.

The brigadier gave me an example of the exaggeration. He said that in a street near him in Rathcoole three houses were lying empty. There had been a row involving a man from the UVF, men from the UDA, and a UDA man's elderly mother. She got beaten up, someone got put out ('well, not exactly, but his house was trashed'), and then relations of the man who was put out left as well. 'Now, nobody told them ones to go,' he said. 'Yet and all, they told the Executive they were intimidated. There's a lot of that.'

'A HOUSE DIVIDED . . .'

I met UUP MP Roy Beggs for the first time in Larne, at the launch of a book about the 1798 rebellion. Gordon Lucey of the Ulster Society, which published the book as part of its mission to promote 'Ulster-British heritage and culture', said the Presbyterians were the only real republicans in 1798. He spoke of the bitterness they felt, which led to mass emigrations to America in the aftermath of the failed rebellion. He said that when the *Clyde Valley* landed its cargo for the UVF at Larne in 1912, 'the guns were for men whose forefathers might have shouldered pikes in 1798'. They were let down by the Catholic Defenders, and their own people. A local Presbyterian minister said that members of his family had been out in 1798 and again in 1912. The author of the book, local journalist David Hume, quoted a poem by one of the Antrim weaver poets, James Orr, describing how the Presbyterians were failed by 'the men from Donegore', who stayed at home, raking their hay, while the United Irishmen went out to fight.

'I don't think anything changes very much,' said Beggs. 'There's still a lot of Donegore men around.' Gareth, a young student who was sitting next to me, whispered: 'He'd be referring to Drumcree. There was a rally here and there wasn't that many at it.' It was the summer of 1998. Gareth was home on holiday from university at Middlesbrough. He said he was surrounded by republicans there, and that English people were scared of him. 'They say, "The Orange Party? They kill people don't they?"'

Beggs agreed to meet me at his constituency office in Larne, a small converted terrace house under a railway bridge, its door surrounded by security cameras and lights. He had represented much of Rathcoole in Westminster from 1983 until boundary changes in 1996, when Rathcoole became part of the North Belfast constituency. The UDA had not changed its territorial boundaries though, so the Rathcoole brigadier's men were still active within Beggs's present constituency of East Antrim. He denounced the loyalist paramilitaries with controlled fury. 'It has reached the stage that ordinary decent people who are unionists would find great difficulty in calling themselves loyalists because of the murders, bombings, destruction, robbery and violence these paramilitaries have created. In Rathcoole you had the UVF at one end and the UDA at the other and an awful lot of decent people in between who wanted nothing to do with them.'

Now in his sixties, Beggs was a school teacher and farmer before he got into politics. The Ulster Unionist Party he joined was still strong and he was on its militant right wing – he was vice-chairman of the Ulster Loyalist Association. He disapproved of O'Neill's reformism, and after the B Specials were disbanded, he joined Paisley in the DUP. He was elected as a councillor for the United Ulster Unionist Council (UUUC) in 1974, and had been on the council since. He scorned the loyalist paramilitary claim that respectable unionism had relied on the paramilitaries to bring down powersharing in 1974. 'The strike could have worked without them,' he said coldly.

The blockade of the port at Larne on the first day of the strike had been crucial to its success. Businesses in the town which had not closed voluntarily were visited by masked men with cudgels, and there was a barricade across the entrance to the harbour. Beggs later became chairman of the local strike committee. He conceded that 'there is no doubt but that there was physical muscle', but said he did not approve of some of the things that were done. He added that the unionist community had been walked over precisely because it was law abiding and reluctant to get into conflict with authority. As for his former allies in the loyalist paramilitary camp. His face darkened and his voice grew harsher. 'There has been an obsession and a concentration of policing on republican terror, and a failure to really clamp down on their [the loyalists'] activities. It may be that now is the opportune time.

'The first two Roman Catholics in my house came to talk to me about Co-operation North. It seemed to me one could have normal neighbourly relations without sacrificing principles.' Co-operation North, renamed Co-operation Ireland in 1998, was a voluntary body devoted to setting up cross-community and cross-border activities. Beggs's party, then the DUP, was outraged when, as mayor of Larne, he accepted an invitation to a function in Dublin. He was suspended, resigned, and rejoined the UUP. He was elected to the short-lived Assembly in 1982 and has been an MP since 1983.

I asked him about the attacks on Catholic homes and businesses which had been taking place in his constituency. 'I don't think it is a simple matter of loyalists attacking Roman Catholic homes. There are families on both sides in this area that if there was peace they'd still be at each other. Every time there's an attack by these thugs on Roman Catholics it gets a lot of attention. The hassling on the other side gets a lot less attention.'

He defended the respectability of the Orange Order and said it had no connection whatsoever with violent activities which went on in the days around Drumcree. 'Orangemen on orderly parade to their breakup destination do not provoke riotous behaviour – it is a case of eyes front, follow the band. The disturbances have always arisen from obstruction and attack by extreme republicanism in the community.' Beggs delivered his militant analysis of unionist innocence in an un-relentingly hard tone. A man with no doubts. He said he slept at night with a clear conscience.

It was not surprising that Beggs had rejected the Belfast Agreement right from the start. It was, he said, simply 'a reward for the terror which had been imposed by the IRA on the people of Northern Ireland'. It gave the Republic far too much say, it was a massive waste of money, there would be more Omagh bombs while there was still Semtex out there. The next step was a united Ireland, and if Trimble pushed on with it, the only supporters he would have behind him would no longer really be unionists. 'Trimble must draw a line, we will not form an executive until there is decommissioning.'

Beggs spoke of his party leader as a professional might speak of an amateur. Certainly not with respect. He said that under James Molyneaux's leadership the UUP had almost reached the end of a 'powerful struggle' with the DUP, and that Paisley's party had started to wane. 'There might have been hope at one time for assimilation into one unionist party again, after Paisley,' he said. The old dream of the united unionist family. 'The horror of it all is that just when there was on the horizon the possibility of coming together . . .' Beggs shook his head, angrily. 'A house divided between itself cannot stand.'

The Belfast Agreement was worse than Sunningdale, he said. He wouldn't be surprised if Trimble destroyed the Ulster Unionist Party by going for government before guns. After all, hadn't Trimble said there was life after politics? He had. In a 1998 British television documentary Trimble had delivered this throwaway observation, his nonchalance belied by the fact that he repeated it several times.

'THIS IS THE REAL WORLD . . .'

Rathcoole in the seventies and eighties had a bad name. It was easy to get a house there, because so many were empty. But it wasn't always so. Ivy was one of the first batch of residents. 'It was like the Ritz when we first moved here. I was born in York Road in a two-up, two-down kichen house with an outside toilet. My father was in the army and then in Courtaulds, wet spinning. He couldn't stand the fumes. He was fifty-one when he died.' She left school at fourteen and worked in the mill. 'When I got married, we lived with my mother in the old house. You didn't know you were poor because everyone was the same. I'll never forget moving out here. We had a bed, a settee, and no curtains that would fit these big windows.'

In the early days, she said, it was 'like the wee streets of Belfast, everyone helped each other'. The next door neighbours were Catholics, the first she had ever met. 'It would have been the start of something good if we'd been left alone. It broke my heart when they left. Bad boys put good neighbours out.' She blamed it all on the type of people who moved to Rathcoole after the start of the Troubles. 'Scum of the earth from the Shankill and the Crumlin. They were like Red Indians. I was reared on a wee side street but I never heard language like it, men swearing in front of women . . .

'They had been up to no good in Belfast and they started it up out here, putting decent people out of their homes, firing stones, drinking. We were tortured. You can still pick out those people's houses. They paved over their gardens and they sit in their houses all day. It is the sons of those people creating all the trouble now. My house never idled. These Belfast ones, all they ever did was fight. We were always in everything, the church, the youth club . . . These ones did nothing and they think they know everything. My kids call them the Simpsons.'

Ivy was proud of her house, and her garden. Her tiny conservatory was overflowing with jasmines, geraniums and gladioli. Her living-room wall was decorated with swords and guns and medals, including her husband's grandfather's UVF badge, a sword from the Somme, Gurkha knives and medals from both world wars.

I was surprised by her answer when I asked her about the role of paramilitaries in Rathcoole. 'Only for the UDA, you couldn't have lived on this estate. You have youngsters growing up here never knew anything but strife. If someone is giving a lot of hassle to their neighbours, people call the paramilitaries in. No one gets a beating without forewarning. Drugs is a big thing. I know the top ones well enough that I can go and say to them what I think. I said to them if I ever find out youse are dealing drugs, I'll report you.

'People say to me, "I wouldn't get involved." I say, "Well, what do you do? If crowds of young lads are roaming the streets terrorising people? This is the real world." The police will say to you, "We can do nothing." I've gone down to the UDA and said, "Don't hurt them. Frighten them but don't hurt them." I don't agree with punishment beatings, but the ones that gets them has been warned and warned. When they get put out of the country and they come back, it's a different kettle of fish. They have to toe the line.

'I don't agree with war. I don't agree with taking life. A relation of mine did time for murder, but he was just the fall guy. He did two degrees in prison and holds down a good job now. The guy who did the murder became a Christian and then he died. The law suits the well-off. I don't like the police or the authorities, but I leave well alone.'

'THE ROT HAD STARTED'

Taxi driver Alec Crumlin was one of the generation which grew up in Rathcoole in its early days. His father, a shipyard worker, was in the vigilantes. 'In good faith.' One of Crumlin's football mates was Bobby Sands, later to become a republican martyr when he starved to death in prison on the IRA's 1981 hunger strike for political status. A favourite piece of loyalist graffiti for a time was, 'We'll never forget you William Sands.'

'Protestants were being put out of their houses, or were moving out of them for fear, and there was nowhere for them to live out here. So the vigilantes started putting the Catholics out. The rot had started. The people they brought in were scumbags. I remember the day they put a bin through the Sands's window. It was those people drove Bobby into the hands of the IRA.' Grug had referred to Bobby Sands as well, except he said that those who put the family out had been proved right, because Bobby 'turned out to be an IRA man' when he grew up.

Crumlin and his wife and children moved to Liverpool, where he had relatives. For a while life was good, but then recession hit. There was no work and no decent housing. They moved back to Rathcoole. 'Nobody wanted to live there. The estate was run by the organisations. All the shops were paying protection. It started off with a few pickaxe handles, now it's a multimillion-pound operation. They've stopped the killings now, but everything else seems to be business as usual. Feuds included. I was more a trade union man myself, very militant, a big mouth.

'In the eighties I was out of work for a long time. I got involved with the self-help group, myself and Mark Langhammer and Bo Dwyer. Mark is an Independent councillor now, and Bo is a Mormon. We went our separate ways. We started benefit take-up campaigns, raising issues about playgrounds, community centres and all. The local MP was Roy Beggs. All the politicians were embarrassed by us. They wrote to the papers calling us Marxists and everything evil under the sun. The attitude was, only taigs do things like that.

'My nickname was "the fenian-loving commie bastard". We got our windows put in by local heavies. Threats. It ended up we met Andy Tyrie, the head of the UDA. He decided we were all right, and even let us use their premises, the Eastway. But by that time the older ones were being pushed aside by the younger, more bloodthirsty ones. I started working in the Unemployed Centre. It was seen as republican until I took a test case for some Harland and Wolff shipyard workers and won it. We went to the city council once to get some money to bring children to a cross-community games at Mosney, outside Dublin. It was just after the Anglo-Irish Agreement. There was a DUP mayor, Sammy Wilson. The council said there was no way they were paying for us in the Free State – they paid the fares to the border.'

Crumlin had reservations about the Belfast Agreement, but voted for it. 'I'm not so sure now I was correct. The prisoners are coming out, but there's no sign of the guns being handed in. I did a thing you might find strange recently. I joined the Apprentice Boys. I did it because of the Sinn Féin orchestrated residents' groups. They have caused a lot of bitterness.' He had friends who were 'sucked in' to violence. 'One close friend of mine is fifty. He spent fifteen years of his

life in jail for murder and fifteen before that running about being a
terrorist. He feels now he made a mistake, big time.'

Looking back, Crumlin said he could see the civil rights movement
had legitimate grievances. 'But they were designated as a Catholic
organisation by the Unionist politicians and the Order, the ones you
had to give backhanders to for a job or a house. We were all living in
the same conditions but the Protestants were told not to shout about
it. Nothing was going to happen while the Unionist Party was linked
with the Order.' He had spent years arguing for class consciousness,
and the breakdown of the old Orange–Unionist arrangement. But he
had come to see things differently. He said that the Order should have
run the vigilantes. And now, thirty years on, he'd become an Apprentice Boy.

'IS THAT ALL THERE IS?'

'I was five when we moved to Rathcoole, from a cottage with no
running water. The house was like a palace,' said Adree Wallace,
another veteran of the self-help group. She had continued to pursue
ideas of community development and, when we met, she was working
for the Northern Ireland Co-operative Development Agency, promoting community businesses in Rathcoole.

She gave me a book her brother, Roy Wallace, had compiled. It was
a history of Rathcoole which got really interesting when it reached the
period of the Troubles, when people who were teenagers told how
Rathcoole changed: 'Sectarian life had began. As a kid . . . we found a
new identity as Protestants. What makes the situation so remarkable,
was the bitterness as children we could inflict on those outside our
identity.' When the 1974 strike began, 'euphoria swept through the
estate . . . we didn't really know who we were defending ourselves
from, or why, but we played along' (Wallace, p. 42).

The children began to write 'UDA' and 'No Surrender' on the walls,
but they also had to prove themselves through strenuous 'cultural
rituals' and participation in gangs. They watched the riots in the
Diamond – the older boys took part. Wallace offered another reason
why young people joined the paramilitaries. Those who did not join
did not have protection and could find themselves 'targets for the men

with sticks and baseball bats'. He described the gangs, combined with the paramilitary youth wings, as making up a 'vast destructive force' which the UDA tried, with some success, to control.

Then there were the bands – loyalist bands, some of which had official 'wine carriers' and whose marching routes were based on the location of pubs. The gangs and their bands went on day trips to seaside places like Bangor and Portrush and caused as much mayhem as they could, wrecking trains and terrorising people. 'It was about who could go the furthest to be the big lad.' One of the main gangs, the KAI, had as its 'official drink' QC British sherry. A former member of the KAI explains in *Goodbye Ballyhightown* that while the initials started out simply as a reference to a Rangers footballer called Kai Johannson, they had gone on to take on more sinister meanings, like Kill All Irish and Kill All Informers (Wallace, p. 47). Rathcoole had its own branch of the National Front, which took part in rallies and riots. Large contingents of skinheads would march to rallies to hear Paisley, and wreck Catholic streets on their way home.

By the mid-eighties Rathcoole had 17,500 residents and a lack of amenities which was described as 'chronic' in an academic study at the time. The big factories which had opened in the sixties in the surrounding area were closing, and Belfast's traditional industries were in steep decline. 'At one time I was the only one in our house with a job,' said Adree. 'I was eighteen and I was the breadwinner, working in the office of a shirt factory. My parents would have had this typical Protestant thing that it was a shameful thing to take anything from the state. You didn't complain about the state either. You hid your problems. My theory is that the Protestants lost out twice – they didn't recognise how badly off they were back then, and now they feel that Catholics have overtaken them. I've had this conversation with a republican friend of mine in Portadown. He says he was discriminated against. In fact, he was better off than me.' Adree had written a thesis disputing Fair Employment Commission statistics.

The self-help group had liberated Adree. She started as an Action for Community Employment (ACE) worker. There was a music workshop: 'It was the punk thing – what the young people wanted – not five-a-side football. There was none of this nonsense about were you talented or not talented.' She laughed. The refusal of the

Unionist-run local council to fund a community festival was a galvanising moment. In 1984 the self-help group contested the local government elections, claiming that the council was dominated by self-interested middle-class business people. Their candidate, Hagar the Horrible of the All Night Party, was fictional, nineteen years old, and unemployed. 'The terrifying thing was, he nearly got elected.'

In the nineties the population of Rathcoole was ageing. More than a third was retired, compared to a Northern Ireland average of 15 per cent. Less than 10,000 people lived on the estate. The tower blocks had been refurbished, with security gates and concierges in place and strict rules about who could live there. Young trees had been planted to replace those torn up for bonfires. Adree and others of like mind had built up cross-community initiatives with Catholic estates like Bawnmore. 'We take kids to an old farm in the Glens of Antrim. We used to bring them to Holland but then when they came home they had nowhere to meet. The people we work with wouldn't want to go to Corrymeela – it's too Christian.' The Corrymeela Community at Ballycastle in County Antrim was set up by clergy in 1965 as a meeting place and residential centre for reconciliation.

'We take kids on trips – some of them had never been to the beach – we have outdoor pursuits, and structured sessions to debate things. We have programmes for 18- to 25-year-olds. They argue passionately about issues. In some ways, the young people from Bawnmore are more optimistic. The Rathcoole ones have this feeling that they are losing everything. You have to try to build up their confidence. We talk about culture and there again the Protestants see it all as being about losing. But they can't say what it is or was that they are losing. In the end they say, "They won't let us down the Garvaghy Road." And it makes me think, is that all there is?'

Adree said that destructive ways of thinking were prevalent among Protestants. 'I see it all the time with community groups. They moan – "The other side gets this and the other side gets that and we get nothing." They point to a community centre in a nationalist area and they say, "Look, all the amenities, everything they want." You say to them, "Yes, they got that because they sat down and applied for this grant and that grant – why don't you go for it?" They say, "Och, what would we want that for? What would we be doing with a big monstrosity of a building like that?"

'There is also this thing of wanting to drag people down. You know, "Who does he think he is? What would he know anyway?" You try to encourage the young people, and then they go home and they meet this defeatism. I've only ever known apathy in Rathcoole. You have to fight every step of the way.

'If we called a public meeting, we'd maybe get fifty people along, whereas Paisley could fill a field. Young men still go to the UDA for all the old reasons, power, status, a bit of money. A lot of the UDA ones still follow Paisley, even though they know what he's like. He used the rabble like a shield. We are involved with projects that have UDA people among those running them. Some of them are OK blokes. We know what they are – but they are just part of the community, same as anyone else.' Adree was pleased to have cut through the macho culture of the Eastway fitness suite, where Grug worked. 'We've managed to get local women in to use it.'

I told her what former UVF man Billy Mitchell had said about Protestant professionals deserting their roots. She nodded in agreement. 'I actually know people who deny that they are from Rathcoole! You meet them and you say, "Do you remember such and such a street?" And they say, "You must be mistaken, I was never there." The funding bodies all want committees for community groups to be full of professionals. In Protestant areas those people have cleared off. I sit on about nine committees. Our ones leave and don't look back.'

'TRYING TO GIVE A VOICE TO THE ANGRY MEN'

One man who has not left and who looked back with pride was Gary Mitchell. Mitchell's stage plays have been critically acclaimed in Belfast, Dublin and London, and have won prestigious awards, with productions on Broadway and on television, and film deals pending. The young playwright was appointed writer-in-residence at the National Theatre in London in 1997. But he continues to live with his parents in the house in which he grew up in the middle of Rathcoole. His intention of staying there is almost militant. A *Sunday Life* feature on 2 August 1998, headlined 'The Pride of Rathcoole', was subtitled, 'Playwright Gary vows to stay on his home patch'. When I asked him about it, he replied, 'Why should I leave?' It is his seriousness about writing that keeps him there, still and listening in the place he knows so intimately. 'It is important for me to stay here and keep in touch with the people I'm in touch with. If you are not aware of how things are changing, you'll lose the detail and you'll write a lot of nonsense. I can be in touch with the world because I have a computer, and I can fly to London and back easily.'

The plays are violent. In *In a Little World of Our Own*, the brutal Ray rapes and murders a young woman who slighted his disabled brother and went out with a Catholic. As Mitchell put it, 'When something happens your precious family, your blood just cries out for revenge.' He compared the loyalist male attitude to Protestant women going out with Catholics to the attitude white men might take to a white woman going out with a black man. 'Catholics are the blacks of the North,' he said.

His play *As the Beast Sleeps* catches meanings of the peace process which have been missed by most. Its protagonists are violent, foul-mouthed, inarticulate. They hate peace because it has brought them nothing and has taken away their livelihood. They want to go out and start robbing banks and killing Catholics again in order to pay for Rangers bedspreads for their children, and pints of beer. These are the people who 'all right-thinking people' have deplored for thirty years. Mitchell understands their rage, their dilemma. Caught in a period of transition, they have been taught never to change. They were warriors. In peacetime, they would be lucky to get a job sweeping the street. Alec, the cynical politician who used to lead them in war, tells his lieutenant to talk to his foot soldiers. Larry replies, 'They don't talk; they don't listen. They follow orders. I made them that way.' The question of one of those foot soldiers, Freddie – 'Why can't everything stay the same?' – reminded me of what Grug had said about UDA men voting for Paisley – that craving for the old certainties. This was what the evangelical church on the Shore Road was promising too. No change. The leader of Freddie's unit, Kyle, tries to explain that what is going on is politics. Freddie explodes: 'Fuck politics, fuck talking, fuck all that shit ... Taigs hate us and we hate them. That's the way it is and that's the way it's going to stay. They were fighting like fuck because we were on top. Now we have to do the same ... we need a war and we need it now.' This seems a very accurate depiction of the real spirit of Drumcree. Young men spitting with rage, women demanding a civil war to sort things out once and for all.

Mitchell was on the side of the modernisers. He was glad that Billy Hutchinson had won an Assembly seat in North Belfast. 'The PUP and the UDP are trying to give a voice to the angry men.' He had a certain amount of sympathy with the Drumcree protesters. 'There is a view within Protestantism that your culture is being continuously eroded, and people just decided to draw a line and say no more, this is where it stops. I do share that view in certain ways. People remember the month of July as a festival time when you went out and enjoyed yourself and got in touch with your friends and family, and talked about just hanging out and being Protestant and the virtues of being Protestant. Playing the music and getting excited about your community again, every year. I think it's a hard thing to ask people to stop. People will tell you that there used to be twelve marches in Portadown and they compromised and it ended up eventually nothing was left.'

He took issue with my use of the word 'assassinations' to describe the killings carried out by the UDA. 'That is not how Protestants would see it. In Rathcoole you grew up on stories about attacks on the Protestant community, and any bomb or shooting was seen as an attack on us, so people thought it was good there was an organisation to defend us. People don't see the UDA as the bad guys. If your community is under constant attack, it is hard to find a strategy. I'm not saying that going into a housing estate and shooting a Catholic is a good strategy – it is a dreadful one.

'But still, the kind of strategy that I would have backed and a lot of people would have backed was the RUC and the British government doing everything in their power to track down the terrorists and put them in prison. That doesn't seem to have been the case.' I took it he meant republican terrorists. He agreed that Protestants tended to regard Catholics as outsiders. 'They think the police are our police – that it is our state, and therefore our security forces. They are brought up to believe Catholics are bad, inclined to criminality, whereas if a Protestant breaks the law, he must have had good reasons. When Protestants say, "the prisoners shouldn't be released", they mean the republican ones.'

Mitchell said Protestants were offended and confused by Bill Clinton's role in the peace process. 'The president of the United States, supposedly the most powerful man in the world, who says he is going to fight terrorism wherever it occurs in the world. Yet he comes to Northern Ireland and shakes hands with the man who in Protestant eyes is the biggest terrorist in the world. That confuses Protestants because they are all for America. They think he is telling us the bad guys are the good guys. I would say most of the 25 per cent of people who voted against the agreement were Protestant, and I'd say about 80 per cent of Protestants would vote against it now. Because of Drumcree, and a sense of betrayal.'

Politics, he said, was not his primary interest. He was utterly committed now to his writing. However, he said he found that in the artistic circles in which he had come to move, he was often the only Protestant. 'Well, that is to say, a working-class Protestant who isn't ashamed of his roots and isn't prepared to avoid an argument by saying Catholics are always right. We have suffered a lot from that. Niceness. People refusing to be drawn in to political talk because they don't want to be seen as bigoted. So they let people walk all over them.

'In terms of strategies, Protestants are limited. It comes from being the defenders. To use a football metaphor – a team which is based on defending is boring. They don't have a lot to offer in terms of flair and entertainment, whereas the team which is on the attack seems to be more creative. It is also easier. In the area that I work in, theatre and the media, it is easy to talk about nationalism and republicanism and the great strides they are making, the changes they are going through. Continually I hear the word "sexy" – whereas in terms of Protestants, it is seen as very boring and nasty and dreadful.' He laughed. ' I don't agree, but then, I'm biased.'

He always wanted to write, since he was about four. He liked telling stories. He passed the eleven plus, without being enveloped in the nervous hysteria that afflicts many children as they go through the ritual sorting-out of the sheep from the goats. 'I knew it didn't matter whether I passed or failed. I would be going to Rathcoole secondary school around the corner. I didn't want to go to grammar school, anyway. My dad told me they didn't play football, they played rugby.' His brother became a minister at the huge Church of God at

Whitewell, between Belfast and Rathcoole, and moved on to have a congregation of his own. But initially young Gary felt that it was not open to him to be a writer. 'I felt it wouldn't be allowed for someone from my background. I felt I had a predetermined place, manning the barricades.'

Most of what he learned in school, he said, was in the playground. 'How to talk my way out of difficult situations. How to take punches and kicks. How to get up and walk away. I hated it.' He used to go to the Alpha, when it was a cinema, before it shut down and became the UDA club. He used to get records from a man who ran the kind of record shop where young people were encouraged to develop their musical tastes, but it was shut down. People said it was because the owner wouldn't pay protection money to the paramilitaries. Mitchell has written a play about it.

'So you had to go to Belfast instead. You'd have heard all these stories about these terrible people called Catholics who would be running around looking for people who were wearing red, white and blue or Rangers tops, to beat them up and kill them. It seemed quite dangerous. So you travelled in what people would probably call a gang – you would call it your friends.'

He acted in school plays, and then decided he could write better ones himself. 'I went to the school's careers adviser thinking he'd tell me how you got to be a writer or an actor. I was very naïve, completely without any understanding of the world. So he said, "What do you want to be?" And I told him. He said, "Well, you can forget about that for a start." I said, "I don't want to." He said, "Well, you've no choice, you've no chance." Then he told me how to go and sign on.'

There followed six or seven years of doing just that. 'I was doing nothing. Nothing that I can say, anyway. It's a murky area in my life. I was like any other young man going down a hard road and doing terrible things. I had remorse but I do feel as if I was psychologically damaged before I was born. I was led. I made the journey through violence and out the other end. I learned that you *can* talk, you *can* compromise, and everyone can win so there's no loser.'

He settled down, got a job in the civil service. 'It was horrendous. This was my reward for having decided not to be involved in bad things. It was a hideous reward. I found it unbearable. It made me physically sick to be in that place among those robots.'

However, he had had one brilliant break. 'I did this six-month youth opportunity programme in drama. The guy told me that when they approached Catholics they called it drama, and when they approached Protestants they called it "further development". Being the youth opportunity programme it was for the working classes, and working-class Protestants had no time for drama. People told me to wise up, that that kind of thing was for Catholics and homosexuals. Well, "taigs and faggots" was what they said. In the local clubs, people would say to me, "Well, Gary, did you get a job? Ha ha!" I'd say, yes, I was doing a drama course and they'd say, "What, poofy acting stuff?"'

He was twenty-six when he wrote his first play. 'A late developer,' he said. He felt people welcomed his work because it was long overdue. 'I've had to fight against all the stereotypes. The Protestant as the hardworking, decent, upright, very religious person, well, man, actually. The working classes as scum. I want to look at Protestants in a realistic way.' He has been troubled by the lack of respect shown to women in Protestant culture. 'I know, looking back, that part of what I found degrading in my civil service job was that my boss was a woman. I found it hard to take women seriously. When I was growing up, men were unemployed and women were working, but the jobs were slave labour. Women were going out and doing these terrible, boring jobs, doing a thing maybe 5,000 times and being under pressure to do it 6,000. Then coming home and starting into cooking and cleaning. I took years fighting against it in my own psyche, this thing of not respecting women.'

In the drama world, Mitchell said, women were treated as equals. He had come under pressure to write strong parts for women. 'It's a dilemma. I couldn't show women in roles that were not real. I had to search around to find stories I knew to make up the character of Sandra in *As the Beast Sleeps*. She is a strong character, but even so, she mostly operates at the level of trying to influence the men around her.' The loyalist ideal is definitely male. Sandra derides her husband, Kyle. 'Some super Prod he turned out to be,' she says sarcastically.

'Protestant men *are* violent, and their language is riddled with violence,' said Mitchell. 'They regard women as weak, unable to think for themselves. Their attitude is to silence them, keep them at home, protect them – don't allow them to do anything. It is a lack of respect. Shame even.' It is the same with the disabled character in *In a Little World of Our Own*. Deborah, the Christian sister-in-law of the hard man in that play, tries to break through the fact that the men are not listening to her by invoking God.

But the God Mitchell knew was a violent and a vengeful God, the God who told Abraham to kill his son. 'God is a character in the play,' said Mitchell. 'He plays himself, jealous and terrible. Gordon loves his brother more than God, and God won't tolerate that.'

PORTADOWN
Bitter Harvest

'Whenever the name Portadown came before my eyes
it was nearly always bad news.'

from Two Lands on One Soil, FRANK WRIGHT

'HATRED'

'Hatred,' said John. 'Hatred.' It was 1 July 1998 and he was describing what Portadown loyalists felt about the ban on the Orange Order's march from Drumcree church down the Garvaghy Road. I had asked John about this the previous year, and his answer had been the same. 'Hatred.' This time, though, John was elated. His eyes shone. The ruling, which had been denounced by unionist and Orange leaders, had filled him with a fierce rapture. 'I hope and pray Mo Mowlam will stick by what she says. The Ulster people will be united again. There's too many organisations, too many Churches, too many political parties. We're too split. If the Orange Order is battered here, it is going to unite the people. It could end up bad, but at least it'll unite the people. It'll take something like this. This will be our Alamo. This'll be Custer's last stand.'

John was an Orangeman but his sash was worn over a shoulder which also bore a UDA tattoo. There was something of the old soldier about him and he liked to hint that he had seen service. He took a hard line, and his pronouncements usually had a harsh simplicity, ideal for the international media. 'Soundbite' was too flimsy a word for such utterances. It was not unusual in early July to see a queue of camera crews and reporters outside his home. Drumcree was known around the world. It meant a place, a series of events, a state of mind. And what a state of mind. John, a typically militant Portadown Orangeman, prayed that the right which he claimed he cherished above all others would be denied him. 'When the British people see British subjects being battered on the streets of Portadown, when they see British blood running down the faces of people that is only looking to walk the Queen's highway, they will think, hold on, those people has the right,' he explained. Then, most revealing of all: 'This will be our Bloody Sunday.' He clasped his big strong hands together and grinned.

Bloody Sunday. Derry, 1972. Fourteen unarmed Catholic civilians killed by British soldiers. Innocent victims. Their community was seen by the world to be the innocent victim of a bullying state. Seen not least because of television and newspaper photographs. It was a defining moment. The republican movement had used the touchstone of that innocence, faced with that brutality, to neutralise antipathy towards its own bloody campaign. To take away the stains. On the verge of a new century, John craved such a martyrdom for his people. He wanted blood sacrifice, filmed and photographed. Blood to wash away the image of Protestants as triumphalist bullies, and show them as the true victims.

John supported the Concerned Protestants group. Set up when the Drumcree parade became controversial in 1995, it was part of the Ulster Civil Rights Movement (UCRM), again, the title a claiming-back. In 1968 the Northern Ireland Civil Rights Association had fought for equality for nationalists, for 'one man one vote', for access to housing and employment. UCRM spokeswoman Pauline Gilmore told me that the 1995 movement, open only to Protestants, was all about Protestants claiming equal civil and religious rights. Once they reached something like equality, they might consider allowing Catholics to join. Gilmore said that everything had changed, that whereas in the sixties 'RC rights were at the lowest of the low', things had now turned full circle. Protestants were afraid to speak, 'unless you're standing with two men on either side of you with a 9 mil'.

The movement's groups attracted their share of such men, and rallies drew rough crowds, which included maverick paramilitaries. 'I don't ask what side of loyalism our support comes from. Within Protestantism, another Protestant is not your enemy. We want strength from all sources,' Gilmore had told me when I interviewed her at her home in east Belfast in 1996. She was a bone thin, intense young woman with black hair, scourged with her sense of grievance. The UCRM in practice was about the right to march. The right to march, which became the right to break the law.

The Portadown group set out to highlight allegations of intimidation by nationalists of the mainly elderly Protestant population of Park Road. Its members would make sure that the lampposts and walls on the frontier with the militantly nationalist Garvaghy Road were properly bedecked with unionist flags and colours. Skirmishes with nationalists routinely occurred when loyalists were putting up the Orange arch, important because Catholics would have to pass under it.

'What is happening on Park Road is ethnic cleansing at its worst,' said John. 'Years ago Catholics and Protestants used to run about together. The Catholics would have come out and watched the parades and everything. Then McKenna and his boys come in and tried to get the Protestants out. The hatred now is unbelievable.' Breandán Mac Cionnaith – loyalists refuse to give the name of the reviled republican leader of the Garvaghy Road Residents' Coalition the Irish pronunciation. 'I know the score. People know my background. They look to me. I've had ladies coming up to me saying, "John, what do you want me to do?" I had a pensioner ringing me and she said, "Do you want me to make sandwiches?" There's good-living people backing the Orangemen on this. Even the lady folk is in on this.'

He did not only offer advice to old ladies – he boasted that the younger generation of paramilitaries in the town looked up to him. 'The Loyalist Volunteer Force took an oath to defend the Protestant people. They'll not let the Protestant people be beaten,' he said. Ceasefires, he implied, can be broken. 'There is dissent among the ranks of the UVF and the UDA. They are saying they've been conned. It takes very little to spark things off.' It was obvious that John included the paramilitaries in his wish for the unionist family to be reunited.

John was in demand. The phone rang and he made brisk arrangements, punctuated with angry, excited laughter. Billy, a stout man in the stained clothes of a labourer, arrived at the door and came in to sit across the narrow fireplace from his friend. 'If there's one Orangeman shot out there, the whole country will go up,' predicted John, clapping his hands. Billy reckoned republican pressure on the government might work in the Orangemen's favour. 'I think,' he said, 'the IRA has told Mowlam – if you let the Orange down the road, we'll hit the mainland.'

However, the men took the view that both British Prime Minister Tony Blair and Irish Taoiseach Bertie Ahern would, in the interests of the Assembly, prefer the march to go ahead, and that they wanted to persuade Mac Cionnaith to drop his opposition to it. This worried the Orangemen. The Order had to be seen to stand up to the combined forces of the republican movement, the British and Irish governments and the pro-agreement unionists. They had to do it alone, David against Goliath. The new powersharing Assembly was meeting for the first time that day. The Orange Order's county grand master for Armagh, Denis Watson, who had been elected on an anti-agreement ticket, had demanded that the Assembly devote its first day to a debate about Drumcree. This had not happened.

John's face clouded. 'I think the Northern Ireland Office might push this march through to make Trimble look good,' he said. Billy nodded significantly at me. 'There's men in the army camps refused to come out, but, against their own people. We have people in high places too, you know. I mind cutting grass in those fields where Garvaghy Road is now. It was all outsiders has come in dictating. That is the way Sinn Féin works. The fear is put in the Catholics. I laugh at these ones, these nationalist ones gets their brew sent out every Wednesday. They don't want the British but they'll carry it in their pocket.' The brew is the dole, unemployment and other state benefits. This is one of the most popular and enduring grievances held by loyalists right around the North. The taking of the Queen's shilling. Catholics, they said, were loyal to the half-crown but not the crown. Recently, the Orange Order's newspaper, *Orange Standard*, had carried advertisements urging its readers to find out about their rights to benefits: 'As British citizens, these benefits are yours by right. Many who are enemies of the union with Britain are claiming their rights. Don't be foolish and miss out on what is rightfully yours.' Credit unions had been opened in Orange halls, and the same thing was said: 'The other side has been at this for years.'

'The Catholics stick together. One time I was working on a site and these two Catholics were saying, "Youse have that many breakaway groups,"' mused Billy. 'This is the first time the Grand Lodge has got off its fucking knees,' said John. 'It has said it'll back the local lodges. The Spirit of Drumcree has redd out the dead wood.'

The hardline Spirit of Drumcree group, led by the bulldog-headed Joel Patton from Dungannon, County Tyrone, had opposed compromise of any kind, and denounced as a sellout any kind of talks with residents' groups. 'The Drumcree ones is prepared to sit,' said Billy. 'You like to see the crack when it starts. You'll find people shot. If you're a Catholic and you come up to a blockade, you'll just be shot. The other side got everything by violence. Daddy is dead and gone this fifteen years. I mind him saying, "The day is coming that the Orange will be like the Masonic. You won't be let walk. You'll have your collarette in your pocket and you'll have to put it on behind a bush before you go into the field." Aye. It's the truth. The parades is finished if Portadown is bate.'

The chalice of Orangeism is passed down the male line, from father to son. Men say, 'My father marched, and his father before him.' There was a joke I heard in Portadown. Why did the chicken want to cross the Garvaghy Road? Because my feathers crossed it. And my feathers feathers before them.

'If Trimble walks, my collarette will be off,' said John. Billy shook his head, smirking. 'Trimble is afraid to put his foot in Portadown. He'll be pinned against the wall and pinned right,' he said. 'He has pushed the Ulsterman down the road –' 'Trimble is a traitor,' said John, fiercely. 'He'll be swinging from a telegraph pole if he comes to Portadown.'

I lost track of John and Billy's conversation. Billy had a sort of chorus line: 'Aye, the dirt was done on me. The dirt was done all right.' There was talk of a man who went off with another man's wife in the toilets of an Orange hall. 'The dirt goes in,' said Billy. 'Oh aye. The dirt goes in. I'm telling you, if I meet them in the barbed wire, they'll not go out. When I hit, I hit hard.' He punched the fist of his right hand into the palm of his left hand, his cheeks quivering angrily. John returned to the main theme. 'If you want a civil war, you stop Drumcree. When the Ulsterman's back is against the wall, he'll fight.'

That night loyalists burned down nine Catholic churches across the North. One of them was St James's church at Crumlin, near the international airport at Aldergrove. Just a few weeks earlier a young student, Ciaran Heffron, had been buried in the graveyard there. He was a Catholic, killed by loyalists after a rally in support of the parades at Drumcree. Crumlin was a village turning nationalist, its population increasing as nationalists, who had been intimidated out of Antrim town, moved there. The LVF carried out the murder, and a group linked with it, the Red Hand Defenders (RHD), claimed the burnings.

'THIS IS HOW THEY REPAY US'

She was standing on the path, a small, elderly woman tugging her cardigan around her. Emily. She lived near Park Road, where soldiers were stopping cars at the huge steel barriers they had erected. She was taking her leave of a young woman in jeans when I stopped to speak. The disputed Drumcree parade was now just two days ahead. Emily looked at me warily. I told her I was writing a book and asked if she would talk to me. 'Wait,' she said. The two women walked slowly to the gate, through the small, flowerless garden. 'So you're sure you don't need anything?' asked the young woman, turning as she reached the pavement. 'No, dear, I'll be fine,' said Emily.

The young woman headed off towards the park and the Garvaghy Road, the frontier marked by the end of old Victorian housing and the start of modern estates, the yielding of Union Jacks on the lampposts to tricolours. 'That wee girl is my home help,' explained Emily. 'I didn't like to say too much in front of her. She's one of the other sort.'

The house was part of an old terrace, beyond the railway bridge. There was an air of decline about this small redbrick enclave, but it had been grand in its time. 'My family has this house this 120 years,' she said. 'I laugh at all this fuss about the Garvaghy Road. There is no such place. The parish of Drumcree runs from there' – she pointed towards town, then swung her arm round to include the other way – 'up to Seagoe church and Tartaraghan on the Armagh Road. Marley Terrace used to be up there, belonging to one of the Miss Marleys. They're Catholics. From Cecil Robb's big white house down is Ballyoran. A man came and took the sign down for Victoria Terrace. I said to him, "What are you doing that for?" He said, eff off. The Garvaghy Road isn't a real address. There was never any trouble till that estate was put up.'

The estates, Churchill Park, Ballyoran and Woodside, were built in the sixties. Churchill Park provided new houses mainly for Catholics from the Tunnel and Obins Street areas of the town. In the seventies, widespread intimidation led to ghettoisation – Catholics from other parts of town moved to Churchill Park and Woodside and Protestants moved to Killycomain and Brownstown. After the republican hunger strikes in 1981 residents renamed Churchill Park in Irish after the dead hungerstriker Martin Hurson – a martyr in the eyes of republicans; in the eyes of loyalists, a murderer.

Garvaghy Road was a sweeping avenue of tall lampposts trailing bright new tricolours. The housing estates were set back from the road, with gable walls facing out with defiant graffiti. 'No talking, no walking'.

'We took them out of a rat-infested hole down there and we put them in here and this is what we get. They got beautiful houses and this is how they repay us,' said Emily bitterly. She shook her head. The narrow terraces off Park Road were heavily festooned with red, white and blue bunting and Union Jacks hung from the metal brackets on the housefronts. Emily's house flew no flag. 'There's a Union Jack in a box upstairs somewhere,' she said. 'But I don't bother with it.

'The carpet factory out on the road there used to be called Castleisland factory,' she said. I asked if her family had worked there. 'Oh no, we never worked in any factory,' she said, indignantly. 'My father was a tradesman, and my sisters worked in shops. I had brothers in the armed forces and any amount of relations fought in the wars. Another sister gave blood. She gave so much blood in the wartime that she got meningitis. I've three brothers under the soil.' She spoke with bitter pride. Her family had worked hard, and given their all for their country. And it had come to this. She was full of disgust. 'What do these people want? They've all the pubs in the town only two, all the bookies, and they're working as doctors and solicitors and I don't know what else. There's a lot of them in Wellworth's and the post office. What more do they want? I know Protestant boys and girls have got good education and they're working in that carpet factory. What more do the Catholics want?

'My nieces and nephews wouldn't live here. They've moved away to Australia.' She proudly named the professions her family had gone into. She was annoyed about the state of the old streets around her, and blamed local landlords for letting the area go downhill. 'There was never a Catholic till now in the houses round here. Now they are putting every Tom, Dick and Harry in. This area is not what it used to be. There are people living here who are not married and they have families.'

The army barrier on Park Road and the fortifications at the far end of the Garvaghy Road meant that Emily was effectively barricaded in with the nationalists. 'I used to go to Drumcree church,' she said. 'If I had my way, I'd burn every one of those tricolours down. If they are nationalists, they shouldn't be here taking our British money. Let them go to the Free State if that's what they want. I have had every window in the house broken. On Monday and Tuesday you couldn't get into the post office for prams and there they are, getting their children's allowance. Oh well. I never go out, anyway. Except to go to Woolworth's for books. I love books.' She showed me a stack of romantic novels in her hall. The houses in the area were regularly vandalised by nationalist youths, and in the evenings elderly residents could be seen hoisting metal shutters onto windows, locking themselves into potential firetraps.

'My aunt was a nurse. She was in every house in that Tunnel and every one of them had thirteen or fourteen children. It's their offspring now who are causing all this bother. I know all about them. I could tell you more, but I won't. I'm keeping it to myself. Gerry Adams' – she spat out the Sinn Féin leader's name – 'I have to laugh at them. This was only an island with nothing on it. It was the Norwegians came here first because we are quite close to Norway. They came here.

There is no such thing as an Irishman. We all intermarried years ago. If only they'd read their history books.'

There was a leaflet from the Orange Order on the hall table. It had been put through the letterbox that morning, said Emily. 'There will be clear directions given shortly as to how you can meaningfully assist us,' it read. 'Do not listen to the propaganda or rumours. Maintain regular contact with leading members of the Orange institution.' I asked Emily what she thought about Drumcree. 'It's a dreadful thing these men can't get down from their place of worship,' she said. 'That's why they are burning down these chapels.'

'I REMEMBER THE ROSES ...'

Armagh is known as the orchard county, and the apple orchards start on the edge of Portadown. Drumcree church has orchards behind it; wheat fields in front of it. Local history has it that just before the Battle of the Boyne, William, Prince of Orange, sent his cider maker, Paul le Harpur, to the town to produce cider for his army. However, the Armagh apples are 'cookers'. A farmer told me they are not suitable for cider. Too bitter. Nineteen ninety-eight was a bad year, the farmer said. Most of the harvest was lost. Frost in May, and a cold north wind.

Out in the apple orchards a few miles from Portadown, Hilda Winter runs a ramshackle museum dedicated to the history of Orangeism, in this, its source and heartland. Her ancestor, Dan Winter, also known as 'Orange Dan', was one of those who fought at the Battle of the Diamond. The Diamond field was across the farmyard from the thatched cottage which Hilda claimed was the place where the Order was formed in 1795. A big tall woman who strode about in wellingtons, Hilda made tea and threw long branches onto the wide, cottage hearth, before sitting down to talk. She had two sons. One voted for the Belfast Agreement, the other against it.

'We want to live in peace with our neighbours,' she said. 'I was of the belief that when we had this agreement the Roman Catholics would accept our parades and our culture. I can't understand them, the hatred they have of the Orangemen. They would need to look into themselves to find out what has got into them to hate people. Is it a

Sinn Féin push to goad the Protestant people into a civil war?

'I'd like to think people would be sensible. We have a lovely country. A dead man is no good. I was just reading there about the twelve tribes of Israel. Some of them rebelled, but you have got to get together and respect one the other. I don't see the parades as triumphalist. Lord save us, look at the reception Gerry Adams gave the murderers coming up to the referendum. That was a sword turned in everybody's heart in the Protestant community. Now, we had to accept that and forget about it and go and vote. Surely the ones on the Garvaghy Road should forget Trimble lifting Paisley's hand . . .' said Hilda. In 1995 Trimble and Paisley had stepped through the centre of Portadown holding hands in triumph after a violent five-day standoff which ended with the RUC allowing the Drumcree parade to go ahead. Despite the involvement of the Mediation Network and other intermediaries, Trimble insisted there had been no negotiation. The traditional route had been ceded, that was all.

'Why should the Orangemen bend the knee and beg to do something they've done for two hundred years?' demanded Hilda. 'To bend the knee' meant to talk, negotiate, compromise. Orangemen vowed they would not do it. 'Soon it will be that every parade that passes a Catholic house will be stopped. I heard on a programme the other night a lady from Londonderry and she actually shuddered at the idea of standing at the war memorial. Now, she had two uncles who had fought, one of them a Protestant lost an arm and the other a Catholic was killed. Yet she shuddered at the thought of standing for the Queen at the memorial. Why should she? John Hume's uncle fought at the Somme. Some of those ones on the Garvaghy Road, their own ancestors probably fought there too. They should recognise it. That parade from Drumcree is to commemorate the Somme.'

The cottage was damp. Books were disintegrating on the shelves, pictures had mildew creeping under their frames, and guns and swords were rusting. Mrs Winter did her best, but said the rats had already got some of the stuff in the attic. She had found weapons in the thatch from several eras. In the corner of a tiny bedroom was a UVF helmet, a B man's hat, while on the iron bed lay folded garments made from flour bags. A few years ago there was a grant won and lost because of a dispute in the family over which of the Winters' cottages was the right one to restore. This was still the subject of vehement correspondence in the *Orange Standard.*

Faith was the heart of it, said Mrs Winter. Saint Patrick had brought Protestantism to pagan Ireland. Later the Bible had been published in English but not in Irish, so the Protestants had supported King William because they understood the 'simple faith' for which he was fighting, whereas the Gaelic-speaking Catholics did not, she said. A hundred years after the Battle of the Boyne, the Protestant faith had again come under threat. 'Again men stood up for their simple faith,' she said. She struck her hand against her heart. 'Your faith. Men died for the Bible. When I was young the big family Bible stood in the parlour open. I read that the Bible gave liberty to the poor. It's in the qualifications of an Orangeman that they read the Bible. The bibles nowadays is lying gathering dust.'

The 'qualifications' require that an Orangeman should 'cultivate truth and justice ... obedience to the laws; his deportment must be gentle and compassionate ... he should honour and diligently study the holy scriptures ... abstain from all cursing and profane language'. He should, above all, be a Protestant 'never in any way connected with the Church of Rome' whose 'fatal errors' he should 'strenuously oppose', while 'abstaining from all uncharitable words, actions or sentiments' towards Catholics.

'The first Orange parade took place in Lurgan in 1796,' said Mrs Winter. 'It was like a big picnic. Joyous. The Order kept men from going out and committing crime, shooting. Orangemen wouldn't do that sort of thing. Harold Gracey said, "Remember, men, you are wearing your collars." Any trouble at Drumcree, it is outsiders. I don't agree with Billy Wright being there. He was not an Orangeman. The Orangemen stood shoulder to shoulder to keep the roughnecks from attacking the police. Mind you, I could be saying a wrong thing to call Billy Wright rough. At our Bible study group one night there was an Orangeman and he was at Drumcree and he said that Paisley had said something that ignited the crowd and it was Billy Wright came down and calmed the roughnecks down. He had great control over the roughnecks.

'Then again, I have heard people say that the loyalists only did what a lot of other Protestants hadn't the guts to do. Murder is murder. But if anyone took Gerry Adams's life, would any of us shed a tear? We are hypocrites, I suppose. The Unionist Party should be more like the Orange, and go forward with one spake. Look at the way the RCs can all back each other. What does it say in the Bible? If you are not for me, you are against me.' Mrs Winter's talk ranged across the centuries, as if she had been at the joyous picnic in 1796, as well as at the Bible study group with the man who watched Billy Wright in 1996. 'Roughneck' seemed a good word for the crowds at Drumcree.

She said the Order had helped put down the 1798 rebellion and that in 1914 Orangemen had fought for their country. 'It was never against your Roman Catholic neighbour. This terrible hatred has only come from 1969 when this trouble started. Before that, it was great.

'I remember after the war all the schoolchildren got flowers to celebrate and we went out and sat in the fields where the Garvaghy Road is now. Another thing about those houses, there was a lot of houses in the town, two-up, two-down and an outside toilet. A builder campaigned to get good houses built. He encouraged the council to buy the land off Sam McGredy, the rose man, who had his rose gardens there. The builder built a house for himself there too. He was tied to his chair and burnt. Now. That is what the downtrodden minority did to him when they got their houses.' The builder Mrs Winter was referring to was the late Alderman William Wright, who had been a UUP mayor of Portadown and chairman of the Borough Council. He had campaigned to get the estates built and had built two big houses for his family at the same time. He and his family had survived the fire. Mrs Winter shook her head with disgust. 'That was the thanks he got,' she said. 'It is all Catholics there now. But however.' She sighed. 'I remember the roses.'

'A PROBLEM WHICH DID NOT REALLY EXIST'

Portadown loyalists were fond of remembering the roses. There was 'never any trouble' about parades until Breandán Mac Cionnaith turned up. Their conviction that Sinn Féin was behind the strategy of opposing parades was confirmed when Radio Telefís Éireann (RTÉ) revealed that Gerry Adams, speaking at a private Sinn Féin meeting in 1995, had commended the work of Sinn Féin activists in residents' groups. Certainly, Mac Cionnaith's background could hardly have been more provocative. He had been jailed for his part in blowing up the British Legion hall in Portadown.

However, the history of Orange parades in Portadown has been anything but peaceful. The town was planted with British settlers by James I in 1610. During the 1641 rising, local chieftain Manus Roe O'Cahan drove eighty Protestants – men, women and children – into the River Bann, 'and there instantly and most barbarously drowned the most of them. And those that could not swim and came to the shore they knocked on the head, and so after drowned them, or else shot them to death in the water' (quoted in Bardon, p. 138). In 1646 the town was burned by the Irish. In 1657 it was occupied by Cromwell.

In 1741 the canal was opened, and Portadown became a prosperous linen centre. Among the peasants and weavers of County Armagh, sectarian violence was rife, with Protestant Peep o' Day boys clashing with Catholic Defenders, in part over competition for land to rent, and for work. The Protestants were better armed. Catholics were not allowed guns, under the remnants of the Penal Laws, and some records show Protestant gentry lending arms to Catholics to protect them from 'these fanatick madmen', described by Lord Gosford as 'a low set of fellows'.

The gentry smelt rebellion. The constabulary was 'a jest rather than a terror to evil doers,' wrote Colonel William Blacker of the situation prevailing in Portadown in 1795 (quoted in the *Portadown Times*, 18 July 1969). Blacker, a local squire, set about remedying this 'dastardly state of affairs', helping 'our side' to make bullets from the lead on the roof of his house. He relied upon the Bleary Boys, who were, by his own account, 'stout Protestants of a character somewhat lawless'. In the crucial matter of loyalty, however, they could not be outdone.

The Battle of the Boyne was first commemorated at Drumcree in 1795, when a Reverend Devine of the Established Church preached what seems to have been a strong sermon, after which his congregation 'gave full scope to the antipapistical zeal with which he had inspired them, falling upon every Catholic they met, beating and bruising them without provocation or distinction, breaking the doors and windows of their houses and actually murdering two Catholics in a bog' (Francis

Plowden, quoted in *200 Years in the Orange Citadel*, p. 4).

Blacker witnessed the Battle of the Diamond, and he was one of the first of the gentry to join the new Orange Order. 'A determination was expressed of driving from this quarter of the county the entire of its Roman Catholic population ... A written notice was thrown into or posted upon the door of a house warning the inmates, in the words of Oliver Cromwell, to betake themselves "to hell or to Connaught",' he wrote (Bardon, p. 226). Potential informers about the activities of the Orangemen were warned to desist. Otherwise, to quote one threatening letter from the time, 'I will blow your soul to the Low hils of hell And Burn the House you are in' (Bardon, p. 226). Bardon notes that looms and webs were destroyed along with houses, reducing competition during a slump in the linen industry, and driving seven thousand Catholics out of County Armagh in a two-month period.

Lord Gosford, who declared himself 'as true a Protestant as any in this room', berated local magistrates for failing to uphold the law by dealing with the 'lawless banditi', as he dubbed the Orangemen, who were persecuting those whose only crime was to be Catholic. When the yeomanry were formed in 1796 to put down the United Irish movement, Orangemen from the Portadown area were among the first to join. Historian A.T.Q. Stewart has noted that United Irish societies 'did not flourish in areas where Protestants had been massacred in 1641'.

There was also the ambivalent relationship between the gentry and the likes of the Bleary Boys. David Jones, the Portadown spokesman for the Orange Order, is one of the authors of a commemorative history of Orangeism in the area. He wrote that the Order depended on the support of the gentry, which had education and expertise, and, crucially, 'considerable influence ... with the authorities' and 'considerable power to influence and encourage the tenants on their estates to follow in their footsteps and join the Order' (Jones, *et al*, p. 3).

Irish Patriot leader Henry Grattan took a less benign view, deploring the fact that clergy were also part of this alliance. In the House of Commons in 1805 he referred to those who stirred up panic, so that 'then walk forth the men of blood', leading to 'atrocities which he dare not commit in his own name' (*200 Years in the Orange Citadel*, p. 7). Throughout the nineteenth century, attempts to ban the Orange

Order were defied in Portadown. In answer to a request to make local Orangemen obey the law, Colonel Blacker replied: 'It was a law made by the Whigs and they had made many laws as well as it, which ought not to be obeyed' (quoted in Wright, 1996, p. 55).

In 1832 Orangemen defied the new Party Processions Act by marching along 'the Walk' (now the Garvaghy Road) to Drumcree. A parliamentary select committee of 1835 found that 'the obvious tendency and effect of the Orange society is ... exciting one portion of the people against another ... to excite to breaches of the peace and bloodshed' (*200 Years in the Orange Citadel*, p. 19).

Armagh magistrate William Hancock, a Protestant, told the committee that, 'For some time past the peaceable inhabitants of the parish of Drumcree have been insulted and outraged by large bodies of Orangemen parading the highways, playing party tunes, firing shots and using the most opprobrious epithets they could invent.' He added that the Orangemen had gone 'a considerable distance out of their way' to pass a Catholic chapel on their march to Drumcree church (*200 Years in the Orange Citadel*, p. 17).

A further Royal Commission after riots in Belfast in 1857 found that the 'Orange system' and its celebrations led to 'violence, outrage, religious animosities, hatred between the classes and too often bloodshed and loss of life' (*200 Years in the Orange Citadel*, p. 21). Jones and his co-authors took these findings in their stride, claiming that 'nothing, of course, could have been further from the truth. The Orangemen were not out to provoke anyone, but rather to enjoy and celebrate their distinctive culture and heritage. Roman Catholics had often attended these parades and had not been offended by them. It was once again a heavy handed approach to a problem which did not really exist' (Jones, *et al*, p. 21).

In 1863 the vehement Orange MP Sir William Verner was decrying the failure of 'our so-called liberal rulers' to 'attach the popish faction to the throne or make them respect the law. The times are too perilous and the conspiracy too active for us to remain silent for, as our would be Parliamentary leaders say, "the sake of peace".' He warned that 'unless Protestants remain in an attitude of watchfulness, many Diamonds will have to be fought ere treason is trampled out of the land and they are permitted to enjoy the freedom and protection a

Protestant paternal government should secure to them' (quoted in the *Ulster Gazette and Armagh Standard*, 7 August 1942).

In 1873 Orangemen marched through the Tunnel. According to an account in the *Portadown News*, when they were en route they hoped 'that the inhabitants of this unenviably notorious locality would manifest for once a forbearance peculiarly foreign to their training and inculcations'. However, they were attacked in a most 'dastardly and despicably sneakish' way. Crockery and stones were thrown 'with a violence ... perfectly compatible with the skulking poltroonery that dictated such a plan for waylaying a number of peaceable men whose only crime was that they were Protestants and loyal subjects' (Jones, *et al*, p. 24). When, later that year, the police cordoned off the Tunnel to prevent an Orange parade passing that way, an 'indignation meeting' was called at the town hall. The 'sacred right' to march was proclaimed, and Portadown was described as 'a Protestant town'. The *Portadown News* declared that it was a 'simple struggle for freedom'. The local Orange gentry opposed the banning of parades, claiming it diminished its ability to exercise 'wholesome' influence.

In 1881 Michael Davitt told a Land League meeting at Loughgall, County Armagh, that the landlords of Ireland 'are all of one religion – their god is mammon and rack-rents, and evictions their only morality, while the toilers in the fields, whether Orangemen, Catholics, Presbyterians or Methodists, are the victims' (quoted in *For God and Ulster*, p. 21). The Grand Lodge moved quickly, denouncing the league as a conspiracy against property rights, Protestantism, civil and religious liberty and the British constitution.

Portadown Orangemen traditionally drape a sash over the statue of Colonel Edward Saunderson in Portadown's town centre every Twelfth of July. Saunderson was the Unionist MP for North Armagh during the home rule crises. During a Westminster debate of the 1893 bill, he stated that 'Home Rule may pass this house, but it will never pass the bridge at Portadown' (Jones, *et al*, p. 30).

Colonel Stewart Blacker, a descendant of the Orange founder, was given responsibility for raising the illegal anti-home rule Ulster Volunteer Force in 1912. Mrs Winter showed me a photograph of her husband's father, Robert Winter, in the ranks of the UVF in front of Ardress House in County Armagh, presided over by Captain Charles

Ensor, the landlord. Ensor would subsequently lead his force, many of them local Orangemen, to the Battle of the Somme, where he was injured and four hundred Portadown men were killed. Jones recorded that many of the Orangemen went 'over the top' with their sashes on.

The current editor of the *Portadown Times*, David Armstrong, showed me a framed scroll in his office, listing the 'names of the fallen' in the First World War. 'That is a great commentary on Portadown,' he said. He pointed to names which were obviously Catholic. 'Look, Trooper Thomas Lavelle from Obins Street – the poppy wasn't a political symbol to him, or to Private Patrick McVeigh of the Tunnel or Private Francis McCann. In 1914 these people paraded down to the railway station in Portadown never to be seen again. But Catholics wouldn't be seen now at the war memorial.'

Mrs Winter had letters about the distribution of guns to UVF men, and a framed letter from the Unionist prime minister, James Craig, about the Special Constabulary. Craig recorded his appreciation of 'the splendid bearing and discipline' of the men, and praised 'the loyal spirit animating the ranks'. The government of Northern Ireland, he wrote, 'thoroughly understands its indebtedness to the constabulary forces'.

I drove out to Ardress one day, wondering if they would have other photographs. The big farmhouse, aggrandised in 1760 by the addition of a façade and fine interior plasterwork, is run by the National Trust. No sign of Captain Ensor with the UVF, nor for that matter of the B Specials, even though he was known as 'the father of the force'. I asked the administrator. He said he'd have a look in the attic. There they were, in their dusty frames. He got them down. Captain Ensor with the troops. The administrator said the trust felt it best not to display them. They might cause trouble.

In Belfast, I called to see Ethel Ensor, a descendant by marriage of the captain. She opened up a wooden chest full of old pictures and papers from Ardess. The family had continued to work for the security forces. Mrs Ensor's late husband had been in the B Specials and the army, and her daughter was in the UDR. Mrs Ensor gave me tea with a plate of her home-made shortbread, gingerbread and cakes. When she saw me writing down the words of a song entitled 'The Fenians' Defeat at Loughgall, August 1873', she said, 'Isn't that rather provocative?'

According to Jones, after partition, Portadown Orangemen rescued Protestants from south of the border, 'victims of ethnic cleansing ... whose only crime had been loyalty to the Crown and the Protestant religion' (Jones, *et al*, p. 34). Sir John Lavery painted the Twelfth in the town in 1928, noting 'the austere passion' of the occasion. He remarked upon the drummers, 'whose lives seemed to depend on the noise they were able to make ... their wrists bleeding and a look in the eye that boded ill for any interference'. The Victorian novelist Thackeray had, on his travels, noted a similarly defiant look in the eyes of the men of these parts.

All the MPs who set up what was to become the Ulster Unionist Party were Orangemen, and the Order became 'a central organisational link in the unionist political machine'. All of the North's prime ministers were Orangemen. It was Lord Craigavon who stated in 1934, 'I am an Orangeman first and a politician and member of this parliament afterwards' (Bardon, p. 539).

Jones described the years after the Second World War as the golden age of Orangeism in Portadown. The Order was regarded as 'noble and honourable' and to be a member 'elevated a man in sight of his peers' (Jones, *et al*, p. 42). In the late sixties the Unionist Party was attempting to join Lurgan and Portadown into a new city, named Craigavon by William Craig after the North's first prime minister. It would be a predominantly Protestant city in the predominantly Protestant east. The then minister of development, Brian Faulkner, opened Craigavon's first private housing development. 'I would like to take this opportunity of dispelling the gloom of the "Dismal Johnnies" who have recently denied progress with the new city,' he said. 'We have put our hand to the plough and there is no question of our turning back' (quoted in the *Portadown Times*, 11 July 1969). Twenty-five years later, whole estates in the failed city were being demolished. Craigavon did not prosper.

The so-called 'Portadown parliament' of twelve Unionist MPs met in February 1969 and called on Prime Minister Terence O'Neill to resign. In the subsequent general election, Paisley came within a thousand votes of taking O'Neill's seat.

In July 1969 the cinema in Banbridge was showing Kirk Douglas in

The Brotherhood, while Lurgan had Carroll Baker in *Custer of the West* and Portadown had Dean Martin in *Rough Night in Jericho* and Marlon Brando in *One Eyed Jacks*. At Drumcree church the Reverend Dermot Griffith told the Orangemen that it was a time of great danger and that they should remember Colonel Blacker's injunction to uphold Protestantism but to be 'charitable to Roman Catholics'. He said many Catholics were horrified by the 'communism of Bernadette Devlin' but that Protestants needed to present a more attractive image to encourage them to support the state. The North's battles were now being filmed for television, and speeches from the period refer to 'the eyes of the world'. There was an awareness that what was being seen was ugly.

There has been sporadic trouble over marches in Portadown throughout the Troubles. After the signing of the Anglo-Irish Agreement, in 1985, Jones claimed that since Orangeism represented the antithesis of republicanism, Portadown was chosen by the British to face down unionist opposition to 'the diktat'. During the fierce riots that followed the decision to reroute a parade away from the Tunnel, a DUP spokesperson said, 'loyalists should not feel ashamed of confronting policemen who bowed to the demands of Dublin' (quoted in Jones, *et al*, p. 50). Enthusiastic Orangemen in full regalia overturned a police Land Rover, an incident discreetly explained by Jones. 'The unfortunate incident of the overturned landrover occurred because in the midst of what was a highly volatile situation a policeman had stepped over the parameters of his professionalism by seeking to taunt Orangemen by use of a physically obscene gesture' (Jones, *et al*, p. 53).

It was at this time that the idea of Portadown as the Orange mecca, the place where Protestantism in Northern Ireland would make its last stand, really began to flourish. In 1986, during rioting, the RUC fired plastic bullets and killed twenty-year-old Keith White, the first Protestant to be so killed. Loyalists attacked the homes of policemen and women, and borrowed slogans from republicans for their anti-RUC graffiti, including, 'Join the RUC and come home to a real fire.'

Despite Orange claims in the nineties that opposition to the parades down the Garvaghy Road had been whipped up by the IRA, it was SDLP leader John Hume who in 1986 objected to the rerouting of parades from Obins Street and the Tunnel down the road. He said it represented capitulation by the authorities to Orange bullying, since the Garvaghy Road was predominantly Catholic. The reroutings went ahead, setting the stage for the first 'siege at Drumcree' in 1995. 'We will die if necessary rather than surrender,' boomed Paisley with his usual afflatus. 'If we don't win this battle, all is lost. It is a matter of Ulster or Irish Republic. It is a matter of freedom or slavery.' Trimble's staunch performance that year reasserted his radical roots in the hardline Vanguard movement, and played a big part in his winning of the UUP leadership.

In 1996 Billy Wright's gang, defying orders from the UVF leadership in Belfast to keep away from Drumcree, murdered Michael McGoldrick at Aghalee (see p. 4). They also managed to bring a muckspreader full of petrol, an armour-plated digger and other home-made weaponry to the church – unhindered, it seemed, by the loyal Orders. Spokesmen for the Order continued to speak of dignified and peaceful protest.

Wright was frequently to be seen at Drumcree with Portadown's Orange district grand master, Harold Gracey. Ruth Dudley Edwards's sentimental and blinkered account of the Order, *The Faithful Tribe*, has its revealing moments. She quotes an Orange friend who told her bitterly, 'Billy Wright has filled the vacuum that is Harold's head' (Edwards, p. 343).

British journalist Peter Taylor noted that Trimble and Wright had a meeting during this crisis (Taylor, 1999, p. 240). Trimble said his aim was to try to stop Wright – but in an interview with the *Sunday Tribune* on 28 July 1996, he said he had told the secretary of state what the paramilitary leader was threatening. Trimble remarked that it was shortly after this that the banned parade was pushed through the Garvaghy Road. The parade was again pushed through in 1997. The chief constable, Ronnie Flanagan, said he believed that, otherwise, loyalists would kill Catholics. They did so anyway. Before the month was out Bernadette Martin and James Morgan were dead. When it came to matters of life and death at Drumcree, death seemed to be dealt to Catholics.

Orange historians claim that Portadown has 'almost a sacred status' for loyalists. The Order has made a series of videos about Drumcree.

On one of them, Gracey described the siege at Drumcree as the siege of Ulster. 'For twenty-seven years the bomb and the bullet have tried to destroy us, but now the tactics have changed. It is about the right of our community to exist.' He said the Order would not yield to the Irish government or to Jesuit priests. The Church of Ireland rector at Drumcree, the Reverend John Pickering, spoke of 'a great sense of God's presence' among the Orangemen there.

The Order refused to meet the Garvaghy Road Residents' Coalition. 'As a matter of principle, we cannot be involved in talks with convicted terrorists because of what they have inflicted on our community,' wrote County Grand Master Denis Watson and County Grand Chaplain William Bingham in an open letter of 1997. If the 'community' was taken to mean the whole population of Northern Ireland, there was a breathtaking hypocrisy about this position, for the Order, while it condemned violence, appeared quite comfortable with loyalist killers like Wright. Jones approvingly quoted the mid-Ulster UVF analysis of Drumcree in his book. Orange leaders were to be seen in close conversation with Pastor Kenny McClinton, who had murdered twice for the UDA, during rallies.

Sometimes, Orange leaders and Unionist politicians have said that they can talk to former loyalist paramilitaries because of the expression of 'abject and true remorse' in the loyalist ceasefire statement of 1994. However, Wright had rejected the ceasefire. Norman Coopey, one of those who brutally murdered young James Morgan in the poisonous summer of 1997, was a member of the Order, and no action has apparently been taken against him by the Order. The issue was highlighted in a cartoon by Ian Knox in the *Irish News* on 10 July 1998. One Orangeman says to another, 'There's no comparison between McClinton and Mac Cionnaith!' The other responds, 'You mean Mac Cionnaith never repented?' 'No,' says the first. 'He never murdered anyone.'

It was Gusty Spence who delivered the loyalist ceasefire statement in 1994. Back in 1967, after Spence had carried out one of the first sectarian murders in the recent Troubles and was in Crumlin Road jail, the Orange lodge to which he belonged stopped the Twelfth of July parade outside the prison in tribute to him. Spence was also in the Black preceptory and the Apprentice Boys. There are lodges in Belfast which commemorate on their banners members of the Shankill Butchers. But the Order's position is not hypocritical. It is brazenly consistent with its sectarianism. An exclusively Protestant organisation, it is solely interested in what has been inflicted on the community it regards as its own. Catholics are not part of that community.

'ORDINARY RESPECTABLE PEOPLE'

Respectability was the key to Orangeism, according to Malcolm, a tall, amiable-looking businessman. 'Respectable means law abiding, not wanting to be in dispute with your neighbour,' he said. I met him before the 1998 parade, and he had invited me to his home to talk. He lived in a fine big house surrounded by well-kept gardens. He was sorry he couldn't offer any hospitality, his wife was away. His father was in the Order, and his father before him. He was also in the Masons and was an active member of the Methodist Church, which was once the predominant Church in Portadown. The family had a tradition of involvement in the UUP.

Malcolm described himself as 'an ordinary, decent – dare I say it? – middle-class, respectable person'. He expressed mixed feelings about Drumcree. 'I don't even know if I'll go to the service this year. Indeed, I'll likely just go and play golf,' he said. He glanced at up at a framed photograph on the wall. It showed an aerial view of a bungalow in a mountainy place, overlooking a beach. 'We won't stick around. We'll probably head for Donegal.'

However, he supported the right to march. 'It is said, "Why doesn't the Order take the high moral ground?" It did so last year and what did they get in reciprocation? Look at who they send to speak to us, a convicted terrorist who carried out an atrocity.' He was referring to the Order's decision in 1996 to relinquish its demand to parade in Belfast and Derry on 12 July. Malcolm continued: 'They still hark on about 1995 and the "triumphalism" of Paisley and Trimble. In reality, it was at the end of the parade and everyone was just so relieved. The Ulster people don't like fighting. They like to work hard. These two men just wanted to get together and say thanks.'

I asked him about the role of paramilitary leader Billy Wright and his cohorts at Drumcree. He shook his head. 'Terrible people. Of course, you can say nothing about them. You'd be afraid.' He whispered one last word: 'Vicious.' For the same reason he did not want his real name used, or details of his family history. Here it was again, the refusal by middle-class Protestants to express moderate views, and the claim that it was the cause of fear as to how Protestant extremists might repay their treachery.

They had other fears. Malcolm said he felt he could speak for the silent majority. 'This is their great fear, the erosion of assets they and their ancestors have worked hard for. They have paid their taxes. Lawbreakers should have been dealt with in a manner which wouldn't have festered in the way it has. They could have nipped it in the bud.' How? I asked. 'I can't answer that,' he said. 'I wasn't in the security forces.' This was one of the most widely held opinions among the Protestants. That there was a rising in 1968, a rising in a tradition of risings, and that the armed forces should have put it down, and defeated the enemy, once and for all.

'The majority of Portadown Protestant people are similar to Protestant people all over Ulster. They want to live quietly in a respectable – dare I say? – Christian, no, they want to live as respectable citizens. They are aware that they are British and they want to keep it that way. We could turn the other cheek and we have done so many times.' He characterised the Protestants as 'hardworking people in jobs with their wives out working too. And young people starting on the ladder. Ordinary, respectable people.' Malcolm supported David Trimble and had voted for the Belfast Agreement. 'He is the leader of unionism and at least he is having a go. But there are things we don't like in the agreement and we need the genuine hand of friendship from the other side, not this intransigence.

'In this town, it is the Garvaghy Road that is the problem, not Drumcree. With regard to Portadown, people got on well and to some degree still do. People will tell you about times not long ago when they could walk freely down the Garvaghy Road. Portadown Rugby Club used to play behind Woodside Hill. It used to be a favourite walk on a Sunday afternoon. Sam McGredy's rose gardens were along there. It is foreign and upsetting now.' The roses again. 'Both sides do enjoy different privileges within the town. Life goes on. People commute along the Garvaghy Road, and the Brownstown Road, which would be loyalist. There are Catholic churches in the town and there is no problem. Unfortunately, we had that awful incident with the young fellow Hamill ...'

In April 1997 Robert Hamill and friends were walking home from a club when they were set upon by youths. Robert Hamill was kicked in the head while his attackers shouted, 'Die, fenian, die.' He later died of his injuries. An RUC Land Rover was parked at the top of the street. Hamill's friends said that the police inside it sat and watched the attack. The RUC issued conflicting press statements about the incident, claiming they had done what they could. I asked Malcolm what he thought had happened on the night of Robert Hamill's murder: 'I don't know. I was in bed asleep,' he replied.

'Business is enjoyed by people from both communities,' he went on. 'There are professional people from the Reformed faith and the Roman Catholic faith in business and professional life in this town. There are good Roman Catholic people who enjoy good relations with Protestants. The Drumcree business hasn't been good for Portadown. Both communities want it over so they can get on with business.' He added that the anger and resentment felt about the bombing of the town by republicans in February 1998 was exacerbated because of delays in the payment of compensation. The town centre was badly damaged in the blast. The bomb was one of a number which were placed in predominantly Protestant towns by the breakaway Continuity IRA.

'Protestant people feel a lot has been conceded to the Roman Catholics. The Fair Employment Commission has come in and virtually dictated who you employ. With regard to parades, eight or nine have already been conceded. The new administration is a concession of Unionist rule. Protestant people feel alienated. They have nothing left to give.' This sentiment, that Protestants had passively responded to nationalist aggression by conceding and giving until they could give no more, was ubiquitous. Young middle-class Protestants were leaving Northern Ireland and not coming back, Malcolm said. His own children included.

'GIVE THEM GRACE'

The night before the 1998 Drumcree parade the Orange Order held a press conference at its hall in Carleton Street. Reporters were made to queue up for special press passes. 'It's for to make sure you can get access,' said press officer David Jones. There were mutterings in the press pack as to why National Union of Journalists (NUJ) passes would not suffice. But we queued none the less, knowing that the argument that NUJ cards were recognised by British, Irish and international authorities would cut no ice with an Orangeman who had a mind to block your way. By the time I got to the desk they had run out. 'Sorry dear.'

The Order is uncomfortable with journalists, its wariness tipping readily into hostility. In 1997 it decided this attitude was adversely affecting its image, and called a special press conference at Craigavon's smart civic centre. Behind the platform, the Orangemen had propped up a banner showing the massacre of Protestants in the Bann at Portadown in 1641. The Order had laid on a buffet, a fine traditional spread such as might be enjoyed in Orange halls and marquees across the North on the Twelfth. There was something sorrowful about the way the gesture was made. As if the journalists were bad and ungrateful children being indulged by a pained but generous parent. But the women who served were smiling and gracious, proud of the spread, and the reporters and photographers cheerfully scoffed salad and lemon meringue pie and cakes with the ordinary opportunism of people caught in a place where decent food is hard to come by.

Now, a year later, we had been invited into the gloom of the Orange hall itself, with its portraits of the Queen and King Billy, and its 'No segregation' posters. The poster design was modelled on a road sign, showing a little Orange family with a bar through them. Mindful of the comparisons which were made between northern Protestants and the South African Boers, the Order had appropriated the anti-apartheid stance.

Jones, a small dark man in a suit, was a civil servant as well as the Order's press officer. His father had been the caretaker of the hall so he had lived, as a child, in a flat in its basement. He had sorrowful eyes, a lugubrious air, and a singsong voice. He told us that a statement would be read, and there were to be no questions. Denis

Watson, sleek and prosperous-looking – an insurance executive before he became a politician – spoke of outrage, discredited quangos, iniquitous decisions, cultural apartheid and terrorist-controlled residents' groups. Then Orange chaplain the Reverend William Bingham, his voice taut and strange, said, 'Every year we hit a brick wall. Every year we hit Brendan McKenna.' He said Mac Cionnaith had got everything he wanted and was holding Bingham's community to ransom. The Order has persistently refused to accept that Mac Cionnaith, a local councillor since 1997, is the elected representative for his area, and has insisted that it has a right to demand that the nationalist community come up with a negotiator more acceptable to loyalists. Bingham concluded with an appeal to Orangemen 'to act with dignity in a peaceful manner' and to 'follow the biblical prerogative – conduct yourselves in a manner worthy of the gospel of Christ'. We were left to the silence of 'no questions allowed'. Above us the Saturday night dance was on, and 'The Sash' was being played roisterously on the accordion. It seemed people were dancing to it, stamping their feet on the floor.

On the Sunday the Orangemen massed on the hill, and surveyed the fortifications which had been erected to enforce the Parades Commission ruling. The road at the foot of the hill below the church was blocked by a double layer of concrete and steel, and there were barricades of barbed wire and double trenches stretching along the graveyard and across the fields. John was highly excited. I heard him say to a companion, 'McKenna will get it. No doubt about it.' The friend agreed. 'Catholics won't get into the town,' he said. 'They'll be ambushed.' Malcolm was at the church in his sash. He smiled a slight, nervous smile in my direction, as if abashed to be seen there, after saying he mightn't bother.

They went to church, and then they paraded down the short hill to the barrier, where they stopped, rigid with indignation, chins up, shoulders back, chests puffed out almost to touch the barbed wire. The peculiarly distinctive stance known as 'dignified'. Bending over backwards, but with no question of any bending of the knee. A commemorative video of Drumcree 1996 shows David Trimble in the stance, on the front line, his face inches from that of an RUC man blocking his way. In 1998 photographers scrambled under the coils of wire. Harold Gracey called forth an officer of the RUC to take from him a letter of protest. Nobody appeared from the fortifications. The Orangemen turned, and marched back up the hill again.

From the platform at the top of the hill, Imperial Grand Master Robert Saulters recounted how he'd been approached by a man who said he was meant to be flying out of Northern Ireland that night, but that if the Order wanted to close the airport, he didn't mind. 'I'll abide by whatever you say,' the man had said. Denis Watson described the scene as reminiscent of a war. 'It reminds me of the Battle of the Somme,' he said, 'when many of our brethren died so that we could live in neighbourliness.' Harold Gracey appealed for unity. 'We are all one family,' he said. 'The only way we'll win is by standing together.' He assured the brethren that he knew for a fact that it was not the Portadown police who had decided there should be no one at the barrier to take a letter from the Order. The implication being that the Portadown police were loyal. Outsiders were to blame. The burger-and-chip vans started to roll in.

That night Paisley addressed a rally in the field below Hilda Winter's cottage, the scene of the Battle of the Diamond. The field was surrounded by apple orchards. Paisley was the Big Man. Moderator of the Free Presbyterian Church, leader of the DUP, and MEP, for whom Drumcree was a matter of life or death. Men in Sunday clothes drove their wives and children in big cars and jeeps into the field. They parked in lines, facing the trailer which was to be the platform, rolled down their windows and waited.

The trailer was hung with an Ulster flag and a Union Jack. Beside it stood a tall, oldish man wearing a grey stetson, a suit and a fluorescent vest with 'Jesus Saves' printed on it in big letters. 'Hallelujah, praise the Lord,' he began to call, offering tracts to the few souls who had ventured out of their cars. A group of men walked slowly past me. 'Keep a cool head, Andy,' said one. 'Aye, or I'll end up back where I started,' Andy replied, smiling. Something was said about the UDA. 'I can't see them shooting at Drumcree,' said one of the men. 'They say the Scottish general said he wouldn't fire on British citizens,' said Andy. Someone mentioned civil war.

I recognised Andy, Andy Smith. I had interviewed him in Maghaberry prison in 1997. He was a former British soldier who had, while serving in the UDR, passed classified security information to the UFF, which murdered Loughlin Maginn at his home in County Down in 1989. The UFF claimed that the material Smith provided showed that Maginn was an IRA officer. His family denied this. Smith was convicted in 1992, became a born-again Christian in jail, and was released in 1997. He said he had left his past behind him. Hypocrisy about loyalist violence angered him. He told me that when he was out on parole, he had been approached by several RUC and RIR men who congratulated him on his crime. 'At least you were able to do something for Ulster,' they had said.

Smith was now a member of the Free Presbyterian Church. He invited me to join him on the field. The Reverend John Gray of Loughgall was on the platform. Smith said he knew him because he visited the prison. The Reverend Kenneth Elliott praised God for the 'religious liberty which we still enjoy', and prayed 'the men may stand fast' at Drumcree. 'Give them grace and enablement,' he prayed. 'We pray that they may soon walk down that main arterial route into Portadown.'

A young woman, introduced as Sister Catherine Mitchell, sang in a strong, sweet voice. 'There's power in the blood, power in the blood . . . wonder-working power in the precious blood of the lamb.' Andy nudged me. 'There's the doc,' he said. Paisley, accompanied by young Paul Berry, the new DUP Assembly member for Newry and Armagh, mounted the trailer. Young Berry prayed 'that we may stand for God and Ulster'. Then he sang, 'It's always darkest before the dawn.' His voice too was sweet, like country tea. It was dusk. Midges and moths and daddy-longlegs flitted about the field. Elbows, which had been perched out of windows, were withdrawn. Paisley stood forward. 'I'm delighted to be here this evening to celebrate the anniversary here in the famous battleground of the Diamond,' he began. He raised his voice. 'And of course the same battle has to be fought today as in the eighteenth century.' The voice rose again. 'The same enemy still would take our liberty. The same traitors are amongst us who would betray us and sell us out to popery.' Popery was a shout full of contempt. He crushed the word as he uttered it, then let it fall to the ground. It was his thirty-third year to address this rally.

His preaching voice swung upwards. 'We have set over us a

quango . . .' he said, the new word hanging incongrously in the biblical cadence. He warned of great trouble if the men were not let down the road. He suggested that Stormont minister Adam Ingram should be given 'another ride of the goat before he goes'. The reference was to an initiation ritual in the loyal Orders, described as 'the most daunting of all the Orange ceremonies' (Haddick-Flynn p. 437).

Then the thunder was back. There would be complete anarchy. We were living under a fascist administration. 'Now they want to set the constabulary at the throats of the Protestant people,' he roared. Mowlam was a republican; Blair was near enough a Catholic.

Paisley was screaming now. 'You'd better let the Orangemen up the hill at Drumcree and down again. If you don't, you'll rue it. You'll reap what you sow.' His words hit the earth on the sloping orchards like missiles, their echoes springing back. It was the DUP's favourite biblical threat. Paisley had warned Terence O'Neill in the sixties that he would reap the whirlwind. In 1997 the Reverend Willie McCrea had warned the voters of mid-Ulster that they would reap a bitter harvest, after they elected Sinn Féin's Martin McGuinness to Westminster instead of him.

Paisley boomed on: Trimble would go, Mowlam would go, Blair would go. 'But the Ulster people will not be going. We will still be here to fight the battles and fly the flag ... What is the root of Ulster's trouble? How did this province which was dreaded by its traditional enemies lose its strength? How was it robbed of its defiance? The blame lies in one place. The ecumenical movement. It was Milton who said, when God is going to destroy a nation for its sins it starts its leprosy in the churches.' There were 'papists' and 'apists'. Church of Ireland Archbishop Robin Eames was, he said, the latter. 'If he loves Papa, he should go and join him,' he sneered. 'The ecumenical movement is out to tear the heart out of our Protestant faith ... the Bible says Rome is the mother of harlots and the abomination of the earth. The book says the Pope is the Antichrist,' he boomed, and again the words ricocheted back from the hillsides. 'I don't believe any of these rascal priests. These paedophile priests are as rotten as hell itself.'

He spoke of the Protestant enclave at the end of the Garvaghy Road. 'They put it into the rebel area,' he said. 'They locked them up with the rebels ... Mr McKenna the IRA terrorist will have to be put in his place. It is time that terrorists realise that we as Protestants and law-abiding citizens will not stand for it. There will be a price to be paid.' I looked at Andy. He was gazing at his leader, mesmerised. He turned to me smiling, whistled in admiration at the speech. 'He's good, isn't he?' he said.

There was more. Trimble had shaken the hand of Seamus Mallon, 'the reviler of the UDR'. This was an insult to the memory of 'those who gave their lives that Ulster might be free'. 'There is a time of terrible need. There is a time of terrible catastrophe. There is a time of imminent disaster for our country,' he roared. 'But thank God' – his voice sank to a theatrical whisper – 'we can pray.' He prayed that God would 'cut out the cancer of ecumenism' and 'send us a great revival'.

In the silence of the field, swallows whistled and swooped. The Reverend Gray stepped forward. 'Now we will all stand for the Queen,' he said. There were sounds of car doors slamming as the people got out slowly for the anthem. Another minister urged the people to 'go forth a band of prayer warriors'.

I walked down to the street preacher in the stetson and Jesus Saves vest. An elderly couple were standing with him. They had the look of people from another time, in old-fashioned Sunday clothes and hats, and the woman with her grey hair swept up in a bun. There was that feeling about the whole event. Despite the jeeps and the big modern cars, it seemed like an event that had taken place in some sort of time warp. The old people looked as if they were in a trance. 'There is a conspiracy to take over the country,' murmured the old man. 'It's a disaster.'

The apocalyptic cast of mind, which flourishes at Drumcree, is fuelled by heavy doses of such fire-and-brimstone preaching. The message is essentially anti-historical – disaster is always imminent, and the rebels have always to be put down. We must look to our baleful God. In the fraught weeks leading up to Drumcree 1997 the *Porta-down Times* published an article by the Reverend Gray, who wrote a regular 'paper pulpit' column. The article was a response to a contribution in early February from Father Eamon Stack, a young Jesuit priest who was then a leading figure in the Garvaghy Road Residents' Coalition. The Jesuits have run a community house in the area for many years. Stack's article was headlined: 'Jesuit cannot understand why Christians are divided'.

The Reverend Gray understood all too well. The Jesuits, he stated, had been formed with one explicit purpose: 'to stamp out Bible-believing Protestantism'. He quoted from a document which he said was called 'the Jesuitical oath', and from another called 'the Knights of Columbus Oath Fourth Degree'. The Jesuit swore that he would 'wage relentless war, secretly and openly, against all heretics, Protestants and Masons . . . to exterminate them from the face of the earth . . . I will spare neither age, sex or condition, and that I will hang, burn, waste, boil, fry, strangle and bury alive these infamous heretics; rip up the stomachs and wombs of their women, and crush their infants' heads against the walls in order to annihilate their execrable race . . . I will secretly use the poisonous cup, the strangulation cord, the steel of the poniard, or the leaden bullet . . .'

I rang the Reverend Gray. I said I was writing a book. 'Is it to blacken the name of Protestantism?' he asked sternly. No, I said. It was not. It was to try to understand. He gave me directions to his home. 'You'll see a scriptural text at the bottom of the lane,' he said. Ballymagerney Free Presbyterian church was a small, plain building in the middle of the orchards outside Loughgall, a few miles from Portadown.

The name of the village carried a potent charge. It was the site of Sloan's parlour, where the Orange warrants were first handed out. The song I'd found in Ethel Ensor's wooden box, 'The Fenians' Defeat at Loughgall', was about how the crows at Drumilly were looking forward to feeding on the blood of 'those rebly dogs, the fenian mobs', a celebration of how the brave village boys determined that 'no fenian crew' would ever take Loughgall. It urged Protestants, 'Be not beguiled by fenian smiles; be this the cry of all,/ No surrender, no home rule, long life to old Loughgall.'

The village was the scene of an ambush in 1987 when the SAS murdered an IRA gang on its way to bomb the RUC station. Nine men died including a passing motorist. Loyalists commemorated this event, described by republicans as a massacre, with victory songs. T-shirts celebrated the 'SAS world tour', which included Mogadishu and Gibraltar, along with places like Coagh and Carrickmore. Loughgall was presented as a score, 8–0, and held up by loyalists as an example of what the security forces could do if they 'got their finger out'. The village was pretty, a winner of Best Kept Village awards, home to antique shops and hanging baskets of flowers.

The Reverend Gray was a craggy young man with black hair and bushy eyebrows, informal in his bedroom slippers. He said that Eamon Stack was one of the instigators of the trouble in Portadown, and had been sent there for that purpose. 'Have the Jesuits suddenly changed? Look at the 1641 rebellion. The facts are that it was the RC Church and its priests who orchestrated it and sent out the rebels to murder innocent Protestants.'

Gray explained that the basic belief of evangelical Protestants was that Roman Catholicism was a 'false religion', which, among other things, promoted 'Mary worship', preaching that Christ's mother was 'born sinless and died a virgin, that she is the Queen of Heaven and that RCs can get to heaven through her'. He said the Bible contradicted this. 'We say there is only one way. "Jesus said, 'I am the way, the truth and the life; no man cometh unto the father but by me.'" He said, "He that entereth not by the door into the sheepfold, but climbeth up some other way, the same is a thief and a robber."'

I had listened to him preach in the little church, and wondered at the equanimity with which about fifty of his congregation got up and obediently left early after he said that only those who were saved could stay for the Lord's table. This was communion. The rest were bound for hell and could not break bread with the saved. They had been banished, yet they seemed cheerful.

Gray told me that when God looked down at the earth he saw two types of people, the saved and the unsaved. Protestants needed to be saved as well as Roman Catholics. 'But you see, that is where the Protestant has the privilege and maybe the advantage of coming into church and hearing the gospel preached to him, whereas the poor Roman Catholic doesn't. He goes to chapel and he is taught his false religion and many of them never hear the truth.' According to this version of things, the only hope for Catholics was to become Protestants.

He condemned 'the Romeward trend'. 'I believe many Church of Ireland, Presbyterian and Methodist ministers have turned away from what their forefathers believed. Their forefathers condemned the false

religion of Rome.' Free Presbyterians and other evangelical Protestants stressed that the Reformed Churches were all also based on
theological ideas of Roman Catholicism as unscriptural.

Repentence was the way to be saved, and repentence came to the
Reverend Gray when he was thirteen. His parents were Church of
Ireland, but his grandmother had been saved at a mission barn at the
Birches, a few miles from Portadown, by a preacher called Leonard
Ravenhill. 'Shortly after that, my grandfather was coming home in a
drunken stupor. My grandmother and her friends were praying in a
mission hall, and he walked in and they thought he was going to cause
a row. But he was so much under conviction that he got down on his
hands and knees and asked the Lord to forgive him and he got saved.'

His grandparents were a big influence on him. 'I had a great fear of
going to hell and being lost. I knew I was a sinner and needed to be
saved. I went to the tent mission and the Lord spoke to me. The
gospel says clearly that God sent his Son into the world to die on the
cross and shed his blood and that if sinners yield to God and trust to
Calvary, they will be saved.'

Despite the *Portadown Times* article, he was not, Gray said with a
diffident air, particularly political. He did not preach politics. The
editor had told him about complaints from Catholic readers about
parts of his material, but he did not believe it. It wasn't Catholics – it
was priests, Gray said. 'Well, there's times you have to bring politics
in. I did preach a sermon about why Christians should vote no in the
agreement, but I was looking at it from a scriptural angle. That's my
responsibility as a preacher.'

He gave me a copy of this sermon. It described the Belfast Agreement as a 'surrender agreement to the IRA and the Dublin government
... deceptive and wicked ... a recipe for disaster'. There were three
reasons to vote no. One, because the agreement gave a foreign government executive and law-making powers in Northern Ireland. Two,
because it appeased terrorists, giving the IRA seats in government and
dismantling the RUC: 'The main function of a government is to punish
evil and reward good, Romans 13:3–4.' Three, because 'there is going
to be tolerance of sexual perversion ... this type of sexual activity is
totally condemned in the Word of God. Sodomy is a sin – Leviticus
18:22, Deuteronomy 23:17–18.' The sermon ended: 'For a Christian

to vote yes in this agreement means voting against God. Therefore a Christian must vote NO.'

He went to look for some books he said he'd lend me. I stood outside looking at the orchards. 'The apples were destroyed by frost this year,' he said. One book was called *Catholic Terror in Ireland*. Another, by Paisley, was called *No Pope Here*, the title printed in the style of a piece of graffiti. 'Don't mind the title,' he smiled.

'BIG BABIES'

'I'm just an ordinary person who potters about,' said Lorraine, who ran her own business in Portadown. She was reserved with me initially, asking those hedging kind of questions familiar to all northerners, which are designed to find out 'are you one of our own?' I said I was from a Protestant family. She was evidently greatly relieved. 'See that wee pup Brendan McKenna,' she said. 'I'm ready to go through the screen every time I see him. Jumped-up wee bastard with his wee wasp's face. There he is sitting in one of those houses in Churchill Park surrounded by phones and wires and computers and if a sparrow flew past the window, he'd be on to some international observer about it. Us Prods are like big babies walking around with our nappies down to our knees beside these people.

'We were in an expensive restaurant in Armagh the other night and we met this pair, and the first thing the man said to us was, "What are you?" Then he started on about Billy Wright and calling him a murderer and then it was all how much money they had, how much their car cost and how much they had sold a house for, and they had a flat in Dublin for the races. And, of course, dripping with Jacques Vert and gold jewellery. Jumped-up taigs. I was fit to be tied. Robert had to hold me back.'

I told her that I thought the Orangemen were uncomfortable with the female journalists. She was not surprised. The Orange Order, was, she said, very old-fashioned in its attitudes to women. Her late father would have disapproved of her, divorced, running her own business, speaking her mind. She agreed with me when I observed, mildly, that there were some rough Protestants about, and that some of them indeed seemed to be up at Drumcree. 'Oh yes, there certainly are.

And when a Prod is rough, he can be awesomely rough,' she said.

'But where would we be if it wasn't for those people?' she added. 'It is them who are keeping the line really. The secretary of state and all the rest of them would be quite happy just to wash their hands of us. They aren't going to pay attention to ordinary people like us. It is left to people like that, who probably don't pay taxes, don't pay their bills and maybe are of no fixed abode, and it's them who are setting the agenda. I mean, look at Billy Wright. Some people say he was a psychopath, but he was intelligent, and at least he was *our* psychopath.

'See these Garvaghy Road women, with their lank hair down round them ...' She dragged at her own hair and made an ugly, miserable face. 'They are there shouting about the danger to their kids, when any decent mother would know not to bring her children within an owl's hoot of the thing. And then they say they are under siege, but if you look into Dunnes any day of the week, it's packed with them.'

Her partner, Robert, joined us. He said that things were better in the old days, when, if you went to the Twelfth, a Catholic neighbour would offer to do your milking for you and save your hay. 'I don't agree with burning chapels,' he added. 'Yes,' said Lorraine, 'but by the same token, Drumcree church has to be guarded 365 days a year. A thousand jobs there recently came into Portadown and not one of them went to a Protestant. Your name has to be Seamus or Eamon now. That Bob Cooper and his Fair Employment Agency was on TV and he was asked about that and he hummed and hawed and eventually he couldn't deny it.'

She would not like it at all if any of her children wanted to marry a Catholic – 'too messy'. She said they were 'getting in everywhere' now in Portadown. The tricolours extended further and further out from the Garvaghy Road every year. I mentioned big new houses which had been built near Drumcree church. 'What are they?' Lorraine asked her daughter. 'Catholic,' said the young woman, not taking her eyes off the television. 'You see,' said Lorraine.

'WAITING FOR ARMAGEDDON'

Things were getting nastier. A local journalist showed me a press release he had obtained. It was from someone claiming to represent the Portadown Action Command. It claimed that

> As and from midnight on Friday 10th July 1998 any driver of
> any vehicle supplying any goods of any kind to the Garvaghy
> Road will be summarily executed.
>
> This order also includes any driver of any vehicle supplying
> or maintaining services of any kind on the Garvaghy Road. Any
> such driver who chooses to disregard this order and proceeds
> onto the Garvaghy Road with a police or army escort would be
> well advised to keep such an escort with them for a very long
> time to come.
>
> We in the PAC also give notice to Mr B. McKenna. It is a sad
> day when a convicted bomber can hold to ransom the good
> people of Portadown. You, Mr McKenna, have contaminated
> the ground on which you walk long enough. Your day is almost
> over. The PAC wishes to point out that it is in no way affiliated
> to the Orange Order but does share its view that any citizen
> should be free to walk any road anywhere at any time. END.

It was signed, 'RJM, OC PAC'. A codeword was given, and would be
used, the statement claimed, on further communications.

'Ulster Scots' was what it said on the woman's placard. She had
devised her own little parade within a parade, by pressing the button
which controlled the pedestrian crossing in the town centre of Portadown. When the signal to cross flashed, she would march across the
road, press the button on the other side, and march back again. A
young policeman watched her, shaking his head in exasperation. 'Flip
sake,' he muttered. I approached the woman. 'I was just noticing your
placard,' I said. 'Aye, Ulster Scots,' she said belligerently. My pen was
poised over my notebook, waiting. She stared. 'What does that mean
to you?' I asked. 'Ulster Scots,' she said. 'That's my heritage.' I wrote
this down and waited. More silence. 'Can you tell me a bit about it?' I
ventured. 'It's my heritage,' she said. She pressed the button again
and resumed her protest.

It was two days since the men had been stopped on the hill at
Drumcree. The 'womenfolk' were parading in the town centre.
Children in pushchairs waved flags and babies were wrapped in Union
Jacks. 'You are just waiting for Armageddon,' said Connie Tedford, a

young woman from the loyalist Rectory Park estate. 'This town is totally divided. It is so fundamental to us, the right of our Orangemen to march. People are very angry and tense. All this talk about dialogue, dialogue. What is there to discuss?' Her friend, Sandra Gamble, nodded. 'There is so much bitterness in this town,' she said. Her eyes, magnified behind big glasses, loomed out, glazed with the bitterness she described. Another young woman shouted at me. 'We don't get anything. Them ones gets it all. See if one of my young ones is sick, the doctor won't come out. If one of theirs sneezes, the doctor's out. The Housing Executive and everything. It's McKenna. He rules with an iron fist.'

Many of the women came from big, working-class housing estates with little in the way of amenities. Even the children were taken up with the dispute at Drumcree. One day I saw little children playing in a garden. They had set up an arch made of sticks, and garden gnomes, painted red, white and blue, were parading through it. In the spring of 1997 I had met people involved in setting up a community house in one of the poorest estates. They were angry about the 'appeasement' of the IRA. They said they needed organisations like the LVF to protect them. The man who had brought me to the meeting said as he was leaving me at my car, 'Don't be landing me in any trouble now, over the LVF.' I thought he meant I shouldn't say that some of the people had said they supported its violence. It turned out he meant the opposite. 'Make sure that's clear,' he said.

At the women's demonstration, I met a man I'd spoken to before at Drumcree. He said he had been accused of withholding information on the murder of Adrian Lamph. He was cleared of any involvement in it. He said it had been a very frightening experience. Lamph, a young Catholic council worker whose family lived near the Garvaghy Road, was murdered in Portadown in April 1998. In the months that followed, Catholic binmen came under attack from loyalist youths throwing stones.

The parade did a circuit of the town centre. There were chants: 'Mo must go.' 'Tony is a phoney.' 'McKenna won't believe us – we'll always walk Drumcree.' They sang the first few lines of 'The Sash', then let it trail away. Someone started: 'What do we want?' 'The right to march.' 'When?' 'Now.' The women missed the rhythm of the original: 'When do we want it? Now.' Because of this, the chant didn't take hold.

We passed the Classic bar, from which Lavery had painted his Twelfth parade. Outside another bar, a woman pushing a baby in a buggy turned to her friend. 'Isn't it fenians owns that?' she asked. 'No, an ex-policeman,' said her friend. The footpath on one side of the road was blocked by scaffolding – the damage done by the republican bomb was still evident. In front of us, three police Land Rovers swept to a halt, partially blocking the way. 'Fucking black bastards,' yelled a woman. 'How *durr* you!' 'Youse are doing a great job in Portadown,' shouted another with heavy sarcasm. 'Youse'll be on the brew next year anyway.' She meant they'd be unemployed. Under the agreement a substantial downsizing of the RUC was anticipated. Beside me, Jim said quietly, 'This is the way they treat British subjects.' The handful of policemen who had got out of the Land Rovers seemed undecided about what they were to do. Several held batons, but did not use them. They did not block the footpath, so the parade simply moved sideways off the road, and resumed its route to St Mark's church, at the centre of the town.

The marchers were furious. A middle-aged man in a belted raincoat over a suit stormed up to me. His face was scarlet with rage. 'I witnessed the entire incident,' he said in a refined accent, brandishing his furled umbrella. 'The behaviour of the RUC would have been considered a disgrace if it happened in any totalitarian state in eastern Europe. The same police force protected an illegal Sinn Féin march in Belfast at the city hall. But here, they drew their batons! I suggest you print that.' He stalked off.

The rage seemed disproportionate. The craving for victimhood. Righteous indignation gone hysterical. I had no doubt that this citizen had been entirely in approval when, during Drumcree 1997, the RUC drew their batons on nationalists who were protesting by sitting on the Garvaghy Road. In the early hours of Sunday morning, 6 July, the batons were put to use. Men and women from the RUC, wearing black flameproof riot gear including face masks, were lined up in double ranks with a solid line of Land Rovers forming a barrier right along the road. Solicitor Rosemary Nelson, inside the estate, demanded access to her clients on the road. She was ignored. The RUC created a sophisticated valve in their defences. The protesters were grabbed, beaten, lifted, carried through the first line of police, which then closed behind them. Then they were flung out through the second line. I had watched them land, bloody-headed and bruised. Ambulance personnel were attending to their wounds while the Orangemen passed down the road beyond the RUC lines, marching towards the thousands of loyalists who were lining the streets from Park Road to the town centre, ready to cheer their heroes home.

The 1998 decision to stop the march and, for the first time, to stick by that decision was, to the Drumcree supporters, a matter of betrayal and surrender. 'I'm sixty years an Orangeman and I'm walking fifty-five years,' said an elderly man. 'Now there's a dozen of these boys holding the entire country to ransom.' Connie nodded. 'McKenna has brought shame to this town,' she said. 'If they'd showed this much force dealing with the real enemy ... if they had put this much effort into defeating the IRA ...'

A young man of about twenty stood in a circle cleared by the incandesence of his anger. As he shouted, sparks of saliva flew from him so that he looked like a firework exploding. 'They're nothing but fucking animals them bastards on the Garvaghy Road,' he roared. 'If we are not down that road by Monday, we'll wreck Drumcree and we'll wreck the fucking peace process. If they don't give us the Garvaghy Road, we'll fucking take it by force. I'm telling you. You ain't seen nothing yet.' Then they sang, 'The Lord is my shepherd'. The last time I had heard the beautiful psalm was at the funeral, in the summer of 1997, of James Morgan, murdered by an Orangeman.

'IT HAS ALWAYS BEEN PROTESTANT AROUND HERE'

The young man spitting with rage and threatening mayhem was uncannily like Freddie, the 'fuck politics' character in the Gary Mitchell play *As the Beast Sleeps*. Mitchell had also written a radio play about Drumcree, in which two brothers, one an RUC man, the other an Orangeman, find themselves on opposite sides of the barbed wire during the standoff in 1996. It was a common enough situation in Portadown and at other marching flashpoints. Cheryl, a young farmer's wife from the Portadown area, talked about it. She was from a family with long involvement in the security forces. When I rang her just before Drumcree in 1998 to say I was coming to Portadown, she urged me to stay away. 'Oh flip, don't come near this place,' she said. It was dangerous. The Catholics had banners up on the Garvaghy Road saying, 'No Protestants here'. She'd heard that, anyway. (It wasn't true.) She was terrified, the way things were going. One lot was as bad as the other. 'You'd be ashamed to be anything.'

She knew the strife Drumcree had caused in families. 'There was one couple and the husband was in the police and his wife was in the reserve and he was beating into the Orange and she was on the other side getting held back. There were police studying the security videos with a view to making arrests and seeing their own relations. They feel they shouldn't be made to go there. My brother is six foot seven and by the time he gets his helmet on, he stands out like the night. I ring him on his mobile and ask him where exactly he is and I bake. I bring them in tarts and scones and all to the Land Rover.'

As for the parade itself, she had a finely balanced view. 'The way the Protestants go about it, they don't deserve to go down, but the Catholics don't have a right to stop them.' Her house was on a hill, looking out over the pastures and orchards of her husband's farm. It was bright and spotlessly clean, with a smell of fresh baking. 'I couldn't live without baking,' she said, presenting a plate with apple pie and chocolate muffins. She worked at home while her husband worked the farm. 'I get up about seven, get the kids to school for half eight, and when I get back I make James his breakfast. He has the milking done by then.

'Then it's the washing, the ironing, the dishes, the windows, the dusting and the cleaning. I make dinner at one, collect the kids, and make tea for six. During the afternoon James might send me a message to the vet's to collect permits and things, or he might need me to chase calves or whatever.' She had never thought of working outside of the home. 'What's the sense in having children if you are not there for them?'

Cheryl and James met at a youth group in Portadown in 1986. She was from a small town in another part of the North. 'My father was in the security forces. The IRA blew up our house and loyalists tried to shoot Daddy. A lot of our family friends were shot and murdered. One man was helping Daddy in the house. He was to come back the next day and Mummy was baking tarts, but he never got back, he was killed. We used to offer our sweets to police and security people. We grew up with uniforms around us. I remember being caught up in bombs when I was about nine. We had to move from shop to shop and the shops kept exploding. It was the biggest bombing the town ever got.'

She dreaded Drumcree every year. 'There's that many truck-headed Protestants around here. I honestly think they'd be disappointed if they get down this year. I go to a Catholic butcher in Portadown – he's the best butcher by far. But you daren't be seen going in to him at this time of year. You'd be liable to get a nail up the side of the car.' She and James had stopped having anything to do with the Orange parades. 'I remember as a child sitting at the side of the road on rugs, waving our wee flags. There are very few kids now.

'James used to walk in the Orange. But it has turned into a drinking session now. They have a drink in the morning, a drink after the parade, and then they drink all night. I wouldn't go near them. I like the Black on the Thirteenth of July in Bangor. It is straight as a die, white collars, white gloves, bowler hats. It is very dignified, everyone so clean-and-tidy-looking, walking up the main street. The pipe bands and accordion bands are fine, but as for the proud-to-be-a-Prod bibs, kick-the-Pope bands, "The Sash" and "The Billy Boys" . . . no. No way.' She voted against the Belfast Agreement. 'I didn't want Gerry Adams telling me what to do,' she said. 'If it wasn't going to be Dublin rule, I'd have voted yes. Most people round here voted no.'

James came in for tea. He talked about the hard times farmers like him were facing, with the failed apple harvest, the aftermath of a TB outbreak, and of the only recently lifted ban on Ulster beef in the European Union because of BSE. They had thought of selling up and moving, but had not done so. One of the reasons, Cheryl explained frankly, was because they did not want to see their house fall into Catholic hands. 'Everyone round here knows who is who,' she said. 'You'd be friendly, but you'd be careful.' She said there were stories of one family of Catholic apple growers hiding explosives among the apples that were being exported to England. I asked her if it was true and she said she didn't know. 'This house was paid more for because there was a Catholic interested. My father-in-law bid more for it. James would want this house to stay in Protestant hands. We wouldn't sell up because even if we sold it to a Protestant, they might sell it on to a Catholic.' I asked her why they were so determined about this. 'It's just that it has always been Protestant around here,' she said.

James employed casual labour in the apple orchards during harvest time. 'We would have got Catholics pulling apples but they won't come now,' he said. In the past, though, he did employ them. He made an observation which seemed to puzzle him: 'I'd rather Catholics as workers.' Why? He shrugged. 'They are more reliable. They are better workers.'

Religion was important to the couple. They were Baptists. 'We are all saved. We go to church on Sunday morning and evening, and the children go to Sunday school,' said Cheryl. 'I feel that at the end of the day, God owns the future.'

'YOUR BLOOD DOES BE UP'

In the days after the halting of the 1998 Drumcree parade, thousands of Orangemen turned up, many of them camping in the big fields across the road from the church, behind the large home of the Reverend Pickering. The evangelical rector said he could not forbid the use of his church to the Orangemen. Nor would he contemplate following the example of the Catholic church at Harryville in Bally-mena. After loyalists had picketed the Saturday evening mass, shouting abuse and physically attacking parishioners for almost a year, the local priest suspended the service.

Cows milled about in the far corners of the crowded fields, and where the fields swept down to a stream, the British army was to be seen daily, reinforcing fences and digging trenches. Soldiers with chainsaws were hacking down branches from the big willow trees, which are one of Portadown's more attractive features. Sometimes soldiers and RUC men could be seen playing football behind the lines, while the bulldozers rumbled through the deep mud. 'They're digging our graves, that's what they are at,' said John, with grim satisfaction. 'They are using the Paras. There has to be a reason. That's the re-giment was responsible for Bloody Sunday. Thirteen dead.' He said the Scottish soldiers were wearing sashes under their uniforms and would mutiny rather than shoot loyalists. The Welsh were different. Catholics. He was confident still of a showdown.

By day the Orangemen and their families milled about, eating burgers and chips from the dozens of vans parked around the site. There was a constant pall of greasy smoke. Big drummers beat out rhythms on the Lambegs in impromptu competitions. The women were there with their men. One couple with a caravan and several small children had been about to go away on holiday but had cancelled to make their stand. The children clutched Union Jacks on sticks and stared about the mucky field. Not the beach they had been led to expect.

At night the scene was more sinister. Busloads of big men from Antrim, Carrickfergus, Belfast and elsewhere piled into the fields. I watched as two large white vans pulled up near the church. Out of them climbed hard-faced, muscular young men of the LVF, moving purposefully off into the crowd. Blast bombs and fireworks were flung at the security forces, who responded with plastic bullets. One young woman lost an eye. The loyalists directed laser torches across the lines. They lunged at barbed wire fences, and staggered back, bleeding and roaring abuse at the baton-wielding policemen on the other side. Huge concrete bollards were painted with paramilitary graffiti and upended like loose teeth in a mouth that has been landed a heavy punch. The work of stout Protestants, somewhat lawless.

British newspaper reporters recoiled from the scene. One woman began her front page report with an account of seeing men ramming a pig's head onto a stake and waving it at the police lines. She said it was medieval. Another reporter observed a young man getting down on his knees to propose marriage to his girlfriend, and then standing up to punch his fist in the air and shout: 'No Surrender!' Two Scottish Orangemen, naked and mud-covered, danced obscenely. I used to buy newspapers in the garage near Drumcree church, but one day it was closed, its shutters down and 'Stay shut' daubed on the door. I did not need to be told that its owners were Catholic.

Elsewhere, by night, loyalists were petrol-bombing the homes of Catholics in predominantly Protestant towns. The initials KAT started to appear on walls and road signs. Kill all taigs. Orange leader David

McNarry stated that the Order could paralyse the country, and all over the North, Orangemen and their supporters were blocking roads and hijacking cars. I was staying in Derry and my shortest route there from Portadown was a Protestant one, through hard villages with painted kerbstones and 'Welcome, Brethren' arches.

I decided to ask David Jones for a press pass. Obligingly, he wrote something on a page in my notebook and took it into the church hall at Drumcree for Harold Gracey to sign. 'To whom it may concern,' it read. 'Susan McKay is working on a publication and is known to us. Please grant her safe passage. Signed, Harold Gracey, District Master, Portadown LOL.'

That evening, just outside Maghera, County Derry, I met a road-block. Twenty or so men in sashes, and others with Rangers scarves wound around their faces, woolly hats pulled down low on their foreheads, were stopping cars and ordering their drivers to turn back. I parked at a distance and walked past a lot of other parked cars, quite a few of them big flashy ones. I approached the apparent leader, who was wearing a sash and an anorak. 'You can't get through here,' he said. I showed him my Orange pass. 'Right,' he said. 'Go ahead.' Just then two RUC Land Rovers pulled up. The men shuffled off the road. They got into their cars, the ones I had passed, and drove off.

In the fields at Drumcree the torrent of bitterness was endless. 'Mr Trimble has done more to damage the unionist people than the IRA in thirty years ... Every time the Protestant people fought alongside RCs, the RCs turned and massacred them. Look at 1641. Their priests were out in front saying, murder without sin. Our names is on IRA hit lists. We lived in Churchill Park. My son was three years old. A knife was run around his neck in 1971.'

After he disappeared into the crowd, I regretted not asking the man if his son, who would now be thirty-one, was at Drumcree and did he remember the terrifying incident. I had heard versions of this story from many Portadown Protestants. Some spoke of people whose throats were actually slit. There was that strange feeling about it, a sense of fear that was somehow archaic, as if they might be talking about 1641 as easily as 1971 or 1991. There was something about the particular crime too. The IRA has used many brutal methods of killing and had slit the throat of at least one of its victims, a south Armagh

UDR man. But in general the slitting of throats would be associated during the present Troubles with loyalists.

Little knots of people would gather when they saw me writing in my notebook. 'They're gypsies, them ones down there,' said a man, gesturing with his umbrella towards the Garvaghy Road. 'That is the most untidy-looking place in the world. It's their culture. You go into Killycomain and you could eat your dinner off the footpath. But see that place ...' Killycomain was a Protestant estate. I looked around the field at Drumcree. Burger wrappers, chip boxes, milk cartons, babies' nappies, beer cans, strewn around as far as the eye could see. 'It's not very tidy round here, is it?' I suggested. 'No, it's not,' he said.

'A whole lot of them doesn't want to work,' added another man. 'If I wanted work in the morning, I'd get it.' 'Sitting on their fat ass,' said a woman. 'Big fat women and the men sitting there smoking all day. They are the same as the Iraqi people, worshipping the rosary beads. The women work and the men sit on their fat ass. They sit in bed and lie till dinner-time and then they come out of the house at night and throw stones.'

Overheard conversations were just as fierce. There was constant derision of the then Secretary of State Mo Mowlam, who was referred to as the 'pig in a wig'. Dr Mowlam had lost her hair as a result of medical treatment for a brain tumour. 'She needs a hair transplant and a facelift,' sneered a man. 'She needs to be shot,' said a woman. Then she shouted. 'A civil war! That's what we need. We need to sort this out once and for all.' A man who was talking to me at that moment, added, 'Hopefully it'll not come to anything worse than a war.' I asked him what sort of war he had in mind. 'Full contact, face to face,' he said. 'Religion is a funny thing. Why did Bosnia have a war, or Israel? This protest will stay here till the dying death.'

John's theory, that once an Orangeman was shot it would unite unionism, including the paramilitaries, was widespread. This was 'Ulster will fight and Ulster will be right' all over again, with the loyalist workers' strike of 1974 as a more recent precedent. There was a fervent desire to see Trimble toppled and the Assembly brought down. John reckoned the Catholics could be starved into submission if the food routes into their areas were cut off. I thought about the Portadown Action Command document, which aimed to do just that.

'We have been abandoned by Blair because we are such a tolerant people,' he said. 'We weren't prepared to be violent.' 'That graveyard is packed with UDR,' said one of his companions. 'Major Harris Boyle of the UVF is buried in there,' said John. 'The PUP is up there in Belfast hobnobbing with Sinn Féin IRA. What would Major Harris Boyle have to say to that?'

Boyle would have been a contemporary of John's. He was the leader of the mid-Ulster UVF gang which murdered Fran O'Toole and other members of the Miami Showband in 1975. The showband was driving home to Dublin after a gig in Banbridge, County Down, when it was stopped at a roadblock manned by UVF men in military uniform. Several members of the gang were, in fact, also UDR soldiers. Boyle, who was twenty-two, was killed along with Wesley Somerville, when the bomb they were planting in the van exploded. The UVF claimed the band had been transporting a bomb and commended its members for attempting to intercept it. One of the death notices in the UVF's *Combat* magazine was from a UDR company.

Up at Drumcree's church gate a middle-aged man helped a very elderly woman in her Sunday best out of a car. They posed for a photograph, smiling proud, no-surrender smiles. He helped her back into the car and she was driven away. I asked a stout, cheerful-looking young man in a T-shirt if he had seen the riots of the previous nights. 'Yes,' he said. 'I was here. It was just a bit of fun.' He swigged his can of lemonade, wiped his mouth with a tattooed arm. It didn't look like that on the TV, I said. 'That's because the TV cameras are against us,' he said, swaying off to join his friends. 'Morale here is great,' said a man. 'I'm just so proud and happy with the feeling among the people.' 'I don't agree with what has went on here this last few nights, but it is not what the Orange Order wants,' said a wiry man in a suit. 'These are people on the fringe. We can't control them. I can understand their frustration but. Your blood does be up. It's all very well Gerry sitting now, saying, forget the past. We are not supposed to remember all the ones belonging to us that we've buried. If we don't make a stand now, in twenty years we'll all be in Lough Neagh with our throats cut.' That archaic fear again. And Gerry Adams as Jerry, the Hitlerite general. 'We'll fight to the death,' said a woman. A passing man added, 'Put No Surrender at the bottom of that.'

In a small field beside the orchards a group of ex-servicemen had set up their own little camp. Old soldiers, they sat around on picnic chairs, with rugs across their knees, drinking cans of beer and reminiscing. Bobby Todd served in the army for sixteen years, in England, Germany, Kenya, Swaziland, Uganda and Aden. Then he joined the UDR and served twenty years. 'I was born and bred in Portadown,' he said. 'And my father and grandfather before me. The republican element has taken control of the Garvaghy Road. I was speaking no later than last week to a man in Churchill Park, who told me he was not only sick of McKenna but also of his so-called coalition. People are terrorised into paying out money to them. I know a man bought a poppy in the Legion and had his windows smashed. His father and grandfather had been in the forces.

'In my company of the UDR, nine men were killed and many more maimed. Tony Blair has bowed to Gerry. The British have dealt with insurrection before, except in Aden where they gave up and withdrew.'

Abey Rusk, who had a similar record of military service, said Drumcree was a disaster for Britain. 'We laid down our lives. We fought for freedom and liberty and we paid our rates. Now we can't walk down the road. It's a bloody disgrace,' he said. An English ex-soldier spoke up. 'These men were more loyal to the crown than the English,' he said. 'It wasn't till I came here that I realised what these citizens of the empire had to put up with. I'd love to give Mo Mowlam an enema with a six-inch gun.' One of the Portadown men smiled. 'You're a Paddy. You're one of us,' he said affectionately. 'This is Custer's last stand,' said one of the men. 'Abey Rusk's last stand.' They raised their cans in a toast to that.

'IF BILLY WAS HERE . . .'

Outside the Drumcree church various stalls selling loyalist tapes and badges had been set up. I spotted the LVF's *Leading the Way* booklet, a new issue I hadn't seen. In front of me in the queue to be served, a boy was wanting to get a tape exchanged. 'That's melody,' he said impatiently to the vendor. 'I told you, I want kick the Pope.'

I bought the magazine, which promised that my one pound would be used 'to further the cause of true loyalism', a ghostly photocopied photograph of Billy Wright on the front cover, with Drumcree church tilting its steeple at the black sky behind him. *Leading the Way* was part of the cult of Wright. King Rat's reputation for having orchestrated the killing of dozens of Catholics made him a hero in loyalist circles. He had been regularly arrested, and would whistle 'The Sash' during interrogations, but was never convicted of murder. Loyalists colluded in making Wright a byword for terror in the Catholic community, allowing him 'credit' for actions in which he had no part. Nationalists believed that Wright was helped by the security forces, while some loyalists claimed he was an MI5 agent.

Among those who appeared on platforms with Wright after the UVF threatened to kill him was the DUP politician the Reverend William McCrea, who said he upheld Wright's right to free speech. Wright was finally jailed in 1997 for threatening to kill Gwen Reid, a Protestant woman who had witnessed members of Wright's gang beating up her daughter's boyfriend, and who had gone to the RUC. During his trial neighbours on the estate said they had seen and heard nothing of the beating or the threats to Gwen Reid and her family.

Wright described himself modestly as a community worker. In prison his LVF gathered together a collection of some of the most frightening loyalist killers from other organisations. The belief took hold that Wright ran a clean wing, where church, gym and education were compulsory. His rules also stated that 'under no circumstances shall physical force be used to impose rules or as a punishment'. After the prisoners wrecked their wing in a protest, journalists were invited to survey the damage, and found walls painted with 'Yabba dabba do, any fenian will do' and pornography among the wreckage. Drugs had been intercepted on their way to the wing. One of those accused of the murder in Poyntzpass of Damien Trainor and Philip Allen in March 1998 was murdered by fellow LVF prisoners in the wing because he was suspected of informing on his colleagues.

Wright was murdered in prison by INLA gunmen in December 1997, in circumstances which suggested that elements among the authorities may well have, at the least, turned a blind eye. His father called for an independent inquiry. A spate of killings of Catholics followed, in which the LVF was joined by UDA members. The LVF threatened tourists, community workers, people in the Republic, virtually everyone. Security and loyalist sources suggested that the LVF was close to organisations like the Red Hand Defenders and the Orange Volunteers.

Portadown's loyalist estates display massive murals of Billy Wright, 'a true son of Ulster'. He was the warrior hero of all the young bloods. His close friend Mark Swinger Fulton, a convicted extortionist, had a tattoo of Wright over his heart. Many of Wright's followers, women as well as men, are tattooed with his image. There are ballads and poems extolling his prowess and his martyrdom for Ulster. He was 'prepared to fight the fight' and he knew no fear because he 'read his Bible'.

I had interviewed Wright several times, but I could not find the charisma of which some journalists spoke. He had a bullying manner and was narrow-minded and dogmatic. He addressed women journalists as 'dear' in a scornful way. But he was articulate and obviously a leader. Swinger turned out to be the author of much of the Drumcree 1998 issue of *Leading the Way*, and it was easy to see why the organisation had foundered since Wright's death.

Swinger's thoughts were basic – Brigadier Billy was the UVF hero who 'knew that his job was to protect The Civil Rights and Culture of his people'. He did so by ensuring that the Drumcree Orangemen would be allowed to parade the Garvaghy Road. Threats of violence had played their part. Swinger echoed the words used by Gerry Adams when he praised Sinn Féin's efforts in residents' groups – here he praised the 'tireless work' put in by the LVF. According to *Leading the Way*, Wright was the man of action, where others were 'talkers not do-ers', and traitors, communists like the INLA. This was a clear reference to Swinger's former colleagues in the UVF. Wright had taken to reiterating traditional Protestant values, from which he said politicians like Ervine had strayed. It was like Grug with his objection to anything 'lefty'.

In a semi-literate article called 'Have Faith', *Leading the Way* exhorted loyalists to reject the idea being imposed on them of reaching out the hand of friendship 'to those who are genetically violent inherent in the Roman Catholic church', a church 'sly as a fox and vicious as a tiger'. Catholics would reserve their worst violence to follow a period of spurious reconciliation with its enemy. Garbled accounts followed of devious ploys engaged to get Protestants off their guard and slaughter them. In 1641 pregnant Protestant women 'had their foetuses cut from their wombs and fed to dogs', while 'thousands' of Protestants were drowned. Another article attacked the Alliance Party for backing 'integrated education and other cross community initiatives which are designed to rob all our young people of all knowledge of their culture'. The LVF, which was fond of the slogan 'our only crime is loyalty', issued threats to named individuals and suggested to its readers that if they were ever in the area of the Alliance headquarters 'and just happened to have a petrol bomb with you …' The back cover featured a photograph of five armed and masked LVF men in front of Ulster flags, and the slogan was again a quote from Gerry Adams, who said it in relation to the IRA. 'They haven't gone away you know!'

Alan Milligan, a member of the Church of Ireland's select vestry, and a central figure in the Drumcree protest, was standing outside the church. I asked him what he felt about the fact that this magazine was on sale. He glanced at it. 'I don't know what that is,' he said. I showed him the back cover photograph. Milligan glanced at it. 'We know nothing about that.' I pointed out that it was being sold from a stall at the church gate, just a few feet away. 'It is being sold from private property,' he said. 'It is nothing to do with us. Excuse me.' He walked away.

A thin young man wearing Jesus sandals and a tracksuit had watched this conversation. He laughed and introduced himself. Mark, a social worker, lately moved to Portadown from Belfast, and a cousin of Billy Wright. He said he had been put out of Belfast by the UVF and that the INLA was after him in Portadown. 'There is no doubt about it,' he said. 'If Billy was here, we'd be down that road.

'Protestants have always thought, we are so obviously right, we don't need to say so. I'm a kick-boxing pacifist. I had real difficulty with the taking of life. I was talking to a UDR man from Tyrone here the other day. He said to me, "I was always against terrorism, but look at the east Tyrone brigade of the IRA. They said they were the best. The mid-Ulster UVF ripped them apart and scattered them." The IRA killed Protestants in the name of socialism. Now the PUP has taken on the same politics.

'We have a biblically driven condition. There are no grey areas in fundamental Protestantism. Everything is good or bad, black or white, Catholic or Protestant. Protestants make bad terrorists – they always need a justification. They are bad lawbreakers – they don't do it with a clean conscience. Billy used to say to me, it is easy to get a Protestant to go out and shoot someone. The difficulty was to get them not to talk about it or take to the drink over it. But Billy was a brilliant judge of people. He knew what he could ask of them.

'The Prods are learning ambiguity. Instead of refusing to apply for a grant because you have to be cross community, they are saying they are cross community to get the money, though they know rightly no Catholic would come near them. A lot of these people here are country people. They join the Orange Order for a social life. There isn't a great deal of teenage rebellion here. They are old men before they are fifteen. The pressure to conform is very strong. I'm into cordon bleu cooking myself, and hill walking. I went for a job in Dublin recently, as a drugs counsellor in the inner city. Didn't get it. I'll probably go back to the mainland.'

'I KEEP MY MOUTH SHUT . . .'

Ballyhannon was smart. Very smart. Big modern houses with double garages, big windows looking out over landscaped gardens. On a hill, it looked down on Portadown. This was where Alistair and his family lived. His parents were professional people. He was at Portadown College, and was about to go to Scotland or England to university, to study politics, medicine, law, history maybe.

Alistair was 'not fond of' Portadown. 'I'm on the outside of it. The whole bigotry and sectarianism of the place is appalling. Drumcree is desperate. People say it is a minority but they have the support of far too many people. You are definitely second class in this town if you are a Catholic, and the Garvaghy Road is definitely discriminated against. It is an Orange town. Where I live is a pleasant sort of suburb, and we have Catholic neighbours. But in the working-class areas it is nearly totally segregated. The reason for the ghettoisation is Protestant discrimination.

'I heard helicopters last night but I've never seen any of the trouble. We usually go away for the Twelfth. We have a house in Donegal. I love Donegal. Being here is just depressing. It gets more and more tense. It really gets to me. We go abroad too, to France or Italy for camping holidays. This year I may go away with friends.' Alistair did not socialise in Portadown. 'I go to Lisburn to the cinema. We have two cars. I go to concerts. As a family, we go to a restaurant in Hillsborough quite often. My parents and their friends visit each other's houses. The chance to socialise across the community is minimal. There is no cinema, no bowling alley, and a mixed disco would lead to horrific riots. There is one mixed pub and that is really good, but the rest of the pubs are red, white and blue or green, white and orange.'

He was in a mixed-religion choir and had travelled to the United States, where they entertained the president at the St Patrick's Day gala in 1997. 'We do quite a lot of Irish stuff, "Danny Boy", "St Patrick's Prayer" . . . that was written by Father Terry Rafferty. It was his response to the murder of Michael McGoldrick. He was the one had to break the news to the parents.' David described Billy Wright as 'a dreadful man, a murderer'. The choir had been 'absolutely fantastic'. However, he said there were some risks for Catholics. If you ran into your Catholic choir friends in town and greeted them, anti-Catholic schoolfellows might notice and go after them. One choir member had been beaten up. 'Others have got called names by ones from the tech.' The tech was what used to be called the Technical College, latterly the Upper Bann Institute for Further and Higher Education. Traditionally, it catered for the largely working-class students who would leave to become apprentices at the age of sixteen.

'These people are just incredibly blind,' continued Alistair. 'They have never even talked to Catholics. At the end of the day it is a class thing. My parents brought me up to be open-minded. A lot of the people who stand over at the hill at Drumcree were brought up staunch. I don't see any difference between Catholics and Protestants, and that is why Ireland should really be united. The British government never needed to get involved. If I ever came back to Northern Ireland – I'm definitely never coming back to Portadown – I'd join Alliance or the SDLP.' He supported the Belfast Agreement. 'If you want peace, you have to compromise. In my school most people think the Orangemen should march, that it is their God-given right and all that. I don't think they have any right to march at all. But I keep my mouth shut.'

'CATHOLICS DEFINITELY GET THE WORST OF IT HERE'

At seventeen, Henry left too. He didn't intend to – he didn't get the place he wanted at Queen's University in Belfast, so he went to England to study town planning. That was in 1977. He came back and worked as a truck driver for a couple of years, then left again to do a master's degree, and went on to live in London. He had married a Scottish woman, and they lived with their children in an estate of bungalows in Portadown. 'I always kept up a strong link,' he said. 'I lived with and was friends with lots of people from here and other parts of Ireland. We'd go out together on Friday nights.

'One of the fellows I shared a house with in London was, as he says, the token Catholic at Portadown College. Another of the guys I shared with was from the Birches, just outside the town. He married a Thai girl and when they came back here she opened a Thai restaurant. Another Thai girl we know worked in the restaurant and lived in a bedsit on Park Road. She got a lot of intimidation – her door kicked in and the like. She worked in Dunnes Stores for a while and the time of the maggots brigade she was the one given the job of finding the maggots.' The maggots brigade? 'It was a bunch of thugs went up the town and into Dunnes and they were throwing maggots all over the place because Dunnes is an Irish store. My friend had to go through all the clothes and stuff and pick out the maggots.'

Loyalists had rampaged through the High Street shopping mall, shouting that 'fenian bastards' were to get out. Several Catholic-owned businesses were burnt out after Drumcree 1998.

Henry was brought up in Killycomain in a small council house. His father was a Protestant, his mother a Catholic. 'She converted to the Church of Ireland. Which of course to loyalists is the next worst thing to Catholicism. A lot of her family would have been from Obins Street. They used to live in an old house near the railway station.' These would have been the people Emily's aunt, the nurse, had worked among. 'As the Troubles developed, the families became distant.' He had no time for the Orange Order. 'I heard a joke about

Drumcree. Did you hear the Orange Order had ordered a half hun-dredweight of Viagra? Yes – it was to keep a crowd of dicks standing in a field for as long as possible. Why the hell don't they catch themselves on? But then again, my mother would say, why don't the Garvaghy Road residents catch themselves on. She remembers the bands on Obins Street, and that they used to enjoy it as kids. They didn't mind. Then again, is it the residents who object or is it Mr What-do-you-call-him, Eamon McKenna? Why don't people get a life?

'This estate has mixed-marriage couples and they get on well with people who have Union Jacks hanging out of every window. I would never have regarded Portadown as a sectarian town but that was be-cause I knew how to avoid it. Catholics definitely get the worst of it here, but Protestants are intimidated by their own kind as well – who you can talk to and where you can go. The quiet majority has never felt inclined to stand up and say, this is our town.'

The Portadown Henry remembered from childhood in the late sixties was less segregated than the town he returned to in 1994. 'My dad went around farms collecting sacks and selling them back to the mills. He also worked as a train driver with Northern Ireland Railways. He mixed with everyone. Portadown was a linen town and working-class people were an integrated workforce in the factories. At first when we lived there Killycomain was mixed. In the seventies, when thugs were going around putting people out, Catholics at the top of our street were being put out and my father and other neighbours went up and said, "If you throw these people out, you'll have to throw us out too." But the Catholics did leave eventually. That was done on both sides.

'A Catholic relation of ours also worked on the railways, and his brother was murdered a few years ago by loyalists. The family moved away after that. After my dad left the railways he started to grow mushrooms, and then he kept chickens. Dessie Hamill, a neighbour of my aunt in Obins Street, raced greyhounds. He came to help my dad. His son Robert died last year after being beaten by loyalists. It just leaves you blank. These boys are criminals not loyalists. They have nothing to do but draw the dole and fight. But the real threat is from the respectable middle-class establishment who are quite prepared to orchestrate these people for their own ends.'

Henry and his wife sent their children to the integrated school. 'I think people need to mix. Most of my friends here have travelled – the Far East, America, London. I got on very well with Asian people when I lived in England. People here in Portadown can be very blinkered. But the worry I have about integrated schools is that it is very much middle class. It is needed in working-class areas like Killycomain and Obins Street, where people are being manipulated.'

'NOTHING GOT TO DO WITH US'

In the week following the blocking of the Drumcree parade, loyalists attacked over 130 Catholic homes across the North. Orange leaders condemned the attacks but said they were not responsible for them and could not stop them. On the morning of 11 July, five Catholic families in the Carnany estate in Ballymoney, County Antrim, received bullets in the post. The UVF was blamed. Partying on the Eleventh night is always frenetic, and in 1998 bonfires blazed as usual, some of them under banners which said, 'Kill All Taigs'. But it was an angry year, with roadblocks and riots, as well as bonfires. In Carnany at 4 a.m. on the Twelfth, loyalists hurled a petrol bomb made from a huge Bushmills whiskey bottle into the home of a Catholic woman, Chrissy Quinn. Her three little sons, Jason (aged eight), Mark (nine) and Richard (ten) were burned to death.

Within hours the RUC said the murders were sectarian. The Reverend William Bingham, the chaplain closest to the Orange leadership in Portadown who had urged biblical behaviour upon the brethren, said in his church at Pomeroy, County Tyrone, that no road was worth a life, and to get down the road after the boys' deaths would be 'a hollow victory'. Orangemen who had been picketing Hillsborough Castle in protest at the parade ban left three bouquets of flowers at the gates and departed. David Trimble, who had supported the right to march, said the only way the Portadown Orangemen could dissociate themselves from the murders was 'to come down off the hill'.

At Drumcree they saw it differently. The mood was volatile, defensive. Reporters were not welcome, but were crowding in again. In the church the Reverend Pickering mentioned the murdered children, and the security forces, in his prayers. Sandra Gamble said, 'The other side has killed and maimed our side and look what they've got out of it. There's going to be a lot of lives lost. Those poor wee children. But we have the right to march.' 'This has nothing got to do with us,' said a man. 'You get that element anywhere.'

A German television crew were filming a young man in a suit, who was standing on the muddy grass verge screaming at them. 'What are youse talking about children for? What about the children the RUC was firing plastic bullets at? Orangemen has been put in Maghaberry prison without a change of clothes. The Church of Rome declared war on us years ago. Who has killed the most children in this war? The IRA. We are a law-abiding, peace-keeping people.' He whisked his walking stick at them. A passing woman hissed at the journalists, 'Scum.'

I saw Malcolm coming out of the church. He said the murders of the children were terrible. He felt things were getting out of hand. But it was obvious he was not comfortable talking to me. Mark Swinger Fulton stood surveying the barricades. 'I've pulled more young ones than enough off them barriers,' he said. 'We are doing our best to keep the peace.' David Jones said that any trouble there might be, any-where, was attributable to Alastair Graham, the chairman of the Parades Commission.

Down at the barrier, a young Scot, reeking of beer and covered in bleeding scratches, was streeling about being filmed by Sky News. 'Ah couldny get through the wire,' he said. 'Ah couldny get through the wire.'

The RUC entered the Drumcree encampment a few days later. They found weapons including grenades and made a number of arrests. David Jones said at the time of the raid that there was nothing to prove that any of the weapons and missiles found were loyalist in origin. The IRA might have planted them, he said. Lurgan Orangeman Richard Monteith, the solicitor who has represented many loyalists, was ar-rested for taking part in a roadblock. He was later convicted.

'Ulster will always be British.' 'We haven't gone away you know.' The placards were out again on Portadown's main street. A week after the Quinn murders the town was rife with lurid theories about what had really happened in Ballymoney. There was an abundance of pastors at the rally. Beside the platform, the Reverend Gray, chatting to Reverend William McCrea, nodded at me. Pastor Kenny

McClinton was in close conversation with John and two leading Portadown Orangemen. On the platform, the Reverend Tom Taylor, the retired Church of Ireland rector of Tynan, County Armagh, prayed. 'I will lift up mine eyes to the hills from whence cometh mine aid . . .'

The Reverend Hugh Ross, a Presbyterian and leader of the Ulster Independence Movement, told the crowd of several hundred that 'La Mon and all the other Abercorns and Enniskillens have been forgotten'. These were all IRA atrocities. The Reverend Ross spoke of 'the terror that dwells in our land'. He said, 'I have come to see that these men who lead Portadown are reasonable men. They have the characteristics of the Ulsterman – tenacity and determination to do what is right.'

Brother Gracey, to cheers and applause and banging of placards, said the Northern Ireland Office (NIO) had 'turned out black propaganda, using the tragedy at Ballymoney for to blacken us'. He attacked the media, and said there was no connection between Ballymoney and Drumcree. 'I would ask the county grand masters to get their finger out and get their people organised,' he concluded. I caught the smoky whiff of the ubiquitous burger vans.

A leaflet was circulating in the crowd. It showed a photograph which had been widely used in the press of Tony Blair standing with a priest in the ruins of the church at Crumlin after the loyalist firebombs of early July. Texts had been printed above and below the picture: 'But thus shall ye deal with them; ye shall destroy their altars, and break down their images, and cut down their groves, and burn their graven images with fire (Deuteronomy 7:5).' 'And the kings of the earth, who have committed fornication and lived deliciously with her, shall bewail her, and lament for her, when they shall see the smoke of her burning (Revelation 18:9).' In huge print at the bottom, 'And again, they said, Alleluia. And her smoke rose up for ever and ever (Revelation 19:3).'

I asked a few people who was giving it out. 'None of your fucking business,' said one. 'You shouldn't be here at all. The media shouldn't be let near our rallies – youse never report the truth,' said another. Eventually I found a small woman with permed hair, in a tweed coat and a little hat, busily handing out the leaflet. I took one from her, then asked who had published it. 'I don't know,' she said. 'I couldn't even tell you what is on it. I never even looked at it.'

'WE DON'T FIT IN AT ALL HERE'

In the middle of the furore at Drumcree a letter appeared in the *Guardian* newspaper saying that Harold Gracey and his Orangemen did not represent all Protestants in Portadown. Its author was Chris Moffat. I wrote to her and she invited me to lunch. She lived in a large old redbrick farmhouse out among the big fields in the rural hinterland of Portadown. You could see the spire of Drumcree from her garden. Chris warned me she wasn't really a Portadown Protestant – she was brought up in England, though her family was originally from Creggan in County Tyrone. She said Creggan had a church used by both communities.

Her husband, Tom Hadden, a law lecturer and founder of the independent review *Fortnight,* had deep roots in the area. 'My grandmother was born here and my other grandmother was born a few miles away. My mother had a Battle of the Boyne sword hidden away under her sofa,' he said. 'The Haddens were all Methodist ministers and doctors. My grandfather was wrecked on Rathlin Island on his way to Scotland. He was told there was a good opening for a doctor in Portadown and he settled here in 1880. My mother's uncle was a Unionist MP. She was the chair of North Armagh Unionists ladies' committee. Making tea.' Chris laughed. 'I came over here as Chris Moffat,' she said. 'When I was in hospital under anaesthetic she told them to change my name to Mrs Hadden.'

The house was full of books and papers, mantelpieces cluttered with old artefacts found in the earth around the house, lovely curved fragments of old pots. Tom produced a fat volume about the plantations, *Settlement and Survival on an Ulster Estate: The Brownlow Leasebook 1667 to 1711.* He searched through it then handed it to me, open at the lease of the house. Dated 1694, it reads, 'Derribrochas sessiagh . . . lease includes five pounds one shilling and eight pence per annum at May and Alsaints and 2 fatt hens and 2 daies work of man and horse from each house or cabin.'

Chris was a founder of the local integrated school. 'Portadown regards integrated education as a stain on its character,' she said. 'They got up petitions and were really belligerent. The Orange Order spends the winter going around trying to get young men into lodges. For me it is just a secret society.

'The council was had up in 1989 over discrimination against a GAA club. Some of the Unionist councillors were stood down and they put up their wives instead. The women saw me as an upstart. But the school does its own thing now. It's a happy little place. You pick up all the stray people, mixed marriages, people who are a bit evangelical, English people, people who want to convert people.

'I'd like to see the integrated comprehensive at Brownlow flourishing. The grammar schools create an élite. Protestants accept this sort of predetermined caste system in education, that some are selected and some are not. I was talking to a teacher recently and children in his class had asked him on behalf of their parents what way they should vote. This society is all based on family, money and position.'

She showed me a newspaper cutting from the *Portadown Times* in 1988, when the Fair Employment Agency (FEA) published a report showing that the council had discriminated heavily against Catholics in its civic centre. The report found that none of the council's chief officers or their deputies were Catholic, that senior personnel were almost exclusively Protestant and that Catholics were concentrated in the lowest ranks. The council had done its best to keep the agency out of the centre and the mayor was quoted as saying in response to the report, 'We in Craigavon have nothing to hide but we do take exception to these people sticking in their noses and creating strife where none exists – the sooner the FEA is scrapped the better.'

'When the Parades Commission came to town last year to meet the people they booked the town hall. Then the Garvaghy Road people said they wouldn't go there. I went along,' said Chris. 'Loyalists were there shouting about the scum of Garvaghy Road. I said, "The Garvaghy Road people are just like you. They wouldn't mind you marching but look at the way you behave."

'The whole hall turned on me. I used to teach and I put on my best teacher's voice and put my case. The police came and said I needed an escort out of the place. The women were shouting louder than the men. It was all about who had fought hardest in the First World War. It was ridiculous. There is this terrific insecurity about here which I really don't understand.' Tom agreed. 'It is as if they think the whole world is against them,' he said.

Chris said she thought that because the Unionists had held onto power 'by dubious means', they now feared that they would be overthrown and the same means used against them. 'There is no tradition of doing things in an above-the-board way. Also, they are against new kinds of thinking and impervious to arguments. The farmers round here use all the sprays they can get hold of, and cut down trees and ruin the environment . . .'

It seemed the area in which they lived was strangely isolated, no buses, no local amenities. Chris said for some local people, a trip to the hospital counted as a big day out. 'There's a laager mentality. Coalisland and Dungannon are the ends of the earth.'

'The Peace and Reconciliation people want to spend money here but they don't know what to do,' said Chris. She said Craigavon District Partnership, of which she was a member, was also trying to spend money on peace, and she thought making a video would be good. 'If people could see themselves . . .' she said. I thought of the Drumcree videos which I'd seen for sale at a stall at the sham fight in Scarva. The County Armagh village holds an annual sham fight to commemorate the Battle of the Boyne. King Billy knocks King James off his horse. Drums are banged and burgers are eaten. The videos were for sale under a banner which read, 'Drumcree . . . as seen on TV'. Obviously those selling, and those buying, felt it looked good.

Neither of the couple felt that the Garvaghy Road people were handling their situation well. Tom said they were making a ghetto of the area, which would make it hard to develop economically. Chris said cross-community work was hard because of the role of the Jesuits, whose connections were largely through the Catholic Church. 'There is no point in pursuing parity at all costs with no quality of working relationships,' she said.

Tom had left Northern Ireland to go to college, and came back in 1969. Talking about *Fortnight*, he admitted, 'I came back naïve. We did security stuff for ten years and then decided we were getting no-where and moved on to political stuff.' 'You were publishing stuff on discrimination years ago and nobody paid a blind bit of notice. Maybe you should have been a bit more political,' said Chris. 'Well, short of founding your own political party,' said Tom with a shrug.

Chris said that after the town hall showdown, people had said she was stupid. 'Maybe it is best to work long term for things like integrated education, behind the scenes,' she said. We ate salad looking out through the big windows at the fields, the willow trees on the long horizons. 'We don't fit in at all here,' said Tom.

There was, though, a sense of permanence about them, there in the old house with its leasebook and its clutter, with the deep roots of Tom's family history around them. A few months later I heard they'd moved. I rang Chris. Oh, she said, laughing. It wasn't their house at all. They'd been renting it and their lease had run out. They were renting another house now, in another place.

'THE LAST THING I'D WANT IS TO CAUSE TROUBLE'

Everyone I met who knew Ruth Turkington said she was lovely. A Catholic friend, who kept her religion quiet among the people she worked with in Portadown, said Ruth was different, a woman who would go out of her way to make you feel at ease. She ran a bed and breakfast from her huge bungalow at Maghery, near the shores of Lough Neagh. It felt like a remote, dreamy place, and the little roads that led to it were narrow and lined with tall willows. In fact, Portadown was just a few miles away across the motorway, which roared past a field or two behind Ruth's house.

Like so many of the County Armagh women I'd met, she was a baker. She had run a small business selling tray bakes and cakes made by herself and a few other local women. She gave me tea and apple tart, with a strawberry on the plate, while she saw off her guests for the day, English people on holiday. 'I live my life quietly – the last thing I'd want is to cause trouble,' she said.

She was born three miles up the road at Derrycoose, and brought up on a small farm. Her family were church-going members of the Church of Ireland and she sang in the choir, was in the Girls' Friendly Society and taught Sunday school. She still sang. 'I make a noise, a joyful one, but I wouldn't do solos.' At seventeen she met Frederick

John Lutton – Eric – on a blind date. 'I'm not dramatic, but it didn't take long to know he was the man for me.' They married in 1967, and lived with her parents, who had no son to take over the farm. As well as farming – an orchard and a few cattle – her husband worked in a factory. Then he had become manager of the Argory, a nineteenth-century mansion run by the National Trust near Moy. One day in July 1998, after long days and nights on the hill at Drumcree, I had gone there for a walk to breathe air that was not polluted with hatred. When I stepped out of the car I smelt the roses, sweet and cool. There was a sun dial in the rose garden, inscribed: 'Here reader mark the silent steps of never standing time.'

'After four years of marriage we had a son, and we felt we wanted a house of our own,' said Ruth. 'There was a lot of trouble brewing in this area and the bombings and killings had started. My husband joined the police reserve to get some money. Four years later, our daughter was born. We had to work hard with not having much. I was cooking meals in a factory and my mum minded the children. Eric came from hard-working people. Gardening was very big in his family. He was a member of the select vestry in the Church of Ireland, he was an Orangeman and a Black man.

'On the Twelfth I went with the church tent, catering. Nigel went with Eric with his lodge. Our tent went to Scarva on the Thirteenth to raise money for the church. Other women with children would be there. We'd chat and make sandwiches and chat. It was a family day. We were happy.

'When Erica was three and Nigel was eight, their dad was coming home from work at the Argory. It was the 1st of May 1979. He had his boss Mr Bond in the car. Mr Bond owned the Argory but he stayed in a suite at the Seagoe Hotel at night. He was the last of the gentry. Eric got out to close the gates and these people, IRA men, stepped out from behind the pillar and shot him dead.'

The phone rang, someone wanting to know did Ruth want to advertise her business with them. She wiped away her tears, said that no, she didn't think so. It was strange to think of Mr Bond and his big empty house, and Eric, saving to build a house of his own. The IRA men, maybe neighbours. 'I didn't think it would happen,' said Ruth. 'Eric was like me, friends with all sides. The day before he died he had been working on a car with some of the opposite persuasion. I didn't think it would happen.'

She recounted every detail of how she heard the news from her minister, what happened at the hospital, how she told her children, how she went into a state of shock which kept her numb for years. 'I lost all hope of living. Mr Boyd, my minister, said the Lord would give me strength. I said, I am on my knees. I was full of anger and hatred. Against all Roman Catholic people, I am ashamed to say. At that time I was working in a shop and half my customers were Catholics. Most of those people came to me and wrote to me. Praise the Lord, I never let that hatred out.

'If I had continued that way, I would have ruined myself, my children and my country. I had to pray very hard for God to take it away, and he did. I will never forget Eric. I still have my tears about it. It was like half my body had gone missing. I am sure that many's another woman in this country has gone through the same. Eric was an ordinary man. A good man.'

After her husband's murder, Ruth built a new bungalow down the lane from her old home, and lived there with her mother and children. She said her son had been very badly affected by the murder. 'He feels he has been robbed. He'd feel very strongly for the Protestant people. He is a strong Protestant. I would say his friends are 100 per cent Protestant. He is an Orangeman. He's been over and back to Drumcree.' It was obvious she was worried for her son. She said the parade should not have been stopped. 'No one has the right to do that.'

Her daughter, Erica, had just graduated from a college in Scotland, and Ruth did not think she would return to Northern Ireland. 'She takes people at face value. She is in the Elim Pentecostal Church herself, but it wouldn't occur to her to want to know what religion anyone is.'

In 1987, she was asked out again, by a man she knew as her local butcher. His name was also Eric. They soon decided to get married, but Ruth was shocked when he said they would build a new house. Although the site was just three miles from her old home, it felt like a faraway place. 'We went for a drive down about Omagh and we saw a bungalow we liked and we stopped. We went to the door to ask the people could we copy it. They were Roman Catholics – they couldn't have been nicer. When this house was abuilding I used to come down here and cry. The bigger the house got, the more I cried. Still at the end of the day, maybe it was for the best. Mum liked it.' Ruth talked as though the move would have taken her many miles from her roots. In fact her mother came 'from a field away from here'.

Ruth's mother was in a home, near Drumcree. 'It was worse than a death to me putting her in there, but I had to in the end. She is looked after very well.' Her voice went into a whisper. 'They are RCs.' It rose again. 'It is brilliant, like a big extended family. Our minister's wife is there too.'

She showed her visitors' book, with comments like, 'Excellent. God bless Ulster.' She even had guests over Christmas. Her church was central to her life. She had been to Paris and London with the Mothers' Union. 'I couldn't stick the pace of the big cities. Mostly we stay in the North of Ireland because some of the women wouldn't want to go to the South.'

Ruth had voted for the Belfast Agreement. 'It is the only glimmer of hope there is. I think we will have a united Ireland eventually, but the agreement will prolong the time before that happens.' She said that the families whose sons 'went wrong' were just the same as ordinary families. 'They would never have been in trouble only for the situation.' However, convicted prisoners should serve their time. 'No one was ever convicted for killing Eric. I don't mind. They have to pass their Judgment Day. They will be dealt with at the end, unless they repent. We all have to meet our maker.'

'THE BILLY BOYS'

Before 1998, Drumcree was something that flared up, blazed, then subsided. But in 1998 it did not end. The Parades Commission stated in its ruling that the Orangemen should disperse after their church service on 5 July. They did not do so, and loyalists continued in the following months to hold regular demonstrations in the town, along the edges of streets in which Catholics lived, and on Drumcree hill. From July to December, more than a hundred demonstrations were held, many of them illegal. A stream of Catholics left the area. In

September rioting loyalists hurled blast bombs at police who were keeping them back from Craigwell Avenue, where Catholic houses were being attacked regularly. Constable Frankie O'Reilly was critically injured and died several weeks later. The Red Hand Defenders claimed the killing.

In October I went to a council meeting at Craigavon, in the civic centre. The councillors talked about Travellers, whose presence near a new private housing development was causing concern. One Unionist councillor said that the Industrial Development Board had been 'very imaginative' in its approach. It was going to make a flat area into a mound, and the Department of the Environment was going to make the verges inaccessible. Breandán Mac Cionnaith made a disapproving remark, and another Unionist retorted that if Councillor McKenna had a site for the Travellers on the Garvaghy Road, he was welcome to them.

At the same meeting the DUP councillors Ruth and William Allen were gravely concerned about an application to open the swimming pool on Sunday mornings. For several years it had been open for a few hours on Sunday afternoons. 'This would open the floodgates,' said Councillor Allen. He and his wife opposed all Sunday opening on Sabbatarian grounds. The Allens, an earnest couple, were advised that other local councils had established that you could not use a Sabbatarian argument against opening.

During an adjournment I talked to local journalist Victor Gordon. As we spoke, UUP Councillor Fred Crowe approached. Crowe was one of David Trimble's supporters in Portadown. 'Victor,' he said. 'They neglected to mention there that I was elected president of the Association of Education and Library Boards. Make sure you put that in your write-up.' Victor introduced me to Crowe, telling him that I was writing a book about Protestants. 'Well,' joked Crowe. 'There's two types of Protestants. Good ones and half-baked ones.'

The council went on to vote in favour of a subsidy to local shopkeepers to enable them to mount a promotion, reducing prices by 10 per cent to try to lure shoppers back to Portadown 'in the light of recent difficulties'. There were bad-tempered exchanges about the nature of the difficulties, with some Unionists deriding nationalist claims that Catholics did not feel safe to shop in the town. On the way out I looked at the display board, which had photographs of all the councillors. Mac Cionnaith's photograph was damaged. The doorman saw me looking at it. 'That's people dunting it as they go by it,' he said. 'They give it a poke.' He demonstrated what he'd seen with his finger, a short, angry stab.

There was another women's demonstration at Drumcree in the autumn. Outside St John the Baptist Catholic church on the Garvaghy Road, a crowd of nationalists had gathered. A few of them were former republican prisoners. A line of police with dogs were standing between them and the road. The parade passed with a clash of drums, and shouts of No Surrender. The police turned their barking Alsatians towards the nationalists. I saw men I knew had been involved in loyalist paramilitary groups. They passed within yards of the republicans. Women on both sides of the line were shouting that they had been spat at. The dogs were going wild. I walked into the parade. A big face loomed into mine, shouting, 'Who the fuck are you?' The parade moved on. Someone shouted towards the nationalists, 'See thon graveyard? There should be more of youse fucking fenians in there.'

At the police barriers David Jones commended the 'ladies'. 'It is a pity we don't have men with the same courage and gumption,' he said. 'We are not a battered-down people. We are a proud people and if we don't have the political leaders, we will stand up for ourselves.'

The huge gathering of Protestants which the Order had hoped for at Drumcree had not materialised. Since the Quinn murders, numbers had been dwindling. Harold Gracey quoted Galatians to show he didn't need a multitude to win his battle. He said the situation would not be solved by negotiation. 'We have given and given and given . . . We will walk the Garvaghy Road in 1998 . . . In the words of Mahatma Gandhi – We must do whatever we can do. No surrender.' He said it as if Gandhi had said no surrender. Women in red, white and blue wigs cheered wildly.

By this time, the women had set up a stall dispensing tea and soup to the marchers. Bands came from around the North, places like Castlederg in Tyrone and Carrickfergus in Antrim. John was often there. One of the bands had a drum with 'Red Hand Defenders' scrawled on it. I asked David Jones about it. 'You must remember

Red Hand Defenders has been the name of a number of bands long before anyone else took it over,' he said.

A few yards down the hill from the jolly canteen, youths were yelling abuse across the barrier at the RUC, while a drunk woman danced and jeered. The centrepiece of the barrier was an army tank which had been smeared by the security forces with a thick gluey substance to discourage anyone from climbing up on it. A man walked me down to find young Paul Berry, who had been attending Drumcree almost every night. The man was friendly. He told me he thought the protest should end. 'Do you say that to people?' I asked. 'Indeed I do not,' he replied.

Berry was standing right against the tank, smiling a beatific smile, wearing a trench coat, his hands in his pockets. Something of the film star about him. He greeted me genially. Alan Milligan, the select vestry man with whom I had tried to have the conversation about the LVF magazine *Leading the Way*, escorted Harold Gracey down to the barrier. 'I don't want any bother here the night, boys,' Gracey said. After he'd left, someone threw a firework across the lines where it exploded. The crowd cheered. 'Away home and change your tights,' a man shouted to the police. This was the way it had gone. The Drumcree view was that the tough women who stood by their men on the hill had more of the warrior about them than the Orangemen who stayed away, and the police were not men at all.

One afternoon I was passing through the area and I drove up to the church. It was late autumn and the apple trees had lost their leaves, their branches like angry arms with fists. John was there with another man, and a little boy of about five. A British journalist, a man, had told me that John had a way of talking about women journalists which was extremely sexually violent. The journalist said it was clear that John had assumed that as a man he could safely be included in such talk.

John had lost the strutting confidence he had had in July. He looked older, and his eyes were no longer blazing with anticipation of a great victory. The parade had been stopped, but the world had not rallied to the Orange cause. The men's talk was grim. They needed a leader, they said. There were no obvious candidates. John said Paul Berry was a 'good lad'. They were furious because crowds had stopped coming to Drumcree. 'The Protestant people is too relaxed,' he said. 'Maybe the IRA hasn't hit them hard enough.'

'Ervine and them in the PUP is cutting the knees out of their trousers apologising,' said John. 'The paramilitaries is sick of the leadership. They are coming out to fight. The young ones has the hatred. You put guns in their hands and you'll see.' The other man, who was about forty, agreed. 'This has come full circle,' he said. 'When we were giving our young ones sashes, the other side were giving theirs petrol bombs. Now it is the other way.'

The little boy stood silently listening to all this. John ruffled his hair. He told me this was his grandchild. 'I'm bringing him up to the gun,' he said. 'Sing this girl a song, son. Sing her "The Billy Boys".' The child stood to attention. Then he sang: 'We are, we are, we are the Billy Boys . . .' When he sang the line, 'We're up to our necks in fenian blood', John grinned, patted the child on the head, and punched the air.

BORDERLANDS
Kangaroo Country

'They have healed also the hurt of the daughter of my people slightly, saying, Peace, peace; when there is no peace.'

from Jeremiah 6:14, quoted in *The True Story of South Armagh*

'AT THE EDGE OF DARK'

'My father used to say, "I'll tell you one thing – there's none of them any good only the dead ones." Some of them wouldn't show it, but it's still there. The sweeter they are, the worse they are. They only get close to you to find out information. That's why Protestants don't trust Catholics. Our side would sell you down the road as quick as look at you. My father used to say, "With the other side you know what you have. With your own side, you don't know nothing." What I do is, I stand and I listen and I don't say nothing.'

She was seventy-five years old, a small angry woman, with a hard, clipped voice. Her answer in the affirmative: Yip. In the negative: Nope. She had reasons to be bitter. She had lived in a hard place through a hard time, and had experienced terror, brutal violence and grief in appalling measure. The IRA had murdered her husband, her brother, her brother-in-law, several other relations and more neighbours and friends. She had sons in the RUC, the Territorial Army (TA) and the British army. 'I come from Kangaroo country,' she said.

'Whitecross, south Armagh.'

I was introduced to Mrs Margaret Frazer by her son Willie, who was a leading member of the Families Acting for Innocent Relatives (FAIR) group. 'We were more or less on our own where we lived,' she said. 'When you went up to the right there was some of the other side and when you went down the road the other way, there was some of the other side too. My father was in the B men, and so was my brother Johnny that was killed, and my man was in the Home Guards and then he went into the B men too. When the B men resigned in 1970, he joined the UDR.'

Her memories ranged from one period of Troubles to another, her father as the man in the house, then her husband, both armed against the enemy lurking in the bushes outside. 'I mind one night when they were hot and heavy against the B men, they came and tried to put the door in. I stood in the bath with a billhook in my hand. The childer was all small then. We were told after that time we had to move. It was your own neighbours was trying to burn you out. I mind one night we had to lie on the ground. Our neighbour was with them, dressed up as a priest. My daddy opened the upstairs window and fired. He got one of them and hurted them. That's how we knew who they were.

'They should never've let this boy Blair in. They should never've let the Free State in. They should never've done away with the B men. The B men knew who they had, where they were and what they were doing. The local UDR wasn't let out on the roads. They weren't let go after them. There was no fancy Land Rovers for the B men. They just put on the uniform, took out the gun, went out and did their job and came home.

'They should've left it to them. This would all have been over long ago. Or left the Black and Tans to them. Some of the two. Did you ever hear tell of them? They were the boys could've sorted them out. I heard tell that when the Black and Tans used to stop people on the road, they'd jump out of the lorry and shout, "Run." If you ran, they opened up on you. Our side was told never to run, you see.'

Mrs Frazer's lament for the B Specials was to be heard from many older Protestants in the North. To them, the disbandment of the Ulster Special Constabulary (USC) in 1970 was an act of betrayal by the British, and the beginning of the end for Ulster. The Specials were set up in 1920, with the B Specials as part-timers – 19,500 Protestant men armed to patrol their own areas. The Black and Tans were the ex-soldiers mobilised to deal with the IRA mainly in the South. Unionists were obsessed with maintaining the border and feared IRA incursions, as well as doubting Britain's commitment to protect them. The B Specials were largely drawn from the UVF and Orange lodges. A British army officer commented that the constabulary had 'a large leaven of a bad type' (quoted in Ryder, p. 8). It was soon embroiled in controversy. The *Manchester Guardian* warned in 1921 that the force had been set up to maintain order, not to operate 'lynch law' over Catholics, 'for in the Ulster Unionist mind Catholic and Sinn Féiner are synonymous' (quoted in Ryder, pp. 9–10). Internment in 1922 saw three hundred nationalists arrested and no unionists.

The RUC was set up in 1922, and was meant to recruit a third of its members from the Catholic community. But half of the first three thousand recruits were former Specials, and five out of six were Protestants. The draconian Special Powers Act of 1922 completed the arrangements. Sir Arthur Hezlet, author of a book written to counteract the 'mendacious campaign of propaganda' against the force, said there were no Catholics in it because of IRA intimidation. He said the Specials, commanded by ex-regulars from the British army, took part in 'retaliatory reprisals' against a 'savage enemy' rather than unprovoked pogroms.

In Hezlet's opinion, the IRA's fifties campaign was ultimately thwarted by the USC's 'steady grip on the Province'. When the Troubles lurched into full swing again in 1968, the Specials were once again accused by nationalists of acts of brutality and sectarianism. The Cameron Commission, set up to investigate the disturbances, reported in 1969 that, 'We have good reason for inferring that in the ranks of the Ulster Protestant Volunteer Force are numbered members of the USC.' In the same year the Hunt report recommended the setting up of the UDR to take over. 'So went a force of dedicated patriotic men,' wrote Hezlet, 'whose only crime was that they were all Protestants.'

The Frazers were a security force family, and Mrs Frazer was constantly alert to danger. 'All the time we lived at Whitecross and Newtownhamilton, I never lay down. I'd have come home from work

and sat and slept in the chair but at the edge of dark I got up again,'
she said. They had moved to Newtownhamilton after a warning that
her husband's brother was to be shot. 'We got moved to a house that
had no heating in the middle of the winter. The door had to be held
closed with two planks. That house was wrecked five times with
bombs. I mind the night they tried to burn the car.

'I used to work for Fruitfield, the jam factory. A woman I know
bought the old barracks and let it out to them. She and I were going
up there one night and we turned back to get a lamp. We turned, and
as we turned, the barracks went up behind us. They must have
thought when they saw it being done up it was for the army. There was
a landmine then. All them things and we never got thon.' She rubbed
her fingers on the palm of her hand, signifying no money. 'That was
the sort of my man. He wouldn't claim. The Catholic woman beside
us, she told me she claimed. Right enough she was expecting and she
lost the child.

'We moved to Newtownhamilton in November and my man was
killed the following August. He was backing the car out of the planten.
He had been putting the sheep in. He must have seen them coming for
him in the mirror. His hand was near beat off him. They left him lying
in his blood.' Mrs Frazer named the man she said helped the IRA men
to get away. She said her husband bled to death on his way to hospital.
'The ambulance had to stop for directions on the way out and them
ones, RCs, sent it the wrong way.

'That was on the Saturday night. On the Monday night they used
his car on the Tullyvallen hall. I knew all those five men that was killed
at Tullyvallen. Six of them foreby that was injured. They got away
after that and took the car up Crossmaglen main street with a bomb in
it.' The IRA ambush on Tullyvallen Orange hall in September 1975
might have left more dead, except that an armed, off-duty RUC man,
who was a member of the lodge, fired on the gunmen.

There had been ominous incidents before the murder of Robert
Frazer. Mrs Frazer named the man she blamed. 'I mind we were
sitting in the car waiting on a band on the 13th July and he came along
and put a boot in my man's face. Another time, I had a broken foot.
There was no lights on the street after a bomb and I fell into a hole. He
tried to jam me against a wall with a load of pigs. That's the get set my

man up. That's what maddens me. They know who they are. Now they say, those things are in the past, over and done with.'

The attack on Tullyvallen Orange hall came during Robert Frazer's wake. Ten weeks later, the IRA struck the family again. 'I lost my brother then and my brother-in-law after that. They shot my brother with an elephant gun. They left it on top of the ditch. Trevor Elliott – he was a cousin, whose brother and sister was married to my own son and daughter.' Elliott was an RUC man shot in 1984. 'Young Willie Meaklin too. He was killed.' William Meaklin was killed in 1975, shortly before Robert Frazer. 'He used to come to my house every morning. See the death they gave him – they cut his private parts off and stuck them in his mouth. They cut his fingers off him. They threw him in a drain and fired shots over him and him dead.'

Mrs Frazer also believed that a doctor and nurse had been at the scene not to help William Meaklin, but to keep him alive so that the torture could be prolonged. Journalist Toby Harnden heard an even more graphic description of the murder of Meaklin from Mrs Frazer's son, Willie. Frazer said that tattoos had been cut out of the man's body, that an arm had been pulled from its socket and that his teeth and fingernails were missing. Harnden looked up the pathologist's report on the murder. He found that Meaklin had been shot at least a dozen times after a bad beating or kicking. The tortures described by the Frazers had not, however, been inflicted (Harnden, p. 141).

'I mind he supplied heaters to pensioners from both sides during the strike in 1974,' Mrs Frazer said. 'The other side owed him a fortune when he died. I don't think his wife ever got a penny off them. He had a great dog. The dog was got in the graveyard trying to dig up his grave the night after he was buried. The local UDR wasn't let go after them. The night they killed my sister's husband, she identified the boy. He had been in her house and had his dinner. He and her man worked in the timber yard together. He shot at her. He was lifted and did five years. When he was in the courthouse, my sister looked him straight in the eye. He said, "I'm sorry, Jennifer, I was made to do it." Her husband was already out of the UDR.

'Every year Belleek hall gets blew up. The man Scott was up a ladder to get drums and they put a bomb under the ladder. The time they were after Joe McCullough, he went into his house and he said,

"I'm going to get my uniform on and my weapon and I'm going out on patrol." But they were waiting for him. The death they gave him . . .' Mrs Frazer exhaled sharply, shaking her head. 'He fought them in and out of the house. The blood was everywhere. He would have been living, only one of them went over and slit his throat.' She jutted her head forward fiercely. 'Now! Then they put a booby-trap bomb on his body but a sow pig knocked into it and was blew half away. And Robert McConnell. They were standing on the roof of a tin shed waiting on him. His brother was dying of cancer and his sister was in a wheelchair. He was the breadwinner.

'About a year ago, a man came to our hall asking for my son to go and do silage. A fellow took my son aside and said, "Do you know who that is?" It was a man working for some of Dessie O'Hare's crowd. And like a cod, he would have gone, only for that.' Dessie O'Hare is a notorious local republican who became known for his violent exploits as the Border Fox.

'Gerry Adams is behind all this dispute about Drumcree. This is going on since 1918. Bridget Rodgers [Bríd Rodgers, SDLP Assembly member for Upper Bann, and briefly minister of agriculture and rural development] and thon McKenna should be transported. Take them off to Africa or some place. I never was in the Free State in my life and I hope I never will be. There's people has went there, mind you, and tells me they got the best of a welcome. Them that goes will pay dear for the grub they get anyway. Do you see the prices on the TV? Go down to Newry and you'll see them in their vans taking food across the border. Then our side is going to get diesel, for it is cheaper down there. I see a boy there caught, he had sheep in the back of the van going backwards and forwards across the border and the sheep was never let out. They were only there to hide the diesel he was smuggling. The poor sheep.'

'IT HAS GOT THAT IT IS NEARLY AN OFFENCE TO SAY YOU ARE A PROTESTANT'

I had met Willie Frazer frequently up at Drumcree, where he was firmly behind the Orange Order's hard line. He was also the president of his local Apprentice Boys club. A publican and owner of a nightclub in Tandragee, he lived in a bungalow a few doors from his mother, on the outskirts of Markethill. Their road, heavily bedecked with Union Jacks, Ulster flags and Ulster Independence flags, faced onto a forest. He vehemently opposed the Belfast Agreement and all that flowed from it.

It was through his work in FAIR that Frazer had come to some public prominence. FAIR was launched in 1998, first, to remember what 'Irish Republican death squads' had done to south Armagh Protestants 'without justification or reprisal'. Second, 'to try to reverse the undeniable fact that good has now become evil and right has now become wrong by the appeasement of Republican terrorists by both the British and Irish governments'.

Its first conference was held in August 1999 in Portadown, with an array of anti-agreement unionist politicians in attendance. It objected to relatives of IRA men claiming the right to be called victims. The idea that IRA men could never be victims is widely held by Protestants. When *Lost Lives*, the epic account of all those who had died to date in the Troubles, was published in 1999, callers to *Talkback* objected to the inclusion of republicans who died in the 1981 hunger strikes.

FAIR had mounted a protest when relatives of those killed in the SAS ambush at Loughgall met a government minister at Stormont in 1998. The group's militant stance appealed to extremists, including those who believed in vengeance. One of those watching the protest – not a member of FAIR – was one of the 'pastors' who was deeply involved with one of the new loyalist paramilitary groupings.

FAIR has insisted that there are 'innocent victims', and, presumably, victims who are not innocent. Many of its members are related to security force victims of republican violence, and the group was incensed by the early release of republican prisoners under the terms of the Belfast Agreement. It has had some influence on leading members of the British Conservative Party. During a demonstration outside Stormont, the BBC's David Dunseith asked Frazer what he thought of the early release of loyalist prisoners. Frazer replied without hesitation: 'They should never have been locked up in the first place.' I asked him about this. 'Obviously, I'm not saying anyone has a right to kill innocent Catholics. But if the security forces had been allowed to do their job, there would never have been any need for the loyalist paramilitaries.' He said it was the loyalist paramilitaries, along with the informers, who had brought about the IRA ceasefire, whereas the British army's very visible presence in south Armagh had actually protected the IRA.

'You take the UDR thing in south Armagh. You take a UDR man. He is in fear of his life. He knows who these boys are. He has the information. He knows the government won't do anything about it. What does he do? He passes it on to the loyalist paramilitaries. If you were in the UDR and your brother was shot, are you telling me you wouldn't? See if a Paki comes from India and kills a Provo? I'm going to shake his hand. Look where violence got the IRA. They have got what they wanted. Our boys were made eejits of. It has got that it is nearly an offence to say you are a Protestant or a loyalist.'

In his introductory note to the FAIR pamphlet published in 1999, Frazer wrote: 'I was brought up to respect my fellow neighbours. We were not allowed to talk about religion and were brought up to identify the difference between right and wrong. Now, however, when I look back at what my family suffered and how murder has clearly paid, how can I teach my children that right is still right and wrong is still wrong?'

He rejected claims that his father was in the UVF or that Joe McCullough, the UDR man whose throat had been slit by the IRA in 1976, had been in the UVF and involved in the Dublin and Monaghan bombings. UDR man Robert McConnell has also been linked to the UVF. His nephew, Brian McConnell, is prominent in FAIR. Frazer said that some of the UDR men shot in south Armagh, including Robert McConnell, had been helping the British SAS in undercover operations against the IRA.

'My uncle was shot on the Saturday, three of the Reaveys was killed on the Sunday, and Kingsmills was on the Monday.' His uncle, a UDR man, survived. The Reaveys were Catholics, shot by the Protestant Action Force (PAF), apparently in retaliation for the murder of three Protestants in a bomb attack on a County Down bar a few days before. The bombing was carried out by the INLA, apparently in retaliation for the UVF murder of a member of the INLA's political wing, the Irish Republican Socialist Party, two weeks previously.

The Kingsmills massacre was claimed by the Republican Action

Force, but was thought to have been the work of the IRA. On 5 January 1976, gunmen stopped a minibus full of workers on their way to Glenanne's textile factory. They ordered any Catholics on the bus to stand forward. Thinking the gunmen were loyalists, some of the men tried to protect the one Catholic on the bus. However, he eventually stepped forward, and was told to leave the scene. The gunmen then shot dead ten of the men. Another man escaped. Frazer had a theory that the British agent Captain Robert Nairac, who was murdered by the IRA, had been acting as a double agent. 'I think he was the man who gave the orders at Kingsmills.'

One of the RUC officers called to the scene in the aftermath of the massacre was Billy McCaughey, then stationed in Armagh. Accordng to Harnden's account, McCaughey had boasted that he and other RUC men were involved with loyalist paramilitaries at that time. 'Our proud boast was that we would never have a Catholic [in our unit] . . . We did actually have a Catholic once . . . The day after he joined we had him dangling out from the back of a landrover with his chin inches from the ground,' he claimed (quoted in Harnden, p. 138). In 1977 McCaughey and another RUC man, along with other loyalists, murdered a shopkeeper in Ahoghill, County Antrim. I'd seen McCaughey at an Ulster Civil Rights Movement rally in Derry in 1996. He was wearing a T-shirt which had 'Harryville on tour' emblazoned on it.

'I grew up with Catholics,' Frazer continued. 'I went to a Catholic school. As a matter of fact, Billy Wright got that from me, you know, when he said he'd played GAA and all when he was younger. I had a lot of time for Billy – he called a spade a spade. Catholics. Some of them went on to shoot members of my family. Now they are saying, let's be friends. They are putting out the hand to us now, when it suits them. I can't afford to let that happen. Last time I did that I lost five members of my family.' He said the UDR had refused to allow him to join the regiment. 'They said enough of my family had died.' He joined the Territorial Army instead.

Frazer stood for election representing the Ulster Independence Party in the 1998 Assembly elections, and got 957 votes. Pastor Kenny McClinton stood for the party in Portadown. Willie said he had recently become saved himself, and was attending the Free Presbyterian Church. He was thinking of selling up the pub. It wasn't compatible with his new religion. 'The man above is the only one can save this country. The like of David Ervine is mocking the Bible, openly saying he is an atheist. How could you vote for such a man? What is the country coming to? There is no morals. My son is not yet five. He came over to me the other day and he said, "Daddy, who shot Granda?" I said, "Bad boys." He went off and got his toy guns. He came back and he said, "Come on, Dad. Let's go and kill the bad boys." If you grow up with a family, it's only later in life the hatred turns.'

Frazer took me out in his car. Along narrow country roads through the small hills he pointed out the spot where someone was abducted, someone else shot, the lane where someone was stabbed, a village square where there had been seven killings over the years, a pub where he'd been sitting when bullets flew. Here and there, a few damaged plastic flowers marked the spot where someone died in a ditch. Some of the memorials had been wrecked by the IRA, Frazer said. There was a ruined building, bombed just before the agreement was signed. It had been bombed before, years ago. He pointed out graveyards where the Protestant dead were buried. A lane down which a wounded man had carried his dead brother. The corner where the Kingsmills minibus was flagged down, the mountain road leading to Darkley Pentecostal church. On a winter night in 1983 the congregation were singing 'Are You Washed in the Blood of the Lamb?' when the Irish National Liberation Army (INLA) sprayed the little hall with gunfire, killing three elders. 'It's all very well David Ervine sitting up on the Shankill Road saying it is all over. How would he like to live on the Falls? That's what it's like here.' Apart from the IRA, Frazer's fiercest enmity seemed to be for the PUP leader.

One of the women in FAIR had said to me, 'All the roads out of Markethill lead to the border.' This part of south Armagh seemed like a place where you could get utterly lost. Narrow, winding roads, many crossroads, lanes that faded out into mangled tracks. Small, steep fields tilting down; high hedges.

'This is Tullyvallen; we're on the border here,' said Frazer, slowing down. On the iron gate into a field, a poster hung. 'The Union is safe – so was the Titanic.' The former part of the slogan was a reference to the loyalist ceasefire statement. Loyalist dissidents had disputed the claim.

Frazer stared across the invisible border. 'That's bad country over there. There's a lot of questions to be answered. Why were the Provies allowed to operate across the border for twenty-five years? I believe there was collusion between the gardaí and the IRA. The least the Irish government could do is apologise to the people living on the border.' This was a position supported by the UUP's security spokesman, Ken Maginnis, who said that if there were to be inquiries into Bloody Sunday, and into allegations of collusion in murders by loyalists, there should be an inquiry into this too.

At a place called Mullyash, Frazer stopped to show me where the border was marked by a narrow river. A man on a skittish red horse rode across an old stone bridge. Man and horse were very thin, the man tall, with long hair and hollow cheeks. He looked at us suspiciously. Frazer stared back. A poster on a tree said, 'Shhh. Don't tell them, it's a united Ireland.'

We drove on. 'That's a Protestant house. I think we're getting into Catholic territory now. Aye. There's a bad boy in there. That's a right nest of them in there.' On a straight stretch of road across a bog, we could see a man ahead of us, walking with a spade over his shoulder. The man turned to watch us driving past him. 'See the other side?' said Frazer. 'They never miss a trick. That's the difference between Protestants and Catholics. If you drive past a Catholic, he'll always look to see who is in the car. In a Protestant area, no one passes any remarks.

'There's a golf course they got. More than a million pounds was paid out by the government for that. The Catholics all claim thousands for the army breaking down their fences. That's the Catholic mentality. One man got £10,000. He claimed he fell down the stairs when a bomb went off. My mother got £6,000 and they took it out of her welfare.' We passed a big, showy modern house, set in the bog. 'That'll belong to one of these poor downtrodden nationalists,' said Frazer with a bitter laugh. 'All that is a lot of waffle. My mother used to babysit for Catholics when they were out in the pub drinking, and they'd be out two or three nights a week.

'We're in Provo country now. There's a monument to them. There's another bad outfit in there. They have taken down all the

signs, "Sniper at work" and all those. They must have media in.
They're trying to make it look like it's all over.' The sniper at work
sign was famous. Its photograph had appeared in the international
press. When the IRA ceasefire was called, it was changed to 'Sniper on
hold'. The eastern swathe of the border is one of the heartlands of
republican dissidents, those who oppose the peace process and the
Belfast Agreement. Some of the men who made the Omagh bomb
come from these parts.

In Cullyhanna, a strongly republican village, Frazer stopped the car
outside a shop. Men stared. It was obvious he had been recognised.
'They'd lift you pretty quick round here,' he said, strangely satisfied.
'You wouldn't know what would happen. They are all the one,
Continuity, Real, Provies. It's just softliners and hardliners.' Then he
got out of the car and walked past the men to the shop. He came back
with cans of coke and crisps. 'I'll tell you one thing, girl. The only
people in this country thinks there's peace is the ones never had a war
in the first place.'

Frazer told me a story about himself. In 1977, a week after Nairac
had been abducted from the Three Steps Inn at Drumintee, near
Forkhill in south Armagh, Frazer's mates in the TA had dared him to
go into the pub. 'I sat up at the bar and drank my pint,' he said. 'There
was complete silence.'

Protestants have been leaving south Armagh for years. A University
of Ulster study shows that in 1971 the Protestant population along the
border was 19 per cent. In 1991 it was just 1 per cent. The Catholic
population had risen from 67 per cent to 91 per cent in the same
period. Furthermore, while the remaining Protestant population was
ageing, the Catholic population was predominantly younger. Protestants were retreating from the border north and eastwards – the
Armagh town of Tandragee saw an increase in its Protestant population from 46 per cent to 64 per cent (Murtagh, 1996, p. 20).

I was told that in Whitecross, where the Frazers lived until they
were intimidated, there was just one Protestant family left in 1999.
The area was as segregated as the urban peaceline zones in Belfast.
Significantly, it also had a killing rate three times higher than average
during the Troubles. A 1991 study shows that 30 per cent of Catholic
men were unemployed in the border region, compared with 13 per

cent of Protestant men, a higher than average differential (O'Dowd, Moore and Corrigan, p. 21). The security forces, full and part time, have been a lucrative employment option for Protestants. One woman described the part-time UDR as 'virtually a type of farm diversification'.

Another study, quoted by Murtagh, found that attitudes in an un-named town in the area were considerably more extreme than any-where else in the North, except among people living on peacelines. Almost 50 per cent of Protestants said they would rather live in an all-Protestant area, and 43 per cent of Protestants said they would not allow a member of their family to marry a Catholic (Murtagh, 1996, p. 29). A large majority of both Protestants and Catholics said that most of their friends were of their own religion – in the Protestant village, the figure was 86 per cent. A 1990 study, also from the Uni-versity of Ulster, identifies as 'cultural blindness' the tendency of people from both communities to say that the area enjoyed good community relations, when in reality there was minimal contact (Murtagh, 1996, p. 31).

'IN LIFE YOU HAVE TO BE AN OPTIMIST'

'Two things I have never owned. A flag and a gun,' said Willie Johnston, a bright-eyed, soft-spoken man of sixty or so. 'Hence, maybe, my attitude to my Catholic neighbours is moulded by that. My view on everything is equal treatment for everyone. I have made a lot of friends and no enemies.' It seemed an impossible boast, and all the more remarkable coming from a citizen of south Armagh, known for the fierceness of its enmities. However, Johnston spoke the words benignly and with a quiet certainty.

He ran a poultry farm at the village of Mountnorris, between Markethill and Whitecross, the place of which Willie Frazer and his mother had spoken with such anger. His offices were an extension of the old farmhouse where he lived, on top of a hill, with the farm in new buildings down the hill below. A big square house, it had little turrets and, on either side of the front door, ornamental trees cut in a twirling design. He showed me the drawing room, stacked high with a display of the wedding presents his son and his new wife had recently received. We spoke in the kitchen, its windows looking out over rolling green hills. 'I was born a couple of miles down the road and I've lived here all my life. I was educated in Newry, a Catholic town,' he said. 'I am myself a Covenanter, or Reformed Presbyterian.

'The attitude of my Church is that one is not recommended to belong to any oath-bound or secret society, so I am not a member of any of the loyal Orders. I would say I tend to take a broader view of how relationships should be with people of other faiths or none. Do right by everybody, is what I believe. That is why I voted for the Belfast Agreement. I believe in equality for all.'

The Covenanters came as Scottish settlers to Ulster in the seventeenth century, and most of their congregations were still in the areas settled at that time, in Antrim, Derry and Down. Their worship is austere – they sing only the Psalms and allow no musical accompaniment. This is based on a literal reading of the Bible. 'Since God has revealed in Scripture how he is to be worshipped, nothing is to be introduced which he has not specifically commanded. Nowhere has he instructed his people to praise him with songs other than those provided in the Book of Psalms' (Donnelly in Richardson [ed.], p. 161).

'On the political side,' said Johnston. 'The break with the Presbyterian Church in the seventeenth century was over the right of the Queen to be head of the Church. We recognise the right of royalty to head the state, but Jesus Christ is the king of the Church.' The Covenanters' attitude to Catholicism is severe. According to Donnelly, liberal theology is condemned by God and Catholicism is not Christian. However, 'There may be individual Roman Catholics who are true believers and all harshness and ill feeling between Protestants and Roman Catholics is to be deplored' (Donnelly in Richardson [ed.], p. 162).

So, while his Church taught that he should not accept his Catholic neighbours' right to call themselves Christians, Johnston was convinced of the need to work with them to bring about a strong community. Economic development and employment were his theme. One of the founders of the Armagh Local Enterprise Centre, vice-chairman of the Economic Development Board, a member of endless local committees and boards, and of the Peace and Reconciliation

Board, he had an impressive record of public service. I was told that when he was a UUP councillor, he had been voted on to boards with the help of Sinn Féin, among other parties.

He showed me advertisements for jobs in the local paper, jobs created by the local enterprise centre which had plans for the town of Markethill. Business units, regeneration of the old courthouse as a 'neutral venue', fine shops and offices, a crèche, sheltered dwellings for the elderly. There were also 'focus groups', a historical society, a gardening club, an art club, a women's group and a youth club. Festivals, flower tubs on the streets . . . Johnston described them all with pride. 'These are genuine mixed groups. They are not doing it because it has to be fifty-fifty. They are doing it because of a shared interest.

'We took part in a New Horizons programme, which brought people from Markethill and Crossmaglen to the United States together. Now, Crossmaglen would be a notorious name in Markethill. Not all the work is with cross-community groups – we on the Peace and Reconciliation Board recognise that some things may need to be single-identity. Anything that keeps people doing something . . .' Markethill was more than 80 per cent Protestant: 'But we have Irish dancing. A lot of work is put in by people who don't say much. Actions speak louder than words.'

It had not all been plain sailing. I knew that a talk at the historical society about the 1798 rebellion had been hastily abandoned after a threat had been issued against one of the speakers, a Catholic priest with strong views about civil rights and state repression. Johnston did not want to speak about it, though he pointed out that, as a matter of interest, the Covenanters had been part of the rebellion.

Protestants had been hostile to certain types of funding. They had told him the money he got for the business centre was 'blood money' because it came from funds set up after the Anglo-Irish Agreement. 'But now they are asking how you go about applying for that money. Realism has dawned.' Others objected to money raised from lottery funds because they were religiously opposed to gambling. 'Now, I've never bought a lottery ticket or gambled in my life, but I see no problem taking the proceeds.'

Johnston believed the Belfast Agreement would work in the end, though he had been against the early release of prisoners without a deal on decommissioning. He said cross-border bodies would not trouble him, as he had been doing business across the border for many years. 'We supply chicks all over Ireland. I have no fear. We have to realise that we are now all Europeans.'

I asked him about anger among Protestants in this border area. He replied carefully. 'Nobody in our family has been killed. We have not been directly affected. That may influence my attitudes. However, there are people in the area who forgive, though they do not forget. The experience of the Troubles in this area was particularly bad in the early seventies when there was a lot of fear and intimidation. You wouldn't have found either Catholics or Protestants out walking of an evening. The IRA killed a lot of members of the security forces.'

He remembered the murders of the Reaveys, and, the next day, the Kingsmills massacre. His company had since bought the old textile factory to which the workers had been travelling, and turned it into an egg-packing station. 'There were funerals for a few days. There was one survivor from each of the two atrocities. I and a number of other people visited them.' He sighed. 'But this area has had virtually no trouble for years now. The IRA hasn't been targeting the civilian population. I don't want to be flippant, but it doesn't concern me. In life you have to be an optimist.'

'THE GHOST AT THE MIDDLE-CLASS TABLE'

It was stormy the night I went to meet Will Glendinning, with snow in the air. The narrow roads of south Armagh seemed to twist and tilt alarmingly in the dark, branches swooping down in the wind, scattering twigs over the windscreen. I had decided I was lost when a fallen tree across the road brought me to a standstill. I reversed the car and saw that I was at the avenue leading to his home, a Georgian farmhouse with bright windows. It was like a Christmas card image appearing out of the wildness of the night.

'Oh my goodness. Oh Lord,' Glendinning said, when I told him about the tree. 'That's on my land.' He rushed off to sort it out. The head of the North's Community Relations Council (CRC), he was also a farmer. I waited by the log fire in the handsome living room. When he returned he said that it was not a fallen tree, merely a branch. The urban visitor had exaggerated.

'My family was originally planted around Beragh, County Tyrone. We are a classic Ulster Protestant family from the linenocracy, starting off as farmers. My great grandfather bought linen from the shores of Lough Neagh and walked to Belfast to sell it with a cart. In the late 1800s he set up a factory in Lurgan.' The pride with which he spoke of his family's progress through hard work to prosperity seemed classically Ulster Protestant too. One grandfather had been a Liberal MP, another a Unionist.

They had lived in big houses. Glendinning had inherited his. Coincidentally, the headquarters of the CRC are in Glendinning House in Belfast, an old linen mill which had belonged to the family. His father had been an Orangeman – the Order expelled him. His mother had left the Ulster Unionist Party around 1960 when he was ten. Something to do with a letter she received instructing her to 'employ the right sort of people'.

This was an astonishing story. I had got used to Orangemen telling me that in the good old days Catholics would do the milking, or bring in the hay for their Protestant neighbours on the Twelfth of July. They wanted me to know how good community relations used to be when Catholics accepted the Order and its rituals. 'The reason my father got put out and my mother got the letter was ostensibly because my father got his hay baled by a Catholic on the Twelfth of July. Funnily enough, the same Catholic came to bale my hay thirty years later on the Twelfth of July. He leaned out of the tractor and said, "Maybe I'll get you into the same bother as I got your father into!" I said, "No, Alfie, you won't, because I'm not in the same things."'

He remembered the start of the Troubles, the police batoning the civil rights marchers in Derry. He remembered anxiously wondering what friends of the family, Portadown Catholics, whose father was a policeman, thought about what had happened. 'It turned out they were horrified, like us.'

He and his siblings had, he said, tested his parents' liberal credentials to the limit. Only one of them had married a white Anglo-Saxon Protestant. 'I have married two Catholics because Pip died and I married again. My parents have never been anything but supportive.'

When the Alliance Party was set up, his older brother Robin got involved. It did not go down well with some members of his family. A political discussion had started in a relative's house and Robin had produced an Alliance keyring. 'We were told to leave, and we were asked did we not know what put the backsides in our breeches. People have no idea the divisions Alliance caused in middle-class families. My mother and one of her sisters stopped speaking over it.'

The Alliance Party went on to become the party many middle-class people felt they *ought* to vote for – it indicated moderation, seen as a virtue. In *Interpreting Northern Ireland*, John Whyte shows that Alliance consistently did better in surveys than in actual elections. The party did badly in the 1998 Assembly election, and followed it with an unseemly public wrangle between its leaders over who should get the Speaker's chair (Lord Alderdice in the end). Glendinning and his late wife Pip had represented the Falls Road in Belfast City Council during the 1980s, relying heavily on Catholic votes. In the 1982 Assembly elections, Gerry Adams had topped the poll in West Belfast. Glendinning took a seat for Alliance. He and his wife retired from politics in 1987.

I asked him about a new report on sectarianism which had referred to it as 'the ghost at the middle-class table'. He nodded agreement. Then he told me a story he had recently heard. 'An antiques class in Armagh, a well-heeled group. After the fourth week a woman came up and said to the tutor, "You know what is going on, the way you are asked to supper after the class? Do you realise that only the Protestants in the class are invited?" He said that no, he didn't. She said if it went on, he would lose half his class.' He said this 'system of avoidance' existed across the whole spectrum of backgrounds.

The CRC is a charitable body, set up in 1990 by the government's Central Community Relations Unit to increase 'understanding and co-operation between political, cultural and religious communities in Northern Ireland'. It funds a huge range of projects, including the Mediation Network, which develops 'creative responses to conflict', particularly in relation to parades; the Northern Ireland Mixed Marriage Association; the YMCA's national council; and Counteract, the trade union body which aims to eliminate sectarianism in the workplace. Controversially, it has also funded Orange Order projects.

'It confronts sectarianism,' said Glendinning. 'Most community groups have it in their constitution that they are non-sectarian and non-political, and that is all very fine and sheltered. But it has to be examined, because sectarianism affects every part of our lives. You have to try to get people beyond the insistence that all is well; you have to get them beyond the point of denial. In the voluntary sector people have been prepared to confront the issue, and move on from being non-sectarian to being anti-sectarian. We've got to look at how it feels to be a Protestant in Newry or a Catholic in Carrickfergus, or we'll end up with apartheid.'

The CRC has been accused of disingenuousness in its attitude to sectarianism. One of its critics, Robbie McVeigh, academic and human rights activist, wrote that the insistence in community relations work on the symmetry of 'one side is as bad as the other' masked the reality – that 'sectarianism is institutionalised by the nature of the state in Northern Ireland and as such it empowers Protestants and disempowers Catholics'. McVeigh accepted that there was Catholic sectarianism, and cited the Kingsmills massacre as evidence. However, he argued that anti-sectarian work which did not acknowledge that sectarian discrimination proportionately disadvantaged Catholics was corrupted and debilitated. The CRC was state-sponsored, and the state was sectarian. The analysis of sectarianism had been restricted to 'individual pathology rather than institutional culpability' (McVeigh, p. 8).

Glendinning disagreed that the CRC took this approach. He said he accepted that sectarianism was institutionalised in the state, so that the Protestant community was more powerful and therefore better able to deliver its ends. Indeed, McVeigh's article actually quoted a 1994 report from the Central Community Relations Unit which explicitly stated that 'on all major social and economic indicators, Roman Catholics generally experience higher levels of disadvantage than Protestants' (McVeigh, p. 9). Glendinning spoke of the work the council was doing with Portadown's further education college, the Upper Bann Institute. 'When you work with the providers of statutory services, you are saying to them, what are you going to do about developing proper policies and training and procedures to ensure that your facility is open to everyone? It means the staff have to take on board that they may have carried out things which were sectarian. It is not nice handling. But the point is that the process can start creating a critical mass which will change things inside Portadown. OK, it is only a small step and Portadown is the worst example, being Portadown, but it is a step.

'Anyway, I don't really see where the McVeigh argument gets you in the end, because there are other areas where some power rests, and similar things can happen there.' He mentioned another college, the North West Institute in Derry, which was avoided by Protestants. He also quoted John Dunlop, the former moderator of the Presbyterian Church, who wrote that whereas Catholics feared the power of the British state, Protestants feared the power of the Catholic Church.

When he married his first wife in 1976, Glendinning said the priest had produced a piece of paper for him to sign, stating that any children would be brought up as Catholics. 'I didn't mind, because as a member of the Church of Ireland, I say the Apostles' Creed which says, "I believe in one Holy Catholic and Apostolic Church." But Pip put her foot down and said I would sign no such thing.'

When they started to work on the renovation of their house the Glendinnings found that if they approached a Catholic neighbour, they were directed to a network of Catholic workers, and if the neighbour was Protestant, those suggested would be Protestant. 'This is a sectarian interface and there has been a lot of hurt. You'll find in a town like Markethill – it is the last town this far south which has a Protestant majority – there is an element there which is either fearful of takeover, or just doesn't want to change.'

He described the work that went into trying to initiate cross-community activities. 'I've been involved in setting up the community association in Mountnorris along with other people, and the only venue we could use was the state school, so it was a Protestant venue. Everybody turned up, however, and the thing people said was, "Wasn't it brilliant, everyone came and it happened so naturally."

'The trouble was, it didn't happen naturally. There was three months' planning went into it. We had to be careful about how the information went out, that all the local churches were spoken to, that letters went out through both the Catholic and the Protestant schools, so that the message was coming across from all quarters that this meeting was OK.'

'THE OULD SOW'

There were those who regarded the achievement of 'cross-community' activities as the ideal. Others defended segregation, and argued that it did not diminish good neighbourliness. I had met Oliver Gibson during the terrible days after the Omagh bomb in August 1998. A fiery old man, he had been a schoolmaster and DUP councillor for years, and represented West Tyrone in the Assembly. His constituency's border with Donegal includes towns like Castlederg, where significant sections of each of the two communities fear and loath each other.

The daughter of a cousin of Mr Gibson's was among the twenty-nine who died in the Omagh bomb. When I called at his house in Beragh after a day of funerals for the bomb victims, Mr Gibson was kind. He gave me tea and headache pills, and told stories against himself. He described a council meeting during the 'Ulster Says No' period after the Anglo-Irish Agreement was signed. The DUP councillors were boycotting meetings, turning up occasionally to hold their seats. He had arrived late. Something contentious was on the agenda, 'something nationalists wanted that would have been very annoying to Protestants'. He had sat down, and was immediately asked to give his opinion. 'I tore in left, right and centre,' he said. 'I gave them what for.' When he noticed other councillors laughing it made him even more vehement. When he had finished the chief executive informed him that they had, in fact, simply been agreeing the minutes of the last month's meeting.

Gibson said that a typical rural west Tyrone village would have a Protestant hall and a Catholic hall, a Catholic school and a Protestant one, a Protestant youth club and a Catholic one, a Catholic church and several Protestant ones. 'Everyone respects their own culture and ethos, and they go to their own places. But they respect each other. Even in the worst of times the business community and the farmers kept up contacts with the other side and kept going. They soldiered on in their own interests and that held things together. But there is no call for this forcing people to mix when they would rather keep with their own.'

Gibson had said something shocking too. He said of the Omagh bomb: 'The only reason there's this whole "see ho" about it is because there was so many Catholics killed.' It was an ugly thing to say. Particularly since a Catholic neighbour of Gibson's had lost his wife, his daughter, his granddaughter and the soon-to-be-born twins she was carrying. But he said he meant no disrespect to the Catholics who died. It was just that nobody cared when it was only Protestants who were killed.

'What about the ninety-seven murders that happened before? Most of them UDR, police, police reserve. Castlederg cemetery has one solid row of graves of people murdered by republicans. What went on here was ethnic cleansing. What difference does it make to people here whether it was the Real IRA, the Continuity IRA or the Provisional IRA? It's all the IRA and the government has capitulated to them.' His brother had recently died having never fully recovered from injuries he received during an IRA ambush many years previously.

A few months later, Paul Berry was to sing at a function in the little community centre adjoining Gibson's offices in Beragh, and he said I could come along. I asked Gibson if he minded my taking notes. He gave me a hard look. 'That's all right,' he said. 'I'll tell you one thing, though – you'll only break with me the once.'

The hall was plain, but comfortable. The older people sat on armchairs. People looked at me with curiosity, in a friendly enough way. A man played a medley of religious tunes on the organ during the 'gathering in' and then the evening started, like all DUP gatherings, with a prayer. 'In the day of my trouble, I will pray unto thee ... oh Lord, we think of treachery abounding, the enemies that are laughing ...'

Gibson's electoral agent introduced the guests. Of the Oliver twins, who were to sing, he said, 'One has taken unto herself a husband and one who looks as if she is maybe about to.' His lilting, biblical way of talking poignantly recalled Esther, the young woman from the Gibson family who had been killed in the bomb. At her funeral the Reverend Ian Paisley had read out a note she had written in the margins of her Bible: 'Oh Lord, if it please thee send me a man of God that I may be his wife.' In his sermon, Paisley the preacher had cried to God for vengeance.

Paul Berry was introduced as the youngest Assembly member and youngest member of the DUP. 'Everywhere I look I see Union Jacks. This must be a very Protestant part of the country,' he said. The audience chuckled. They sang in praise of King William and the 'green grassy slopes of the Boyne ... our war cry "no surrender"'. Berry invited them to sing along to 'The Sash'. He told them to sing it loud so that the people of Carrickmore would hear it. After a verse, he stopped them and said, 'I'm serious. I want the ones up in Carrickmore to hear it.' Carrickmore, a few mountainy miles from Beragh, was a Catholic village with a strong republican element. As a show of strength, the IRA had once staged a roadblock there, posing for a film crew.

A small, dark-haired man took the stage. He had a slight lisp and a soft Tyrone accent. He said he was William Anderson and he would read some poems his father, Joseph Anderson, had written. His father had been a councillor. One of the poems was about the UUP 'powersharing with the friends of the gunmen'. The last line was, 'No surrender, no Provos, no SDLP'. Another was in praise of Paisley. It was based on the siege of Derry and the idea that it was time to rise again and shut the gates:

> For we've got a blood-bought heritage
> And the enemy is Rome
> And though we'd hate to cause a split
> We'll hold our Ulster home.

There was more singing – 'The Old Rugged Cross', and a song called 'The Battle of Loughgall', celebrating the SAS ambush there. 'What we need from the government is a few more Loughgalls,' cried Berry. 'Now, listen to this wee song. It goes to the tune of "Stand Up, Stand Up for Jesus", and it's called "The B Specials".' The song had lines like, 'disease is rampant where popery reigns' and 'give us back our Specials and give us back our pride'. Then Berry sang, to the tune of 'Who Do You Think You Are Kidding Mr Hitler?' 'Who do you think you are kidding Mr Trimble/ When you say the Union's safe?' His sweet voice allowed no humour into the song.

There was a break for supper. A fleet of smiling ladies swept through the hall, with plates stacked high with sandwiches, cakes, tray bakes and big slabs of home-made apple tarts. An abundance. There was a huge kettle full of tea, which was served in china cups. The women came round again and again, urging us to heap our plates. It was very cheerful.

Afterwards, William Anderson took the stage again and read more of his father's poems – in praise of the B men, and against Catholics who took 'our benefits'. One of them was called 'The Ould Sow':

> The ould sow grunted and keenied
> And dundered her snout of the dure,
> She devoured all we could give her
> She was looking for more to be sure.

The pig kept on demanding more, even though she spilled what she had 'in the muck and the filth of the craw'. Why, the poet asks, was she so obstructive? The answer is plain: 'She was a fenian, as sure as you're there.'

But when it came to polling days, the fenian, far from polling for those who supplied the family allowance and the government grant, 'polled for the bullet and the gunman'. What was to be done? The poem had the answer:

> I think he should get what he's asked for
> And I think he should get it now.

The audience laughed and clapped, and William Anderson's face blushed with pleasure as he left the stage.

In a book published in 1970 by the Bob Jones University Press of South Carolina, Paisley had written about the insatiable greed of the Catholic Church: 'You can never satisfy the Church of Rome. Even if she gets a 65% grant, she is not happy ... she says she wants a 100% grant – she must have it all' (Paisley, p. 12). In the 1920s Lord Londonderry had attempted to bring in a form of integrated education. He was opposed by the Catholic Church, the Orange Order and several Protestant Church bodies.

I talked to Anderson after the function. He told me he was a postman. There was a small collection of his father's poems. He said he'd send me it, and he did. I saw him once after that, marching with a band up and down the hill at Drumcree, then taking tea from the women at the stall. At the foot of the hill, other men were flinging fireworks and abuse at the police. But he didn't see me, with the crowd, and the shouting, and the general mayhem.

'I WOULDN'T TOUCH TALKS'

A country boy from Tandragee who regularly toured the North singing gospel songs, as well as being prominent at Drumcree, Paul Berry was well placed to observe the mood of rural Protestants of the DUP persuasion. Born into both the Free Presbyterian Church and the DUP, he told me that he had become born-again on 10 April 1981 when he was eight. (Precocious – but Paisley's salvation occurred when he was six.) He joined the Orange Order at seventeen. He worked in a hardware store, as a sales representative, and latterly as an examiner in a shoe factory before he stood for the Assembly in 1998. We spoke in the big offices he had been allocated in Stormont. He had just moved in. No books yet, no papers. He swivelled about in his chair, feet up on the desk, a young man well pleased with himself.

Young, but sounding strangely old. 'I have a love for politics but an even greater one for this wee province of ours,' he said, in the singsong preacher's voice which is typical of the gospel branch of the DUP. The Orange Order was 'very special to all of us as Protestants'. He warned that people misunderstood the Order. 'Yes, it was set up to protect our faith, but also to protect our Protestant people. The sooner it gets back to defending the people the better.

'If the people hadn't got into militias in the past, where would we be? Our faith would have been trampled on. I personally believe the Orange Order isn't militant enough. It is getting to the stage that if we don't stand up to the republican element, our wee province is finished, our heritage is finished.' He said if the government did not let the Order down the Garvaghy Road, 'our men are going to have to take it, illegally'. It had been done before, he said. 'Don't forget, Dr Paisley led them up the road one year at night.' As for meeting the nationalist residents' group, 'I wouldn't touch talks.'

He was clearly comfortable in his new life as a politician, but he insisted that the Assembly was 'not for this wee country'. It was really just the road to a united Ireland. 'We are here to fight for democracy and fight for the Protestant people, but we will not sit down with IRA murderers. We could govern this wee country without Sinn Féin IRA men.'

Berry said he supported Willie Frazer's assertion that loyalists should not have been punished for killing republicans. 'Yes, I would agree with him there. They were living in a border area and their families were being slaughtered. They took a look at the government and the way it wasn't dealing with the IRA. The only attack on the IRA was at Loughgall. It was republicans got the B Specials disbanded, because the B men had their eye on them.

'The UDR got more and more organised and had strains and restrictions put on it. You can hardly stop a republican now, but they lift the mobile phone and phone the nearest security base and say they are getting harassed. The UDR and the RIR's [Royal Irish Regiment] hands were tied. They couldn't do anything. Not like the B Specials – they could take the republicans into their own hands and control them.

'It is easy to see why loyalists took the law into their own hands. If we said we supported loyalists killing the IRA, we'd be slaughtered for it, but my own personal view is that if the republicans are out to murder our kith and kin, as they have done, if you live by the sword, you die by the sword. It would be wrong for me to condemn those loyalists, even though God is the only one who has a right to take life, but yet and all, these men have seen their relations killed.

'If my brother was killed by a republican and a loyalist killed the republican, if we were honest to God, we wouldn't feel sorry and that is it. My own uncle, who was a policeman, was blown up to bits in Moy.' He paused. 'That made me want to be in politics, to deliver peace and democracy to this wee province.'

'THE GROUND WAS TAKEN FROM UNDER YOU'

The UDR was set up, along with the RUC reserve, to replace the B Specials and guard the border. It was to have no sectarian baggage, though Lord Hunt, whose report had led to its formation, warned that its name alone would be anathema to many Catholics. Although recruitment was open to all, application forms for both the police reserve and the new regiment were sent out to all serving Specials, and all seven battalions were led by former commandants of that force. The UDR's honeymoon period with the nationalist community was brief.

At the same time, champions of the Specials said from the start that the UDR was a poor replacement. When Bill Craig formed Vanguard, this was his argument for starting a Third Force, which would, if necessary, 'liquidate the enemy'. In 1972 the Reverend Willie McCrea held a press conference at which a masked man in UDR uniform took the platform. There were hints that members of the regiment were 'prepared to take the campaign against terrorism into their own hands'. A Free Presbyterian minister said in 1984 that he would 'love to see rebellion' in the ranks of the local security forces, though he urged them to 'sit tight'.

A UDR commander said that joint UDA–UDR membership would not, of itself, lead to expulsion from the regiment. He was criticised in an editorial in the *Belfast Telegraph*. UDR men were involved in the UVF's Miami showband massacre, in the Shankill Butchers, and in bombings and shooting attacks. UDR soldiers were also convicted of providing arms and arms instruction to paramilitaries. Arms belonging to the Ulster Resistance movement were uncovered in the homes of UDR soldiers in County Armagh.

In late 1981, Paisley inspected some 6,000 masked men in paramilitary-style uniform at a rally in Newtownards, County Down. 'Here are men willing to do the job of exterminating the IRA,' he declared. 'Recruit them under the Crown and they will do it. If you refuse, we will have no other decision to make but to do it ourselves' (Taylor, 1999, p. 177). Some of those present wore berets with UDR badges, and leaders of the Third Force boasted that members of the regiment were involved. However, the UDR on this occasion ordered any such soldiers to resign from the regiment. It was revealed that while 44 per cent of applicants to the UDR were turned down, others who failed a vetting procedure were still allowed to join.

The Stevens inquiry found that there was collusion between the loyalist paramilitaries and the UDR, though it was 'neither widespread nor institutionalised'. However, in 1990, Lord Hunt wrote in the London *Independent* newspaper that he supported calls for its disbandment. He said that his hopes that Catholics would be proportionately recruited had not been realised, and that the distrust with which the minority community had regarded the B Specials had been inherited by that force's successor, the UDR – 'Serious crimes, attributed mainly to the part-time members of the UDR, have tended to discredit the whole regiment – however unfairly' (quoted in Ryder, 1991, p. 207). In 1992, the British government announced that part-time membership was to be phased out, and that the full-time regiment was to be amalgamated with the Royal Irish Rangers to form the Royal Irish Regiment.

When, in 1985, the SDLP deputy leader, Seamus Mallon, had demanded the immediate disbandment of the UDR, claiming that it was the armed wing of unionism, the UUP MP Ken Maginnis retorted that this would be a recipe for civil war. He said that what would result would be a vacuum filled by 'warring militias fighting for territory'. Maginnis, a former B Special who served as a major in the UDR until he became an MP in 1982, has been its most forceful champion. Dismissing claims of institutionalised wrongdoing, he also rejected the 'bad apple' theory, and said that during his twelve years in the regiment he had never come upon a bad apple, only a small number of 'bruised apples', whose 'level of tolerance is breached'. Deploring their 'mistakes', he said they were under enormous stress (quoted in Ryder, 1991, p. 181). He told me that the record might have been better 'if people like Ken Maginnis had been doing the vetting and not civil servants from Dorset'.

Maginnis, defeated by David Trimble in the 1995 leadership contest, had been regarded as a more moderate candidate. A decade earlier he had denounced the Ulster Clubs, which had Trimble as a member, with their rhetoric about the use of 'legitimate force' to oppose the Anglo-Irish Agreement. As the UUP's security spokesman, he had, before the party countenanced entering talks with Sinn Féin, taken part in a televised debate with his namesake, Sinn Féin's Martin McGuinness. While Martin the Sinn Féiner attempted to cajole him, Ken the Unionist refused eye contact and alleged that Martin was on the army council of the IRA, a claim he has repeated on numerous occasions. The IRA has attempted to murder Maginnis on at least five occasions.

When the UUP finally sat down at the negotiating table with Sinn

Féin in 1997, Maginnis stated that he was not there to take part in talks – he was 'refusing to give up political ground'. Recalling UDR friends who had been murdered, he said, 'I have a deep, deep bitterness about the IRA . . . I could never give cognisance to them, not as long as I live' (quoted in McKittrick, 1999A, p. 96).

Maginnis had been Trimble's most solid supporter when it came to the Belfast Agreement. I had met him during the funerals after the Omagh bomb in August 1998. He told me that angry unionists had been telling him that the agreement was a sham, and he had replied that after thirty years of killings, it was time to sit down and start running the government together. A year later, that had still not happened, when I met him again in Aughnacloy, County Tyrone, in his constituency of Fermanagh–South Tyrone.

It was a sunny Sunday morning. He had said he would take me to the top of a hill on the River Blackwater, and show me farms all around on which the IRA had murdered an eldest son. But he decided the ground was too wet for such an expedition. Instead we drove in his jeep through the countryside along the border, and he showed me houses and lanes where the IRA had shot people – farmers, teachers, businessmen. He said there had been a time when he could have named every person who had been killed, but too many had died, and many of the murders had been so long ago, he had lost track. 'When I was soldiering down here I would have known everyone,' he said. He showed me the house of a UDR man who had known he was going to be killed, and who was killed. It was a typical border killing – he was shot in the back by gunmen who emerged from the bushes as he fed his pigs in the sheds at the back of his farm.

Fermanagh had a relatively low death toll during the Troubles, a total of 110 people, 43 of them from the UDR, RUC or RIR, and a further 21 from the British army. Armagh and Tyrone were considerably more dangerous – 114 members of local security forces were murdered in the former county, 99 in the latter (McKittrick, *et al*, 1999B pp. 1478–9). However, the impact could not be measured simply in terms of fatalities. There were those who moved away, those who lived in terror, and those who were demoralised. I'd kept a cutting from the *Irish News*, an interview with a former UDR man called John McClure. He had left his border home in 1972 after the IRA murdered his friend. 'What you have worked for all your life was scattered ... the ground was taken from under you. You were leaving your home,' he'd said. Maginnis saw it as a campaign of ethnic cleansing, designed to make a large tract of land along the border uninhabitable by Protestants. 'It was an area under siege.' Political ground, not to be given up. Many Protestants did not give it up. 'There would be quite a few elderly mothers still holding onto the land along the border, even if there is no one left in the family to farm it.' Swathes of these ruined fields could be seen along the border, gone to ragwort and thistles.

In the village of Moy, further upriver, Maginnis said the IRA had systematically murdered the entrepreneurs, 'the people who had the ability to hold the village'. We drove to Aughnacloy, with its wide main street and its British army checkpoint, marking the border crossing on the main Derry to Dublin road. A young Catholic man, Aidan McAnespie, had been shot and killed by a soldier as he walked through the checkpoint to a Gaelic Athletic Association (GAA) match in February 1988. His father said afterwards that a soldier had told him Aidan was to be shot. The soldier who fired the fatal shot said it was an accident. Maginnis did not speak of this incident.

Maginnis's close friend, Cormac McCabe, who had been his predecessor as UDR company commander, had been headmaster of Aughnacloy High School. He had crossed the border for a meal with his family in a Monaghan hotel in January 1974. The IRA had abducted him. His body was brought across the border again and dumped near his home village of Clogher, County Tyrone. We sat outside the school for a moment. 'He was the kingpin of this little community. The people who were targeted were carefully selected. You destroy the talent. Dishearten the community. It is a takeover.' A disheartened community. It was a powerful description.

Sir Norman Stronge had been the heart of Tynan, a few miles away, he said. I told Maginnis that the former Speaker at Stormont had been mentioned by many people. 'He symbolised Northern Ireland,' he said. 'Tynan Abbey where he lived had some peculiar place in old Irish nationalist thinking. These people are not republicans – they are irredentist late-nineteenth-century nationalists. Whatever peculiar thinking they have, they blew up and burned an irreplaceable library

of books at Tynan. It was the work of vandals, not Irish patriots.'
Portadown Orangemen had gathered in the grounds of Tynan Abbey
for the Twelfth before the war in 1914. There is a polished brass
plaque to the Stronges just outside the debating chamber at Stormont.
The burnt-out abbey was demolished in 1998.

This phrase, 'irredentist late-nineteenth-century nationalists', was
one Maginnis kept repeating. He contrasted it with the 'basic decent
Hibernian ethos, the old Ancient Order of Hibernia ethos' out of
which, he contended, SDLP support came. This ethos had failed in
Fermanagh, he said, when, in 1981, the SDLP 'failed' to put up a
candidate against IRA hunger-striker Bobby Sands. Sands's victory at
the polls might have started the movement towards constitutional
politics for Sinn Féin, but it had been a massive blow to unionism.

I asked him why it seemed people along the west Fermanagh border
seemed so much less bitter than people on other parts of the border,
and why in south Armagh people were so furious. The late Gordon
Wilson, whose daughter Marie was one of those killed by the
Enniskillen bomb in 1987, said he had prayed for the killers and that
he forgave them. A Leitrim Protestant, he had lived and worked in
Enniskillen for many years. His feelings were not shared by all those
bereaved in the blast – one young man sawed one of the doves off the
memorial to the dead because the plaque said the victims were 'killed'
and he wanted the word to be 'murdered'. However, before he died in
1995, Wilson did have a lot of support locally, and the Spirit of
Enniskillen bursary schemes, which he initiated for young people,
were popular. It was hard to imagine a similar stance proving acceptable in south Armagh. Maginnis agreed. 'South Armagh was always a
lawless area. It was always smuggling country. The border never really
existed there.'

We got lost briefly, and found ourselves near the tiny village where
he went to school. He praised the education he had got there more
than fifty years ago. The school was in ruins. 'As I tell people, I'm a
simple country schoolmaster,' he said. He pointed down a hill. 'We
used to be sent down there with two pails to get water from the Priest's
Well. You wouldn't ask a six-year-old to do that now.' The village had
been a Cooneyite settlement. The Cooneyites were a small austere
sect with their roots in evangelical Presbyterianism. He didn't really

know who lived there now. He was skilled in the ways of the constituency politician. When we met someone on the road and he
couldn't immediately put a name to them, he would greet them
warmly, looking down from the high window of his jeep. Then by a
roundabout of genial questions and comments, he'd extract the name
and introduce me.

I asked him about an incident a few months previously when DUP
supporters had physically attacked him as he went into a meeting in
his constituency at which Trimble was to speak. 'Those people believe
in free speech for everyone except others. They know I won't lie
down.' He described Paul Berry as a 'revolting young man'. He had
taken a hard line himself on Sinn Féin decommissioning. Those who
thought the UUP should have accepted the British and Irish governments' line that there had been a 'seismic shift' in Sinn Féin's position
simply did not understand.

'I was at a rugby match yesterday and this came up. Somebody said
to me, if you get them into government the guns will become irrelevant. I said, "You don't understand guerrilla warfare. What would
happen is this. Violence continues and is tolerated within the administration. You create a vacuum. You discredit the establishment
and you fill it with your own people." Sinn Féin IRA has no intention
of decommissioning and that is endorsed by intelligence sources on
both sides of the border.'

Maginnis had a tendency to cite such sources for robust and controversial statements. He had said of Pat Finucane, the solicitor
murdered by the UFF in circumstances which suggested security force
collusion, that he was 'inextricably linked with the IRA'. The Finucane
family demanded a retraction. He said of Rosemary Nelson and
Robert Hamill, also murdered by loyalists, also in circumstances
which raised questions about the role of the security forces, that they
had both been 'at worst IRA sympathisers'.

He dismissed claims that Unionists were just using every ruse to
avoid sharing power with Catholics, pointing out that he had been one
of those who pioneered powersharing arrangements within the local
councils. A few days after we met, the then Secretary of State Mo
Mowlam announced that despite recent violence, including a murder
and the attempted importation of guns, she believed the IRA ceasefire

had not broken down. She would therefore impose no sanctions on Sinn Féin. Maginnis voiced unionism's rage, demanding Mowlam's resignation, declaring her unfit for office.

Mowlam, well aware of how her decision would be received by Unionists, had been trying to be careful of her image. The night after her announcement on the IRA ceasefire she had appeared on comedian Paddy Kielty's television show, but she had been restrained, remembering, no doubt, gaffes made by previous secretarys of state. In 1992 Peter Brooke had gone on Gay Byrne's *Late Late Show* on RTÉ and sung 'My Darling Clementine' the same day as the massacre of seven Protestant workmen at Teebane; an eighth died later. Patrick Mayhew had told the presenter of the BBC's *Newsnight* to 'cheer up, for God's sake'. This was during a spate of tit-for-tat killings.

But Maginnis was not impressed by Mowlam's efforts. He said in a BBC interview that she seemed to prefer the company of 'marginal people', alluding to her attendance at a huge rock concert featuring Robbie Williams at Slane in County Meath that weekend. The *Irish Times* carried a photograph of her at the event. She was hand in hand with Lord Henry Mountcharles, the owner of the stately home in whose grounds the concert was held. They were, according to the newspaper, close friends.

'IF . . . PEOPLE HATED LIVING IN NORTHERN IRELAND, WHY DIDN'T THEY MOVE?'

Sir Basil Brooke made the infamous speech in which he claimed that he 'had not a Roman Catholic about the place' and appealed 'to Loyalists . . . to employ Protestant lads and lassies' at a Twelfth of July gathering at Newtownbutler, County Fermanagh, in 1933. Catholics, he said, were 'endeavouring to get in everywhere' and were out to destroy Ulster. Two summers later, after riots left thirteen dead, the Belfast City Coroner noted that the people were 'easily led' into bigotry, and that it was 'not good Protestantism to preach a gospel of hate and enmity' (Bardon, p. 541).

If the 3rd Viscount Brookeborough, and 7th Baronet of Cole Brooke, Alan Henry Brooke, was tired of being asked what he thought about his grandfather's call for sectarian employment practices, he didn't show it. In fact, he shrugged it off lightly. 'I don't know why my grandfather said it, because the thing is, he did employ Catholics at that time. Perhaps it was because it was soon after they had failed to capture his eldest son. It is terribly easily to quote someone out of context. I mean, something is said, perhaps at a dinner party, and the next thing, it is made into a controversy.'

The current viscount lives with his wife, Janet, in the stately home last occupied by his grandfather, near Rosslea on the Fermanagh border. The village had one of those names – Roslea to Catholics, Rosslea to Protestants. Pronounced the same. Alan Brooke's manner was polite, slightly diffident. He went off to the library and returned with a local history book about a mountainy community which used to be part of the huge Brookeborough estate, and quoted from it to show that his grandfather, who had been prime minister of Northern Ireland from 1943 to 1963, had gone to some trouble to help Catholics. 'When they were building a chapel and steel was in short supply, he got them steel,' he said. 'There was a woman in Rosslea who said "They supplied a car to get me to mass." The man who used to help us fishing was a Catholic.'

It would have been pleasant to accept this rubbing out of the significance of the statement by the mild-mannered grandson, but unfortunately, the militant old grandfather had sought out occasions to reinforce his message. He told Derry's Unionist Association that he recommended that loyalists should not employ Catholics, '99% of whom are disloyal. If you don't act properly now, before we know where we are we shall find ourselves in the minority instead of the majority. I want you to realise that, having done your bit, you have got your Prime Minister behind you.'

A Protestant minister across the border spoke out against him, and another Fermanagh landlord, Captain T.T. Verschoyle, condemned Brooke's remarks and wondered whether 'the Colebrooke Hitler' would be rebuked by a 'responsible member of the government'. However, far from rebuking him, Prime Minister Lord Craigavon insisted, 'There is not one of my colleagues who does not entirely agree with him and I would not ask him to withdraw one word he said' (quoted in Farrell, p. 91). Craigavon went on to make his infamous speech putting Orangeism before politics: 'in the South they boasted

of a Catholic state. They still boast of Southern Ireland being a
Catholic state. All I boast is that we are a Protestant Parliament and a
Protestant state' (quoted in Bardon, pp. 538–9). Those were the days.
'Look,' said the current viscount. 'Times were different. Things
change.'

The Brookes were Anglo-Irish planters who arrived in Ireland in the
1590s and became governors of Donegal. They played their part in
putting down the 1641 rebellion and were rewarded with 28,000 acres
of land. Their stately home, Colebrooke House, was almost as os-
tentaciously splendid as the massive neo-classical Castle Coole, its
neighbour, a few miles away towards Enniskillen. Fermanagh has a lot
of stately homes, and a smattering of remaining British aristocrats. A
local school teacher and historian suggested that the county also still
had 'a kind of deference'.

Under various nineteenth-century Land Acts, all but around a
thousand acres of farming land were sold. It was Sir Basil who re-
claimed the house from the disrepair into which it had fallen and who
made the estate work (courtesy of the labour of many Protestant lads
and lassies). However, by 1939, he was considering felling the trees on
the estate to clear his overdraft. 'All might have been well,' noted
Country Life in April 1995, 'had some tax planning been made before
Lord Brookeborough died in 1973.' No such planning took place,
however, and when the Honourable Alan Brooke inherited it in 1980s
it was, according to *Country Life*: 'A sprawling barracks of a country
house, in the heart of terrorist torn Northern Ireland, encumbered
with death duties and overdraft.' In short, 'an unenviable inheritance'.

The viscount did not think so, though he remarked that it was death
duties which had destroyed the place. For him, and for his wife, the
restoration of the house was a labour of love. 'I was brought up at
Ashbrooke on the estate and we used to ride up to the house on our
ponies as children. When my grandfather was prime minister we used
to go and stay at Stormont. The estate reached to the border, and the
whole mixed population of this area were looked after by it. I could
take you up the hill there and you'd meet people who'd say, "Your
father used to ride here and other members of your family, and they
were good people." There isn't a house up there I couldn't walk into,
and have a cup of tea.'

This notion of walking into people's houses to seek testimony of their approval seemed a rather feudal one. Incongruously, it reminded me of an interview I'd done with Billy Wright, in which I asked him about reports that the local community was sick of him. He invited me to tour a local estate (housing estate, on this occasion) where he assured me he would be welcomed on every doorstep.

'As children we went to school in England,' said the viscount. 'You were proud that you lived on a border and you had a customs post. All our holidays were spent at home. Horses were the family business and that meant show jumping all around Ireland. Talk about cross community. I won a competition at Castleblayney when I was twelve – my uncle had won it in 1937. The border meant nothing. The Fermanagh Harriers' hunt lives across the border in Scotshouse. My opinion of Ireland is that it is your home. I came back because I wanted to live here.'

He and Janet, an antiques expert from County Antrim, ran the house as a business as well. They were redecorating it bit by bit, with Northern Ireland Tourist Board support. Their guests were of the wealthy corporate classes, who came to combine hunting, shooting and fishing with conferences and executive training courses. The couple were known to those who stayed in their house as Alan and Janet. 'The great Edwardian house parties were held not only for the benefit of the guests who came to stay but for the hosts – they wanted to share their house, their park and their sport with their friends. They needed entertainment. They regarded it as a favour to them,' the viscount told a business magazine. Colebrooke guests were warned not to be alarmed if a peacock landed on their windowsill. The flamboyant birds paced the huge lawns in front of the house, their colours exotic and outrageous in a place where the normal colours were muted lakeland greens and greys.

Lord Brookeborough had been an army officer in England, and when he returned to Fermanagh in the early seventies he wished to join the local regiment, the UDR. There was a complication about his transfer, and he went to see his local MP about it. That was Frank Maguire, a well-known republican. 'I went to see him at his office above his pub. On top of a chest of drawers was a silhouette. I asked him was it Roger Casement. Casement was a cousin of my mother's.

He was impressed. He wrote the necessary letter for me, even though he knew it was a sort of joke. He was a good sport.'

The viscount's idea of community comfortably included the big house. His role as a lieutenant colonel in the local regiment was the traditional one, and he was an Orangeman too. 'Just an ordinary Orangeman,' he stressed. His grandfather had been one of the founders of the B Specials, returning from the First World War to 'defend my birthplace'. He had organised local vigilantes. In 1918 Nationalists had won control over key local councils along the border and Sinn Féin was strong in Fermanagh.

Sir Basil had got out the old UVF rifles stored in Colebrooke and armed his men, urging that the British commander in Ireland recognise them. Otherwise, 'hotheads will take matters into their own hands'. It was suggested that he arm his vigilantes with whistles to summon the Royal Irish Constabulary. Brooke and his men treated this with derision: 'Dublin can go to hell . . . we'll look after ourselves' (quoted in Bardon, p. 474). In 1925 the Boundary Commission proposed to trim out of the North part of south Armagh, part of south-west Fermanagh and part of west Tyrone, reducing the 300-mile border by 50 miles. The North would have gained a little of Donegal and of Monaghan.

However, the Unionists were determined to yield not an inch. The Specials fought many small, hard battles with the IRA, and had shown that they could virtually seal the border. The commission's work was scrapped. The small village of Pettigo, which was to have become part of the North, was instead cut in two. The houses on the west side of the River Termon, still called Pettigo, remained in Donegal in the South, while on the other side of the river, the village of Tullyhomman in County Fermanagh was created. Pettigo has a statue of an IRA man pointing his gun across the river. Locals called it 'the Quiet Man'.

Alan Brooke joined the UDR 'because I wanted to contribute to peace and security'. I asked him if it wasn't divisive, given the hostility of nationalists to the force. He said most people supported the soldiers, and welcomed their checkpoints. 'I joined for several reasons. I was unmarried, and had time available. On the roads one would be stopping and meeting friends from both sides of the community. And, while I'm not really political, I support Northern Ireland. When things were bad, it was tremendous to have a right to know what was going on. I could go to the mart and know what people's problems were. It is a matter of being aware of your surroundings. In my view, 97 per cent of the people are against terrorism.'

He was critical of the business classes for their failure to actively support the security forces. The UDR was drawn largely from the farming and working-class communities. 'There was a lot of killing around here for a time until the border checkpoints went in, in 1981. They were killed off duty. I would say we are soft targets. I had soldiers living right on the border. By and large the business classes, while they supported peace, didn't support the fight against terrorism. They complained about the disruption checkpoints caused, and they jumped in their Jags and headed for tennis and tea parties.'

He insisted that Fermanagh was a well-integrated county, not polarised like south Armagh or west Belfast. Quite a few local Catholics had joined the UDR. 'We would say there are a lot of Fermanagh Catholics who are unionists with a small u. Any Protestant you meet here will tell you they have Roman Catholic friends.' Then he offered one of his benign and simplifying explanations of how things really were. 'The IRA will tell you it is hard for Catholics here in Northern Ireland. How is it then that these people didn't move five miles to be south of the border? In England, when there was the oil boon, people moved north. People are relatively mobile. If it was true that these people hated living in Northern Ireland, why didn't they move? The answer is because they were quite happy.'

As a hereditary peer, his future in the House of Lords was uncertain given New Labour's reforms. 'It is by an accident of birth that I am there but it is a wonderful opportunity to say what you want and ask questions about things that affect Northern Ireland. Gerry Fitt would happily say he is a good friend. We co-operate. He is a good guy.' There was an eagerness to present references – Lord Fitt, erstwhile Republican Labour MP for West Belfast and founding member of the SDLP, joined the people living on the mountain to vouch for the viscount's good character.

In the Lords he had raised farming issues – seeking a rescue package for the hill farmers of Fermanagh and other west-of-the-Bann areas, a return to the farm diversification schemes which Labour had frozen pending a review, and, promoting the interests of the FEAR group. FEAR, which predates south Armagh's FAIR, stands for Fear Encouraged Abandonment of Roots, and was a group of Protestants from along the border who were seeking compensation. Some of them had been forced to move out and sell their land, others had kept the land but were unable to farm it. Explaining that property had been allowed to become severely run-down, he told the Lords in 1998 that the border was 'a dangerous area'.

Janet Brooke came in, eager for the interview to finish. 'Now. How are we doing in here?' she asked briskly. It was evident that there was work to be done. People in wellingtons passed to and fro outside. The viscount wanted me to visit the church in the demesne before I left. On the way across the gravel in front of the house, he told me that he was a lord-in-waiting to the Queen. When I asked what that was, he seemed surprised by my ignorance, and rather offended. 'I represent the Queen at certain functions,' he said.

The church, a pretty stone building from the eighteenth century, was packed with memorials to the Brookes, commemorating, by and large, their military service to the empire, from the Battle of Waterloo to the Afghan campaign of 1880, to the UDR's border duties during the most recent Troubles. There was Field Marshal Alan Francis Brooke: 'He was a Knight of the Garter and Order of Bath. So was his nephew, Sir Basil Brooke. It was unusual to have two Knights of the Garter with only five years between them.' There was a Francis Theophilus Brooke who was killed by the IRA in Dublin in the 1920s. Major General Edward Basil Brooke, according to his plaque, 'scorned delights and lived laborious days'. 'Makes him sounds like a right old bore,' murmured his descendant.

The famous Sir Basil was commemorated in a glass screen engraved with scenes from his illustrious life. 'Basil Stanlake Brooke 1888–1973. 5th Baronet, 1st Viscount, CBE, Military Cross, Knight of the Garter, Croix de guerre. Minister of Commerce. Raised B Specials, county grand master, deputy grand master of Ireland, Minister of Agriculture, her majesty's lieutenant for Co. Fermanagh, Captain 10th Royal Hussars, MP for Lisnaskea, 20 years Prime Minister of Northern Ireland.' He and his wife were, the plaque stated, 'widely respected in all walks of life ... for their courage and leadership in preserving peace in this province'.

Lord Brookeborough drew my attention to a memorial to Henry Francis Brooke, who served with the Bombay army and was killed on the walls of Kandahar. 'He was the last to leave and lost his life in the noble endeavour to bring to safety a wounded brother officer,' it said. 'Quite a duty for a brigadier general!' said the viscount. He gestured around the church. 'It doesn't entirely explain our attitude, but . . . the family has sometimes been known as the fighting Brookes.'

'THIS IS A VERY CATHOLIC PLACE'

'It has got that there's only one Protestant living in Rosslea village, and that is our son,' said Doreen. 'It has been nerve-wracking betimes, living out here on the border. Quite a few people have been shot around here. A young girl was blown up at the bus stop, some good friends were shot, policemen, a shopkeeper. He was the last Protestant shopkeeper in Rosslea, a God-fearing man who did no harm to anyone. These times would leave you very nervous. You sort of forget. We never passed any remarks living up here. We get on OK with our neighbours. This is a very Catholic place.'

Doreen and her family lived just a mile or two away from the splendours of Colebrooke Park, in a typical Fermanagh farmhouse, plain and simple, an old house comfortably modernised. The house sat on top of a hill, surrounded by tidy barns and sheds. There was a long winding lane up to the 'street', or yard. There were several other houses along the lane. The house overlooked the big green hangars of two British army checkpoints, now abandoned. This had been the 'home place' of Doreen's husband, John, the place where he grew up and had lived all his life.

In 1883 Rosslea had been the scene of the 'Invasion of Ulster', when nationalists called a meeting as part of the campaign for a government in Dublin. The 5th Baron Rossmore, who was the Orange Order's Monaghan grand master, organised to bring some seven thousand counter-demonstrators. He called the nationalists, five thousand of whom had gathered, 'rebels and scavengers'. The flooded River Finn kept the two sides apart.

The fields around John and Doreen's house were bounded by a

tributary of the Finn, a stream the local people called the Border River. 'Most of our land you've to go through the South and back into the North again,' said Doreen. 'It was very inconvenient when the roads were blocked. You had to make a big detour.' Nevertheless, she had been happier when there were blocked roads, barriers, checkpoints and soldiers in the army post. 'You felt safer,' she said. 'We did go through a hard time here. On the third of September 1991 my husband was at a vestry meeting – we are in the Church of Ireland – and I went out for a walk. The children were in bed. This van drove up in the street and some of the children said, it must be the IRA. Karen hid behind the piano. Norman took his gun and pointed it. They caught Irwin on the stairs. They threatened to kill him if Norman didn't drop his gun. He has never got over that. He is nervous yet.

'Kenneth jumped out a bedroom window. Leanne was asleep in bed. They tied up three of the children. They took Karen and Norman with them. They took a shotgun belonging to David, our son, and they took them to where the bomb was, in a trailer down by the Border River. They wanted them to drive the bomb to the checkpoint. But the trailer had sank into the ground and it couldn't be got out. They sent the children home in their bare feet.'

Her husband, John, joined us while she was telling the story. He had been out working late on the farm. It was late summer and there was a lot to be done. 'How long ago it is and you've still that fear,' he said. Doreen nodded. 'It took a lot of work with the children,' she said. I was puzzled about the references to the guns. How could children have, and be prepared to use, guns? And Doreen didn't seem the sort to go out and leave a houseful of children unattended. John talked about the son who was supposed to drive the bomb as 'our cub'. But it turned out that the older children, including David, Norman and Karen, had been over the age of eighteen. Families stayed together late in rural Fermanagh, and children were children till they married.

The incident had not been the first of its kind. The proxy bombs represented one of the IRA's most shocking tactics – in October 1990 Patsy Gillespie, a Catholic man who worked in the canteen of a British army base in Derry, was forced to drive such a bomb into a checkpoint on the edge of the city. He was killed, along with five British soldiers.

The following April a woman was forced to carry a bomb in her bag into Belleek RUC station, where she worked as a part-time cleaner. The bomb exploded but no one was hurt.

Another Protestant family in Fermanagh had left after the father was beaten and tied up in the house while the son was made to drive a bomb to the same checkpoint that was the intended target the night Doreen's family had been kidnapped. In that case the IRA had beaten the young man's knees with iron bars so that he was unable to get out of the tractor when he reached the checkpoint. British soldiers had to drag him off the vehicle. The bomb, containing 3,500 pounds of explosives, had the distinction of being the Provisional's largest. It failed to go off. That was in November 1990, a week after the then British Prime Minister Margaret Thatcher had visited the army on the Fermanagh border and had stated, 'We must never, never, give in to terrorism, never' (quoted in Bardon, p. 804).

Neighbours of John and Doreen had gone from Rosslea after their homes were burned, or they were threatened, and the couple had once again witnessed the IRA's capabilities when, in 1994, a local woman out walking her dog had found the bloody body of a young woman on their land. Caroline Moreland had been tortured and shot in the head before she was dumped behind the 'dragon's teeth' barriers with which the British army blocked border roads and lanes. She was a young republican from Belfast. The IRA had claimed she was an informer, but there were suspicions that her murder had more to do with a settling of personal scores before the ceasefire.

Despite all this, John said he and his family would never leave. 'Maybe it's the type of us,' he said. 'That is what they would like.' But both he and Doreen were very angry. 'This is what Sinn Féin IRA has been doing on the border this thirty years,' said John. 'The idea is to get the land into Roman Catholic hands. I don't belong to any organisation, I'm not in the Orange, I'm not in politics, and I'm not in the security forces. I drive a school bus and I farm my land and I go to my church. Why was I picked on? I'm just an ordinary Protestant. That's why I'm so bitter about it.

'Over the years you see what is going on. The IRA didn't get a boy to come up here from Dublin without local help. I know that some of our neighbours helped to plan that, to let it happen. Some of the Roman

Catholics about here would be kind of bitter.' He didn't go into any possible reasons for such bitterness. 'I live neighbourly. I'd get up at three in the morning to go out and help with calving. But the IRA Sinn Féin is pressurising people. You can read between the lines and you hear what is going on. The RC people can't say anything because they daren't. Look at Lisnaskea, Enniskillen, Rosslea. You've an IRA presence in all these towns. There is no doubt about it, they have control over the Roman Catholic people. See if a Protestant got shot tonight in Rosslea – would those ones come out and say what they seen?' He shook his head disparagingly.

But believing that neighbours acted, or failed to act, out of fear, did not excuse them. 'We got no support after that happened. Our friends came, but no one else,' said Doreen angrily. 'No Roman Catholics.' John laughed bitterly. 'Aye, and a funny thing,' he said. 'None of them ever saw anything.' 'Yet there's times John would land in the street and the phone would ring and they'd be looking him to come over and help,' said Doreen.

A documentary film had been made about John and Doreen, and the experience their family had been through. Doreen said they had been inundated with calls from reporters, and that some of the reports which appeared had exaggerated the incident, and that had embarrassed her. The BBC had phoned, asking would she like to contribute to *Legacy*, a two-minute slot before the nine o'clock news every morning, during which people told a story of their experience of the Troubles. And yet, both Doreen and John insisted that the Protestant story had never been told. This was a widely held view. 'According to what I hear, most of the Protestants was drove out of Londonderry,' said John. 'When a Roman Catholic gets thrown out, there's a lot of shouting about it, but when thousands of Protestants have been driven out of their homes there is no word about it.' Doreen agreed: 'The Protestants never spoke up. Never got the message across.' She had taken part in the Long March in the summer of 1999. The march, from Derry to Portadown in time for Drumcree, was led by people with a banner emblazoned with 'The Real Victims'.

For all that the border had brought trouble to them, they were determined that it should remain. They were British and would never be Irish. They had nothing but contempt for the authorities in the

South. 'The night they did that to our family, those boys had a big Shogun jeep waiting across the Border River. All they had to do was wade over to it and off they went. No one was ever got for it. But there was supposed to be a checkpoint on the far side that night. It is always the same story. They just turn a blind eye.'

As a border family, long established in the area, both John and Doreen had relatives in the Republic. 'I don't believe Protestants get fair play there,' said John. 'I've seen things happening over the years, in farming. There came out a law when Charlie Haughey was in charge. The Land Commission took land off farmers. I know small farmers, Protestants, looked for some of that land and didn't get it. These were men had no other jobs. But I know Roman Catholics that had jobs and they got land. My own cousin lived where there was a whole estate dividing up, and his Catholic neighbours all got their big plots.'

Land was the thing. John defended the right of Protestants not to sell it to Catholics, because of his belief that Catholics were complicit in the 'Sinn Féin IRA plot' to drive Protestants away and seize their lands. However, he was resentful of the fact that Catholics would not, he said, sell to Protestants, so that his farm was made up of 'wee parcels of land, here and there'. The BSE crisis, which saw Northern Irish beef banned in the EU, had played havoc with his livelihood, and his income had dropped. 'The farmer isn't in a good way of going. Our beef should never have been banned. There never was any ban of their beef across the border. The funny thing about it is, we can't go up the South with our cattle and yet they can come down here with theirs.'

They were pessimistic about the peace process. 'You are not going to see peace in Northern Ireland,' said John. 'It is just going to keep travelling on and on. When the people was asked to vote, we were told there would be decommissioning. They were conned into it. There can be no peace with guns. Where was the shift in Sinn Féin? If anyone gave in, it was the unionist people. The other side gave nothing.' 'If you started to think about it, your nerves would go,' said Doreen. 'They never tried to defeat the IRA,' said John. 'Neither North nor South.'

John suggested I talk to Canon Edwy Kille, the local rector. The canon had written a leaflet about the kidnap. It described the effect on the youngest of the girls, 'it was the horror of those hooded hoodlums that haunted her tender heart'. He wrote that when the bomb got bogged down, 'The masters of the murderous minions ... could only shout "abort".'

Canon Kille was extremely wary of talking to writers or reporters. He said he had been 'stitched up' before. However, he agreed to speak to me, on condition that I showed him what I wrote. I had read some of his sermons, which were published as booklets. In one, preached at the cathedral in Enniskillen in 1981, he said, 'It has often been said that it is not a religious war in Ireland. I would beg to contradict that thought. I would say that at the very heart of our troubles we are in a religious war ... I speak of the warfare of good and evil ...' In the same sermon he called for more police along the border, because of the murders.

There were also leaflets published by the Irish Church Missions in Dublin, where he had trained. These were a response to a 1995 encyclical on ecumenism by Pope John Paul II, and argued that the Roman Church's interpretation of the Bible was wrong on key issues. These included papal infallibility, the role of Mary, 'the Lord's Mother', and the meaning of the sacraments. When I showed him how I'd written up his interview he said I had misunderstood everything and I could not publish it.

'THE SOONER A UNITED IRELAND, THE BETTER'

One of the effects of segregation in a community is that people who do not exclusively identify with one side find themselves displaced. This had been the argument of some socialist opponents of the Belfast Agreement that it institutionalised sectarian division. Proportionality was achieved by describing people as unionist, nationalist or 'other'.

Eileen was a social services worker who lived on a farm on the Fermanagh border with Cavan. There was an ongoing dispute in the area involving a local school at Aughadrumsee, which had been picketed by Protestant parents after jobs in the canteen had been given by the education authority to Catholics, jobs which the parents said should have gone to Protestants.

'I come from a mixed marriage, though we were brought up as Protestants,' she said. 'My parents had liberal views. Speaking disrespectfully of Catholics would not have been allowed in our house, and we were never let get involved in skiffs between the children from the two schools.'

The house she lived in was her husband's 'home place'. A big old farmhouse on top of a hill, it looked out over rolling fields – and the empty army posts. Because of incidents such as the one Doreen's family had been caught up in, the checkpoints had been closed. 'When they built those in the early nineties I felt it was an affront to our privacy,' said Eileen. 'I'm sure they can see into our rooms. But we came to look on them as protective.' She had, however, worried about the risk that her family might get caught up in booby trap bombs or attacks on the army. 'We didn't really go cycling or walking so much any more.'

In the eighties she had been horrified when the IRA murdered a succession of Protestant businessmen in the nearby border village of Newtownbutler. 'I wanted to show my abhorrence. But the meetings which were held in protest were addressed by people like Paisley, and I didn't want to be connected with a very strong Protestant voice. I never wanted to be aligned with Orangemen or paramilitaries either. In the end I went to the meetings to be a number in a crowd, but I took no part. You knew even by being there you were potentially making yourself a target – the nationalist feeling would have been very strong too. They'd have been watching who was there.'

Her children had suffered for their liberal upbringing too. They had stopped taking the school bus because of taunts from Catholics, but had also got into trouble with Protestants when they wouldn't sing anti-Catholic songs. 'It's a difficult course for them, but I'm proud of the way they've managed it.' Her daughter, rushing around, in and out of the room, getting ready for a school trip to France, smiled at her.

After the murders, Eileen said, a lot of her Protestant neighbours moved away from the border. 'That left us very isolated and the community very polarised.' The nearest village to her home had a cluster of Union Jacks and Ulster flags, but she said that, in general, in the area, the villages were Catholic, while the land was owned by Protestants. She said there was no way land would be sold across the religious divide. Protestants banded with Protestants to hold on to the land they had, and Catholics who had land did the same. Her parents had defied this unwritten rule. 'My parents sold their land to the highest bidder, who happened to be a Catholic,' she said. 'My mother used to say, "We are all made of flesh and blood." They reared nine of us, and they did it successfully. There is not one of us a strong Protestant, and there are mixed marriages in the family. My parents were ordinary country folk.' She associated 'strong' Protestantism with sectarianism.

She had been active in the local community association, and had worked hard to persuade Protestants to get involved. 'The idea is to build up community spirit and pride. But working together is very much surface working. It would take very little to topple it. Deep down, I don't believe there are cultural bonds. There's very little tolerance here for the Protestant tradition. They have a great sense of loss. They feel that no matter what they give, they are going to be bullied. Protestants are more reticent than nationalists – they don't want to hurt the feelings of the other side.'

Protestants were less community-spirited than Catholics, she felt. 'Catholics look on grants as getting something they deserve from the system. The Protestant work ethic really is very strong. You are really only valued for your work and you work all the time. You are responsible for yourself and your family. You stand on your own and you look out for yourself. It is very individualistic. The converse is that you don't share much. You have not been taught to have trust in the community, the communal. It is really almost impossible to get Protestants involved in community things.' She said Protestants tended to base their social life around the Orange hall, and church.

Eileen seemed always to try to look at things from all sides, before making up her mind. As a child, she had known about the IRA, through stories of the burning of buildings back in the twenties, and then again in the fifties. She spoke of the B men as their Protestant equivalent, and said she knew that Catholics saw the UDR as 'armed Protestants'. She saw both sides of the Orange parades dispute too. Her family had attended the parades when she was a child, but by the time she was a teenager, she felt uncomfortable at them. She believed that the bewilderment of Protestants as to why they should be stopped doing something they'd done for years was genuine. 'But equally, Catholics would tell you the bands used to taunt them. They'd even name the drummers.

'My father-in-law, who was a Protestant, used to say that if the Orange Order had behaved itself, this wouldn't have happened. Some of the Orange lodges would be very opposed to the community association. They'd see people like me as being, well, sort of treacherous.' Oddly, though, the old people mixed. Eileen thought maybe it was because they had been integrated when they were children, before partition.

'Protestant society is more staid. Catholics are more fun-loving. I see that at work too, even in hotels – the ones run by Protestants are different. Protestants are more reserved, shyer. You don't let yourself go. Protestants are worriers too. And they have difficulty asking for help. Catholics will ask for help, but they'll also give it. The thing about the work ethic is, you can lose your soul in all that.'

She had refused to vote for the Belfast Agreement, though she broadly supported it. She did not like the way it had been presented, as though anyone who demurred in any way from it was against peace. She supported Trimble's refusal to govern with Sinn Féin in the absence of decommissioning. 'Why do people need guns in a democracy?' Her political conclusion was, though, that Northern Ireland had not worked, and was finished. 'At this stage I think the sooner a united Ireland, the better. That, and a bit of dignity for the people. I think that might be the only way to stop the futile killings. I'm not so foolish as to think it will happen easily though.'

'IF YOU GET BITTER, IT RUINS YOUR LIFE'

When Simon Bullock was small he remembered his father telling him about how masked men came and blew up Aghalane bridge beyond the house, and about the days the customs hut was blown up, the day the boobytrap claymore mines were found, laid for the army, and the petrol station burned. These things had happened in the seventies. 'It was some handling. But, as a child, it is like some old story. We thought it was great crack. We'd always be asking him to tell us again. It is only when you are older that you realise it wasn't crack at all.'

The Bullocks' house was a lovely eighteenth-century thatched cottage, under trees beside the broken stone arch of the bridge built during the Famine. Simon's mother, Joan, a hospitable and friendly woman, used to bring lost motorists in for tea to her busy farm kitchen. There were plenty of them – a lot of maps did not show which border roads were passable and which were not. A wide, new concrete bridge was opened in 1999 to carry the European highway into Belturbet, a Cavan town caught in a post-partition decline, exacerbated by the recent closures. It looked surprised by this invasion of the modern. Now the callers at the thatched house came on cabin cruisers – the Woodford River was part of the Shannon–Erne waterway.

Now in his twenties, Simon had inherited his father's farm along with his brothers, and he was about to get married. He and his young wife would move into the old family home beside the blown-up bridge. Joan and his brothers would move to Tommy Bullock's old house, a house with a sad and violent history.

Simon was only a baby when a carload of IRA men crossed the border by the bridge outside his home and drove up to his father's cousin's house, a big old stone place up a lane from the road. It was a fine house – Tommy had been the land agent for Lord Erne. He was also a part-time farmer, and a part-time soldier in the UDR. He and his wife Emily were watching the television news. It was a tense time. Internment, bombs, rioting. Locally, three Protestant families along the border had been attacked. In September 1972 the gunmen murdered Emily when she answered their knock on the door, and then they murdered Tommy in the kitchen.

An uncle of Simon's spoke about the murders on television – in response the IRA blew up the filling station he and Simon's father owned. Loyalist paramilitaries blew up the old bridge to stop the IRA crossing from Cavan. When a temporary bridge was put up in its place they used it themselves to plant bombs in Belturbet in December 1972, killing two young people.

Tommy's house lay empty and untouched until 1997, when the Bullocks began the job of restoring it. Joan showed me through the big empty rooms. We entered by the back door, the way the gunmen came, and she described the murders. 'However,' she said with a sigh, 'that's in the past now. It is a beautiful place, isn't it?'

They were big dairy farmers, and had bought the land which linked the old house at the bridge with Tommy's house, so that the brothers between them owned all the land for almost two miles along the Woodford River. I asked Joan if it was true what people said, that land never passed between people of different religions along the border. She shook her head impatiently. 'That's a lot of old nonsense. Some of the land we bought, we bought from a Catholic man.'

What Simon remembered most distinctly about his childhood was its isolation. Once the bridge was gone, the family was cut off from all the nearest neighbours. To visit people three miles away took forty-five minutes. The next village back from the border in Fermanagh was Catholic. School was across Lough Erne in Lisnaskea. There were bridges, and then one of them was blown up too. 'It was a major mission to go and hang out with your mates.' His father had land on the other side of the border, half a mile from the house. But without the bridge, it was a twelve-mile journey, so he sold it. Joan remembered an ardent bull swimming across the Woodford from the fields of Cavan to get at the Fermanagh cows.

It was a society of farmers, soldiers and policemen, and many of them were killed. 'It seemed like half the kids in my brother's class had lost their father. The headmaster was shot and killed. I wouldn't have minded joining the army – my uncle had been in Egypt and all, but the recruiting officer said they couldn't take me because they didn't want people from families that had already been bereaved. Obviously, I couldn't join the UDR and come back and farm on the border.'

Simon said he considered himself Northern Irish first, British second. 'We are part of the United Kingdom. We're going to have a united Europe so a united Ireland wouldn't be so ...' He paused, considering the import of what he was going to say, and changed tack, slightly. 'I have little respect for some of the politicians down south. They seem to be very ignorant of the North. It is all right for them in London and Dublin to dictate to us, but unless they know what they are talking about ...' He did not think that Sinn Féin or loyalists should be allowed into government without giving up their guns. 'The violence didn't stop with the ceasefires. I remember going in to the cinema in Enniskillen to see *Titanic*. We found the cinema had been blown up. That was the year before the Omagh bomb, and there was another bomb at the Killyhevlin Hotel. Nobody was making any fuss, but you could see Omagh coming.' The bombs he mentioned were the work of breakaway republicans. Simon's fiancée, a physiotherapist, worked with people who had been injured in the Omagh bomb.

The reopening of the border had been a revelation. Simon and his brothers had taken to going for a drink in Belturbet and the other small towns in Cavan. 'It is like as if we were living on an island and we didn't know it. They speak with a different accent. Mum said when she came here there was no difference. A woman in one of the pubs thought I was from Glasgow. The towns are so different too. Our towns have been bombed and wrecked and rebuilt – theirs are so old-fashioned. The pubs have old counters with wooden shelves behind them.'

He said he had no problem mixing with Catholics, and did so through the Ulster Farmers' Union and the Enniskillen Diving Club. 'You have to rely on people to help you in diving. I'd risk my life for any of those guys, regardless.' His fiancée was, like him, a regular attender at the Church of Ireland. 'I suppose there's a bit of pressure to marry into your own Church. People who stay here tend to do that. For people who move away, it is different. If I have kids, it wouldn't bother me.'

Not long before our conversation, Simon had walked in late to a farmers' meeting in County Fermanagh, a Department of Agriculture briefing about soil analysis. The hall was packed, but nobody had sat down beside a local Sinn Féin councillor. Simon took the seat. 'I didn't feel any the worse for it.' His mother said more than half of her friends would be Catholics. 'People round here weren't aggressive. They agreed too well. I would have hated to bring up a family wanted nothing to do with the other side,' she said. 'If you get bitter, it ruins your life, and you embitter your family and the thing goes on.'

BALLYMONEY
More to That Than Meets the Eye

'And Aaron shall lay both his hands upon the head of
the live goat, and confess over him all the iniquities of the
children of Israel, and all their transgressions in all their sins . . .
And the goat shall bear upon him all their iniquities unto
a land not inhabited . . .'

from Leviticus, 16:21–22

'THIS IS NOT A SECTARIAN TOWN'

'There was more to that than meets the eye,' said the woman, leaning forward confidentially. 'You wouldn't know what it was about, but there is no way it was sectarian. This is not a sectarian town.' We were sitting in the spacious drawing room of her bungalow, its big windows looking out over well-tended gardens, the bungalow next door just visible through a discreet line of shrubs. She was talking about the murders of the little Quinn children, Richard, Mark and Jason, who had burned to death in the early hours of 12 July 1998, after loyalists threw a massive petrol bomb into their home in a Ballymoney housing estate.

Along with the traditional Eleventh night bonfires and partying, there had been roadblocks in the area in protest at the continuing ban on the Orange Order march at Drumcree. UVF men, and men wearing their Orange sashes manned the roadblocks. The RUC had cleared one from the road at Carnany shortly before the killers arrived. This was the dawning of the day Paisley had called 'the decider'. He predicted that the Orangemen would get down the Garvaghy Road: 'They'd be far better letting them down before 12 July because anybody here with any imagination knows what's going to happen on 12 July.'

The Quinn children's grandmother, who also lived in the Carnany estate, had been among the hundreds of Catholics intimidated out of their homes across the North, particularly in County Antrim, in the preceding week. Five Catholic families in Carnany had each received an envelope containing a bullet and a message from the UVF. 'Get out now.' On the morning of the Twelfth, within hours of the murders, the RUC stated that they were treating the deaths of the Quinn boys as sectarian murder.

This woman, middle-aged, kindly, an evangelical Presbyterian from the professional classes, was saying what almost everyone else I met from the Protestant community in Ballymoney said, in one way or another. 'You wouldn't know what goes on in these housing estates.' 'There may have been other factors involved.' 'We don't know the whole story there.' The Protestant people of the town were adamant: 'It was not sectarian. This is not a sectarian town.'

From a distance Ballymoney had seemed a peaceful enough place over the long years of the Troubles. It was predominantly Protestant, small, nestled on the western edge of Paisley's Bible Belt heartland in north Antrim, but a town where a Catholic minority seemed to live quietly. Paisley had represented the area in Westminster for almost thirty years. It would have been what the RUC might call a 'soft area', which is to say, one in which it was not threatened by the IRA, although one woman, a Protestant, had been killed by an IRA bomb on Main Street in 1972.

Parades, and disputes about them, brought confrontation. In 1995 hand-to-hand fighting broke out in the nearby village of Dunloy, and there were claims that ceremonial swords and hurleys were drawn. The village is almost entirely nationalist, but has an old Presbyterian church and a big, plain Orange hall, which had been daubed with republican graffiti. The loyal Orders refused to meet the residents, and efforts at mediation were unsuccessful, largely because of the intervention of the Spirit of Drumcree group. On several occasions the RUC had stopped the loyalists outside the village. Some protesters shouted out the names and personal details of RUC men, one of whom was Constable Greg Taylor. In another menacing incident, just days before the Quinn murders, hundreds of Orangemen and their supporters blocked approach roads to the village for several hours.

The dispute about Dunloy turned particularly bitter when supporters of the loyalists set up pickets at several Catholic churches in the region. One of these, at the Saturday evening mass at Harryville chapel in Ballymena, lasted twenty months, at which point the local priest suspended the service. Although the Orange Order condemned the picket, leading Orangemen took part, including Ballymoney DUP councillor, and former Irish rugby player, David Tweed. Portadown hardliners attempted to revive the picket in April 1999, without success.

The picket at Harryville was frightening. The demonstrators attacked Catholics, threw bricks through their car windows, and on one occasion broke into a house and beat up people in their beds. They also hurled abuse, grunted like pigs at the worshippers, and tried to burn out both the chapel and the priests' house in its grounds. Placards referred to the local mayor, UUP Councillor James Currie, as 'chicken Currie', because he had opposed the action and shown solidarity with the Catholics. Pastor Alan Campbell preached a sermon in the town, in which he claimed that what was really going on in Harryville 'is the ancient battle between the true church, Protestantism, and the Whore, the Beast, and the Baal worshippers within Catholicism' (quoted in Brewer, p. 124).

But Ballymoney remained quiet. Then, in June 1997, a loyalist mob set upon Greg Taylor, who was off duty, having a drink in a bar in the centre of town. They kicked him to death in the street. Witnesses said the crowd, a local flute band and its supporters, had recognised the constable from the barriers at Dunloy. Two men were convicted of murder, two admitted manslaughter and others were found guilty of affray.

People in Ballymoney disputed the evidence about this murder too. 'That was nothing got to do with Dunloy,' said a teacher. 'I doubt there was more to that than meets the eye.' Others said it was 'just drink'. Certainly drink had played its part. The murdered man had been drinking, and one of those who killed him had been in a drunken sleep in the bar before he joined the rampage outside and set upon the policeman. Witnesses described Taylor's head being kicked like a football.

'AM I A DARKIE?'

The stout country man was indignant. The young man in a suit appeared to have neglected to give him the handout and he was up in arms. Rising from his seat in the main chamber of the town hall, he shouted, 'Am I a darkie?' The young man turned, slightly alarmed. 'Here, boy, am I a darkie?' the older man shouted, while his friends sniggered. When he got his leaflet, which asked for responses to the meeting, he didn't read it, but threw it ostentatiously on the floor.

It was Ballymoney's turn to host the Independent Commission on Policing for Northern Ireland, the Right Honourable Chris Patten's roadshow designed to elicit the views of the North's public about the future of the RUC. The commission had been established under the Belfast Agreement, and had roused strong feelings in the unionist community. Patten, a Tory wet, had been the final governor of Britain's last colonial outpost in the Far East, and this was seen by many as an ominous portent. As anti-agreement UUP MP Willie Thompson put it, 'Most unionists will remember Mr Patten as he stood lowering the Union Jack on Hong Kong and what we find in Northern Ireland is that the British government are slowly but surely lowering the Union Jack here' (quoted in the *Sunday Tribune*, 3 May 1998).

The Ballymoney meeting was held in the afternoon, and the town hall, with its red velvet drapes and sombre portraits of former Unionist grandees, was not packed. Most of those who had come were in late middle age or were elderly. A lot of grey heads, mostly men. On the platform, Sir John Smith, a bluff Englishman who congratulated Ballymoney on having the best cheese-and-pickle rolls in Ulster, conveyed apologies from Chris Patten who was unable to attend. Rowdy old men in the back rows muttered, 'Lies.' 'Chicken.'

Bill Mathews, a well-known local surgeon and Alliance Party figure, spoke about the honourable role the RUC had played in bearing the brunt of terrorism. However, he urged that since Northern Ireland had six counties and Ulster nine, it would be more accurate to change the force's name to the Northern Ireland Police Service. There were hisses from the back rows, and murmurs of, 'Shame.' John Robb, retired surgeon and founder of the liberal New Ireland group, agreed with the proposed name change. 'After all, the RUC originated in a paramilitary-type force defending the frontier,' he said. 'Thon's one buck eejit,' one of the back-row men muttered. A middle-aged woman said she was very angry at Robb and Mathews. 'They want the Royal out of it and they want Ulster out of it,' she said.

Then a man who described himself as an 83-year-old Presbyterian said that Dublin was a safe haven for terrorists, that he supported the police but that 'unlike nationalists, law-abiding soft touches were discriminated against'. He said that a man who had justified stoning the police had been made a lord in England. That was Gerry Fitt. The government and Church leaders 'got off the hook' after the Enniskillen bomb by using Gordon Wilson, who, despite losing his daughter, had said he forgave the bombers. The old Presbyterian said that after the IRA bomb in Coleraine in June 1973 (which killed six pensioners) the council had said it brought people closer together. This was a disgrace. Finally, he said a Union flag which had flown at his premises for thirty years had recently been removed. The police had caught the perpetrator but he was not prosecuted: 'Yet and all, they arrest members of the Orange Order.'

A mild old man told a homely story about how his house had been burgled and the RUC had been 'so pleasant'. They had even taken the fingerprints of his little grandson because the child was upset. The people heard him out. Then a succession of people stood up and said the commission was a 'con trick', like the Anglo-Irish Agreement before it. That all the British were interested in was appeasing the IRA so as to keep bombs out of English cities, that there was no peace, that there were hidden agendas. That the 'so-called' agreement was signed 'at the behest of mumblers and groaners' from the nationalist community.

Former councillor James Simpson said we would have been ruled by terrorists if it hadn't been for the RUC. He said police morale had been damaged by the release of prisoners. 'Think of the lives that were lost putting them in prison,' he said. John Leslie, former local UDR commander, big house owner and father of James the UUP Assembly member, said the Hunt commission's ruling thirty years previously that the RUC should be disarmed had been wrong, and that the RUC was 'as uncorrupt a force as you'll find'. He was applauded.

The DUP mayor, Frank Campbell, said the council had in the past offered the RUC the freedom of the borough, and it supported the force. Someone said that you had to remember that one section of the community had tried to take control by armed insurrection. 'You don't fix something that is not broke,' said a man. 'The RUC won the peace – now they must be let maintain it,' said another.

Mo Mowlam was described as a 'Johnny come lately, throwing her arms around terrorists'. Unionists hated Mowlam's demonstrative ways, the kisses and hugs she dispensed, the way she threw off her wig and scratched her head, kicked off her shoes and cursed. They were incensed to see her kissing their enemies.

A GP spoke of the sense of failure among the police, and the fear they had of the IRA. The RUC needed weapons and it would be un-reasonable to expect the force to take in ex-paramilitaries and crim-inals. The only reason Catholics didn't join was because of republican intimidation. Then a Christian from Portrush spoke: 'I speak for the quiet God-fearing people of Northern Ireland,' he said. 'We have heard a lot about consent, but God's emphasis is different. You don't consent to authority – you submit.'

There were contributions from several serving or former members of the RUC and other branches of the security forces. One man said he had served for nineteen years in this 'gallant force', and his father, also a policeman, had been shot in 1981. 'His crime was to serve his country,' he said. 'He gave up his life in guarding its judiciary, after years of picking up the mutilated bodies of murdered colleagues, and carrying their coffins.'

Another RUC man mentioned that the commission's terms of re-ference stated that the force was 82 per cent male and 90 per cent Protestant. He said senior officers had 'bent over backwards' to change this. 'We all have Catholic friends in the force. I've never known any of them to state that they were harassed. Catholics came up to me at Drumcree and thanked me for what we were doing. Our crest has the crown, the harp and garlands of shamrock. Why should that change because 20 per cent of the population has spent twenty years trying to destroy this society?' 'This force is a proud force but it is completely and utterly demoralised,' said another.

A 'ratepayer from Ballymoney' said he had spent twenty-five years in the armed Special Constabulary, the UDR and the RIR. 'We never defeated terrorism because we were shackled,' he said angrily, to applause and cheers. 'If we'd taken the same stance against Hitler, we wouldn't be standing here. You have to defeat terrorism, get the thugs off the street and the drug addicts. In places like Carnany you have known thugs running the streets. After twenty-five years' service I am crippled. Now they want to dump me in the street like a dustbin. That's the thanks I get.'

'THE LIBERAL TRADITION'

Alec Blair, head of the history department at Dalriada school, was Ballymoney's historian. He gave talks in the town hall and conducted walking tours 'roon the toon'. His local knowledge was immense. A decorous middle-aged man, he lived with his mother in the house in which he was born, near the village of Kilraghts, where he was an elder and clerk of sessions in the Presbyterian church. His mother sat by the range in the kitchen. When her son introduced us, she looked at me seriously. The parlour was full of books, and looked out on a garden bright with marigolds, lupins and hollyhocks. Blair said he had a man in to look after it.

'There wasn't much bother ever in Ballymoney. Protestants and Catholics work together here, and always have. The drama society has been a great healer. In Larne certain groups, like the Dunloy Players, weren't allowed to play. In Ballymoney they won a cup. It's the liberal tradition.'

The area was heavily planted with Scottish Lowlanders in the early part of the seventeenth century, and the 'displaced Irish' had beaten them in the 1641 rebellion. The Scottish were restored by force, and thereafter 'worked the land with a plough in one hand and a sword in the other'. There was a big lodge of United Irishmen in the town in 1798. 'Nearly everyone in Ballymoney was for the rising. The only people who were loyal were the Catholics.' Henry Joy McCracken had been defeated before the Ballymoney men could reach him. They retreated. 'The army entered and burned their houses on the Sabbath day, which to Presbyterians was seen as heathen. People were hung, had to leave and so on. The Presbyterian minister took a nervous breakdown and died. It was rough times.' The magistrate, known as Bloody Hutchinson, gave money for the building of a new chapel, a reward for the loyalty of the town's Catholics.

Ballymoney had the biggest flax market in the country, and flourished in the late nineteenth century, when it was known inelegantly as 'cow town'. Its claim to a liberal tradition rested largely on the figure of J.B Armour, a Presbyerian minister. 'He was born a few fields from here. His father was a tenant farmer. He founded Dalriada school, which has always been mixed. Whereas Presbyterians were never good at putting their case, it was said that he "brought a tongue of fire" to his cause. When it came to home rule a lot of the tenant rights people turned Unionist overnight. They knew what side their bread was buttered on.'

Armour claimed that 'Home Rule is a Presbyterian principle' and denounced his fellow ministers' 'senseless fear of Romanism'. He described Carson as 'a sheer mountebank, the greatest enemy of Protestantism in my opinion existing, inflaming men to violence' (quoted in Bardon, p. 440). 'Armour would have disliked the Anglicans more than the Catholics,' said Alec Blair.

'He organised a big meeting on home rule in the town hall in 1913.' Sir Roger Casement made his first public speech at it. 'It was seen as the test of liberalism. It would show the government how Protestants would react. But the liberals were rare birds, no longer making the running. The meeting was not a success.'

The audience of five hundred people was asked to sign an 'anti-Covenant' based on, but opposed to, the Solemn League and Covenant. Carson's covenant, including the separate women's Declaration, had been signed by almost 500,000 people. Outside the anti-Covenant meeting, an Orange drumming party had been got up, literally to drown out the liberals. A week later Unionists got a crowd which filled the town hall, the Orange hall and the street.

Local landlord James Leslie, ancestor of the current Assembly member, had been behind the founding of the Orange lodge. It was to Leslie's big house, Leslie Hill, that Protestants paraded to sign the Covenant.

Historian J.B. McMinn, author of a study of Armour, has cautioned against the 'Ballymoney legend' of radicalism, noting acerbically the popularity of a misleading biography of Armour by his son among 'political polemicists seeking the holy grail of Protestant Nationalism or the equally elusive political middle ground' (McMinn, *Irish Historical Studies*, no. 89, vol. 23, May 1982, p. 17).

Armour described the Stormont government as a 'bastard parliament', remarking that, 'For years they have been yelling against Home Rule, and now they have got a form of Home Rule which the devil himself could not have devised' (quoted in Stewart, p. 173). 'He said Stormont would maybe last fifty years,' said Blair. 'He said, "I doubt it won't last." He wasn't far wrong.

'Ballymoney was almost exclusively unionist through the twentieth century. The gentry were returned mainly, though Paisley turned all that around. He has tremendous support around here. I like him immensely as a person. He is a great character, a very friendly and gracious man. He'd do a tremendous amount for you. I know a lot of Catholics would say he has righted wrongs for them. He is very jolly – he'd say, "How are you, brother?" He is one of the last great characters. But his politics wouldn't be mine.' Blair recalled a visit to Ballymoney by both Paisley and the then leader of the UUP, James Molyneaux. 'You'd hardly get a word out of Molyneaux, but I did learn that he is obsessed with the saints of the Church of Ireland.'

Blair supported the Belfast Agreement, and described James Leslie as 'a right fellow – he is gentry but he has the common touch'. I asked him about nearby villages with a reputation for being hardline loyalist, places like Dervock. 'Yes, that would be strongly loyalist. It was a village built by a landlord, so the thing was to toe the line by being strongly loyal. But it has a chapel, the only chapel with an earthen floor maybe in this island. Mind you, it has a bit of graffiti on the door. But it is still there and it is well attended.' This seemed a good and simple definition of loyalism. Toeing the line.

Blair said it was significant that the protest about Dunloy was happening in Ballymena rather than in Ballymoney. 'We had no

Harryville. If you look at the Quinns, Methodist and Presbyterian ministers took part in the funeral prayers. The prayer of the Presbyterian moderator was beautifully crafted. It was quoted in the *Irish Times*.' On several occasions he spoke with pride about Ballymoney events which had been written up in the *Irish Times*, which he clearly regarded as being a paper of note, a cut above the local dailies.

He spoke about the Quinn murders. 'It was terrible, of course. The people of Ballymoney were very hurt by that. The silence of the people lining the streets was eloquent. I know very little about Carnany. There are always rascals. A very small minority. It doesn't take many.' Blair had suggested during a BBC discussion programme after July 1998 that it might help bring peace if people learned more about the shared history of their townlands. But nobody talked about Carnany.

What was most striking to me about local working-class people was their strong accent. It was, like the Ballymena accent, Scottish-sounding. I asked Blair about it. 'The Scottish planters brought that accent. It isn't a language, it is a lovely sort of injection into English. This Ulster Scots language is very artificial. It is really an attempt to have a Protestant language because the Catholics have Gaelic. But the Presbyterian ministers here in the seventeenth century "had the Gaelic". The name Ballymoney is an anglicised version of two Gaelic words meaning the town of the bog. Our placenames are Gaelic. That accent is English pressed into a Gaelic structure.

'These people should look to their culture instead. They have a strong Scottish background, and we are in Ireland. But Protestant alienation from being Irish was due to the way the Catholic Church appropriated Irishness – they took the music and the language ... if you look at the feis in the Glens of Antrim, the ones who promoted that first were Protestants. Irish dancing and so on. When the lord lieutenant came to Ballymoney to open the technical school, the banners across the road said "Céad Míle Fáilte". Nowadays there would be objections to that.'

Unionists have long resented being cast in the role of the original baddies – the Planters who came and dispossessed the Gaels, whose victim role was inherited by nationalists. Councillor Ian Adamson has promoted the idea of the Planters as a returning people. His books claim that the Scottish Planters in the seventeenth century were the descendants of the Cruthin people who had been forced out of Ireland in the fifth century. A.T.Q. Stewart also describes western Scotland as 'an extension of the Ulster kingdom of Dalriada'. Stewart cautions against relying on modern notions of nationalism to describe a situation in which geography was possibly the most significant factor: 'we can easily forget that mountains, forests and marshes were at one time greater obstacles to man than the open sea' (Stewart, p. 35). He quotes a geographer who described the Irish Sea as having been the centre rather than the frontier of a cultural province.

Adamson's books have been written off as amateurish propaganda by some historians, and popularised by Michael Hall, a community worker who felt that young loyalists needed to know their history if they were to have any self-respect. In *Ulster, the Hidden History*, Hall quotes another of the Cruthin school of historians who said descendants of the Cruthin had returned 'as canny, hard-headed Scots who became the majority Ulstermen of today – ardent Irishmen at a rugby international but retaining strong ties with Britain' (Hall, p. 41).

In the *Sunday Tribune* on 11 April 1999, journalist Neil MacKay claimed that 'the most significant migration in the British Isles is that from Ulster to Scotland'. These Protestant emigrants were 'fiercely proud of their Scottish roots' and saw 'their fellow brethren there as supporters in the fight against republicanism'. He also claimed, paradoxically, that they wanted to get away from sectarianism and the Troubles.

Ulster Scots was part of the same project as the Cruthin. Adamson wrote to Assembly members, claiming there were '100,000 native Ulster Scots speakers'. The north Antrim region, from Ballymena to Ballymoney, is recognised as one of its core areas. In 1999 the UK government announced its intention of signing up to the Council of Europe's charter for regional and minority languages, committing itself to recognising Ulster Scots. When the Assembly was set up, advertisements were placed seeking an Ulster Scots translator for its proceedings. However, it proved impossible to fill the well-paid post, fuelling the derision of those who regarded Ulster Scots as 'DIY language for Orangemen'. In the *News Letter* on 5 March 1999 Queen's University linguist John Kirk said that a lot of the words in the advertisement had simply been made up. 'A language needs a political and social momentum and structure. It is more than a dialect written down.'

The language movement is part of the construction of a kind of loyalist nationalism. Republicans have successfully promoted and politicised the Irish language, with one activist claiming that every Irish word learned was the equivalent of a bullet in the freedom struggle. The project was not without its difficulties. In 1999 Castlereagh Borough Council erected street signs in Ulster Scots in east Belfast. Incensed local loyalists, who thought the signs were in Irish, tore them down immediately.

Depressingly, the imagined community the architects of the Ulster Scots movement had in mind was already proclaiming its victimhood. UUP Councillor Nelson McCausland is 'heid yin' of the Ulster Scots Heritage Council. In a 1998 editorial in the council's journal, entitled 'Tha Wittens o tha Ulster-Heirskip Cooncil', he laments 'the years of neglect, underdevelopment and discrimination that the Ulster-Scots community and culture have had to endure' (*Ulster Scots Heritage Council News*, no. 3, 1998).

'OLD STOCK'

An elderly silver-haired man living in a big bungalow on the edge of the town, Tom McIlderry was definitely what Ballymoney called 'old stock'. His great grandfather, a farmer called Thomas McIlderry, set up market yards in Ballymoney in 1835. The contemporary Tom McIlderry had run the family bacon curing business until recent years. When the factory was accidentally burned down in 1998 it caused a crisis in the North's already declining pig industry.

McIlderry saw himself as an inheritor of the liberal tradition. 'In 1798 the United Irishmen hid their pikes in the kitchen of my great grandfather's house. My ancestors, right down to my father and myself, always employed people from both sides of the community. We were unionists by name, but I was very annoyed when a leading light in the Unionist Party came and warned us that we were employing too many Catholics. A lot of other employers in the town didn't employ any. That was their explicitly stated policy. I told him we didn't discriminate.'

He spoke of Terence O'Neill as the courageous lost leader of liberal unionism, except that he gave up too easily. 'Things fell apart very badly after that.' He had not trusted Brian Faulkner, though he had supported the Sunningdale accord. 'What went on in Ballymoney during the loyalist workers' strike in 1974 made a lot of us ashamed. A Unionist politician sat in the Orange hall, sent for the shopkeepers one by one and issued instructions. Paisley is more responsible for the trouble in Northern Ireland than any other politician. I still remember him organising men on the hillsides at Ballymena. He was the one who encouraged thoughts of armed struggle.'

McIlderry said thirty years of the Troubles had embittered Ballymoney people. Another businessman told me that a lot of Ulster Unionist voters in the town felt ashamed because in 1985, in response to the hated Anglo-Irish Agreement, they had swung to Paisley. McIlderry joined the Alliance Party when it was formed, supported the Belfast Agreement and felt confident it would succeed. 'Maybe the time will come when Trimble will seem to have the same sort of liberal attitude which Alliance supports.' However, he reserved his warmth and enthusiasm for Seamus Mallon, the SDLP's deputy first minister. 'Come to think of it,' he said, apparently surprised, 'I have a lot more respect for the SDLP than for the Unionists.'

'IN THE POLITICAL WILDERNESS'

'The Presbyterian,' according to A.T.Q. Stewart, is by nature radical. 'The austere doctrines of Calvinism, the simplicity of his worship, the democratic government of his church, the memory of the martyred Covenanters, and the Scottish refusal to yield or dissemble – all incline him to that difficult and cantankerous disposition.' However, his situation and history in a predominantly Catholic Ireland has made him 'defensive, intolerant and uncritically loyal to traditions and institutions' (Stewart, p. 83).

James Simpson was a disillusioned Ulster Unionist who described his own background as being 'the son of Presbyterian tenant farmers'. He was an agricultural consultant, who, like Tom McIlderry, saw himself as part of a political line which went back to Armour. However, his politics were quite different to the Alliance man's. 'There is a north Antrim radical tradition which has died. I feel I'm part of that. I wonder why I'm in the UUP at all. But there's nowhere else to go.

'There is no radical centre party in which I could express the views I hold passionately. I'm a one-nation Conservative, like Enoch Powell in 1950, or Edward Heath. The market is important but isn't the be all and end all. There have to be protections for those who don't benefit from it.

'I'm in the political wilderness. I would have been attracted by the UK Unionists. They recognise that the Union can be broken by stealth. Nationalism is clever. They are devious as well – they take advantage of Unionist stupidity. I suppose you can't blame them for that. Sectarianism is inherent in Irish life. It exists between the Presbyterian Church and the Church of Ireland in this area. And, of course, they said home rule would be Rome rule – well, it was. Their system of education made Ireland the jewel in the Vatican crown.

'I would have been quite sympathetic to the organisation of the Conservative Party here too. That would be a tremendous advance, an end to parochial politics. But they were too evangelical about it. The zeal of the convert is a curse. Union First could have potential. They are forcing people like Leslie to answer the questions.' The hostility between the Presbyterian farmer and the big house Unionist was alive and angry in Simpson's heart. Simpson spoke more vehemently about his opposition to the son of the big house than about his opposition to the Belfast Agreement. Deference, he said, was at the heart of unionism's problems. The gentry were responsible for unionism's downfall.

A former councillor, Simpson voted against his party in the 1998 elections. 'They should never have selected Leslie. He came out of the blue and some of them nearly fell over themselves because he's landed gentry. It's the old tradition. Son of the big house goes off to Africa for a few years and then comes back and gets a seat in parliament. Leslie came back here and in no time he was standing for Westminster.' Simpson had voted for an anti-agreement Independent.

'The whole movement against home rule was led by the landlords, using the Orange Order as their machine. They got the labouring classes in that way. And then there is the deference. I remember my mother saying, "You must never get beyond yourself." There was a pecking order, a strong class system, and you didn't move outside that. There is a bit of mobility now, but the barriers are still there.' Simpson said the UUP was now overwhelmingly middle class. 'They lost the working classes to Paisley, because he seemed to be doing something for them and because he defended them.' He said that if Gregory Campbell, the articulate Derry Assembly member who is prominent in the DUP, had been in the UUP, 'he would never have got anywhere' because he was from a poor family. 'In the UUP it is fashionable to say, "We aren't involved in politics." These people actually vote for the party because it has no politics.' At his party conference in Enniskillen in 1999, Trimble admitted that there was a problem even getting members of the UUP out to vote.

'The vast majority of unionists haven't read the agreement and don't know what's in it. They voted for it because Trimble told them to. If he'd told them not to, they would have followed him. It's the deference – the person at the top knows best. I know a fellow teaches in an élite college. He said there was no discussion of the agreement in the staffroom.' It was certainly true that few Protestants I spoke to referred to the agreement in anything other than general terms except for what it said on decommissioning and prisoner releases.

'My family was bitterly opposed to the Masonic. My father used to say it perverted the course of justice. People were able to get off, or be treated leniently in the courts. If you had a network of contacts, you were invited to join. A chap I know well, an accountant, I said to him, "Why did you end up in accountancy?" He said, "My father was a Mason. He went to a Masonic dinner and he found himself sitting beside someone who ran an accountancy firm. The man said, 'Tell your son to come to my office on Monday morning.'" That's how he got the job. It's not a matter of discrimination – it's a matter of favouritism. That's a mistake Catholics make. Mind you, I think rugby has probably led to more favouritism than the Masons.'

There was no interest in history. 'Education was regarded as having a great importance in my family. And there was that tradition – the second son of tenant farmers often went on to train as a Presbyterian minister. But, to give you an example, I grew up beside a Norman fort and no one ever told me what it was. If you look at the Catholic community, they have a huge interest in history. Protestants hark back

as a way of anchoring themselves. That is different. There is a phi-
listine attitude to the arts in the Presbyterian community too. Things
have to be seen to be useful.' Respectability was the key: 'prominent
church connections, being in the Chamber of Commerce, rugby club
membership, service in the Boys' Brigade'.

Simpson opposed the Belfast Agreement because he thought it
contained 'the seeds of its own destruction' and because the South got
too big a role. 'Trimble doesn't seem to realise he has to sell this
agreement. People who voted for it feel betrayed. Unionism is totally
disorganised. They have to work out how to convince Catholics to
vote for the Union, given that they may soon form the majority.

'That's another thing about north Antrim, they way they imposed
this girl Campbell. So naïve. Did they think Catholics were so stupid
that they'd vote for her just because she is a Catholic?' The selection
as Assembly candidate of Patricia Campbell, who previously ran the
UUP's London office and had taken a case against the party alleging
religious discrimination, had led to bitter public wrangling. The UUP
criticised the *Ballymena Guardian* for reporting it, but in September
1998 the newspaper went on to describe a further 'sometimes ill-
tempered debate'.

Campbell, who was not elected, later wrote in the nationalist *Irish
News* on 16 April 1998 that loyalists had a 'Serb mentality towards
Catholics' and that if those who protested at Harryville had their way
'there would be no Catholic churches left to picket'. Simpson was one
of those who opposed Campbell. He admitted he would have liked the
nomination himself. What he did not tell me was that he had been
heavily defeated during the selection process for the 1997 general
election. The successful candidate was James Leslie.

'The Catholic community got so much more out of the agreement
than us, far more than Sunningdale offered. They'd have been fools
not to go for it. The SDLP is slick, it really delivered the agreement, and
Sinn Féin has a tightly controlled machine. The Catholic Church is a
tighter operation too. They control the Church, the GAA and the
schools. The GAA has the same role in nationalism in terms of advancement as the Orange Order in the Protestant community.

'The Protestant community is in disarray. The loyalists have moved
away from being a God-fearing community to being a hooligan

community. A degeneration. There is a whole section of the community which used to be the manufacturing industry. Back then, their energies were channelled. There were apprenticeships. Now industry has been decimated. Where are their sons and daughters now? In rough estates. There is no middle leadership in the unionist community. Nor is it encouraged.'

Simpson said Ballymoney had a drinking problem and a paramilitary problem. He took the more-to-that-than-meets-the-eye view of the Quinn murders. However, he went on to say that the expulsion of Catholics from the town's housing estates was not a new phenomenon. 'I remember in 1987 coming back from holiday on the Eleventh of July and six families had been put out of Glebeside. There was no publicity about it. I went to one of the houses – they said the priest had been, but no Protestant ministers. The police said they didn't know anyone in the area.

'A Presbyterian minister said to me, "Oh, that's a terrible place. We have only one or two families in there." Clergy used to visit people. That attitude of paternalism is gone. If not enough people are attending a church, they shut it down. They don't try to reach people. They have no social outlook. The evangelicals are so heavenly minded they are no earthly use.'

'THE MOST CHARMING TOWN . . .'

Leslie Hill had diversified. The Leslies had cannily seen the decline in farming coming, and had started an open farm, popular with tourists on the Causeway Coast. James Leslie, Assembly member, lived, and had his office, in a fine old farmhouse in the grounds. His jeep was parked in the yard. He said he'd had to stop playing Rory Gallagher tapes because the music made him drive too fast. 'I'm quite fond of Van Morrison too, although even by Ulster standards he is pretty cussèd,' he said.

He had no worries about being regarded as a blow-in. 'We've lived here since 1660. We built up the farm to a considerable acreage over the years. There is a tradition in the family of working overseas – my grandfather was in the colonial service, as was my father. I was sent to public school in England because my parents took the view that if one had the wherewithal, that gave one the best chance in life. But I always intended to come back to the farm. I am Northern Irish. I used to get awfully angry with people at school who would call me Paddy or Irish. I'd say, "Look here, I'm sorry, I'm not Irish, I'm an Ulsterman."'

After school, he went to Cambridge, and then had a career in merchant banking which took him to Dubai and Hong Kong, with a brief spell in Dublin. He was part owner of a bank in the end. His father had been chairman of the North Antrim constituency Unionist Association in the sixties. Leslie said that for years he had been frustrated by the 'lack of vision' in the party. 'I read everything there was to read.' He returned to the North in 1996 to stand for the Forum elections. 'I was only back for the last ten days of the campaign because I was bailing out of Hong Kong. But it was fun. There was no chance I could win – I was learning the ropes. The following year I stood for Westminster. I did very well, got the vote up to 10,000 from 8,000. Paisley's majority of 15,000, which had been regarded as unassailable, fell to about 10,500. In the 1998 Assembly elections, I took a seat.' So did Ian Paisley Junior.

Deference had nothing to do with his selection, he said. 'When Stormont was set up, the attitude was, put the guy in the big house in charge – he'll know what to do. But that has diminished. It's gone, actually. If I wanted to be really naughty, I might say I'm not sure you got better government as a result. The resentment is stronger than the deference. I get both and I don't like either. I mean, I've come up through a meritocracy career – merchant banking is cutthroat. Let's see what they get – if I do a good job, I'll be selected again.'

His father was commander of the local UDR, and young James spent summer holidays from Cambridge as a private in the regiment. He strongly identified with the security forces. Unlike many in his party, though, he had every confidence in Chris Patten, who was in the middle of his review of the RUC when we spoke. They had Hong Kong in common, and were old boys of the same public school.

'It grieves me terribly the state Ballymoney seems to have got into because it is so contradictory to the town's tradition of liberalism. The 1798 rebellion was quite well supported in the area.' I mentioned that his family had opposed it. 'That's true, although my relevant ancestor went and pleaded for the lives of some of the ringleaders because he felt they had just been misled and rather carried away. That liberal tradition carried on right up until Paisley won the seat in 1970.

'We have never been a sectarian family – we have always employed Catholics. When the sort of battle started in 1969 I had to ask my parents what was happening, and who was fighting who, and my parents had to explain that unfortunately it was Protestants and Catholics.' He had disliked the Belfast Agreement at first sight, because of 'the survival of parts of the Anglo-Irish Agreement ... and that it is so finely balanced as to be unworkable'. He was veering towards support when Tony Blair got his infamous blackboard out at Coleraine, a few miles up the road, and started promising things that were not in the agreement. 'I damn near voted no at that point because I thought, he is fudging and it won't work.'

He stood on a Yes platform in the end, while insisting that Blair must honour his blackboard promises, which chiefly related to the requirement that paramilitary arms would have to be decommissioned before the formation of an executive. I asked him if, a year on, he still believed it could work. There was a long silence. Then he said, 'Only if everyone remains pessimistic, funnily enough. If anyone was optimistic it would imply they were getting unfair advantage.

'Life would get a lot easier if the broad swathe of people would regard the constitutional issue as settled. Sadly, most people on the unionist side are convinced that it isn't, and that there is danger round every corner. That is a really bad backdrop because what is really required for the new regime to work is for people to cross party lines on issues and build consensus on an interest rather than a party basis.

'Unionists have a chronic naivety about negotiations. It is this Presbyterian ethic that everybody has to be involved in everything. But we were prepared to split our party to go with this agreement. Sinn Féin was not. It makes us wild when they say we will have to show courage. If this fails, it will take more than ten years to get another reformist leader.' This was important, because it went some way to explaining something about Trimble's apparent paralysis as a leader. Repeatedly he made himself a hostage to anti-agreement elements and to the party's unwieldy bodies. Unionist leaders never lost the party's support for being too conservative. It was when they tried to move forward that the trouble started.

The Alliance Party was reprehensible, according to Leslie. 'They should have toughed it out. They could have helped to reform unionism, and those from a nationalist background could have stopped the SDLP drifting towards violent republicanism. The big machine is the Ulster Unionist Party. That's the one you have to get pointing in the right direction. Now that Alliance is in decline, those people should come back.'

Leslie said the UUP had changed and traditional unionism had been discarded. 'It just ain't going to work any longer. It has a strong underlying sectarianism and its distrust of the other side is pathological. Whilst I think a healthy caution is a good thing, I think you've got to extend a measure of trust and if that is returned, then in time you advance a further measure. The anti-agreement people are not willing to do that. They cannot see the macro-political picture, which includes the Single European Act, the Maastricht Treaty and the Amsterdam Treaty. That is pretty significant for the sovereign integrity both of the Republic of Ireland and the UK. UUP MPs like Willie Ross are pursuing a political philosophy which no longer applies.'

He said there was a lot of work to be done on unionism's intellectual 'raison d'être'. 'There is a lack of intellectual substance to Unionist politicians.' I asked him did he think the party had sold the agreement well to its electorate. 'I think it's unfortunate that Unionists don't realise that all of the things which are good for unionism in the agreement will arrive when the executive is formed. Bingo – the Anglo-Irish Agreement will be gone. Unionism will have a veto over North–South activity. There will be the ability to control expenditure, and the Irish constitution will change to drop Articles 2 and 3. The Irish will open a consulate in Belfast – recognition that it's in a foreign country.' This wasn't entirely true. The hated Anglo-Irish Secretariat known as Maryfield was replaced under the agreement by the Anglo-Irish Intergovernmental Conference. There would be no consulate.

Leslie spoke knowledgeably of the disastrous state of farming in Northern Ireland. Oddly, Trimble had made him spokesperson on social affairs. 'It's the "brew" and housing, basically,' he told me. He drew out the local word for social security benefits, as if holding it up between fastidious fingertips. His use of it brought his family's background in the colonial service uncomfortably to mind. It came as no surprise to learn that he believed there were 'two tribes' in the North. When power was devolved to the Stormont executive in November 1999, Leslie became the UUP's spokesman on finance and personnel.

Despite the Anglo-Irish Agreement, many of the liberal unionists I met retained a grudging admiration for Margaret Thatcher. *Thatcher – The Downing Street Years* was to be seen on many bookshelves, including those of Alliance voters. Leslie was a full-blown supporter of the mistress of monetarism. 'Because we have not had responsibility for socio-economic policy here for twenty-five years, people have not experienced the collapse of socialism. They are stuck in some early seventies ideas. New Labour is a disaster – it thinks it understands markets which are the most powerful in terms of driving economies, but it doesn't.

'Gordon Brown as chancellor is making the most dreadful mess. They are still wedded to this idea of helping everybody, whereas my view is that people can help themselves given the right cirumstances. We have got to move from a dependency culture to a motivating one. The SDLP thinks it knows about business but it is woefully naïve about money.'

A phone call interrupted the interview. It seemed to be someone asking advice about the prospect of opening a shoe factory in Bulgaria. Leslie spoke fluently about floating labour costs, the relative costs of labour in China and Bulgaria, material costs, the Deutschmark, the weakness of the lira and the peseta. The language of international capitalism in action.

When he came back I asked him to explain the abdication of the middle classes from northern politics. 'They were scared,' he said. 'To be blunt about it, there is no question but that there has been an easy living for a middle-class person in the east of the province over the last twenty years if you kept your head down. You'll find a lot of middle-class people are incredibly bigoted and entrenched in their views but they daren't let it show because they feel that being middle class, they shouldn't feel that way. If they do start to come back to politics, I hope they realise you have to start at voluntary level and not by getting into representing.'

Leslie reckoned that the old Stormont regime was 'better than it's given credit for', though he added that he had no doubt that 'there was severe discrimination in terms of housing policy and definite jiggery-pokery in the drawing of electoral boundaries'. He worried that there was 'a very deeply imbedded disrespect for law of any kind' in Northern Ireland. 'The 1977 loyalist strike didn't work anywhere else and it did work here, and that was achieved through intimidation. Paisley has been a horribly malign influence around here. People in Ballymoney, middle-class people as well, are in denial about the sectarian problem here. But there is a problem and the sooner we take it on the chin and deal with it the better. I mean, where you have a thumping great Protestant majority, there is far less willingness to address these things.

'Take the case of the Quinn children or the murder of Greg Taylor. People have come up with every conceivable explanation to excuse what happened. Incredible. I mean, Greg Taylor was kicked to death in the street. The tragedy of it is, Ballymoney is the most charming town. The people are utterly charming.'

I asked him about the claim made by loyalist paramilitaries, that what they did helped the security forces, whose hands were tied. He condemned the paramilitaries roundly. However, he added that whereas in the early years loyalist killings seemed indiscriminate, 'the '93–'94 activities of the loyalists were pretty effective. They were much more targeted. It put the wind up the IRA in a way that very little had done up to then. It was far less safe being an IRA man because people had your number and were looking for you.'

'A PESSIMIST'

Leslie suggested I speak to his assistant, Robert Wilson, a big, shambling, good-natured man. He looked about thirty, but told me he was forty-nine. We met at the office. Leslie was rushing off to Stormont. He asked Wilson to check with the council about reports that dead calves were being dumped in skips. 'Do you have a number for the council?' Wilson asked. 'You might look it up in the phone book,' replied his boss briskly.

Also a former banker, though with experience of Ballymena and Derry rather than Hong Kong and Dubai, Wilson had come home to the village of Broughshane to look after his mother and the family farm six years previously. He had made an ill-advised foray into poultry keeping, and had lately started a farm shop. He had voted against the Belfast Agreement. 'On moral grounds,' he said. 'I don't think murderers should be in government. Not just Sinn Féin. The loyalists too.' However, he said he was a democrat and therefore had no problem about working to implement it. He said Paisleyism had split his family.

'Various accusations were made against my grandmother by certain people. There were things said at my uncle's funeral which had no right to be said. Questioning her Christianity. That made a big impression on me. I had nursed her and read the Bible to her.' I asked what religion she was. He was startled. 'Presbyterian. I just assume that goes without saying.' His grandmother had 'made provision for the Paisleys'. He added, rather spitefully: 'They weren't always as affluent as they are now. They weren't in a great way of going.' He remembered an aunt bringing soup to the Paisleys, and that the blocks for the original tabernacle built by Paisley's father in Ballymena were made with sand from the Wilsons' land. 'A very poor sandpit it was, as far as I understand,' he said, and I felt there was some vague biblical import to this remark. The tabernacle that is built on poor sand ...

As a child, he had been discouraged from making noise on the Sabbath. He still tried to keep it holy, and a family day. He was an elder in the church, and an officer in the Boys' Brigade. He was a fundamentalist. 'To me that means believing in the Bible.'

He disapproved of 'kick-the-Pope' bands and said a great many of the Orangemen of north Antrim would be DUP people, 'gravely misled' by Paisley. He felt the Orange Order was a nuisance, blocking roads and causing disruption, but that in the past it had been culturally inoffensive. His wife was from a part of Ballymena where Catholic children used to hold the strings of the banners in the parades. 'And they weren't condemned as heretics.'

Harryville was a disgrace. He said the protesters were a type of loyalist who were 'idiots, total cretins who couldn't spell loyalism if you asked them'. He was annoyed at the priest too, though. He said he had slighted unionists who had 'gone out of their way' to support the Catholics. 'Some boys went along and tried to break the doors of the chapel open. The priest came on TV and said it was typical. I thought that was really anti-loyalist and anti-unionist, terrible rhetoric for a man professing to be a preacher of the gospel. I wouldn't like to think a preacher would go out and rile up the rabble against the other community. There were Protestants who stood up against that protest and people took business away from them for it, which was petty in the extreme.'

When I asked did he think the agreement was going to work, he said he was not an optimistic person. 'I'm a pessimist,' he said, adding slowly, 'Maybe that is why so much goes wrong for me.'

'THE SCAPEGOAT'

At the Ballymoney Independent Christian School the children were working their way through the Old Testament. There were thirty-five children at the school, ranging from five to sixteen years old, with four full-time teachers and a teaching assistant. Parents paid fees and the Free Presbyterian Church paid a subsidy. I rang the minister, the Reverend David Park, and he invited me to sit in on his scripture class.

The Reverend Park was young, dark-haired, with big eyebrows and an intense look. He looked like the Reverend Gray, in Loughgall. He lived in the big square manse in the same grounds as the church and the school. The children in the class were about ten to fifteen years old. They had reached Leviticus, chapter 16. 'Wesley, tell us what the scapegoat means?' asked the minister. Wesley said that the priest was to take two goats, one for the Lord and the other for the scapegoat, to be sacrificed. 'It was to take away the people's sins,' he said. 'Yes,' said the minister. 'The sins of the people were symbolically laid upon the goat, signifying the sins of the people. Christ shed his blood, and the scapegoat removed our sins away out into the wilderness never to be remembered against us any more. Beverly – what does the scapegoat mean?' 'It means we've got a way to heaven,' Beverly replied.

Park explained to me that the children write out memory verses. He asked David to read 'the one about the blood' in Leviticus 17. David read, 'It is the blood which maketh an atonement for the soul.' Park nodded. 'The New Testament tells us that without shedding of blood there is no remission, no forgiveness, no taking away of sin. We also have a reference to capital punishment. As Bible-believing Protestants, this is very significant. Andrea, will you read Leviticus 24, verse 17?' Andrea read: 'And he that killeth any man shall surely be put to death.' 'Andrew,' said Park. 'What is a Protestant?' 'A person who stands up for his civil and religious liberty and the freedom to worship.' 'Where does it go back to?' 'The Reformation.' 'What do you protest against?' 'Error.'

The principal of the school was Noreen McAfee, a stout young woman with dark hair, worn long. She was dressed in austerely long dark clothes, and had a shy smile. 'We teach from a scriptural viewpoint,' she said. 'In science we teach that this is what God created. We do not teach sex education because that is the priority of the parent. We do not overlook evolution, but we teach it as a theory that is wrong. We do not take part in Education for Mutual Understanding and we do not participate in any inter-school activities.' This included other Protestant schools. 'We could not control what would happen if the children mixed with others.' Education for Mutual Understanding (EMU) is a government scheme to bring about an element of mixing between schools of different religions.

'The ethos here is that God and God's Word is central to everything. We do still use corporal punishment.' Corporal punishment is illegal – I asked Noreen McAfee what they used. 'A wooden spoon,' she replied with a small smile. 'Usually it is not necessary.'

After I had seen around the school, which was spartan and remarkably quiet, Park invited me to the house for coffee. 'My wife is away but I can boil a kettle,' he said. He rehearsed the reasons why Roman Catholicism was in error, and ecumenism was wrong. He spoke of Moses and the symbol of the burning bush which was the school badge. 'Moses was instructed by God to take the blood of a lamb and smear it on the doors and God said, "When I see the blood I will pass over you", so when the death angel came that night all the homes marked by the blood were sheltered. The New Testament tells us that death and destruction are coming but all those who are sheltered by the blood will be saved. The scapegoat is another example.'

The daubing of houses reminded me of a house I'd seen in Belfast, in the loyalist Village area in Belfast. 'Get out or burn out' was scrawled on it in huge white letters and it was empty. Also of Krajina in Croatia, where I saw villages in which all the houses had been marked, and those marked to denote Serbian occupants had been burned out. Then I thought about Larne and Carrickfergus, and Carnany, where Catholics were not 'sheltered by the blood'.

Park spoke about a local Free Presbyterian missionary who had recently been home from Spain. He hunted out a copy of the *Ballymoney Times*, dated 14 October 1998, to show me an interview with him, which was in an issue of the newspaper that had as its front-page story an interview with Park himself, about the death of his brother-in-law. Frankie O'Reilly was the RUC man who was hit on the head by a blast bomb thrown by loyalists in Portadown and died later, in October 1998, from his injuries.

'Frankie was brought up a Roman Catholic but had forsaken it,' said Park. 'He attended a Presbyterian church with my sister.' In the newspaper article, Park movingly described the family's loss. He also took the occasion to attack David Trimble for not visiting Constable O'Reilly in hospital, while proving 'able to meet Sinn Féin during that period'. He defended the right of the Orange Order to march 'the Queen's Highway' in Portadown and said that those who called for the Drumcree protest to end after the murder were 'sickening'. 'At the moment the RUC are poor pawns in the middle, carrying out the policies and decisions of a government which refuses to take the terrorists on,' he was quoted as saying.

Constable O'Reilly's murder was claimed by the Red Hand Defenders. This group, which emerged in July 1998 in support of the Drumcree Orangemen, considered itself to be conducting a holy war, and used bloodthirsty quotations from the Old Testament to support its violence. Orange spokesman David Jones said in the aftermath of the murder, 'Unfortunately, when you are standing up for civil liberties sometimes the cost of those liberties can be very high.' He added, 'Our protest will go on.' A few months previously, the Orange Order had stated that it was not responsible for the Quinn murders, and would not be made the scapegoat for them.

'WHOEVER SHOUTS THE LOUDEST WINS THE DAY'

Evelyn had been brought up as a Catholic, but decided as an adult to become a Baptist. 'I realise now that God had been speaking to me for years,' she said. 'I wanted to walk closer to him. The church I have joined has a lovely fellowship about it.' It was set up by a missionary who had come 'church planting' to the area, and soon established a Portakabin for his new flock. 'What attracted me was, the pastor made it clear that Orangeism should be totally divorced from your religion. He hates this idea of "for God and Ulster". He thinks God is for everyone, not just for Ulster. When I hear someone is in the Orange Order I do question if their loyalty is to God first. If you are in an organisation which is quite openly sectarian, how can you follow the gospel of loving one another and respecting one another?

'At times I feel within some of the evangelical Churches there is a lot of naked sectarian hatred. I can't understand how they can carry such hatred. But by their fruit ye shall know them. My daughter goes to a school which is mostly Protestant and she says, "Mummy, you have no idea how bitter and narrow-minded some of these people are."' Evelyn's teenage children had also been baptised as Baptists, and were debating issues in Bible studies such as, can Christians drink alcohol? Her Catholic past had not been an issue. 'The attitude is that everyone needs to be saved.'

She had strong doubts about ecumenism. 'I am in a dilemma about that. In ways I feel you need to mix with other denominations in order to bear witness to them, but it doesn't really work like that. Our pastor compares it with the bad apples in a basket. The bad ones destroy the good ones. The person speaking for Christ doesn't get heard. I don't want to share services with Catholics. I feel more anti-Catholic than many who haven't been there. There is a shallowness about their worship. I gave my mother a Bible, but I don't think she reads it. That annoys me about Catholicism, that lay people don't feel they can open the Bible and read it themselves.'

Although now convinced that 'salvation is of the Lord and not of works', Evelyn had recently been involved in efforts to provide a cross-community facility in her village. 'The village is fifty-fifty, but there is no neutral building. I remember hearing Will Glendinning from the Community Relations Council talking about the glass door, people pretending to get along fine, but really, if there was the slightest wee thing that might tip things the other way, the bitterness comes up.

'In our village we just simmer along most of the time and people talk to each other and share shops, but then if something contentious happens, people go into their own wee camps. The first year I saw it happen was the first year of Drumcree. Catholics resented the ones in the bands. Then the GAA was planning to build a pitch and a petition was got up and it was decided the village didn't want this. But they only went around the Protestant houses.'

Some Protestants claim that the GAA is offensive to their culture, because games are played on Sunday, because of noisy cavalcades of cars trailing tricolours, and because of the ban on RUC membership. A DUP politician said that, to Protestants, the GAA was like 'the IRA at play'. Paramilitaries have killed Catholics connected to it, like Sean Brown who was abducted from Bellaghy, not far from Ballymoney, by the LVF in 1997. Evelyn said that around the Twelfth, Protestants put up Union Jacks on one side of the street, and Catholics put up GAA flags on the other. 'The flags stay up till they are in tatters. It shows no respect to either.'

The cross-community facility was to be based in a public building in the village. 'Then one night a woman got up and said, "There is no way Catholics are getting into this building. This has always been a building for Protestants." She said she was speaking for everyone. Now, other people came to me quietly after and said she wasn't, but they daren't speak out. I suppose whoever shouts the loudest wins the day. Protestants feel very threatened about going to a Catholic building. I think they feel very threatened by community development. They feel they had the upper hand but now they are losing their grip.' The group fell apart. 'With the Twelfth coming up, people drifted away and that left just the broad-minded Protestants and people would say they are half Catholic anyway.'

Evelyn voted for the Belfast Agreement 'because I couldn't see any alternative', though she said she hated the prisoner releases and wanted to see decommissioning. 'I am Irish, but I am also British, because that is the system we live under. It doesn't bother me. I like Irish culture, but I think the way the language is used is quite divisive. A man told me recently that two men started talking Irish in his company and he felt excluded. You always have to take into account other people's feelings.'

'I'M NOT VERY STAUNCH'

Ballymoney did not have a youthful air about it. A lot of shops were boarded up. The clothes stores were far from fashionable, and the entertainment pages of the local paper advertised old style country-and-western bands. Plenty of religious services to go to, and a big leisure centre (which sometimes hosts concerts by the likes of Charlie Lansborough) but not much for the young. The university at Coleraine is only a few miles away, and is a big employer, but students away from home favour the nearby resorts of Portrush and Portstewart, where there are discos and bars and flats in tall houses overlooking the Atlantic.

The Youth Council, which is a cross-community venture, was set up by local community workers, through the borough council, to provide a forum for young people in and around the town. I met Victoria and Donna in the town hall, where the group was having a meeting. My request to speak to Protestant members was at odds with the whole idea of the group, and the girls were concerned not to seem to slight their Catholic friend who had arrived at the same time as them.

Victoria, a tall, smiling girl with long blond hair, and Donna, smaller, with tumbling red hair, were both fifteen. Victoria lived in the suburbs of the town. Her parents ran a shop. Donna lived in the country, where her parents had a small business. Victoria had just finished a history project on Northern Ireland from 1920 'to last Monday'. 'It was interesting but it kept repeating itself, people blaming other people for everything. It made me angry,' she said. It also made her pessimistic. 'I would like the agreement to work, but after reading about so many failed initiatives, there isn't much chance it will. I hope it will but.' She was at Coleraine High School. 'I think it's all Protestant.' And she belonged to a Presbyterian church. 'It is very boring, very set in its ways. I do believe in God and what I've been taught, but I'm not strongly set.' She was a Sunday school teacher and said that one day a row broke out among some little boys, who started shouting at each other, 'You're a fenian.'

Donna had grown up in Dunloy, knowing Catholics. 'I'm not very staunch,' she said. I asked her what 'staunch' meant. 'It means being in a loyalist band or a paramilitary organisation and saying "Catholics out" and "We hate Catholics", giving them the fingers and calling them fenians, even though you don't know any. There's a wile lot of people like that in Ballymoney. They don't know anything about Catholics but they have all these stereotypes. There is only one Catholic in my class at school. He is pure dead on.'

Her family had moved out of Dunloy recently. 'The people were friendly. We just felt it would be better.' The school bus she got also served a Catholic village. 'The Catholics sing "The Soldier's Song" just to annoy us. We don't sing "The Sash" back. I have a friend at the Free Presbyterian school. He has a Drumcree keyring and he's out blocking roads and all. I don't get that. They are blocking their own people. When they divert the Apprentice Boys away from Dunloy they send them down our wee road. I hate those two weeks in July. It goes kind of hyper round here.'

'I used to love that time,' said Victoria. 'We had a caravan and we'd have a bonfire and a big party. We had a family of Catholics used to come and celebrate with us, but we can't have it any more. It has changed. The summer before last, we stayed in. Someone else had a bonfire and it was all flags and things. The next day a wee girl of about eight came up to me and said, "Why weren't you at the bonfire? Are you a fenian?"'

'We race cars. It's called autocross and it's a mixed thing,' said Donna. 'The chairman is a Catholic and my dad is vice-chairman. Politics never comes up. You can't paint your car green, white and gold or red, white and blue. Mind you, one day this wee girl we race with says to me, "I hate him, he's a Protestant." People don't give the other side a chance. I got a job in a shop in Carnany. I couldn't have worked there if I was a Catholic because the customers wouldn't have let me. There's a lot of pure psychos in Carnany. It is not a place I'd like to live. My mum has a friend who is a Catholic married to a Protestant. She goes to the Twelfth and all, but they put a brick through the window of her house.'

The girls said they didn't talk politics with their Catholic friends, because politics was stupid. But then Victoria said she hated that her friends didn't do anything to change things. 'I'm going to write to Mo Mowlam, the secretary of state. The Assembly needs a youth input.

I'd like to be a politician.' Donna suggested she could join Alliance, or the Women's Coalition. 'There's only a small minority willing to sit on the fence,' she said. Donna didn't like Gerry Adams because of the 'obvious' links between Sinn Féin and the IRA, but she liked John Hume. 'You know what is great? *Give My Head Peace*. It shows how stupid people on both sides are.'

Give My Head Peace is a satirical television show from the Belfast-based Hole in the Wall Gang. Episodes have names like 'A Land Rover Named Desire', and there was a feature called *Two Ceasefires and a Wedding*. It features a Catholic family, headed by Ma and Da, a Sinn Féin activist, and a Protestant family, consisting of Uncle Andy, a UDA-style loyalist and his son Billy. Billy is an RUC man married to one of Ma and Da's daughters and then another, after the first one leaves him. At the wedding, as he drinks to drown his sorrows, Uncle Andy roars: 'Not my Malibu! I was saving it for a happy occasion, like the collapse of the Belfast Agreement.' Andy is the star of the show – a loud-mouthed, vain, foolish bigot with a Zapata moustache. The character is popular with loyalists – tapes of the show are on sale at stalls at all the big parades. The BBC has used him in its advertisements warning people to get their TV licence in order.

'I'm Irish,' said Victoria. 'I wouldn't care if we had an all-Ireland. I'm neither nationalist nor unionist.' 'I'm Northern Irish,' said Donna. Victoria said she was middle class; Donna, working class. Neither saw much future in staying in Ballymoney. They spoke of a friend of theirs who had her life planned out and it revolved around training to be a chef and then returning to her home village. Victoria said she wanted to travel the world. However, both agreed they wouldn't settle too far away. 'It would be too hard to get home if anyone died,' said Victoria.

'On the day of the referendum my friends were asking each other what way would you vote,' said Donna. 'I said I'd vote yes, and they said, "Traitor." In Victoria's school they had debated the agreement, which was pinned up on the wall, and local politicians had come in to argue for and against it. Then they had a vote, and 73 per cent voted for the agreement. Donna said marches shouldn't be stopped because roads were neither Catholic nor Protestant. Victoria said she couldn't see why it was so important to march. 'But I see both sides,' she said with a laugh. 'That annoys people about me.'

'THE GENERALS HAVE TO LEAD'

After Greg Taylor was kicked to death in 1997, Gil Warnock wrote an angry letter to the London *Independent*, saying that Ballymoney was radiating hatred because it had been irradiated for thirty years 'by people who'd created a situation in which such a killing was waiting to happen'. Warnock was a business consultant and former Irish chief executive of a multi-service company. He lived in the stylishly renovated farmhouse in which he grew up, on the outskirts of Bally-money. The lethal hatred, he told me, was created by the fusion of hardline unionism with the violence of the IRA.

He spoke of a 'leadership deficit' in the Protestant community. 'Take the Presbyterian Church,' he said. 'It is clearly the dominant Church and it had the capacity to make a powerful difference. But it hasn't. There have been outstanding individuals, like John Morrow, who set up the Corrymeela community, and John Dunlop – shining lights in a sea of darkness. But it would be interesting to know how many Presbyterian ministers know the phone number of their local Catholic priest, or would address them by their Christian name.

'Here we have this army of Christians, and if you believe as I do that "love thy neighbour" is to the core of Christianity, then this is the message that needed to be preached. But it isn't happening. The generals have to lead.' He felt people in Ballymoney simply couldn't cope with the appalling reality of the Quinn and Taylor murders. 'There is a lot of denial. However, both cases were far more complex than at first sight they might seem.'

Warnock had hopes that David Trimble might be a leader in the mould of Brian Faulkner, 'someone with the bigness to reach across the divide and take the Unionists to a place where they can really be confident'. He described the old Unionist establishment: 'You'd have had the local squire marching in front of his lodge, business leaders with their gold-tipped umbrellas – a large, strong, well-oiled machine. It was powerful. It elected the majority and it had its hands on all the levers to the very top and the very bottom.' Unionists had not re-covered from its break-up. 'You had direct rule which discredited them in the eyes of the world, and you had Paisley like a Rottweiler snapping at their heels. They had ruled without competition – they did not know how to cope.' He believed a lot of unionists would not speak about their politics, out of fear. 'We are lucky, sitting in the upper echelons of the middle classes. You can say what you want to your own circle of like-minded friends.' The middle classes had opted out of politics because 'there was nothing in it for them', and moderates feared a backlash from loyalists.

Having worked in Brussels and in Dublin, Warnock saw great advantages in cross-border trade and co-operation. 'In Dublin I saw a much more vibrant and self-confident set of institutions than in the North.' But change would have to be managed judiciously. 'The unionist is like a child who has been slapped around the ears for thirty years. He may have deserved it, and he is going to have to grow up, but he needs help to get his confidence back.' Sinn Féin was adopting cynical strategies to make sure that unionism remained trapped on issues like Drumcree. There could be trouble ahead if that party 'has already digested the meal of Easter '98 [the signing of the Belfast Agreement] and is hungry for more'. He said it was like trying to plough with two horses. 'If one of them is a born kicker, it won't work.'

As president of Ballymoney's Chamber of Commerce, Warnock offered leadership he felt had been effective in revitalising local traders. They had produced an attractive leaflet called 'Ballymoney – Ireland's best kept secret', to entice tourists heading for the coast to leave the bypass and see the town. There had been controversy about the photograph on the cover. It was of the pub from which Greg Taylor was pursued to his death. Warnock had no qualms about the choice. 'Kelly's pub is a metaphor for what is happening. The provincial press keep digging it up as a symbol of a bad past. The tourists who pick up our leaflet come because it is attractive, and return because it is so peaceful and friendly. Maybe it is an omen.'

I had read a travel article in the *Independent* on Sunday, 21 June 1998, which captured one of the oddest ironies about Northern Ireland. Gareth Lloyd wrote of small-town loyalist Ulster that 'the patriotism which drives places such as these to paint their kerbstones red, white and blue, and to have Union Jacks fluttering from every lamppost, can be strangely unnerving'. Ballymoney was that kind of town.

'AN UNSETTLED PEOPLE'

'I think the Protestants are in a terrible state,' said John Robb. Seeing both sides had long been his mission. A retired hospital consultant, he was one of the founders of the New Ireland group. The name was taken from the writings of William Drennan, another doctor, who described the first Volunteer convention at Dungannon in 1782 as 'the birthday of New Ireland'. In 1972 Robb wrote an inaugural pamphlet which imagined 1990, the third centenary of the sieges of Londonderry and Limerick, and asked: 'Would it be too much to hope that Orangemen and Hibernians of Ulster might congregate in the ecclesiastical capital of Armagh and, after attending the appropriate cathedral, join in a long march south with their bands and banners to meet a similar contingent coming from Limerick for a gigantic festival of the people around an arena for the first ever inter-provincial Games of the New Ireland?' Obviously, yes.

Robb lived in an imposing redbrick house on Charlotte Street. The street was handsome, with a brief terrace of tall Georgian houses, though these were followed by the ugly fortifications of the RUC barracks. Robb's huge study was overflowing with books and stacked papers. 'I've watched Ballymoney go down the tubes,' he said. 'There has been a terrible loss of morale in small towns, with the closing of hospitals and schools. There has been no effort to sustain the idea of a community. It shouldn't be just a commuter place.'

His own background was 'very privileged'. His father had been a surgeon. His mother was the daughter of the last solicitor-general. They had lived in a big house with servants – 'and guns, by the way'. He was sent away to public school in Scotland at the age of eleven. 'It was quite a feudal setup, and the boarding school bit was really a preparation for running an empire.' He studied medicine, travelled, worked in Soweto, where he was horrified by apartheid, and was working in a Belfast hospital when the Troubles started. 'You didn't hear Protestants talking about why this was happening. All you heard was talk of communism and IRA manipulation. When I had to deal with the victims of the first riots I cried my eyes out. I was totally and utterly ignorant. I started to read Irish history and realised that this was a terribly unjust society.'

He wrote his first letter about the New Ireland to the papers in 1971. 'I remember being terrified. You felt you were breaking ranks.' His associates in the movement included Dick Ferguson, 'who left the Orange Order and got a bomb in his garden', Barry White, who became a political commentator, and Roy Johnston, 'one of those who got the Official IRA to give up violence'. They launched the group in a Belfast hotel 'in a blaze of middle-class glory'.

He said he wrote to stimulate young Protestants into a new way of thinking. There was something of the naivety of the autodidact about the enterprise – the long, complicated letters, the heroic vision. In 1972, convinced that a great leader was needed, and that such a person could expose the Protestant ascendancy as 'out of date and going nowhere', Robb had in mind the young Reverend Ian Paisley. A decade later, in 1982, he thought of Bob McCartney.

He was a signatory to the MacBride Principles on fair employment. These were based on principles which had been devised in Washington DC, and were named after Sean MacBride, the former IRA leader in the twenties who had won the Nobel Peace Prize in 1974. The principles called for increased Catholic representation in the workplace, including managerial and administrative posts. Companies planning to invest in Northern Ireland would be obliged to apply them. They were strongly resisted by the British government, but latterly endorsed by President Clinton.

Robb had consistently challenged unionist orthodoxy on controversial issues, including decommissioning. 'The Protestant people have a tremendous reticence bordering on inability to discuss abstract ideas. There is a who-does-he-think-he-is attitude. The Bible does that to them. They seem to be lamentably poor at reading the situation they have got into. They don't realise that if this agreement falls apart, the fallback position will be the Anglo-Irish Agreement. The one comment James Molyneaux ever made to me was, "Beware of losing the landmarks too quickly." You need a sense of place and the relationships that go with it and Protestants are losing that. They have not been accustomed to being the underdog.'

Robb referred to a comment by PUP leader David Ervine, who had said that if an agreement about forming an executive was not reached and the government instead imposed an arrangement, loyalist para-militaries might go back to violence. 'If the IRA said that, there would be outrage,' said Robb. 'This is about democracy. Protestants are defensive and full of denial about their own violence. They feel in-creasingly demoralised and threatened. They are an unsettled people.'

Looking back, Robb said he wondered if he should have joined the SDLP, instead of trying to start a movement for 'communitarian democracy', with its emphasis on empowerment. 'But at least one has tried. This is such a caste-conscious society. The Protestant middle classes haven't retained any leadership link with the working classes. There are people in this town to whom I will always be "Mr Robb", the consultant. I was educated to be able to walk into the Gymkhana Club in New Delhi, or the Polo Club in Durban. After that I got a labouring job and found I could not communicate with the other workers. I am on the management committee for a local estate, and I'm on a community relations group. But a lot of what I think is abstract and esoteric. Is it practical to imagine a feeling of social in-clusivity? Maybe it is more realistic to try to give people confidence within their own areas. What do I know of Carnany?'

'NAE DIFFERENCE AT ALL'

Carnany is a very basic estate. Green spaces, but no landscaping. Small gardens mostly untended in front of plain, terraced houses. Although it was built twenty years ago, it looked like a newly planted place, cheap and disposable. But it had a community centre, and was soon to have a playpark, a memorial to the Quinn boys. When I visited first, the burnt-out shell of the house in which they were incinerated was still there, a desolate reminder, an ugly monument to something unacknowledged. It was demolished in April 1999.

I met Josie at the community centre. The blackened walls of the Quinns' house were just a few yards away. Gable walls across the green had been painted with 'UDA' on one side and 'UVF' on the other. Both had been painted over and partially erased. A stunted tree had a Union Jack painted on its bark. Josie, a warm, friendly woman who didn't look old enough to be a granny, but was, said of the Quinn family. 'They've been here that lang, it's sad tae see them go, like.

'It is mixed here. Everybody got on with everybody. It's all good people here on the estate. The centre here is mostly for the weans. I hae nothing against Catholic people, only the ones that's going out killing and maiming. My father was a Protestant and my mother was a Catholic, so she turned. My grandfather was a Catholic and my grandmother was Protestant. He turned and it didn't work, so she turned and stayed. There is fourteen of a family of them. Some of them stayed Catholic, some turned. You'd get that a lot here.

'We are Protestant. My eldest is going with a Catholic. She is living with him. I like him. He's a nice chap. But at the end of the day, if she came in and said she was for turning, I'd be annoyed.' I asked her why. 'She's a Protestant,' she said, with a shrug and a smile. What if her daughter married her boyfriend – would Josie mind? She laughed. 'I don't think she'll ever marry. She's too wise. My other daughter has a wee baby. She has her own wee house here on the estate. That's the way I like it, to have them close to me.'

This was a surprising thing. Chrissy Quinn was a Catholic whose former partner was a Protestant, and whose partner at the time of the murders was also Protestant. She had Protestant uncles, a Catholic mother. The friend who was in her house on the night of the fire was a Free Presbyterian. From what Josie was saying, none of this was unusual in Carnany. And yet, from what I'd heard, and from the graffiti, I assumed there was a loyalist paramilitary presence in the estate. It was like what I'd been told about Carrickfergus, where UVF men were married to Catholics. Or Lisburn, where several Catholics were in the UDA.

It is one of the sordid mysteries of sectarianism – the way it turns on individuals who had believed they were tolerated. I thought of Bernadette Martin staying overnight with her Protestant boyfriend in the home of the man who would, eleven days later, murder her.

A tall, lanky young fellow in a tracksuit came through. He started telling Josie about an Irish dancing contest they'd had at the disco. 'It was "I'll tell me ma",' he said. 'It was cracker, so it was. You want to have seen them. Blooter won in the end.' Josie introduced us. 'This girl's writing a book about Protestants,' she said. He half-turned, and gave me a look which seemed to be full of contempt. Then he left.

Josie had lived in Carnany for almost twenty years and loved it. She was angry at media coverage of the Quinn murders. 'They made a mountain out of a molehill,' she said. 'They went overboard. They were crawling all over the place. Now people say about Carnany, "That's a bad place." If it was, I wouldn't be here.' The community centre ran courses and 'fun days' and had darts and snooker and TV for the children. On St Patrick's Day, 17 March, they had an 'Irish stew night'.

Josie said that it was said there was a drugs problem. That 'people said' that drugs were being sold from a house which she pointed out to me from the window of the centre. I asked her what the drugs were. 'I dinny know,' she said. Ballymoney is twenty miles from Ballymena, which had become the hub of a small but growing heroin trade in the North. It seemed strange to worry about your children's exposure to drugs without finding out more. I realised Josie was not being entirely frank.

She invited me to come and meet other women at the mother and toddler group which met at the Carnany centre. They were friendly, but wary. Tilly, a cheerful woman with permed hair and a lined smoker's face, lived in a pensioner's bungalow on the estate. She said there was nothing wrong with Carnany, but that Ballymoney was a dead town. 'You've nae bother getting up the street for it's empty,' she said. What did she think the town needed? A big shopping centre. Jobs, she said. Something for the youth. 'I was a spinner in the mill at Balnamore from I was fourteen till I got married when I was nineteen. I worked myself up. I went back to work after my first child was born. I had to. I cleaned houses and worked in the shirt factory in Coleraine. I did home help too. I had seven children. In our day ye didny get it easy. You didn't get running aboot. You'd to work from eight in the morning till six at night. You'd tae carry water from a pump and you in your bare feet. You had no TV. But we were happier in them days.'

The women weren't church-goers and said the churches were only concerned with money. They all said they had no interest in politics. Tilly said she didn't know who the political representatives for the area were. The MP and MEP has been Paisley for decades. 'I sat and read thon book they sent around the houses,' she said, referring to the

Belfast Agreement. She had voted against it. 'There was a wheen of things in it I didn't agree with.' I asked her what the things were. 'I dinny mind.' Doreen, who said she'd left school at fourteen 'and started to smoke', was against it too, but when I asked her why, she replied, 'I dinny mind. There was a wheen of things in it . . .' Tilly was pessimistic. 'We're no any further forward since this agreement. I canny see any peace coming out of it.'

Most of the women were involved with the Orange Order in some way. Doreen had been in a woman's lodge for a while, and she took her children to band parades. 'My daddy was a drummer in a flute band,' said Josie. 'It wasny a rowdy band. My husband is in the Orange Order and the Apprentice Boys.' Tilly's husband, a tradesman, was in the Orange Order. 'I wouldny miss the Twelfth,' she said. 'It's a day oot.' She liked the supper dances the lodge organises. 'But I'd rather the Black. It's a far better sort of people.'

This brought us back to the Quinns. The boys had gone to the local state school, which is, in practice, the Protestant school because most Catholics go to the Church's own 'maintained' schools. The experience of the Quinns was a caution against expecting too much of integrated education. They were boys who were well integrated. They went to school with Protestant children, ran about with them and used the same community centre. They spent the evening of 11 July 1998 at the loyalist bonfire they'd helped to build. Hours later, their house was ablaze and they were dead.

'We were all right devastated,' said Josie. 'They were good weans. It was terrible. I heard the glass breaking and I ran down. It's terrible to stand there knowing someone needs your help and you can't give it. I greet about them weans yet.' The other women all said they grieved for the children, and it was obvious their sadness was real. They hated the sight of the burnt-out house. But they were adamant. 'In my heart I know it wasn't sectarian,' said Josie. 'Everybody gets on round here. There's nae difference at all,' said Tilly.

I asked the women why they felt Chrissy Quinn said she didn't want her children buried in Ballymoney. 'I can't understand why she said what she did,' said Josie. 'I don't think she should be bitter against the people on this estate.' The women said they had not talked to Chrissy since that terrible night. They did say, however, that she had been seen about town. They said this to show that she had not taken against Ballymoney in the way she had said she did. Her surviving son was back at his old school too, they said, resting their case.

I asked them about other allegations of intimidation. 'There's a lot of lies told,' said a young woman. 'People jump on the bandwagon. There is people after intimidation grants. Some of them is coming back now.' Doreen nodded. She looked out the window. 'See thon woman thonder,' she said, indicating a woman walking with shopping bags across the green. 'She was told to get out of Carnany and she stayed.'

A local UVF man told me the UVF cards with bullets enclosed had not been sent by the UVF, and that, anyway, there was no connection between those threats and what had happened to the Quinns, which was nothing to do with the UVF either.

The women said the people who killed the Quinn children were 'cowboys', 'smart alecks with time on their hands'. Josie said she couldn't believe any of the loyalist paramilitary groups would have done such a thing. 'It's not their style to target weans. The way I look at things, if the UVF or the UDA goes to someone, they have a reason for it.' She said people in the estate had no problems with the police. 'We hae community police and we get on good wi' them.' I asked about the roadblocks and petrol bombs on the night the Quinns died. 'I suppose they did it because everyone else was doing it,' Josie said. The women said there was no trouble around the Twelfth or the marching season in Carnany.' Tilly insisted: 'There's never nae bother at all.'

'THERE IS ANOTHER WAY TO LIVE'

Alison, who worked as a teacher in the north of England, had her first proper political discussions when she left the North to go to college there. 'I met an Irish lad whose background was the opposite of mine. He was from a republican family, and I was from a security force one, and we became friends. We used to argue and talk about everything.' She liked that. 'At home you have to be so cautious and secretive. When you do discuss something and you disagree, people get very excited and voices are raised. People get nasty. There is a lack of freedom here that you don't recognise until you go away. I like it that in England people don't care about your religion.'

She came 'home' to Ballymoney regularly, to see her parents, but said she could never return to live. 'My husband is a Catholic. Actually, religion in itself is not important to me. It's people who count. We are both Christians. I don't think of myself as a Protestant. The church we go to is non-denominational and forges links with all the Churches. But I know some of my family avoid telling people that my husband is Catholic. If they have to, they say he used to be but now he goes to a Protestant church with me. I have heard some terrible things said, that Catholics aren't Christians for example.

'I am Irish. My family doesn't like me saying that. I have friends from Northern Ireland over in England and they feel the same as me. They have dissociated themselves from Northern Irish politics. I honestly don't think it would be such a bad thing if we were joined with the Republic. The economy there seems a lot better than here. Britain is not what it's made out to be – the part of England I live in has a lot of poverty and disadvantage. This clinging to the crown is ridiculous.

'My brothers and sisters who stayed at home still see things the traditional way. Northern Irish Protestants deny their culture and heritage by dissociating themselves from their country. We look silly to other people. They see Paisley on TV bawling his head off and getting thrown out of parliament and they think he's a clown. They can't tolerate him. They change the channel. Whereas Sinn Féin are very poised. They have good speakers and people in England listen to them. I think that once you link politics and religion it becomes brainwashing. Worse still, Paisley has schools.'

Coming back, she found that the North has a 'post-war feel' and she sensed that Ballymoney was 'a town in decline'. She was upset about the Greg Taylor murder. 'The level of hatred was shocking. He was a Protestant murdered by Protestants, and people helped some of those responsible to get away. And then they more or less tried to make out he was to blame.' Then she spoke about something that had happened near Ballymoney when she was a young teenager, in the early eighties. A friend of hers was beaten to death. 'It was a sort of punishment beating gone wrong. It was over something really stupid, like he had taken a ball belonging to one of them.' So she had seen Protestants turn on their own.

She was in England when she heard about the Quinns. 'I felt so sick. Those poor little children. When they said it was a mixed marriage my first thought was, that could have been me. Though I suppose these things are more likely to happen in these council estates. But when I came home my mum had the local paper laid out to dry the floor in the kitchen and I was reading this stuff about how the Orangemen in Ballymoney were very angry because the chief constable said it was sectarian.'

Alison thought band parades and marches through nationalist areas were provocative. Her family did not agree with her. They said those who objected to the parades were 'just against Protestants'. She recognised a lot of bigotry and sectarianism in people she knew. 'They won't recognise it though. Drumcree is only an issue because the Orangemen have allowed it to become one. There is another way to live. In England people ask me what these parades are about and I try to explain, and they say, "And when was this battle?" Then you have to say, "1690", and they are just bewildered. To be part of a community, you have to respect people whose beliefs are different to yours.'

'SHAME'

Jailing two men for the murder of Greg Taylor, Lord Chief Justice Sir Robert Carswell said that while they had not intended to kill the RUC man, 'this does not take away from the fact that it was a vicious assault, a disgraceful episode which has brought shame to the community in which it took place' (quoted in the *Irish News*, 22 December 1998). The men appealed their conviction.

Just over two months later, there was fury in Ballymena when author Peter Taylor mistakenly stated in his book *Loyalists* that the Quinn children had been murdered at their home 'near Ballymena'. The Ulster Unionist mayor of Ballymena, James Currie, demanded a public apology to the citizens of Ballymena, while DUP councillor Maurice Mills said the error 'could hit Ballymena's image in a big way'. Alliance Councillor Jayne Dunlop said it could affect investment in the town. 'We could be perceived as a load of hooligans,' she said

(*Irish News*, 12 March 1999). Even after Taylor had apologised and promised that a correction would be made in reprints of the book, Currie, while welcoming the news, said it could never take away all of the damage.

And yet, strangely, no one spoke to me in Ballymoney about shame or damage after the Quinn and Taylor murders which were committed in the town. Instead, they offered reasons for the murders. Some went to the brink of justifying them. Chrissy Quinn's house might have been attacked by someone who mistakenly thought a drug dealer was living there. Or it might have been something to do with her former partner, who had been ordered out of the North by paramilitaries. Some of the Quinns had been in trouble with the law: 'Not a good family, you know.' Paisley said the IRA had carried out 'far worse murders'. Greg Taylor's killers were drunk – they did not know what they were doing. It just got out of hand. There was 'bad blood' between Taylor and his attackers.

People insisted that the murders had nothing to do with Drumcree, nothing to do with Dunloy, nothing to do with sectarianism, nothing to do with the Orange Order. Ballymoney was not that kind of town, they insisted. First Minister David Trimble denounced the rumours and claims about the murder of the children. 'There is no doubt in my mind that the house was petrol-bombed in the context of a spate of sectarian threats in that area. To suggest anything else is quite despicable,' he said (quoted in the *Irish News*, 14 July 1998). But the rumours, ugly and poisonous, kept on proliferating. At Drumcree they were particularly offensive.

Middle-class people said that some of the people involved in the killing of Taylor were 'from respectable families'. By contrast, Taylor had jeopardised his own respectability. He had been separated from his wife for a time, for example. One mild-mannered businessman told me that people had been leaving the remains of Chinese takeaways on his grave. 'There has to be a reason why they are doing that,' he said meaningfully. In short, a shocking range of Ballymoney people chose almost to blame the victims of these appalling murders, rather than face up to the violence in their community.

One woman, who had known and liked Greg Taylor, said that if he was killed for stopping the loyalists from getting into Dunloy, it had all been a tragic mistake. He had told her that while on duty there, he had been ashamed of his RUC uniform. He shared her view that opposition to the parades was a smokescreen. That these residents' groups were actually just 'against Protestantism'. In other words, he was not disloyal. He understood the frustration of those the politicians had made him stop. She said local police should not be made to man the barricades. The implication somehow was that this kind of thing was the inevitable result of 'bad law', the loyalist term for rulings by the Parades Commission. A policeman told me that on the night of the Quinn murders, some people in the crowd that gathered in Carnany blamed the RUC for the deaths of the children. They said it wouldn't have happened if the police hadn't blocked the road at Drumcree.

Respectable middle-class Ballymoney people tended to distance themselves from Carnany as a whole. There was no 'old stock' living there. A lot of blow-ins from trouble spots in Belfast. They spoke of it as a place they disapproved of, and into which they would never venture. One man explained that middle-class people resented being smeared by the murders. He said he imagined a white-carpeted drawing room in one of Ballymoney's nicer areas. Comfortable people are drinking sherry and eating shortbread. Suddenly the little pet dog, which has been sitting on the rug, gets up and shits on the carpet. The dog is called Quinnie. Nobody knows what to say.

In an essay on fundamentalist Protestantism, academic Duncan Morrow quoted Ken Maginnis, who had said that the Protestant community saw itself as 'more sinned against than sinning'. The Reverend Kille had restated this in his sermon on the battle of good against evil. So had those on the long march, with their 'the real victims' banner. It was the 'ferocious attachment' to this idea which explained the importance of fundamentalism, and why its influence reached beyond those who shared its religious doctrines. The ritual re-enactment of the Protestant myths, especially the Orange parades, said Morrow, 'does not unite the political nation but divides it into two – those who belong and those who are seen as enemies'. He quoted the French social critic René Girard, who said that all myth was structured around the memory of expulsion of a scapegoat, reinforcing the unity of the group (Morrow in Shirlow and McGovern, p. 59).

The struggle of the Orange Order in the late nineties was to prove that while the rest of the world might look on the Quinn children and others as the scapegoat of a violent loyalism, the truth was, it was the Protestant people who were the victims. The expulsionists were the pan-nationalist front, Unionist parlance for the combined forces of the SDLP, Sinn Féin, the Catholic Church and the Irish government – in other words, Irish Catholics. They had been aided in their project by a treacherous Britain.

There was a terrible lack of humanity in the way many Ballymoney people, of all classes, spoke about the Quinns. One man even said that, despite what Chrissy Quinn said about not wanting to come back to Ballymoney, he didn't think the people of the town were bitter against her. A minister warned me 'to tread very carefully because you are on dangerous ground, the truth has not come out yet'. His wife spoke about a television interview which Chrissy Quinn gave a few days after the murders: 'That reporter asked her was it to do with Drumcree. He should have been skinned alive.'

The claim that the murders were not sectarian implied that there were other reasons, more acceptable reasons. This in turn implied a tacit acceptance that men who used petrol bombs were in some circumstances justified in doing so. People said, on the one hand, paramilitaries don't go after people for no reason, and, on the other, we have no paramilitaries here. They said that nobody got put out, and they said that a woman was told to get out and she refused.

James Leslie spoke of his anxiety about a lack of respect for law and order. But then, he also said the paramilitaries had been 'pretty effective' against the IRA in the period leading up to the ceasefire in 1994. Leslie is a politician from the class whose line loyalists traditionally toed. He condemned loyalist violence, and said Protestants must face up to sectarianism. There was no doubt about his sincerity. However, those seeking justification for continuing paramilitary activity were liable, albeit wrongly, to regard descriptions like 'pretty effective' as endorsements.

The deputy leader of the UUP, John Taylor, said in 1993, after an eight-day period in which loyalists had murdered five Catholics, that 'in a perverse way this is something which may be helpful because they are now beginning to appreciate more clearly the fear that has existed for the past 20 years as they have been killed at random by the IRA' (quoted in the *Irish News*, 9 September 1993). John Taylor also told journalist Peter Taylor that 'the loyalist paramilitaries achieved something which perhaps the security forces would never have achieved, and that was, they were a significant contribution to the IRA finally accepting that they couldn't win' (Taylor, 1999, p. 234).

I tried to imagine the reaction in Ballymoney if a crowd of Catholics had set upon Greg Taylor in a bar and kicked him to death. Or if Chrissy Quinn had been a Protestant living in a predominantly Catholic estate, and, on the night of a republican festival, her children had been murdered. And if the chief constable had said that he believed nationalists were responsible and that their motivation was sectarian. There would have been overwhelming rage and fury. People would have called it ethnic cleansing. Some at the angrier edge would have said that it proved that nationalists were filled with destructive and murderous hatred of Protestants. That when it came down to it they were all republicans, and that what was needed was a security clampdown. Some would have said this should include shooting to kill, internment and even capital punishment.

On 12 July 1997, a year before the Quinn murders, Paisley addressed the Independent Orange Order at Ballycastle, on the Antrim coast a few miles north of Ballymoney. Prominent members of the Orange Order at Ballymoney, including John Finlay, later to be elected as a DUP councillor, were present. After the parade reached the field, the young crowd cleared off to the pubs. On the platform, a long, solemn line of mostly ageing Independent Orangemen made dreary speech after dreary speech.

Then Paisley spoke. The older people sat on the grass munching sandwiches and drinking sweet tea from flasks, while Paisley made smutty jokes about the ability of good Protestant ladies to breed just as well as Catholics. He told them 'the entire pan-nationalist front' was 'seeking the reincarnation of the beast of fascism', the IRA. World War Two was being fought out again in Northern Ireland: 'the jackboot and the gas chamber murder mentality is the driving force of the leadership of the pan-nationalist front'. He told them that 80 per cent of the Protestant population of the Republic had been 'eliminated' and that the attempt to stop Orange parades was 'the prelude to the elimination of Protestants' in the North. Rome was the ecclesiastical front; the IRA the political front. Their shared dogma was 'submit or perish'.

Orangemen are inclined to wax sentimental about the old days when Catholics would watch the parades, but it was hard to imagine that any Ballymoney Catholic, persuaded along to share the cultural highlight of his Protestant neighbours' year, would feel anything other than appalled by such a speech. But the sandwich-munching crowd chuckled at the jokes about breeding, and nodded and clapped for the rest.

The speech was frightening in a different way to Protestants, with its claims that their co-religionists in the South had been eliminated, and that the actions of nationalist residents' groups were a 'prelude' to the elimination of Protestants in the North. This had echoes of the real horrors of Rwanda, where genocide had followed hate-filled tirades the previous year. But there had been no genocide in the Republic of Ireland.

Paisley had raised his Third Force, marched people up hills with gun licences, and urged people to fight to the death. But he had never stood on a platform and said, 'Go forth and hate Catholics. Go forth and kill them.' Indeed, he had repeatedly and strongly condemned those who took such meaning from his words. A fastidious exactness, a literal-mindedness, however, was required to understand and accept these distinctions.

While I was visiting the Independent Christian School in Ballymoney, I asked Noreen McAfee if she could send me some information about approaches to reading the Bible. She sent me *An Introductory Guide to Reading the Scriptures*, along with an invitation to a family night at the church, at which a fisherman who nearly drowned in a storm off the Antrim coast was to give his testimony. The material, of American origin, set out to arm Protestants with the facts with which to destroy the arguments of non-believers. It did so by proving the literal truth of biblical stories. Questions such as 'Was Noah's ark big enough?' were addressed. 'The ark measured 300 by 50 by 30 cubits (Genesis 6.15)', this section began. There followed an intricate piece of arithmetic involving cages, food, air circulation and other factors. 'We are discussing an emergency situation, not necessarily luxury accommodation. Although there is plenty of room for exercise, sceptics have overstated animals' need for exercise anyway.' Proof was offered that a million insect species, each pair occupying cages of 10 cm per side, could have been accommodated. However, 'insects are not included in the meaning of behemah or remes in Genesis 6:19 and 20 so Noah probably would not have taken them on board anyway'.

This kind of literal approach led David Jones to state that by 1999 the Orange Order would require to walk down the Garvaghy Road not once but twice, since they'd missed the 1998 march. It also allowed the Order to dissociate itself from responsibility for actions carried out by its supporters. It was true that they told troublemakers to stay away. That was what made the Reverend William Bingham's stand remarkable, after the Quinn children burned up in what poet Tom Paulin called 'Orange flames'. Bingham said the protest should be ended because 'we can't control it'. But it was not ended.

'My son is a very decent, caring and well-brought-up young gentleman,' said Mrs Irene Gilmour. It was 27 October 1999, two days before Mr Justice Liam McCollum was to deliver judgment on her son Garfield for the Quinn murders. I was interviewing Mrs Gilmour for the *Sunday Tribune*. She accepted that Garfield had driven the car in which the killers travelled: 'My son very innocently gave a couple of boys a lift. He did it because he is a very obliging boy. If Garfield had had any idea of what they were going to do, he would have done anything in his power to stop it happening.' He would have been unable to believe that any-one 'could go and do that in cold blood'. It wasn't until he was arrested and taken to Castlereagh five days later that 'he realised what he was involved with'.

Mr Justice McCollum did not think so. In his judgment, he said Gilmour was 'a person of good character' But the Justice told Belfast's Crown Court that Gilmour was also a 'resourceful liar at times in the course of his interviews and I am sure that he has not disclosed his full involvement in the events of that morning [12 July 1998]'.

He was satisfied 'on the basis of his admissions... and on the evidence of the witnesses called by the prosecution that the accused was aware that the house occupied by some members of the Quinn family was going to be petrol bombed by [two others] and that in that knowledge he remained near the scene in order to enable [the two other men] to escape after petrol bombing the house'. He was also satisfied 'from [Gilmour's] visits to the estate he knew that there were young children in the house'.

Mr Justice McCollum noted that Gilmour had been seen driving around Carnany and past Chrissy Quinn's house on 9 July, and had again driven around the estate the morning before the attack. He spent the Eleventh night at a bonfire in another part of Ballymoney. In statements quoted by the Justice, Gilmour said he did not know why he was later asked to drive other men to Carnany, but 'twigged on' when one of them 'pointed out the house' and he saw 'the bottle'. He said it was 'glistening'.

'By the looks of the bottle and that, it clicked on me that they were going to petrol bomb the house,' he said in a statement. 'But I prayed that I was wrong.' He said the third man was left in the car with him 'to make sure I didn't drive off'. Seconds after the two men got out of the car, he heard breaking glass.

The Justice said he was satisfied that once Gilmour became aware that one of the men in the car with him had a petrol bomb, 'he would have realised instantly that its use was to cause grievous bodily harm to the occupants of the house, especially since he recognised that the attack was a UVF attack with the clear inference that its motive was sectarian'. The RUC had found UVF Christmas cards in the house in Ballymoney which Gilmour shared with his girlfriend in July 1998. They were the same as the ones which had been sent to Catholics in Carnany, complete with a little quote from Sir Edward Carson on the subject of freedom. Gilmour denied sending the cards, which, he said, had been bought by his girlfriend at a band parade.

In one of Gilmour's later statements, quoted in Mr Justice McCollum's judgment, he said that after the men came back to the car, he drove them 'down the town'. He admitted that he knew the attack was 'a UVF operation' because, he said, the other men in the car were in that organisation. 'The UVF scare me,' he said in the statement. He said that after they drove away, one of the men said something like, 'They were warned to get out of the estate'.

Inside the blazing house Chrissy Quinn was woken up by 'the weans shouting, Mummy, smoke'. Minutes later, ten-year-old Richard pressed himself against the upstairs window crying out that he was frightened and his feet were burning. The firefighters arrived within ten minutes, and risked their own lives to try to reach the boys. The three small charred bodies, each of them curled up in the foetal position, were carried out of the ruins.

The Justice said that after Gilmour 'was informed [by the RUC] he had been seen driving his vehicle with three other persons in it at the back of No. 41 [Chrissy Quinn's] at about 20 minutes after the fire... he admitted to driving into the estate after the fire although he attempted to explain the number of people in his car by saying that two young boys had got into the car in Carnany'.

Mr Justice McCollum said that Gilmour was from 'a good family'. Irene Gilmour was a staff nurse at Coleraine Hospital, and her husband was a former civil servant. They had done their best for their adopted son. He had gone to prep school and to Dalriada College. He was a salesman, drove a good-sized car. There was a family farm, which he was to inherit. In other words, Garfield Gilmour was a young man from a hardworking and respectable Protestant family, and he had good prospects in life.

But Mr Justice McCollum convicted him of the murder of each of the three little Quinn boys, 'on the basis that he aided and abetted a petrol bomb attack on the house in which they were sleeping, knowing that the intent of the perpetrator... was to cause grievous bodily harm to the occupants of the house'. Gilmour was sentenced to life imprisonment. His counsel had sought a verdict of manslaughter. Gilmour has appealed.

Chrissy Quinn lost three of her four children in the most appalling circumstances. She was in court when Mr Justice McCollum gave his verdict on Gilmour's part in what he called 'this shameful outrage'. The ghost of a smile passed across her face. But there was still, in Ballymoney, little sense of that 'shame to the community' of which Sir Robert Carswell had spoken in relation to the Taylor murder. I was covering the Gilmour trial for the *Sunday Tribune*. 'We could do without you coming round here digging all this up again,' said a local businessman. The DUP continued to insist the murders were not sectarian. The UVF continued to deny involvement. The Orange Order claimed it had been vindicated. The Reverend William Bingham agreed, and apologised to the Order 'if there was any misunderstanding' about his comments after the murders.

I went back to the woman who had said to me in 1998, 'There is more to that than meets the eye.' Back to the bungalow belt. 'We are all very angry about the whole thing. It was a disgrace. Chrissy Quinn went out of her way to blacken the Orangemen at Drumcree when it was nothing to do with them,' she said. 'There is nobody has any time for her in this town.'

PLACES OF THE MIND

'... how this caper will end no one knows'

from 'Drumcree Four', TOM PAULIN

THE CRITIC – 'THERE'S A SORT OF CULTURE WAR ...'

'I felt when I came here it was a very secret place,' said Edna
Longley, the formidable professor of English literature at Queen's
University Belfast. 'There were all sorts of strange codes.' Born in
Dublin, the daughter of a professor, she met her husband, the poet
Michael Longley, at Trinity College and they moved back to his native
city. An intense and rather fierce woman, she was also softly spoken
and apparently shy. We spoke in a study in her house on a leafy
avenue near Queen's. There were fine paintings of nudes by her
daughter on the walls. An enormous tom cat wandered in and out.

Longley's critical work had to a great extent defined the 'Ulster
poets', who began to publish in the late sixties. In an essay written in
the seventies she had described the coincidence of the 'tribal pot
coming to the boil' and the overflowing of the poetic streams. She had
been the champion of the poets, but she had increasingly got involved
in debating the politics of culture. 'There's a sort of culture war,' she
said. 'There are a lot of quite hostile stereotypes about.' She quoted
the Ulster Unionist politician Chris McGimpsey who had summed up

the stereotypical views held about his community as: 'Protestants burn wood.'

Longley was a kind of warrior herself, and had explicitly taken on nationalist ideologies which tended to imply that unionism and culture were contradictions in terms. She was brave. Like the Progressive Unionist politicians she admired, especially Ervine, she was willing to debate with nationalists and republicans on their own ground. Writing about the 'Irish, Irisher, Irishest' approach to identity, which only referred approvingly to 'Patriot Prods (Tone, Emmet etc)', she remarked bitterly that, 'It sometimes seems as if Protestants have to die for Ireland before being allowed to live here' (Edna Longley, 1994, p. 175).

She had gone into full-scale battle with the Field Day Theatre Company, which included writers like Brian Friel and Seamus Deane. 'The whole country abounds in Ancient Orders of Hibernian Male-Bonding: Lodges, brotherhoods, priesthoods, hierarchies, sodalities ... Field Day Theatre Company' (Edna Longley, 1994, p. 187). She noted that unionism was patriarchal too, but bitingly added that at least it 'does not appropriate the image of woman or hide its aggressions behind our skirts'. (She had been proved right about the patriarchal assumptions behind Field Day when it published its massive anthology of Irish literature in 1991 and included almost no women.)

Central to the feminisation of nationalism was the figure of Cathleen Ní Houlihan. Longley noted the enormous irony of the fact that it was the Protestant and aristocratic William Butler Yeats who, with his early play *Cathleen Ní Houlihan*, had propagated this 'feminine mystique'. 'Irish cultural nationalism, thanks to Yeats, is romantic,' she said. The feminine mystique was allied with the idea of woman as victim to male aggression. Britishness was male. Unionism was male.

'There's a lot of political illiteracy among unionists here. It's to do with not having certain traditions. Dublin provided that – look at Carson. There is an extraordinary lack of PR skills. It is almost innocent. New unionism is trying to redress that.' She had reservations about some of the recent crop of Dublin commentators who had rushed to support unionism. She mentioned Eoghan Harris and Ruth Dudley Edwards. 'The zeal of the convert is irritating.' Conor Cruise O'Brien was an earlier, destructive, example. 'New unionism' included historians like Paul Bew, and critics like Jack Foster, though Longley noted that Yeatsian romanticism had proved very resistant to revisionism.

Longley as political commentator has sometimes been disingenuous. In an article she gave me called 'Ulster Protestant Mentalities' she noted that outsiders were more likely to sympathise with the desire of most Ulster Catholics for a united Ireland than with the desire of Protestants to remain part of the United Kingdom. 'Irish nationalism is sexier than unionism, partly thanks to clearer self-articulation and better propaganda, partly to less tangible assets.' These assets were of the Ossianic, Celtic, romantic sort. Unionists, on the other hand were internationally identified with 'an Orange parade!'

This conveniently erased the possibility that 'outsiders' might have well-founded objections to unionism, or the way unionists had treated nationalists, though elsewhere she recognised and criticised Unionist gerrymandering and discrimination. Nor did it allow that 'outsiders' might wonder why, given the 'image problem' which Longley attributed to the Orange Order, unionism was so reluctant to distance itself from it. The Order might urge its members to vote for Paisley in the 1999 European elections, though he was not an Orangeman, instead of the UUP's Jim Nicholson, who was – but the UUP steadfastly refused to break its structural links with the Order, links which gave it power within the party. The Unionist cliché that 'the other side is 'far better at propaganda than us' all too readily became a form of denial.

Similarly, Longley had written off Tom Paulin's fine poem 'Desertmartin' when she referred to his inability to temper the 'extremist techniques of satire' and said that his 'clichéd, external impression of the Protestant community, exposes Paulin's own "parched certainty"' (Edna Longley, 1986, p. 192). British poet and critic Sean O'Brien remarked that this type of writing belonged 'more properly to the right-wing British press than to literary criticism' (O'Brien, p. 186).

'One reason for some of the stereotypes is that, if you take, say, a Protestant renegade like Derek Mahon, his dissidence from his origins is seen in a negative way,' said Longley. 'You see it a lot in his early poems. Also in a recent poem, "Death in Bangor".' The poem she mentioned was a moving elegy to the poet's mother, in which he reflected on 'the plain Protestant fatalism of home'. Its last line describes his return from the funeral to 'blue skies of the Irish republic' – an inversion of the loyalist vow, 'We will never forsake the blue skies of Ulster for the grey skies of an Irish republic.' Longley said that Catholics picked up the sense that there was something in the poet's background that he couldn't forgive. 'They say, there you are, we always knew they were like that. They don't recognise that what Mahon's alienation also shows is that Protestantism can produce its own critics.'

I knew what she meant, but wondered if the Protestant tendency to exclude the non-conformist was not the stronger force. How easy it was to become a Lundy. How unforgiving Protestants were to those who were 'disloyal'. Evelyn, the Ballymoney community worker, had said of the Protestants who supported cross-community work in her village that they would be regarded by other Protestants as 'half Catholic anyway'.

Frustrated by 'stilted political thinking' in unionism, Norman Porter had attempted to define a new 'civic unionism'. As Longley herself noted in a review of his book, *Rethinking Unionism*, Porter had been vilified and shunned by party colleagues for his efforts. I had heard Porter address a gathering of republicans and nationalists at the West Belfast Festival not long after his book appeared. At a manic pace he told jokes, sent up the old unionist certainties, and laughed loudly. He seemed anxious to show that unionists could have a sense of humour. When someone asked a question about the role of the Catholic Church in the Republic, he told a story about waking up with a hangover in a bed and breakfast and seeing the red light of the Sacred Heart lamp. It was left to a stern republican woman to deal with the substantive issue. In her review, Longley said that 'civic unionism', as an idea, 'struggles to be born'.

Longley described Trinity College in the sixties as 'this extraordinary place where you got Protestants and a few Catholics', while at Queen's, 'bright young Catholics' like Seamus Heaney were meeting 'a very English staff'. 'Of course,' she added, 'the universities were at this point also incubating your Eamonn McCanns.' Incubating? The poetic streams and the tribal pot. I found Longley's tendency to divide people into those for us and those 'agin us' a bit parochial and stifling. (Ronan Bennett, she said, was a *bête noire*, and he 'had the ear of the *Guardian*'. Bennett is a Belfast-born, London-based novelist and journalist whose perspective on Ireland is critical of unionism.) When I asked about her role in the 'culture war' she replied, 'I didn't start it.'

Longley was an infinitely more interesting and subtle thinker when she was not propagandising. She spoke of the 'coincidence of talent and history'. 'There is a lot of "spilt religion" in Northern Irish poetry. Heaney's pastoral was Catholic. The metaphysic of Derek Mahon's poetry is post-Protestant. There is lapsed Anglicanism knocking around in there too, in MacNeice. The voice of the preacher is there sometimes. Beckett is a post-religious Protestant who translates a scourging Calvinism into other modes. The sides have been watching each other here for centuries. There are a lot of doubles and shadows and mirrors – a binary relation. It is civil war poetry, really. Twin and twin at each other's throats.'

One of the most interesting examples of this phenomenon was, in fact, her husband's poem 'Ceasefire'. The powerful poem, based on a story from Homer's *Iliad*, ends with the couplet: 'I get down on my knees and do what must be done/ And kiss Achilles' hand, the killer of my son' (Michael Longley, 1995). Like Van Morrison's song 'Days Like This', and Seamus Heaney's poem *The Cure at Troy*, Longley's poem had an extraordinary resonance in an emotional and highly charged time. Published in the *Irish Times*, it became well known, and informed difficult debates about reconciliation, the disappeared, and prisoner releases.

THE HISTORIAN – 'MY SIEGE MENTALITY'

A.T.Q. Stewart's reputation had suffered because of extreme praise. In 1977 he published *The Narrow Ground*, a historical study of aspects of Ulster from 1609 to 1969, including the Plantation, the siege of Derry, and the politics of Presbyterianism. Shortly afterwards, Ian Paisley brandished the book in the air above the pulpit of the Martyrs Memorial Church on the Ravenhill Road in Belfast. 'Brethren and sisters in Christ,' he shouted. 'Here is a great book that tells the truth about Ulster. Go home, friend, and read it' (quoted in Paulin, 1996, p. 28).

Tony Stewart was well aware that such a eulogy was a mixed blessing. 'I can't help who reads my books,' he said. 'Paisley will never change. It's one of those ghastly things – a lot of what he says is true.' We sat in the living room of his house in the south Belfast suburbs. His wife brought coffee and set it out on a nest of tables. 'Oh this is awfully lower middle class,' said Stewart cheerfully.

'The whole question of Presbyterian radicalism is my subject. My father was a Belfast Presbyterian, my mother was from an English Methodist family. My grandfather was a Methodist lay preacher. The Methodists have always been anxious to be seen as on the side of reconciliation – polite critics of the harder edges of Ulster unionism. On the other side, then, you had Uncle Elijah. He was an Antrim Presbyterian, radical underneath, and always critical. He resented people referring to Roman Catholics. He said Romanist.'

Stewart agreed that politics in the North was in some ways strongly defined by place. 'The tension between the Church of Ireland and the Presbyterians in the eighteenth century was not fully worked out and that led to the United Irishmen. But two things came out of Presbyterianism in 1798 – the Orangemen and the Volunteers. In County Antrim you became a United Irishman, in County Down you became a Volunteer. Though only a minority of Presbyterians were radicals. There was no competition with Catholics in Antrim for weaving jobs. Territory is so important – "beating the bounds". We have the Irish identification with the soil. The last residual resistance in the North will be among farmers. What is behind these concerned residents' groups is, they are attempting to take territory.'

He said that different layers operated within the community in the North. 'At the first level, it doesn't matter what religion a person is, or their politics. We don't get on the bus and ask the driver what religion he is. I like to think of myself as someone who could engage with ideas, engage with minds across the world. A lot of people think they are like that. That, because they go to concerts in the Waterfront, they aren't bigoted.

'Another layer is not discussed much. If you live in Surbiton, you watch TV and you think, "Look at those dreadful people but of course, it's understandable, they don't know each other." Then someone sets up a school and they all go there together and the children write poems about peace and reconciliation and everyone thinks, "Isn't that lovely?" But it isn't true that we don't know each other. We've lived with each other for three hundred years and that is a culture in itself. There is an almost visceral hatred between the two communities. People in Kosovo lived together for years – then someone made a mistake. We have a very mild form of that here.

'Every day you hear about reconciliation. You must have concerts and all that. People feel good when they shake hands. But it's all hot air. You don't start with reconciliation. If you belong to a state you subscribe to its law and order but you also expect it to protect you. Until that is resolved, you'll not end violence. You need to strengthen the majority position and then create a federal situation. What they've done since 1969 is to exacerbate the situation. They have created a Konfessionskrieg which the 1920s settlement had taken the heat out of. There is no sense of state. We are not in a united Ireland and we're not in the United Kingdom either.

'I think the government has taken sides. Unfortunately, not the Protestant one. It worked like clockwork. They got rid of Stormont, they got rid of the B Specials, they got rid of the UDR. Now the last defence of the state of Northern Ireland is about to go. They are getting rid of the RUC.' The Patten report had just been published and had been hailed as a disaster and a betrayal by unionists. John Taylor had said that if it was implemented, terrorists would bring about a 'bloody revolution'.

'This state was supposed to provide a shelter for Protestants,' said Stewart. 'There are awful, basic facts. People are actually menaced. This is not understood. Protestants won't live in Roman Catholic areas for fear. Catholics don't have that fear.' This seemed an astonishing claim. He said there was 'a kind of intuitive blood knowledge of history' and wondered if in somewhere like Portadown there was 'Jungian folk memory' of massacres: 'Admittedly, it is hard to see how the drug-taking, disco-attending, couldn't-care-less youngsters of today could be influenced by 1641.' However, he recalled walking out of his 'quiet room' in the university and straying into a downtown riot. As he walked away again he saw two middle-aged men showing some young boys how to make petrol bombs. 'It is handed down,' he said.

'I think the trouble in Ireland is we look through our history backwards.' He made a telescope of his hands. 'We look at 1798 and see the Provisionals. But the politics of 1798 belong to 1798.' However, what he then said was, 'People say the sides have to come together. No. One side or the other has to surrender.' He smiled. 'Maybe it's my siege mentality.'

THE POET – 'THE NEW MODEL ULSTER'

When I told A.T.Q. Stewart I was also to interview the poet and critic Tom Paulin he told me about a clash between them at a meeting of the British–Irish Association dinner at Oxford. This august body, colloquially known as 'toffs against terrorism', is a forum for discussion among academics, diplomats and politicians. There have been several such groups, including the Monday Club and Friends of the Union. After his run-in with Paulin, Stewart had felt obliged to leave the grand dinner and go off alone to a Chinese restaurant. When I met Paulin he was reluctant to revisit his old skirmishes. 'It all seems so long ago,' he murmured, clearing a space for me in the midden of his study in Oxford. He apologised for the mess, balanced a cup of coffee on a precarious stack of books. Before going any further, he had a word to look up. 'Stochastic'. From the Greek *stochastikos*, 'skilful in aiming', as it turned out.

Born in Leeds in 1949, Paulin had been brought up in south Belfast. ('His father was a very nice man,' Stewart had said.) A soulful-looking man, he lectured in English at Hertford College, Oxford. He had left the North to go to university in England, and had stayed away. 'I put in for jobs in Belfast and Coleraine but I didn't get them. I got stuck in Nottingham for twenty-two years, then moved to Oxford.' It had taken him several years away to realise that he had emigrated. I asked him if he still followed Northern Irish issues. 'Incessantly,' he said, and the word was full of torment.

He had written a long essay about Paisley. 'He is a somewhat degraded version of a Yeatsian imagination – that sense of extremity, risk, head-banging, martial, visionary quality. The comparison might seem bizarre, but Yeats said he got his first idea for writing poetry from Orange ballads he heard from his uncle's stable boy.' Paulin brought in a framed print of Jack B. Yeats's painting *On Through the Silent Lands*. 'I think this painting shows a Sligo Orangeman after a march. It's a painting to do with the dereliction of Orangeism. I'm haunted by that painting.' He was planning a book on Daniel Defoe, having found in *Robinson Crusoe* a coded epic about William of Orange. 'It's an allegory and nobody has noticed.'

'It was bizarre to grow up in a statelet that had no future. The root of it all is Calvinism. The sense of being persecuted and a member of an elect minority, feeding its persecution complex. It takes everything to the limit. When it's crumbling, it has a change of heart.' He had reviewed Stewart's biography of Edward Carson, and described Carson's maiden speech at the House of Lords as 'a spectacular example of the contradictory, self-pitying, childish and festering sense of grievance which is at the centre of the loyalist mentality' (Paulin, 1996, p. 78). In another essay he described the 'aggressive feeling of cultural inferiority' which afflicted the loyalist imagination.

'I'm reluctant to talk in terms of national minds, but I spent years writing a book on Hazlitt and his view on the English mind was that it was flexible and subtle. My own way of thinking and arguing is simplistic and confrontational, seeing everything in terms of polar opposites. That is severely damaging, I think. It is puritan but with an emphasis on communication, but only to one's own. There is a monomaniacal aspect.'

Paulin has become better known as a cultural critic and essayist than as a poet. He is a regular contributor to the BBC's *Late Review* programme, and has a style which is often witty and penetrating, but sometimes resembles a parody of his own description of his way of thinking. He can be relied upon to be cranky, difficult, dissenting, hard to please. When it seems he is putting himself on as an act, it can get tiresome.

The Northern Irish state had been 'stillborn', he said. It was only meant to be a holding operation. There had been no vision. It was symptomatic of the lack of creative imagination in unionism that 'they had to import a bizarre romantic maverick' like Enoch Powell, who was a UUP MP for South Down from 1974 to 1987. Paulin said there was a case to be made for unionism, and for Protestant grievance.

'There is no doubt there was gerrymandering and discrimination, but if you put that on one scale and the IRA on the other, you can say, these atrocities are worse. And indeed they are.'

The trouble with Paulin's balancing of competing grievances in this way is that it was not just the pre-1968 behaviour of the unionists which had been unacceptable to nationalists. In a collection of essays to mark the twentieth anniversary of the start of the Troubles, journalist Ed Moloney wrote that the reasons for nationalist support for organisations like the IRA had to be addressed: 'What was there about British policies in the security and economic fields, in the behaviour of the British army, the RUC, the UDR, the courts and the unionists that led thousands of normal and otherwise peaceable people to believe that the only way to deal with them was through the bomb and the bullet?' (Moloney in Farrell [ed.], p. 141).

Suddenly, Paulin moved into celebratory mode: 'With no sectarian intent, every bloody thing I've written has been an attempt to represent what I had access to by the good fortune of growing up in Belfast. It's a *mentalité*, as the French would say. My book on Hazlitt is an attempt to describe that ideal, a kind of active address to the world where the imagination is capable of abstract, intellectual argument, but is also sensuous. You can feel ideas.'

Edna Longley had accused Paulin of obsession with the wilder reaches of Protestantism. His poem 'Desertmartin' depicts a place 'in the dead centre of a faith', a 'bitter village': 'Here the Word has withered to a few/ Parched certainties, and the charred stubble/ Tightens like a black belt, a crop of Bibles' (Paulin, 1993, p. 43). He had not stayed there, however, but passed through, 'The owl of Minerva in a hired car.' Paulin's 1999 collection included a moving poem about the murders of the Quinn children. There were also two poems about Drumcree, one of them referring to 'the preacher': 'he claims this patch of ground's/ his tribe's alone' (Paulin, 1999, p. 73).

He had written in the *London Review of Books* about going to Belfast the day the votes were counted in the referendum on the Belfast Agreement: 'There is a classical, enlightened feel to the document, but I know that in Ulster there is a deep permanent counter-enlightenment scepticism which mocks and derides any attempt to create political consensus ... an unbudging implacable destructiveness.' He quoted from Maurice Leitch's novel *Liberty Lad*: 'the old deadly derision, the curse which we are all born with in this cold cynical northern province'. By contrast, the *News Letter*'s front page banner headline, 'Say Yes and Say it Loud', indicated to him 'a new spirit ... something joyous and creative and energised'. The paper's editorial was in a new language too: 'It draws on Freemasonry to summon an image of Cromwell's and Milton's republic.' He praised its ' "new sprung modern light", as Edmund Burke would put it'. He said David Trimble and John Taylor were redefining unionism. When the Yes vote of 71 per cent was announced, he wept. 'Yes,' his Belfast Diary concluded, 'the New Model Ulster is rising from the wreckage.'

Paulin said that immediately after the agreement had been signed, 'you got the beginnings of decorous speech'. 'A culture is a living thing which depends on argument to evolve. For a culture to work, you have to have an agreed civility, a discourse drained of emotion.' However, an arid year and a half later, with Taylor back in his old mode of predicting paramilitary catastrophe, it was hardly possible to be so optimistic. The *News Letter*'s headline the day after the Patten report – 'Betrayed'. 'To be honest,' said Paulin, 'I'm sick of the concept of Protestant identity. I wish people would forget about it and get on with making politics work.'

THE SINGER – 'A GREAT JOY OF MUSIC'

She'd caught the grief of the moment, and channelled it through her voice, when she sang at a service in Omagh's town centre, a week to the day after the 1998 bomb. The town was hushed, and police were still sifting through the rubble. People of all religions had gathered to commemorate the newly dead, and pray for the survival of the wounded. Juliet Turner sang 'Broken Things' by US singer-songwriter Julie Miller. 'You can have my heart, if you don't mind broken things ...' she sang, with her own heart in her voice, broken. There was a powerful sense of communal solace.

'I still don't fully understand the depth at which people responded to the song that day,' she said. 'It wasn't me. It was the power of music for healing, which I'm a big believer in. Van Morrison is the only artist who touches me in that deep way. It's partly because he's coming from the same sort of background as me. That born-again scene. He has that sense of a mysterious God.'

After Omagh she was well known, but resisted demands that she release 'Broken Things' as a single, because she felt the idea of advancing her career on the back of a tragedy was appalling. In the end she recorded it on a compilation album which was made to raise funds for the victims of the bomb and their families.

Omagh was her town. She grew up in the countryside, thirteen miles from it. 'I was born on a dairy farm, pretty much in the middle of nowhere,' she said. 'For the first four years of my life we were in a caravan in the grounds of the big farmhouse. My granny lived in it, on her own, and then we moved in with her. We were like wee gipsies – we ran around the fields and spent our life in the river. We'd plaster ourselves with clay like a tan. Nobody worried where we were. We just showed up at meal times. Mind you, I did have a streak of Protestant landownerism in me. The neighbours were Catholic, and they used to come over, and we'd play. Sometimes I got annoyed. I remember standing on the banks of the river, shouting' – she put on a snooty child's voice and shouted, 'Get off our land!'

We were in a stylish Dublin café. A few cappuccino drinkers turned for a moment to see where this strong, clear voice was coming from. She laughed heartily. 'The Catholic children used to say, "Jesus Christ" and "Jesus, Mary and Joseph". In an evangelical home, that was terrible.' Her primary school was mixed, her headmistress a Catholic. 'We never had any bother.'

Religion was a huge part of Juliet's childhood. 'I remember inviting Jesus into my heart when I was about four or five, and after that, whenever I'd do anything bad, I'd get down on my knees and ask him back. We've had the farm for a hundred years, and my parents would have a strong faith in a creative God, the God of nature and beauty. We went to Togherdoo Methodist Church, and Sunday school – the whole thing, from the age of four, till we were teenagers.'

That was where she sang and learned to play piano and guitar. 'The Methodists have a great joy of music. It was really creative. There were a lot of girls and we were all quite strong-minded. We had a lot of freedom. I remember it was very open in a spiritual and intellectual way. We were encouraged to question things. As a teenager, I used to wear ripped jeans to church, and I had a Goth phase when it would be short black skirts, torn black tights and Doc Marten boots. People didn't put me down. They made me feel quite special.

'We really went overboard – rehearsals for our nativity play would start in September. At special times, like the harvest, the singing would be something else. We'd really lift the roof. We'd sing, "Yes, God Is Good in Earth and Sky" and "All Things Bright and Beautiful", hymns praising God for the things around us. We went in for big harmonies. The church would be full of fruit and flowers and it was lovely.' It wasn't all joy, though. 'I began to feel quite stifled as a teenager. I was angry, and I resented all the emphasis on sin and guilt.' Instead of leaving it all behind, though, she went deeper in: 'I got involved in a charismatic thing, where the emphasis was on the gifts of the holy spirit, the Pentecost, speaking in tongues, and people getting healed. It was exciting. There was a magic about it.'

She said she was ugly as a teenager. 'I was very tall. I had buck teeth, glasses and acne, and I wore weird clothes.' It was hard to imagine her in that way. At twenty-six, she was beautiful. 'We used to go to these Young Farmers' Club socials.' She threw her head back and laughed. 'They were the most godawful things ever. They were in the Orange hall, and there was always diluted orange in plastic cups. It would be too strong or too weak. There'd be an accordion player and we'd play games like the Farmer Wants a Wife. That was what it was all about, really. Nobody ever asked to see me home, so I'd trail off alone, feeling terrible. The funny thing is, when I go back up to the North now, people are still doing these things. It always seemed that Catholics were having a better time. They had better songs, and they drank more.'

She'd moved to Dublin to go to Trinity College. 'Dublin was beautiful, and romantic, in a Maeve Binchy way.' The sudden death of her thirteen-year-old brother had brought her home again for a miserable year, when she worked in a village supermarket. There'd been a year working in Glasgow too, but she'd returned to Dublin and stayed. 'I like it here. People are softer, more relaxed. Northerners can be very reserved. It doesn't do to show affection. Religion in the North has echoes in the environment. If you look at the black rocks and sea storms of the north coast – it's cold, and harsh and Calvinistic. It's very unforgiving. I like that cutting, sarcastic northern humour, and it can be insightful, but it can also be a way of putting people down. I used to laugh at people here for being too nice.'

The first song she wrote was called 'Glory to the Ground'. It was a Protestant minister who encouraged her to sing in public, and to record her first album, *Let's Hear it for Pizza*, in 1996. The songs are bitter-sweet, poignant, introspective. The songs of a young woman. Her voice is expressive, her Tyrone accent uncompromised. Her lyrics are not overtly political, though 'Edward' is about a man who won't sit down to talk, ' 'cos there's a fenian in his seat/But when his Catholic friend got killed, his heart went missing.' She said there was 'always this dual thing' in the North. When her father was ill, the neighbours rallied round, as country neighbours do. One of those who came with a gift was an IRA man. 'And it was nice of him,' she said.

'Violence makes me angry. It's not about religion. It's a lunatic fringe thing. I remember coming back from touring Scotland, and there was this burning car in the middle of the road. It was to do with Drumcree. We drove up to it and stopped, and my friend got out. It was a group of old fellows and some young fellows who looked like they'd never done a day's work in their lives. It's ignorance. A frighteningly blank ignorance. People who have never been encouraged to think for themselves – they've just imbibed the whole thing.'

'I want to be an artist, with a career,' she said. Things were going well. She drew good crowds to her own gigs, and had been a support act for artists like Tracy Chapman, Brian Kennedy and the legendary soul and gospel singer, Al Green. She didn't go to church any more, and said she felt stronger than ever in her faith. 'I find religion en masse disturbs me now, and I disapprove of the evangelistic thing. I only realised recently how little of my own thinking I've been doing. Religion herds people together. It encourages that unthinking element. People stick with their own kind.' Her new album – she was recording it at the time we spoke – is called *Burn the Black Suit*.

THE PAINTER – 'WHY NOT CALL A SPADE A FROG?'

Dermot Seymour was born on the Shankill Road to a street-fighting, hard-drinking father who was rarely around, and a mother who committed suicide when he was nine months old. He was reared 'on a street which no longer exists' by his mother's sister and her husband. Ma and Da. The McKeowns. Jimmy McKeown was a shipyard worker who refused to join the Orange Order because it 'wasn't fair'. Maud McKeown charred for people in big houses on the Malone Road. Dermot went to the Church of Ireland until he was thirteen. 'I was bored stiff.' And to Sunday school. 'I never learnt anything. I was never confirmed. So I'm technically doomed.' He laughed. Delighted.

'I always painted. It became a vehicle to detach myself from the absurdity of normality growing up in Northern Ireland.' He was kept away from the bad boys. 'Bad articles,' his Ma called them. 'My primary school class would have been devastated. One of them killed himself in prison. Others shot people. Or were shot by each other.' Lenny Murphy, leader of the Shankill Butchers, was around, a few years older. 'You knew to keep out of his way. I remember being in the Limelight one night when I was about fifteen and he came up to me in a typical bully way and said, "You hit my sister, didn't you?" Then he was interrupted. Beef Campbell came over and told me Murphy was in a mood. I left.'

Seymour's paintings feature cows, vegetation, Northern Irish graffiti, military installations, and human figures, some of them headless. *Who Fears to Speak of '98*, painted in 1988, shows a headless man in a bandsman's uniform, his right hand extended, pressing on the shoulder of a woman, also in uniform, and with a flute in her hand. She is dancing. There is an aggressive feel to the man's stance. In the foreground, an abandoned Ulster flag lies on the ground. Beyond the figures stands a cow, and on the horizon rise the big cranes of Belfast's shipyards. The sky is lurid and menacing.

Seymour has explained the painting: 'Being a Protestant, for me, is like having no head, in the sense that you are not allowed to think. It is hard to hold an individual thought about anything – whether it be in the immediate family circle or in the community, or in the North in general – without becoming a threat, or a Lundy, and it could be something as trivial as listening to rock music ... Out of that inability to think comes a lot of bizarre, extreme behaviour, like the Shankill Butchers ...' (from O'Regan [ed.], p. 17). He described the process, 'your neck being twisted till you've no head'. He said the risk for those doing the twisting was that 'you might talk sense and that threatens their insecurities'. He said northern Protestants had no self-esteem and that there was a 'pride in being ignorant'. This extended to only valuing an activity if you could make money out of it. 'When you're a painter you get wrath because they think you're a homosexual. You get slagged and laughed at. There is this constant putting each other down so that no one moves. It is a world of inferiority complex. Your confidence would be bashed.'

It was easier, he said, 'down here'. He had moved to the Republic in the eighties, and had settled in the far west, in Mayo. 'To hell or Connaught' had been Cromwell's decree for Catholics, and also the Orange Order's. Latterly, Mayo had attracted certain northern Protestants. Brian Keenan had gone there to recuperate after his ordeal as a hostage in the Lebanon. The Longleys had a house there. Gary Hastings, a radical young Church of Ireland minister and musician from Belfast, was the rector at Westport. Seymour said his whole generation of artists had left the North. 'Even the diehards who said they never would.' His work was changing. Less graffiti, more sky. 'Maybe I'll end up with a blank space. To go completely minimal is a very Protestant thing.'

He did not admire the traditional Protestant virtues, like straightness: 'Why not call a spade a frog? They don't meander in a way. Everything is black and white. They never realise that it is what lies in between that is colourful and interesting. They don't understand shading. In their naivety they stick to this unquestioning belief in right and wrong. They miss all the lovely magic.' It was all too small. He couldn't see himself going back. 'My brain's too big.'

Although there was a small progressive minority within Protestantism, he did not think the people could change. 'Republicanism has stunted them even more than their own self-stunting mechanisms. They have got more and more entrenched. There is no such thing as history. Everything is a retaliation for something else. It is a culture based on conflict. It doesn't filter in that 71 per cent is a majority in a democracy. It doesn't matter what percentage are Protestants. If you wanted to save the Union, you might think of trying to make it more attractive to non-Protestants.'

The percentage he quoted was the majority in the 1998 referendum in the North. In the Republic it was 94 per cent. Unionists have been inclined to cite an estimated Protestant majority of 55 per cent and to claim that if the referendum was rerun, the Nos would win. David Trimble has tended to lapse into this way of looking at things too. As First Minister he had bravely spoken in 1997 of a 'pluralist parliament for a pluralist people'. However, after the Patten report was published in 1999, he said there was a risk that 'the community' wouldn't accept it. He meant the Protestant community.

Political historian Frank Wright has divided unionists into two groups – those who want and believe it is possible to get Catholic support for the Union, and those who believe that Catholic unionism would be 'undesirable, impossible or too conditional to depend on' (Wright, *Journal of European Sociology*, vol. 14, 1973, p. 221). Seymour believed that unionism, without the opposition of the Catholics, would collapse. 'If "them ones" became unionist overnight, what would be left? Your culture would be destroyed because it is based on war against "them ones". Protestants see sharing as losing. They are doomed, but it is almost as if they want to be doomed.'

The 1999 report of the Parades Commission has on its cover a photograph which is strikingly like a Seymour painting. In black suits with white gloves and furled black umbrellas, marching along the double yellow line beside red, white and blue painted kerbs, a phalanx of headless men.

DERRY
The Dawning of Realism

'What of the change envisaged here,
The quantum leap from fear to fire?'

from 'Derry Morning', DEREK MAHON

'NO ANGELS'

In 1689 the Protestant apprentice boys shut the gates of Derry to keep the Catholic army of King James out of the walled city. In 1999 Catholics made a sport of throwing stones from the ancient walls down onto the Protestants outside, and two young Protestant mothers nightly locked the gate of a fence which separated their area from the Catholic city. All's changed in Derry, Protestants so alienated from the city that, although they had 'fought for Derry's walls', they had come to hate the name. The Catholics had captured Derry.

That was how it seemed to the people in the Fountain estate, anyway. An ugly concrete enclave, partly incorporating the old city prison, the Fountain clings to the outside of the ancient walls, separated from the Catholic Bogside by what is, in effect, a peaceline, though that term is only used in Belfast. The peaceline here is a low wall with a high fence rearing over it. Someone had written on the Catholic side of the wall, on Bishop Street: 'Boris Yeltsin is a Prod.'

The young people in the Fountain's thriving youth club were

definitely Prods, and they believed they were being punished for it. 'The Catholics think it's their city,' said Carly, whose mother was one of those who shut the gate at night. 'They say, go back into your cage.' It is the last working-class Protestant area on Derry's west bank, known as the cityside. There had been a large migration of Protestants across the River Foyle to its east Bank, known as the Waterside. That is where the big loyalist housing estates are. (It is also where the hospital, the railway station, the port, the city's main industrial area and some of its flashiest houses are to be found.)

We met at the youth club, temporarily using the local primary school while a new one was being built. The school was modern and bright, with lots of children's art on the walls, and a big gym where the younger children at the club were making Easter baskets and cards to give to local old people. 'We're stuck in here and we can't get out. There's nothing to do only the youth club. We've no park nor nothin',' said Carly. She and her friends were all aged between twelve and fourteen.

'The ones in the Waterside can't come over at night cos they'd be scared,' said Lorraine. 'We don't speak to Catholics. Certainly not. Would you speak to people that has broke twenty-eight windows, broke into your cars, stolen them? Them people just demolish everything they see. In town it's Spot the Prods. You get chased. I got a kickin' on my birthday. A gang of girls done it.'

'We do fight wi' them,' admitted Scott. 'But there's not enough of us to go after them. There's a whole swarm of them. They call us Orange bastards and they shout chuckey ar law.' (*Tiocfaidh ár lá* – 'our day will come' – is Sinn Féin's slogan.) 'Aye, there's too many of the fenians,' said Ian. 'On Bloody Sunday about 30 of them naw, 300 – tried to come over. It was a full-scale riot.' He was referring to the annual commemoration of Bloody Sunday. The Fountain is only about a quarter of a mile from Free Derry Corner where the annual commemoration is held.

Exchanges of hostilities were commonplace: 'Brickin', throwing bottles and paint bombs. My brother is eight and he throws bricks. He has to defend himself,' said Ian. 'You can't go to football. Them brickin' and you brickin'. We can't go to St Columb's park across the town – you get spat at. There used to be a big green place and you could run mad. Now we've nothin' only a car park, a school football field, and two wee poky parks, wee square things with rotten logs and rusted ladders.'

The young people said that when they were 'down the town', they knew who was Catholic, and Catholics knew who was Protestant. 'They know to look at us. They have a different accent and they're called things like Majella and Kevin,' said Craig. Linette nodded. 'And the girls have their hair up like a pineapple.' However, just to make it easier for each other, young Derry people wear uniform. 'I went down town in a Rangers top and I got beat up by these boys in Celtic stuff,' said Kyle. 'We were afraid to go down the town at Hallowe'en,' he said. Others agreed. Elaine didn't. 'Youse are lying,' she said. 'We went down the town and no one said a word.' 'I threw a banger at a boy,' boasted Andrew. 'We give them what they give us.' They did, it turned out, spend a good bit of time with Catholics. 'We go on school residentials. Twenty of them from St Brechin's and twenty of us from Clondermot. There's people fight with us on the bus and we get blamed,' said Linette. 'I got called in for "racial language". For defending ourselves.' 'We were forced to make friends with them,' said Ian sourly.

'I keep to my own,' said Emma. Then she said something else. 'See if you talk to Catholics, you get a beating. Some of them are nice.' They talked about a video they'd seen called *Across the Barricades*. 'It's class,' said Emma. 'It's about a Catholic and a Protestant who fall in love.' I asked them if they'd go out with a Catholic. 'My da would beat the life out of me,' said Ian. 'My ma said to me, "Don't you EVER go out with a Catholic",' said Linette. 'I went out with a Catholic,' said Rebecca. 'My mother wouldn't say anything to me.'

'Youse must admit,' said Linette. 'The only ones I'd speak to is half-Jaffs. They're half Prods and brought up as Prods. Even my ma brought one of them into the house and she wouldn't let a Catholic in.' 'I wouldn't trust them,' said Kyle. 'Jaffs' are Jaffas, as in oranges. Young Protestants were often known to young Catholics as 'Orangeys'. 'My ma said, before the fenians burned her out, she'd burn them out,' said Andrew. 'They are just greedy. They don't want our marches but they have hundreds of marches with their oul' priests and all. We're the last Protestants in Derry.' Before I left, Carly and

Linette danced to the theme song from the film *Titanic*.

Alastair Simpson, governor of the Apprentice Boys and a long-time resident of the Fountain, spoke about the murder of local man William King, one of the first victims of the Troubles in Derry. He had been kicked to death in September 1969 by a nationalist gang, watched by British soldiers who had no authority to intervene. 'They used to come up Bishop Street and shout, "We might not have got King William but we got William King!" (Templegrove Action Project, p. 15). A local loyalist band was named after William King.

The Fountain was troubled not just by its conflict with the city's Catholic majority. Many of the more long-term residents had left, and there was a widespread view that 'problem families' had been 'dumped' in the estate by the Housing Executive. 'They just shove all these poofters and prostitutes and weirdos and druggies in here,' said Ian succinctly. The young people clashed with their own elders too. They called one corner of the estate 'the Witchies', because the women there shouted at them when they were 'brickin'' the young Catholics on the walls above the estate. There was anti-police feeling too. The old city walls had telling graffiti: 'Drumcree warriors fear no Peelers. Londonderry loyalists say No Surrender.' The Fountain reminded me of a young man from the area who was quoted in Desmond Bell's 1990 study of youth culture, *Acts of Union*. 'I don't think Ulster is meant to be a place,' he said. 'It's just meant to be the Protestant people' (Bell, p. 138).

But regeneration was in the air, and the isolation of the Fountain and its five hundred inhabitants had been recognised by funding agencies. A recent government study had shown that under the EU's urban initiative, the area had got just over £1 million. The Catholic Creggan, which had a population of 11,000, got slightly less. There was a well-funded local partnership, developing economic and social projects. Jeanette Warke, who ran the youth club, said it was being refurbished with a grant of a quarter of a million pounds, Peace and Reconciliation money. 'They are brilliant kids,' she said. 'They'd do anything for you. But they are no angels, mind you.'

She was from the Fountain, though she had moved, under duress, she said, to Newbuildings, a village of loyalist housing estates across the river. Newbuildings was a fractious place with red, white and blue kerbstones. People had low expectations and hard feelings. At Strabane, a few miles away, Catholics stoned buses carrying Protestants, and Protestants attacked buses carrying Catholics through Newbuildings. During Drumcree one year, youths stopped the car of an RUC man and dragged him and his young son out, seriously injuring the boy. Young loyalists also stoned houses belonging to Catholics in new estates of big, ostentatious houses which reared up on the hills overlooking the Foyle between Newbuildings and Derry. 'I hated Newbuildings at first,' said Jeanette. 'But I've got used to it.'

She was nostalgic, though, for the way the Fountain used to be, before redevelopment in the seventies. 'It was lovely wee old streets and old women out on the street with their arms folded and the windows would be shining and a big fire inside. The shirt factories were the hub of the community, as were the pubs. I remember the Eleventh night. There was dancing at the bonfires. I'm sure there was Catholics came, because Catholics used to come with us to the Twelfth. Och, it was just lovely. You could have spent the whole night wandering. It would be great to have all that back again. I always said the architect who designed the Fountain the way it is now, must have had a screw loose.'

She said she was 'all for cross-community work', and cited programmes the club was involved in, which were both cross-community and cross-border. 'It takes that little bit of bitterness out of the kids.' She wanted loyalist commemorations to turn into carnivals for everyone, Catholics included, but acknowledged that 'blood-and-thunder' bands were a problem. 'They put the fear of God into Catholics. Let's face it, I wouldn't go to a Catholic parade that had IRA in it.' She was about to leave her job in a children's clothes shop to take up a new one as a women's development worker in the Waterside.

I had met Jeanette when we were on a BBC Radio Foyle programme together. It was about the civil rights movement, on the thirtieth anniversary of the famous 5 October march in 1968. The march had been banned, the Apprentice Boys of Derry had organised a counter-demonstration, and when around four hundred civil rights marchers had attempted to get to Craigavon Bridge, to cross from the Waterside, where they'd started, to the cityside, the RUC had attacked them with batons. These events were captured by television cameras and were seen by millions of people. The march had launched the civil rights movement in the eyes of the world, and had done so in a way which reflected very unfavourably on the Unionist state.

Jeanette had not been happy about the radio programme. She had spoken about the poverty in which she had grown up, which was, she said, as bad as anything experienced by Derry Catholics. But she hadn't had a chance to say much. The panel had included Jack Allen, who had been a rising young Ulster Unionist on the council at the time, and Ivan Cooper, a Protestant who had been on the march, and who went on to become one of the founders of the SDLP. As we left the studio, Cooper spoke to her in a friendly way. She looked at him coldly. 'I would never have taken part in this if I'd known you were going to be on as well,' she said, turned on her heel, and walked away.

'OVERNIGHT I WAS A TRAITOR AND A LUNDY'

Ivan Cooper was used to hostility from his fellow Protestants. But as Jeanette Warke had walked away he looked hurt and shaken, none the less. I arranged to interview him a couple of days after a meeting to commemorate the October 1968 events. The meeting was a sorry affair. Widely advertised, it failed to draw a crowd, undoubtedly largely because Sinn Féin was not involved and had not given its blessing. In a room full of cigarette smoke, ageing men who had been fiery youths in 1968 swore that they would smash the 'sectarian agreement' which had been reached at Stormont six months previously. It wasn't for this sellout that they'd had their heads bashed. But it was apparent that whatever those who supported the Belfast Agreement had to fear, it was not from this quarter.

Cooper's office was in a house up on the city walls. His business was sorting out the affairs of bankrupts and others in deep financial trouble. He said it reminded him of constituency work, and that was what he liked about it. His office, a tumble of papers, had a huge window which overlooked the Bogside and a mural for the Saoirse prisoners' rights group, huge hands breaking a chain.

Cooper had no time for Sinn Féin or its associates. He had agreed to take part in the 1968 commemorations only once he was sure that Sinn Féin was not involved. The office was busy. His secretary kept interrupting as clients arrived. 'I double book and don't tell the girl,' Cooper confessed. A middle-aged man put his head round the door. Cooper asked him to come back later. He told me the man was a famous seventies showband singer.

'I was brought up in Killaloo, two hundred yards from the Orange hall and next door to the Church of Ireland. My mother was a sub-postmistress, my father was a supervisor for Derry City Council, which meant he was over all the roadmen who cut the grass, swept the roads, and trimmed the hedges. Before that, he was a policeman. I wear my poppy with pride,' Cooper said.

'The church was very much part of our lives. We were Church of Ireland, and although the Presbyterian church was up the road, that community was very separate to me. They used to have concerts in the Presbyterian lecture hall, and the minister would rope off the first three rows for the gentry. They were the local big Presbyterian farmers. My mother used to go in and lift the rope and sit down there. The old gentry had been Church of Ireland, the Established Church, so their workers had been C of I as well.' The old gentry had run Derry at a time when it was politic for socially climbing Presbyterians to convert to the Church of Ireland, while the working-class Presbyterians had started the Apprentice Boys organisation. Thousands of Presbyterians had emigrated in the eighteenth century. Liberal Presbyterians had briefly allied themselves with Catholics, before the home rule issue united Protestants again.

'My mother used to bring me to St Columb's hall in Derry and you had the Irish dancing there. On a Sunday there were Catholic sports in Claudy, the nearest village to us, but we weren't allowed to go because it was the Sabbath. But when my sister went to live there I spent all my recreation time there and it was a totally integrated village. There was no sectarian divide. There was an Orange band, but there was everything else as well and it wasn't sharp. I played Gaelic football and cricket with Catholic boys.' The cricket club, however, was not just almost exclusively Protestant, 'it was run by big landowners for their own. My father was a brilliant cricketer who taught us all, but he couldn't get into the club, and nor could I.'

Claudy had been bombed in 1972, killing nine people, Catholics and Protestants, and including nine-year-old Katherine Eakin. The atrocity was not claimed, but the IRA is assumed to have been responsible.

'My first employment was in the shirt industry in Derry. Let's call a spade a spade, the only reason I got the job was because I was a Protestant. I was hand-picked as a manager. I've always had a great affection for the shirt factory girls, because only for them, I would never have become a politician. They helped to sharpen and hone my ideas. I had so much admiration for those women. I couldn't begin to tell you how heavy their jobs were. Also, the amazing charity and love they had for each other, Catholic and Protestant. Most snobby shits look down on factory girls – to me they were the backbone of the city.'

He said he had to leave the job when he was blacklisted as a result of getting involved in politics, initially as a Young Unionist. He had supported a working-class Protestant from Drumahoe, near Cooper's home, who decided to challenge the local sitting UUP candidate on bad housing and other social issues. 'There was such a hue and cry – you were splitting the Protestant vote, you were a traitor, a Lundy. He got crucified, and when I stood the next time, I got crucified too. The sitting candidate was a Mrs Milligan, wife of a former editor of the local paper. She was a very authoritarian woman, extremely abrasive. A Mrs Bouquet type of lady, totally removed from anybody living in a council house.'

Through football, and playing it in the Bogside, Cooper came to know Catholics who were 'socialist-minded'. They included the young John Hume. 'We talked about gerrymandering and bad housing. I got involved with squatting people, opposing landlords who threw people out. That was what happened when anyone got into arrears – they were locked out. Protestants did suffer some similar conditions but not to the same extent, and not to the extent of being thrown out.'

In the general election of 1918 the seat for Derry was won by Sinn Féin, whose candidate promptly took up his seat not in the House of Commons, but in the unofficial Dáil Éireann in Dublin. Unionists had secured their control over local government in Derry by a variety of means, despite the fact that the city had a Catholic majority. In 1920, following the introduction of proportional representation, nationalists won a majority in Derry's corporation, as in many of the border towns. Unionists abolished PR and rearranged the electoral wards. Nationalists withdrew, and Unionist control was re-established. But in Derry it was always under threat. The Catholic community was growing, and was growing restive.

Control was maintained by the system of gerrymandering. Derry Catholics were crammed into one electoral ward, so that nationalist candidates were returned with massive majorities there, but Protestants lived in two wards so that their candidates were returned with small majorities, but they had more seats. Company directors had multiple votes, and only householders could vote. The corporation was slow to house Catholics. When a British Labour government changed the local government franchise in 1945, the Unionist regime at Stormont opted out, and further cut back on those who could vote, by excluding lodgers.

It was in Derry that Sir Basil Brooke had warned unionist employers to do right by their own or they would be outvoted. In the absence of employment, there was a steady stream of Catholic emigrants from the city. Unionist employers also persuaded most working-class Protestants in the city that trade unionism was merely republicanism by any other name. Such industry as came to Northern Ireland tended to be based in the Protestant east. In general Unionist councillors were able to use jobs and houses as rewards for loyalty.

The young Cooper saw the debilitating effects of this system on working-class Protestants. 'The Protestant community was very much a law-and-order community in those days. They just accepted that the men of the big house were the men who became the elected representatives and that was it. I remember a very prominent local Mason and he used to take great pride in telling you how he used to organise the company voting structure and got all these Protestants into companies as nominee directors and so on. He was also the Unionist registration agent.

'On the other hand, my father supervised men who were paid next to nothing. Where we lived, there were farm labourers who were near-enough slaves. I used to watch one man who was a great Orangeman going up Kilcatton Hill and he'd be bent double. And another poor woman who laboured in one of the big farmhouses, and she was a slave. The blacks in South Africa were treated as well as she was. You knew your place. But then October 1968 happened and all of that, and Craig denounced us as communists and republicans and overnight I was a traitor and a Lundy. Overnight I was denounced and estranged.

'The local hierarchy of Protestantism organised a boycott of my mother's post office. Local people threw petrol bombs at our home. I remember my mother was at one window with a shotgun and I was at another window with a shotgun, and the mob was outside. The Unionist establishment had so conditioned people into thinking that this was a republican communist plot, that Ulster was under threat, and in the middle of it all was this young Protestant man and he was a Lundy. They were conditioned into thinking that it wasn't about social issues, or about the fact that you lived in a dump, all it was, was about Ulster and Ulster's future.' Reluctantly, the family moved from their rural home into Derry city.

Cooper's home at Killaloo was near Burntollet Bridge, scene of a Protestant ambush on a People's Democracy march from Belfast to Derry in January 1969. The march had been modelled on the march in Alabama in the deep south of the United States three years earlier. That march and the campaign it was part of had brought about reforms which improved the civil rights of black people. As chair of the Derry Citizens' Action Committee, Cooper was to receive the marchers into the city. When he heard what had happened he drove to Burntollet. He named the man who had organised the boycott of his mother's post office, and who had been one of those instrumental in keeping the working classes out of the cricket club. 'There he was sitting in his car, directing operations. His brother and him were the principal organisers. They had organised for three loads of stones to be dumped at the top of the hill above the bridge. They wouldn't have been seen throwing stones, of course.'

The People's Democracy carried out an investigation of events at Burntollet. It found out that the ambush had been organised at a meeting in Killaloo Orange hall the previous night. The men Cooper named were prominent, and other local big farmers and business people played their part.

The Cameron report into the early part of the Troubles found that the organisers of the march had seen it as a 'calculated martyrdom'. It also found members of the B Specials were among the crowd which attacked it. At Stormont, Northern Ireland Labour Party (NILP) MP Paddy Devlin asked 422 questions about Burntollet, largely to do with the role of the Specials. Using photographs taken at the scene by marchers and press photographers, most of the Protestant crowd was identified, and 100 out of 257 of them had records of service with the Specials.

However, the B men's champion, Sir Arthur Hezlet, dismissed in his book any adverse implications of all this for the force. He disputed the authenticity of the photographs, and remarked that even if B Specials had been present, that did not mean that they had attacked anyone. It was, he said, a fine example of Sinn Féin propaganda, and he noted tartly in passing that Devlin's questions had cost the government £3,315 to answer. 'At Burntollet it was not established by the RUC or anyone else that there were more than two serving members of the USC present and that they were other than innocent bystanders who had every right to be there.' Burntollet was the start, he said, of the 'mendacious campaign' against the force. Catholics and mainland British people were taken in – but Northern Irish Protestants knew better. Since 1914 they had been immune to republican propaganda. 'It was their firm conviction that you could believe very little of what the native Irish told you' (Hazlet, p. 9).

Cooper, who had been in the NILP from 1965 to 1968, was elected MP for Mid-Derry as an Independent in 1969, and then joined the new SDLP, led by Gerry Fitt. 'Bloody Sunday changed everything in Irish politics. It was no longer a case of getting rights the same as in Birmingham and London. It had become a national issue and after Bloody Sunday I was very firmly a nationalist. I had decided we couldn't get the reforms in the British system. We had to seek further.

'I was with Fitt and Devlin on the socialist wing, and it was a unique experience. The love you felt for colleagues like that, it is something I have never felt since.' Cooper was an Assembly member for the SDLP and was made minister for community relations in the brief 1974 powersharing executive, but he stood unsuccessfully for the party in the 1974 Westminster elections. He was a member of the Constitutional Convention from 1975 to 1976.

'I've always had this burning passion in me, this great thing in me about redressing the wrong of the past vis-à-vis working-class people. I also harboured a dream that by good constituency work I would get back into the hearts of the ordinary Protestant people. John [Hume] used to argue with me that the function of an MP was to be a legislator, not a social worker, but I knew how vulnerable I was. A lot of people on either side wouldn't trust me. The only way I could hold my seat was by working desperately hard.'

After his political career ended he had his wilderness years, a period of 'clinging on, hoping that politics would evolve again, floating about, trying to find a niche that wasn't there'. He had been a lost soul. But he had come to terms with it eventually. Politically, he said, he was 'yesterday's man'. However, he felt he had got one up on his old adversaries in Killaloo. He took obvious satisfaction in driving through his old area in his shiny red Jaguar, getting up speed. 'All those élitist Presbyterian farmers, I earn far more than any of them do,' he said, smirking unashamedly. 'As well as that, they can't treat their workers the way they used to. The civil rights movement changed everything. It produced better representation for Catholics and then Paisley took on all that constituency side of things for Protestants, so they did well out of it too.'

He was still an SDLP voter and had remained friendly with Hume, but wasn't entirely happy with the way the SDLP had developed. 'All my life I've been very committed to consensus with the Protestant population, recognising Protestant rights. There is a whole new class in Derry, the new Catholic rich. You get Catholic landlords breaking every law to evict tenants.' He said with disgust that Protestants had been driven out of the city of Derry, noting in particular that several churches had been vandalised or burned. He applauded Protestant business people who had stayed.

Many of the new Catholic rich lived in big private housing estates on the west bank of the Foyle, extending out almost to the border with Donegal. These sprawling mock Tudor mansions had been pointed out to me by resentful Protestants from the bleak Housing Executive estates on the Waterside. And it was Newbuildings youths who had attacked the big houses owned by Catholics in the Waterside. They left the Protestant mansions well alone.

Cooper supported the Belfast agreement and he believed it would, unlike the executive on which he had served, actually work. 'Paisley doesn't have the UDA on his side this time, like he did back in 1974. They have come to their senses.

'People looking at me might think, the problem that man has is that part of him still thinks through Protestant eyes, and they are right, I do. I believe we should be facilitating the Apprentice Boys to march in this city – not, mind you, to bring a gang of hoodlums in to spit at Catholics and impose that kind of sectarianism. But it is hard to get across to Catholics how strongly the Orange Order is ingrained into Protestant culture. Out where I'm from, there are lodges all over the place, at Tullyally, Killaloo, Claudy, Fawney, Killdogue, Tullintrain, Drumcrain.

'The identification is with the working-class people. The halls would be used for gospel meetings, and as a community centre. For so many people the Twelfth of July is just a day out, a bit of colour. We seem to have lost sight of that.' But he believed the Order was in terminal decline. It had sailed too close to Paisley, handled the parades issue disastrously.

'I go to church. I am a Protestant. I could never be a Catholic.' He was an attender of many services, having returned to the Church of Ireland from which he had been exiled by the fact that so many people in the congregation knew and reviled him. 'I am a nobody now. There's no one looking at me saying, there's that traitor.'

He also went to Plymouth Brethren meetings, with friends, though he found the religion dry. And he went to the huge Metropolitan Tabernacle in north Belfast, 'an American-style church with a magnificent choir'. He said its pastor had taken a lot of worshippers away from Paisley. Ministers had sent a lot of sinners with money worries Cooper's way. He got a lot of evangelicals, and a lot of security force people. 'They can't handle their money.' He enjoyed opening tightly closed minds. 'I had a client who was a hard-line Protestant and I was able to demonstrate to him that a Catholic would give him a chance, after his own had given up on him.'

There was something of the preacherman about Cooper, a very northern, political preacherman. His need for the people he served. His need to be on the road, travelling to out-of-the-way corners of south Armagh and Ballybeen housing estate on the outskirts of east Belfast. Our meetings were interrupted by calls from desperate people who had just received eviction notices, or were phoning from call boxes outside courtrooms. He dealt confidently and compassionately with those in dire straits.

Over and over, Cooper had spoken about being called a Lundy. A close relation had, he said, spat into his face in October 1968, called him a Lundy, and, thirty years later, was still 'totally unforgiving'. However, a brother-in-law had stayed loyal to him. 'He is a direct descendant of two of the original apprentice boys,' he said, and he said it with pride.

'SUBVERSION, LEFT, RIGHT AND CENTRE'

At their annual pageant the Apprentice Boys exhort the people to 'Lift up your hearts, lift up your weapons . . . No Surrender!' The siege of Derry provided the essential loyalist vocabulary: 'No Surrender' may first have been used in County Cork, but the phrase has become firmly established as the defiant call of the besieged Protestants of Derry in 1689. Northern Protestants have grown up knowing that to be called a Lundy is the ultimate shame, for it means that you represent the antithesis of loyalty, the highest Protestant virtue. Some loyalists are confused about Lundy, however. An Orangeman in Portadown declared that Lundy had burned down the Houses of Parliament.

Derry had been developed into a walled Plantation city in the seventeenth century by the wealthy trades guilds of London. During the 1641 rebellion Protestants had crowded into the city for protection from the 'cruel murtherers and thirsty shedders of innocent blood' (contemporary pamphlet quoted in Stewart, p. 60). In 1688 James II proposed to replace the existing Protestant corporation of the city with a new one which was largely Catholic. A new garrison was also to be sent – again, largely a Catholic force. The anxiety caused by these developments flared into terror when the contents of the so-called 'Comber letter' became known. This was a document which was found in County Down in December 1688 and purported to be a warning that the Irish were about to 'fall on to kill and murder man, wife and child'. The letter was a hoax: 'It was probably created by the fears which it stimulated,' observed Stewart. It was believed genuine because 'it spoke in the ancestral voice' (Stewart, p. 65), and Stewart accepted the view that it probably lost Ireland for King James.

While the corporation dithered, 'an impetuous collection of youth', the thirteen apprentice boys, took action and shut the city gates. They did so to keep the Catholics out, and those Catholics who were in the city were expelled. The siege began. Lieutenant Colonel Robert Lundy, a Scottish Protestant, was made governor.

The Glorious Revolution took place, with James fleeing to France, and William taking the crown. He sent a commission to Lundy – whose existing commission was to King James – requiring him to take an oath of allegiance. The city's council of war decided to hold the city for William, and erected a gallows to deal with traitors to 'the Protestant interest'.

Lundy and his Protestant soldiers suffered a series of defeats by the forces of King James. Lundy was blamed. He was pessimistic, convinced that Derry was about to fall to the enemy. He proposed that the city's leaders should leave, so that the people could make 'a timely capitulation' and better terms with the enemy. The citizens were incensed, and Lundy had to be smuggled out of the city to escape their rage. He was said to have climbed down a pear tree beside the walls, with a load of match wood on his back.

The siege continued for 105 days, during which time those inside the overcrowded city suffered horribly. The new governor, George Walker, drew up a list of foods available, including horse flesh, rats, and dogs 'fattened by eating the Bodies of the slain Irish'. In July, the boom which James had placed across the River Foyle was broken by British ships and the city was relieved.

William promised that the loyalty of the Protestants of Derry would be rewarded and their losses compensated, but they were to be disappointed. Colonel John Mitchelburne, one of the siege's heroes, died in a debtors' prison. The library at Tynan Abbey contained IOUs for monies owed to the Stronge family which were still unpaid when the IRA burned down the abbey in 1981, after murdering Sir Norman Stronge and his son. The majority of ordinary citizens in the city during the siege were Presbyterian, while the officers and leaders were Anglican. The Anglicans played down the role of the Presbyterians, who were subsequently discriminated against under the Penal Laws. Given the loyalist tendency to regard today's betrayals as repetitions of those endured in the past, much could have been made of these matters. That has not happened, perhaps because to do so might involve criticism of the Glorious King William, much-vaunted bringer of civil liberties to all. What remained was the founding parable for contemporary loyalism. According to those taking part in the pageant, 'The action of the Apprentice Boys had saved England, Scotland and Ireland.'

Stewart described how the siege of Derry has been used as a metaphor to preserve the British Plantation interest. The Conservative leader Andrew Bonar Law told the UVF in 1912: 'you hold the pass, the pass for the Empire. You are a besieged city. The timid have left you; your Lundys have betrayed you; but you have closed your gates' (quoted in Stewart, p. 67).

It was an endlessly recurring situation, in which heroic decisiveness covered all doubts. 'This is the permanent duality of the Protestant defence ... when a decision is made a scapegoat must be found for all the misgivings that had earlier been expressed' (Stewart, p. 67). Lundy was the scapegoat, the load of match on his back 'the burden of the city's anxiety and irresolution'. The annual ritual burning of Lundy's effigy is, according to Stewart, the resolution of a crisis of conscience. 'They have made up their minds again: the cry is to be No surrender.'

The Apprentice Boys society was set up in 1823, and its twice-yearly commemorations in August and December have been occasions for trouble, including serious rioting, ever since, the degree of trouble depending on the volatility of the political situation at the time. The society has a fine collection of Derry artefacts and documents in its huge Victorian Gothic hall inside the walled city. A senior Boy, William Coulter, showed me around.

'There's the lock of the old magazine where they kept the guns during the siege. Solid brass and it still works perfectly. This is a banner for the Independent Order of Good Templars, a temperance movement led by old Mr Hamilton who ran one of the factories. It's the derelict building at the end of the bridge now. That's a photograph of a demonstration against home rule – and there's one of the guns smuggled in in 1912, a German Mauser.'

There were photographs of Roaring Meg, one of the cannons still to be seen on Derry's walls. The City of London Guild of Fishmongers had supplied it. 'Historically, the charter for the city was Londonderry. The council dropped the name out of prejudice.' The nationalist council had dropped the 'London' part of the name in 1984. David Dunseith had told me that at that time he got a call from an English broadcaster who explained that his newsroom had received a fax from an organisation called the Apprentice Boys of Derry. What puzzled them was that the Apprentice Boys of Derry were objecting to the fact that the local council had changed its name to Derry City Council. Could Dunseith explain?

Protestants have traditionally called the city Londonderry, and many who didn't have started to do so since the council's action. Some will point out that whereas there was a city called Doire before the London companies arrived, there was no county, so that the county *must* be called Londonderry. Soldiers manning UDR checkpoints would routinely challenge drivers who said they were going to Derry: 'You mean Londonderry?' A response in the negative could well result in a full-scale search of the car. Coulter agreed that the Apprentice Boys called it Derry, and that he did so himself. But if he was writing, he used Londonderry. A member of the District Partnership for Peace and Reconciliation, set up after the ceasefires in 1994, told me proudly that in their efforts to create a 'shared city' this had been the first problem. In the end, he said proudly, they had reached agreement. The partnership's headed paper ended up with 'Derry/Londonderry/Doire', followed by the postcode.

It is common in nationalist areas to see signposts for Londonderry with 'London' painted out. In Limavady, a predominantly Protestant town, there was a signpost for Londonderry and Dungiven. Dungiven, a nationalist town, had been painted off the sign entirely, and Derry had been painted out of Londonderry. The signpost was left indicating that London was just fifteen miles up the road from Limavady.

The term 'blood money' was used to disparage the Apprentice Boys' application to the International Fund for Ireland, because the fund had been set up in the aftermath of the Anglo-Irish Agreement. The Boys weathered the storm, only to end up unable to take the money, because, as their governor explained to me, 'the organisation had to be cross-community, and we couldn't have a Catholic on our committee'.

Coulter raised his arm and pointed to a large oil painting. 'That's a well-known painting, the charge of the 36th Division at the Somme, on 1 July 1916, painted by James Beadle,' said Coulter. 'That's a photograph of the obelisk marking the scene of the Battle of the Boyne. It was blown up in the twenties. There's a photograph of all the men who set up the first Stormont. A very respectable-looking bunch compared with today's.' He was scornful about 'this new liberal cross-community thing', which had led some unionists to call for a break of the link between the Orange Order and the Ulster Unionist Party. 'The party was practically formed out of the Orange Order. If they lose the strength of the Order, they won't get far. It was set up to defend the Protestant people.'

He explained the symbols and emblems on the banners, many of them relating to the Bible and particularly the twelve tribes of Israel. The Orange, Black, Apprentice Boys and the Masonic, were all very different in character and purpose, but they were all brotherhoods, and all related to 'a moral way of living'. He said that people had traditionally joined the Black preceptory for political furtherance, and that the Masonic order suited Derry businessmen better. 'You don't have to parade, and if you have customers on both sides of the community you don't want to be seen.'

'There's someone you may know,' he added, picking up a photograph of a smiling young Paisley with his family, when Ian Junior was a baby. 'There's Bernadette, breaking stones.' He picked up a UUP leaflet entitled *Ulster – the Facts* and dated 1 September 1969 with two photos on its cover. One was of the young Bernadette Devlin, then a newly elected MP, famously raising a paving stone over her head, about to smash it into pieces for hurling at the RUC. It was taken during the Battle of the Bogside in Derry in 1969. The Bogside people had barricaded themselves into their area after RUC men had rampaged through the streets shouting, 'Come out and fight, you fenian bastards.' The Apprentice Boys were celebrating the relief of their siege in 1689. Sir Patrick Macrory, author of *The Siege of Derry*, wrote in a footnote to his concluding chapter: 'On the eve of the march in August 1969, I asked an Orangeman of my acquaintance, the kindest and most decent of men, why it was necessary to keep up these obviously provocative celebrations. He looked at me in mild surprise and then said grimly: "We have to show them who's master, that's why"' (quoted in Lacy, p. 261).

Catholics knew all too well that this was the message, and they were not having it. Acquiescence was a thing of the past. Clashes between them and the loyalists led to fierce riots which went on for two days, and resulted in the British government sending in its troops. The home secretary, James Callaghan, said it was a temporary measure, and that the soldiers would only stay until law and order were restored. By then rioting had broken out in Belfast and other towns, and people were dying in the streets. The guns were out. Republican guns, loyalist guns, RUC guns and British army guns. Thirty years later, the troops were largely back in their barracks, but Protestants were still demanding the restoration of law and order.

The other photograph on the cover of the Unionist leaflet was of a young policeman with a badly burned face and a bandaged hand. The caption over Bernadette Devlin read: 'Young lady with a £60 a week job.' Over the policeman it read: 'Young man with a £20 a week job.' Inside, Ulster – the Facts claimed that the violence which had broken out was all part of a secret IRA plot, which had actually been disclosed in the News Letter in 1966. The details were in a document held by the 'Eire government'. It was 'nothing less than a blueprint for the takeover of Northern Ireland'.

This was the process Ivan Cooper had described, a conspiracy theory which was profoundly unsettling and allowed Unionists to dismiss all the issues raised by the civil rights movement. Like the Comber letter in 1688, it 'spoke in the ancestral voice', the voice in which Brookeborough warned against employing Catholics, '99 per cent of whom are disloyal'. Coulter still believed the voice. 'Everything in this city is swamped by Roman Catholics. The half of Donegal is in this city. They are able to claim all the benefits. If they were good citizens, you wouldn't mind. But there is subversion, left, right and centre. I've seen it. I worked in the hospital. Since the country was divided in 1921, the 26 counties were Roman Catholic controlled and the 6 counties were for the Reformed people.

'The Protestant population in the South has fallen to 3 per cent.

They are so busy telling us in the North about fair employment, but in the South you have to have Irish to get a job in government, but I don't hear them speaking Irish. We never had a united country – it was always the survival of the fittest, like in Africa. Primitive.

'I had to move from the Glen Road because my house was repeatedly burgled, and now I live on the edge of the Fountain, between the two sides. I have grilles on my windows and my gable wall is covered in graffiti because they know I am a Protestant. Catholics make out they were badly off. Look at these photographs of cottages in the old Fountain – the Roman Catholics were no worse off than the Protestant working class. Anything the Protestants got, they worked for. Not like the so-called underprivileged.'

'THERE WAS NOBODY SHOT IN DERRY THAT DAY'

William Coulter's manner had changed, and his voice had taken on a tinge of the kind of bitterness about Catholics I'd heard in the voices of people I'd listened to when I was growing up in Derry, in the early days of the Troubles. Like a respectable old primary school teacher who spat out things like, 'The post office is rotten with them.' She was indignant when Dana, reared in the Bogside as Rosemary Brown, won the Eurovision Song Contest in 1970 and bought a big house in the respectable area where she herself lived.

I went to a grammar school misnamed Londonderry High School for Young Ladies. During the shouting match which our modern history class became, one of my classmates said, 'Sure, they're breeding like rats up in the Creggan.' References to Catholics as animals, or attributing animalistic characteristics to them, are a feature of sectarianism, a lessening of their humanity. A letter in the *Protestant Telegraph* referred to Catholics as 'two legged rats'. In 1970 the same paper had published an article about British army house searches. 'The unfortunate soldiers who had to search the Roman hovels (which were nice terrace houses before the present occupants moved in) were subjected to vile conditions; described as squalid and verminous. It has been reported that a soldier of the Royal Scots had to receive medical attention when he was overcome by the stench of a room being used as an open lavatory ... the great unwashed is an epithet applicable hygienically and spiritually to the natives of the lower Falls' (quoted in Wright, *Journal of European Sociology*, vol. 14, 1973, p. 237). It was frequently said that when Catholics got houses with bathrooms, they kept their coal in the bath. It was against this background that Terence O'Neill made his speech about how if you treated Catholics properly, they would 'live like Protestants'. In 1997 the Spirit of Drumcree Orangemen had the Ulster Hall fumigated before a meeting because Sinn Féin had used it before them.

Bloody Sunday was a huge and defining event for the Catholic community. It had little immediate impact on Protestants. Ellen in north Down had spoken about this. Another woman told me that when she had said something against the shootings in their immediate aftermath at her Methodist Sunday school, a senior figure in the church had told her coldly that the victims had all been gunmen. My school was about half a mile away from the scene of the massacre. There was no formal reference to the events of that day, no acknowledgement that something terrible had happened.

Diane Greer, a Protestant community worker, was thirteen in 1972. She went to the secondary school beside the high school, with a lot of children from the Fountain estate. She remembered the chant: 'We shot one, we shot two, we shot thirteen more than you . . .' Years later, she told me, she had begun to meet Catholic women. Listening to them talking about things like British army raids on their houses, she found herself questioning the things she had been told. 'I realised that these women were not bad, that it wasn't true what we'd grown up hearing, that Catholics who complained or got shot were all in the IRA.'

She began to look again at the events of Bloody Sunday. 'As a matter of fact, I became almost obsessed with it. It was a journey through all kinds of things. I tried to talk to other Protestants about it, but it just wasn't acceptable. I wanted to go on the Bloody Sunday commemorative marches, but I felt I couldn't. Sinn Féin had really taken them over. But I do try, quietly, to support the Bloody Sunday Trust. I tried to bring the Bloody Sunday exhibition into Protestant areas but there was a lot of resistance.'

She vividly remembered one woman in a loyalist estate in the Waterside. Diane was recording reminiscences for a project. The woman spoke of Bloody Sunday. 'She said there was nobody shot in Derry that day. The bodies that were laid out in the morgue that night were taken out of deep freezes. They were IRA men who had been killed in previous gunbattles. I wasn't supposed to interrupt but I was horrified. I couldn't stop myself. I asked her what was the evidence for what she was saying. She said she knew someone who knew an ambulance man, and he had told her the bodies were still thawing out. I was just appalled.' Firemen, ambulancemen and other emergency service personnel, always unnamed, were frequently invoked as sources for this type of outlandish tale.

Eventually, Diane went to visit the sister of one of those who was murdered that day. 'I said to her, "I've come twenty-one years too late to your door to say I know now that your brother was innocent." We talked for hours. I cried and cried. I've grieved buckets. I felt it was guilt.' Guilt, however, would not advance anything. 'I think Protestants have to recognise that things were done in the past that shouldn't have been done. Then we have to say, let's begin to do things differently.'

In September 1999 Diane's teenage son had gone for a drink in a pub on Derry's cityside, the Henry Joy McCracken. It was on the city-centre edge of the Bogside. He rarely used the cityside. He was menaced in the bar, then followed by several men. 'They called him a Jaffa bastard and attacked him on Shipquay Street, right in the centre of the city. They kicked his head and left him unconscious.'

She was contacted soon afterwards by the UVF, the UDA and the IRA, all offering punishment beatings. She declined. 'I know the owner of the pub was horrified by what happened. I work in community relations. We are trying to spin a positive message about being a minority in the city. Every time I hear local politicians on, giving out about how Protestants are second-class citizens, a beleaguered people and all that, it makes me angry. Do they really want a people which feels downtrodden and demoralised?

'Things are changing for the better. Newbuildings community association has links with Carnhill, and Tullyally and Creggan have linked up on the issue of child abuse, which has afflicted both of them.' All the places she mentioned are working-class estates. Carnhill and Creggan are Catholic, Newbuildings and Tullyally are Protestant.

'People are working in a solution-focused way,' said Diane.

In January 2000, Diane was one of the organisers of a discussion about Bloody Sunday which was to take place in a city council premises in the Waterside. But local politicians from the UUP, the DUP and the UDP opposed it, and it was cancelled. Diane said she was bitterly disappointed. She felt frustrated too by 'the immaturity of my people'. However, her patience was boundless. 'We have to look at the positive side of this,' she said. 'Something almost happened.'

'THE FREEDOM OF THE CITY'

There is a special room in the Apprentice Boys hall, tall enough for the nineteen-foot figure of Lundy to hang. Raymond Walker had been brought to watch the building of the effigy since he was a small child. In recent years he had become the builder. It took him about forty-three hours, he said. When I called he had nearly finished the work, and thirteen bales of straw, papier-mâché, wire mesh and wooden staves had been transformed into a black-cloaked, seventeenth-century gent with long hair and a tricorne hat. Walker flashed open Lundy's cloak to show me. A risqué moment. Then he pinned the 'An End To All Traitors' placard on his back.

'He turned out to be a very respectable man,' he said. 'King William got him released from the Tower of London and he went on to fight good wars in Belgium. But he tried to sell this city. He was taking the keys out to King James when he climbed down the pear tree. When we burned him off Walker's column, there used to be rockets in him. Now that rockets are on sale again, people are saying we should start that again. But I'd be afraid of someone getting hurt. They'd take you to the cleaners.' Fireworks had been banned in the North during the Troubles.

Lundy is burned in several towns and villages around the North. Walker said the Apprentice Boys' rituals were relevant to the modern Derry. 'The apprentices showed us not to give up our religion so easily. Our youngsters don't have the freedom of this city the way we did. If the other side knew they were coming in to any of their bars, they'd fall upon them. People has called the governor himself a Lundy for a couple of things he gave away.' The governor, Alastair Simpson, had talked to the Parades Commission, and, through mediation, to the Bogside Residents' Group. The Apprentice Boys felt aggrieved, but had recognised the need to seek agreement. They were trying to make their annual pageant into a tourist attraction. On the touchstone issue of Drumcree, Simpson remained militant.

Walker said he had Catholic friends, and that he worked with Catholics too. 'You have to live with them, and that's it.' He had no time for Donncha Mac Niallais, a former IRA prisoner who was the leader of the Bogside Residents' Group. 'Donkey Nelis had started to shout. Then you've the rabble comes in behind him.'

An elderly man wandered in, a spruce figure with a hat and umbrella. 'An end to all traitors,' he read. He smiled: 'There's still a few of them about.' He lived, he said, in an estate in Lurgan which used to be totally Protestant. 'Mine is the last Protestant house left. I had three windows broken last week. They've a fortune wasted on eggs, pelting my house and my car. They can't pass my house without spitting. I would move out tomorrow but I'm just too stiff-necked.' He was in one of the Orders. 'I'm in a lodge that never meets in the same place twice. It's a travelling lodge, the lodge of research. I can only go so far within it, because I go to the synagogue. After the preceptory, it's Christian.' So he was a Jew. A Protestant Jew.

I stood in the December dusk on the steps of the Church of Ireland's large deanery to watch the burning. The deanery is one of many fine Georgian buildings in the wide streets within the walls. Behind it stands the Church of Ireland St Columb's Cathedral, with its lectern on which is engraved, 'A city that is built on a hill cannot be hid.' Mrs Cecil Alexander had worshipped there, and commemorated Derry in her children's hymn, 'There is a green hill far away,/ without a city wall,/ where our dear Lord was crucified,/ who died to save us all.' The cathedral had fragments of the original crimson flag which, during the siege, had signalled to the Williamite forces that the city was still loyal, and the cannon ball in which proposed terms of surrender were fired into the city.

Thousands of Apprentice Boys had gathered. As the huge figure blazed up, sparks showered out over the crowd. A lot of the men were drunk. The atmosphere was not vengeful or menacing as might be expected of a gathering to watch a ritual burning. It was debauched. I watched a fight which had to be abandoned because the two angry men were unable to land a punch, and kept flailing off after their fists to sprawl on the street. Lit up by the flames, a sober Alastair Simpson shook hands with other dark-suited dignitaries. William Coulter was with him. They looked proud and excited, and oblivious to the drunkenness around them. Behind me, the door of the deanery was slightly open. A glimpse of a crimson carpet and a sparkling chandelier. The young dean and his wife were watching the scene, discreetly.

Downtown, there was a pall of smoke, and sounds of clamour. 'The fenians are burnin' the town,' said a youth. The next day, photographs of Guildhall Square appeared in the papers, the Christmas decorations illuminated by a blazing car.

The summer demonstration of the relief of Derry tends to be more confrontational, because of the huge numbers of Apprentice Boys who come from all around the North. The year the Cloughfern Young Conquerors ran amok, I watched a squalid little riot. It was in the Diamond, the centre of the walled city, where the Boys had laid wreaths at the war memorial while young Catholics jeered. The loyalists were drinking cans and bottles of beer, and when they'd drained them, they flung them towards the Catholics who were behind barriers under the walls.

The Catholics were drinking pints, and when they'd finished they hurled the glasses towards the Protestants. The reporters were caught in a spray of stale beer. Another time, I'd wandered around the loyalist stalls in the Waterside with an English reporter who was looking for a copy of a tape he'd been told about, called 'The Pope's a Darkie'. He bought it to add to a collection which also included a baby's bib printed with 'Born to walk the Garvaghy Road'. After the August 1999 celebrations, young Catholics had engaged in serious rioting, resulting in millions of pounds' worth of damage.

Terence O'Neill had been called a Lundy, as had Brian Faulkner and David Trimble. David Ervine was another so designated. They were unionist leaders who had compromised. Ivan Cooper was a classic Lundy – he'd gone over to the other side. On 16 November 1985, the morning after the signing of the Anglo-Irish Agreement, the *News Letter*'s editorial said, 'At Hillsborough yesterday the ghosts of

Cromwell and Lundy walked hand in hand to produce a recipe for bloodshed and conflict which has few parallels in modern history.' David Keys was a Lundy – he was one of the LVF gang who murdered two young men at Poyntzpass, a Plantation village which straddles the border between counties Armagh and Down, in the spring of 1998. Philip Allen was a Protestant. His friend, Damien Trainor, was a Catholic.

Keys, who had 'helped the police with their enquiries', was found hanging in a cell at the Maze prison. The former RIR soldier had been tortured and beaten to death for his treachery. Afterwards, the prisoners daubed each other with his blood. That summer, as a mark of respect to the Allen and Trainor families, the Orange Order did not hold a parade in Poyntzpass. Lundy, however, was burned as usual.

'YOU LOOKED AFTER YOUR OWN'

'There was no such thing as gerrymandering,' said Jack Allen, veteran of the notorious Londonderry Corporation, which was abolished in 1969 in an effort to meet the demands of the civil rights movement. He'd said the same on the radio programme we were on, and Ivan Cooper had shaken his head and said, 'How can you possibly say that?'

Allen, a genial man with a ruddy face and white hair, talked to me in his big, old redbrick house in one of the Waterside's most established wealthy areas. 'This house was owned by two ladies who'd owned a shirt factory. I bought it in 1975,' he said proudly. It was quite a social leap for a young man raised in the Fountain, where his father was a bookmaker. He had worked his way up, he said.

In 1957 Allen joined both the Orange Order and the Apprentice Boys when he was sixteen and working in Tillie and Henderson's shirt factory. He started a fruit shop and went on to buy a pub on London Street, between the cathedral and the Apprentice Boys hall. While the argument about gerrymandering of electoral wards was raging in 1969, he had got married and bought a house in Belmont on the cityside. Three quarters of the houses in the area were owned by Protestants at that time, he said. He sold it again in 1975, when he 'fell in love' with the big house across the river. No, he said, he was not pushed out of the cityside. He was, in fact, pressurised to sell the house he was leaving to a Protestant, and he did so.

That was the year he was mayor and leader of the Unionist group on the council. 'The Unionists used to assist people to buy houses. They had a fighting fund to help them. They were in a strong financial position. We let out properties. It was our forefathers who made that possible.' The Orange Order still had its Ulster Land Fund. I'd seen notices in the Apprentice Boys hall, offering watches for sale in support of it.

'I was one of the first Young Unionists to be elected to a council in 1966. Bill Craig came to speak for me. The main gripe against the corporation was the lack of housing, but two-thirds of the houses built between 1945 and 1966 went to Catholics. I remember the re-development of the Bogside between 1966 and 1969. That was in-itiated by Unionists. The corporation was a fair-minded council of businessmen who were conscious of the cost to the ratepayer. They were very cautious. Admittedly, Unionists were criticised for the fact that the mayor allocated houses and was a Unionist.'

I asked him about discrimination in employment. In 1951 Catholics made up 43 per cent of the population, but less than 8 per cent of non-manual government employees of the council. In 1971, in Northern Ireland as a whole, Catholics were two and a half times as likely to be unemployed as Protestants, a statistic which had not changed significantly in 1981 (McCormack and O'Hara, p. 6). Jack Allen said it wasn't a matter of discrimination. 'It doesn't matter where you are, Belfast, Liverpool or Dublin – a father will try to get a job for his son. My own father did his utmost to get me a job. Most Protestant employers had Catholics in the workforce, and there were plenty of Catholic employers only employed Catholics. You looked after your own. Admittedly, Catholics in the city were in a minority. But things were changing. The situation was improving.'

David Trimble, in the speech he made on receiving the Nobel Peace Prize in 1998, admitted that Unionists had made a 'cold house' for Catholics when the northern state was set up, but Allen's view was gaining respectability again. Whereas militant loyalists might say things like, 'Yes, there was discrimination in the past but it's gone the other way now', in the mainstream, past wrongdoings were frequently denied. Several people referred me to a book called *Londonderry Revisited* by Paul Kingsley, which starts with Bernadette Devlin's description of Derry as 'the capital city of injustice', and goes on to deride the 'myth of the oppressed Catholics' and to dismiss the Cameron report's findings on the background of the Troubles. Kingsley said it was all aimed at causing a 'guilt complex' and making Protestants feel that some 'massive act of atonement' was required of them.

The book did not demolish the facts. It also degenerated into anti-Catholic ranting: 'We might again well ask of Ulster's minority: What sort of people are they? Well they are certainly not innocents' (Kingsley, p. 219). Catholics were 'cunning and manipulative', and Londonderry's Protestants were 'still beseiged in their frontier town'. Kingsley said Britain's failure to deal with the enemy had 'driven a loyal, law abiding people to resort to the use of Protestant paramilitaries'. Like Viscount Brookeborough, he concluded that if Catholics didn't like Northern Ireland, there was nothing to stop them leaving.

In September 1999 John Taylor said that reports of discrimination against Catholics under the old regime had been greatly exaggerated. In the same month, he announced that he considered the Belfast Agreement to have failed, and refused to take part in George Mitchell's review of the peace process. One of Trimble's advisers, Graham Gudgin, had made similar claims.

Taylor's adviser, Stephen King, had signalled this trend in a review of Kevin Haddick-Flynn's study of Orangeism in the *Irish Times* on 24 July 1999. King was popular with the media in the Republic – he sounded upper class, looked modern, and implied that he took a progressive line. He also boasted that he was the author of the 'Guns before Government' slogan, adopted by Unionists prior to the completion of the Mitchell review in 1999. He said that Haddick-Flynn had trotted out the 'common myth' that there was wholesale discrimination in housing under Stormont. King started by admitting that the 1969 Cameron Commission had presented a prima facie case of ' "blatant manipulation": 8,700 Protestants and 14,400 Catholics elected 12 Unionist councillors and 8 Nationalists'. He disposed briskly with this 'so-called gerrymander of seats in Derry', stating that, 'the Nationalist Party only ever put forward eight candidates and the Catholic vote was split between the Nationalists and the SDLP, while Protestants were almost uniformly Unionist'. Of the fact that 139 of 149 Unionists who sat at Stormont between 1921 and 1968 were Orangemen, he remarked, 'Many, though, like Terence O'Neill, would have joined out of a desire to advance their electoral prospects rather than any great fealty to the precepts of the Lodge.' These were strangely Jesuitical lines of argument.

The *Orange Standard* still makes a practice of listing the Unionist representatives who are involved in the Order. In August 1998 the list appeared beside an article about Trimble, illustrated by a photograph in which he was wearing his sash, his mobile phone characteristically pressed to his ear and a worried look on his face. The article was called 'Trimble's political demise?' The list included 8 MPs, 34 Assembly men and women, and one MEP.

Unionists have not been coy about their intentions in the past. In 1950 Tom Teevan, the chairman of Limavady Rural Council, said, 'In Londonderry City and County, where we should have been on our guard, our majority has dropped from 12,000 to a perilously low figure. How did that come about? Through the ruinous and treacherous policy, pursued unwittingly perhaps, of handing over houses owned by Protestants to Roman Catholics. It is also caused by the great employers of labour in the North of Ireland employing Roman Catholic labour' (quoted in Farrell, p. 89).

An Enniskillen councillor, George Elliott, said in 1963, 'We are not going to build houses in the South Ward [Unionist held] and cut a rod to beat ourselves later on. We are going to see that the right people are put in these houses and we are not making any apology for it' (Farrell, p. 88).

Jack Allen said that O'Neill had 'gone too far, too soon, without bringing people with him'. He was critical of Faulkner's resignation in 1974. 'He shouldn't have walked out. He was captain of the ship.' He repeated that change had been on its way. 'The border would go because we were entering Europe. It would have drifted away.' He had been elected to the Assembly in 1982, and went on to become the chairman of the party, then its treasurer, and the chairman of several committees. He had been a devolutionist, he said.

He blamed John Hume for the failure of the 1982–86 Assembly. 'John never wanted to be part of any establishment that had a pan-unionist front,' he said. He was on a joint DUP–UUP committee to oppose the Anglo-Irish Agreement. The Hume–Adams talks were a nationalist conspiracy: 'When Hume persuaded Adams in, I think he assumed that Unionists would leave.' He was on the UUP's negotiating team, 'a key player', in the talks which led to the Belfast Agreement. 'I don't think anyone thinks it's a good agreement. But you have people like Willie Ross who can't see any way forward. They think every Unionist has to be an Orangeman and look to the past. They can't adjust to change at all. Then you've Jeffrey Donaldson. He wanted to ride both horses. He's with us at meetings and then he goes out and tells the press he's not buying it.'

Allen was also election agent for Jim Nicholson in the 1999 European elections, and worked on the assumption that revelations about Nicholson's extra-marital affair would cost him perhaps 20,000 votes. The campaign had not been helped by John Taylor's declaration that he would not vote for Nicholson. Despite the unwillingness of the UUP to cut its formal links with the Orange Order, the Order urged its members to vote for Paisley, who was not an Orangeman. Nicholson got 119,507 first preference votes, just 2,000 more than Sinn Féin's Mitchel McLaughlin. It was enough to secure the third seat. Paisley had swept in on top, though he was just 2,000 votes ahead of Hume.

'TITANIC SHIFTS'

'At the YMCA you don't have to be young, male or a Christian,' said Mark Patterson, who was, himself, all three. He was director of the YMCA in Derry, and was in charge of a rising young soccer team, many of its players Catholics. Tall, athletic and energetic, he was more upbeat about being a unionist than anyone else I met. 'Old unionism was about keeping the Catholics out,' he said. 'Did you ever read Tom Paulin? He is just brilliant.' He bounced over to the shelves in his brightly painted living room in a terrace in the Waterside. 'Listen. This poem is about how the whole fifty years of Stormont, they only passed one bill that was put forward by a non-unionist.' He read 'Of Difference Does It Make' which describes a bird rapping out 'a sharp code design/ like a mild and patient prisoner/ pecking through granite with a teaspoon' (Paulin, 1993, p. 64).

'That's what it was like. Fundamentally wrong. I am a unionist. But it was a journey of rage. I would have been highly critical of the leadership in the past, so I have a moral obligation to help. I started to observe the peace process where there was a leader with a capital L, taking us out of the old psyche.' He had joined the UUP just before the ceasefires in 1994, and supported Trimble's leadership. He played in a band called Blue Room, and once, during a gig in London, dedicated a song to the leadership of unionism.

He played me a tape of one of his songs. It was called 'Sandal', after the prehistoric site in County Derry where the earliest known signs of human habitation in Ireland have been found. The band sounded a bit like Belfast soft rocker Andy White. Its anger was directed at 'heads full of yesterdays'.

Patterson was 'born, bred and buttered in loyalist Mourneview', a housing estate in Lurgan. 'But I journeyed away. I did a post-graduate course in youth and community studies, and I worked in the Irish communities in London, Cumbria and Kilburn, where I was the only Prod for miles around. The Irish in London had drawn a terrible lot. Unemployment, homelessness ... but they were sparky.' He had been part of the so-called 'brain drain' of young Protestant graduates from Northern Ireland. 'It's a Protestant thing, that dissenting thing, getting out and doing something. The frontier spirit. God's frontiersmen, as one writer put it.

'I felt very passionate about it, coming back. I will stand where thousands fall. I honestly felt I wanted to go back and make things better. Now the shoe is on the other foot. I see Protestants in Londonderry like the Catholic Irish in London, driven out, unwanted. The YMCA is the oldest voluntary charity in the city. It used to be based on the walls. It was a sister organisation of the Presbyterian Working Men's Institute in the Diamond. These are the old Reformed institutions. The YMCA was for apprentices.

'In the seventies it was firebombed, and it joined the exodus. It was like Moses having to get up and go to Israel. We came over with them. They made Harkin's fields into the pitch, just the same as the Glen had gone in houses.' This was the intimate geography of Derry, the seizing and losing of territory, field by field. Harkin had been a Catholic farmer in the predominantly Protestant village of Drumahoe, where the YMCA had built its new base. The Glen had been a Protestant area but had become almost entirely Catholic.

'We gave away 26 counties and only kept 6. No wonder people are fearful. Are we to be given away? Protestants are wary of cross-community things because of their experience of loss. The siege mentality is very real. I was speaking to a Protestant elder in Lurgan recently. He said, "We all know that Protestants had to give away some ground. But we feel we have done that, we have given the ground." Paisley is a fifties man, strong, aggressive against the enemy, principled. But his day has gone. We've observed titanic shifts from Sinn Féin, the UUP and the loyalist people.

'In Mourneview we would have stood up for the Queen when the TV shut down. Granda stood up and saluted. There's a class awareness now. We never identified with blue-collar Catholics. But the deaths were largely boys from blue-collar areas. In the season which we would call the present, they have good leaders now, in Ervine and Sinn Féin.

'I have an abiding contempt for the IRA and what they have done. They shaped my childhood. We were shrouded. We lived in Northern Ireland, a boil on the ass of Europe. My growing up was segregated, suspicious, surreptitious; sneaking about, knowing where you could go and where you couldn't. One wee piece of violence a day, a bomb, a murder. It absolutely paralysed a psyche. Where was art? The Miami band was murdered. It closed people. There was things you couldn't say. That affects a child. I'm still working with kids whose minds are poisoned.'

'Sam Shepard [the US playwright and actor] said the place to be in life was in the middle of a contradiction. Some of us hate Catholics but go out with Catholics. Have a wee sneaky court with Roisín and then go out and play with the flute band. You dodge the lines. Still, there is something in Protestantism which allows you to be free. The Irish identity is leprechauns, Guinness and U2. A tea towel – let's get pissed and pretend. The Ulster Protestant identity is harder to find.

'I am an Ulsterman and a European. I have a regional identity and a Covenantal nationality. When it comes to war, like the 36th Ulster

Division, we'll go with the crown. We got the province. We give our loyalty for our statehood.' He was excited by the work of Ian Adamson, Dalriada and Cú Chulain and the Cruthin and all that. 'There is a marvellous exhilarating journey there to find the identity of Ulster. The IRA's success was to make people believe that we were just visitors here, who came and took everything.' The song he'd played, 'Sandal', was about this, going back 'to get grounded'.

'This past couple of years, I feel completely at home here. There was an industrial free spirit that came with these people, a principle of industry, dissent, individualism, capitalism. You can't take photos of it, like you could of a *seisiún* or a sweet Irish colleen. It's about principles, not images.' Patterson said he had been a Christian since an evangelical experience in his teenage years. He didn't go to church though. 'I don't like what Ireland has done to the gospels. I would be a liberationist and where do you find liberation theology in Northern Ireland?'

I asked him about images of Orangeism. He turned out to be a passionate believer in the right to march. 'Aborigines have to walk the songlines. Orangemen have to walk their traditional routes. It's a vast minority who walk for supremacist reasons. I know hundreds of Orangemen and they are decent people. Pro-state people.

'It is a masculinist thing. If men don't spend time with older men, where do they find collectivity? The churches, the working men's clubs, they are gone. The Order remains. It is a powerful thing, men together. It is to do with forefathers. My dead grandfather is dishonoured if I don't walk.'

'I WOULDN'T TURN MY BACK TO THEM'

The photograph was of a middle-aged man looking mildly surprised in a small boat on the River Foyle. This was Brian Stewart's father, Jim, a Derry shopkeeper, who, after his west bank business had been destroyed by bomb after bomb, finally moved it to the Waterside. The family initially continued to live across the river on the cityside. Between bombs, bomb scares and RUC and army checkpoints, it could quite frequently take two hours to get across Craigavon Bridge. In the seventies the next bridge over the Foyle was fifteen miles away, at

Strabane. So, Jim Stewart spoke to a friend who had a boat, and became a waterborne commuter. Soon afterwards, the family followed the business to the Waterside.

Brian Stewart, now a Church of Ireland rector in Belfast, said Derry had not been as segregated as the bigger city. 'If you read *Holy War in Belfast* by Andrew Boyd, you find it was a Church of Ireland minister ranting and raving in Belfast started the riots there in the 1790s. Derry didn't have that history.' This thesis could be overstated – there had been sectarian violence in Derry before the sixties. In the twenties, for example, the security forces and the UVF had joined forces against the IRA.

'Certainly when I was growing up there, Derry people knew each other, through business and sport. City of Derry Golf Club was mixed. Derry had its own league which had broken away from the Irish Football Association. It was mostly Catholic, but mixed. My brother played football with Martin McGuinness. We grew up beside John Hume. His father was a self-taught accountant and he did my father's books. Fergal Sharkey of the Undertones lived out the back. My father often said his best customers were in the Creggan. You didn't get the tit-for-tat killings because of that intimacy.' Again, caution was necessary. In April 1981 one of those killed in Derry by the IRA had been a young woman called Joanne Mathers, who was collecting census forms in a nationalist housing estate not far from where she had grown up.

'My grandfather was on the council. When I was 12 or so, I realised my father had 2 or 3 votes in the local elections. Everyone uses this as an example of how Unionists disadvantaged Catholics, but it didn't only do that. It disadvantaged Protestants too.' This was one of the most frequent comments made by Protestants in any discussion about the civil rights of Catholics pre-1968. It was often used simply to end the discussion.

However, it was importantly developed at a conference by Ken Rooney from the Fountain Area Partnership. He was reporting back from a group discussion: 'Did the unionist parties ever really look after the interests of the Protestant working classes?' the group had asked itself. 'NO, and they are now jumping on the band wagon,' it had concluded (report of conference on Community Development in

Protestant Areas, Lisnaskea, 1991). This conclusion advanced the argument. Instead of Protestant grievance simply cancelling out Catholic grievance, it allowed room for disadvantaged Protestants to look critically at the politics of the élite within their own community. Stewart said there was a growing awareness of this. 'I know one fairly hardline loyalist who would say of the old Unionist establishment, "They were sore on the people."

'My father prospered. He had two shops on the cityside. One was blown up by the Provisional IRA and soon afterwards the other was bombed by the Officials. He used to joke that it was provisional, then it was official.' He remembered his father listening to the radio on Bloody Sunday. 'He said, "They've gone bloody mad. They've shot ten people dead." He saw it as a massacre.'

One of Stewart's cousins was in the UDA. Another cousin was killed when a bomb he and others were about to plant in a supermarket blew up prematurely. I was surprised. I hadn't heard of a loyalist bomb of this kind in Derry. 'It was the IRA,' said Brian. 'It was something which we didn't talk about much after that, in the family.' Some of Stewart's family had been workers in the supermarket. It didn't make any sense. Earlier that year, the two cousins, who were teenagers just a few years older than Stewart, had marched together in a UDA parade, wearing the gear favoured by the UDA at that time – 'a bum hat, dark glasses and flared combat trousers'. The UDA cousin had done time for armed robbery, and had long since left paramilitarism behind.

'My mother was steeped in unionism. My father was from Donegal and had an Irish passport. He walked out of the Orange Order, and none of us ever joined it.' Stewart was a drummer in a rock band at school, failed exams, travelled, 'bummed around', studied motorcycle engineering and came back to open a motorbike business in Derry. Then he changed tack and trained in Dublin to be a priest in the Church of Ireland. He was rector of St George's, a city centre church with a 'high' tradition, a famous choir and an unusually mixed congregation. 'We get all sorts of people, gays, divorced people, Protestant nationalists, people who were sort of lost elsewhere.' And an Anglican nun, Sister Anna, who came to Belfast with Mother Teresa and stayed. The Northern Ireland Mixed Marriage Association started at St George's.

Since 1995 he had been a member of the Catalyst group. 'In the light of the ceasefires, we wanted to make a contribution to dialogue. We decided to tackle sectarianism in the Church of Ireland.' The group published pamphlets and addressed such issues as the Church's stance towards political unionism, and its association with the Orange Order.

This became highly contentious. After successive years of violence at Drumcree, Catalyst wrote to the Reverend Pickering, asking him to stop inviting the Order to his church. They also wrote to the eight hundred or so ministers around the country, north and south, asking them to back them. Some 162 did so. In its pamphlet *Sectarian Divisions and the Church of Ireland Synod*, published in 1999, the group argued that the Orange Order was a religious political organisation which held sectarian tenets that were 'explicitly at odds with the ecumenical position of the Church'. It said that the Church had to address 'blatant contradictions' and if resolution was not found, there should be a 'parting of the ways'. Northern Ireland was 'still afflicted by theologically inspired hatred' and there were 'people whose minds were so possessed by such formulations that their defence justifies any action, including discrimination, violence and persecution'. At the 1999 Church of Ireland synod the findings of a sub-committee on sectarianism were addressed. Among other things, this committee had called upon the Orange Order to 'show itself a truly Christian movement' by demonstrating that 'love of God, love of neighbours and obedience to the New Testament principles take priority over party advancement' (report of the Church of Ireland Sub-committee on Sectarianism, p. 184).

The synod passed resolutions in relation to the flying of political flags from churches, the use of the language of the Thirty-nine Articles to promote anti-Catholicism, and Drumcree. However, according to Catalyst, the resolutions which were passed 'had no teeth'. One member said that they were so bland that they were almost meaningless, vacuous, 'an exercise in evasion'. Many of the clergy who backed Catalyst were in the Republic, and UUP deputy leader John Taylor questioned what he felt was the disproportionate influence of this section of the Church, considering that most members of its congregation were in the North. On the other hand, when Archbishop

Eames said the Orange Order had to make up its mind whether it was a political or a religious organisation, Orange members of the Church of Ireland pointed out that Eames had also made political choices when he became a member of the British House of Lords.

The Orange Order rejected Archbishop Eames's call for them to 'obey the law of the land'. Union Jacks and Orange flags still flew from church spires, and the Reverend Pickering invited the Orangemen to Drumcree as usual. 'The Church ended up looking foolish,' said Stewart. In 1999 Catalyst subsequently published a strongly worded pamphlet arguing that Drumcree had made a mockery of the Church's ecumenism. Its response to the report on sectarianism 'gives no assurance that the long-standing scourge of sectarianism as it affects the Church is to be tackled with urgency and determination'.

I asked Stewart if he had preached about Drumcree, and if he had advised his congregation on how to vote in the Belfast Agreement. 'I touched on Drumcree. I was critical of the Order and of the Church's stance. On the agreement I took a neutral line, though I said I would be voting yes.'

When we were talking, Stewart had referred to someone he knew as a 'typical Prod'. He was speaking approvingly. I asked him what he meant. 'Prods tend to come in, set their cards on the table, honest and open, no guile, clear cut and unambiguous. They want things in order – steps one to four. They have that common sense Scottish rationalism. They are very honest, and very moral. You can read them like a book. Working-class Prods have a great humanity – in the middle class you'd find that underneath the niceness the bigotry is dreadful.

'Republicans and nationalists are into the bigger picture – ideas – they are more fluid. Catholics have a more relaxed attitude to the details. They sit more easily with guile, a bit of slyness. The Shinners have the Unionists every time – they don't show their cards.' He spoke with some bitterness about Sinn Féin. 'They say they are separate from the IRA. Ha ha. Is the Pope a Catholic?

'The southern government still has the attitude that it was OK for them to put IRA men up against the wall and shoot them. But not for the Brits. I wouldn't trust Adams and McGuinness. They'll take all they can get and give nothing. I wouldn't turn my back to them.'

'THE GOOD OF THE CITY'

The idea that the IRA had succeeded in the twentieth century where James II had failed in the seventeenth, in uprooting the Protestants of Derry and driving them from the safety of their city, was a powerfully emotive one. But not everyone believed it. Brian Stewart had not been bitter about it, though he hated the IRA. Ian Young's motor parts business on the cityside had been bombed in the seventies, and he had relocated to premises on the Waterside, directly across the bridge from the old place which his father had established. But he did not accept the claim that what had happened had been ethnic cleansing.

'The move across the river was a natural one. People go to the place they feel safe. Don't forget there was a movement of Catholics from the Waterside to the estates on the cityside as well.' The Protestants were not a community of victims, he said. The gerrymandering which Unionists had carried out in the city had been a disgrace. 'I believe the Troubles started because of sheer frustration among the nationalist people in the north-west.

'I got to know Paddy Doherty through the Inner City Trust. They call him Paddy Bogside. I got him to understand the Protestant culture. I remember him showing me photographs of Catholics in Derry before the Troubles. He said, "Look at their eyes." You could see the pent-up anger and resentment there that was bound to explode. If the Unionists had made some effort, they might still be in power and we wouldn't have had this thirty years' disaster.'

For all that, Young was a unionist, though some other Derry unionists muttered that he was SDLP in all but name. A pillar of society, leading member of the Rotary Club, outgoing chairman of the Chamber of Commerce, and a member of many boards and committees. 'I'm an unusual unionist,' he admitted. 'I believe totally in economics. You can't eat flags.' He said that he and John Hume were 'like brothers', and he spoke of Hume with a passionate loyalty. 'John looks to me for a unionist viewpoint.' He had urged Hume to continue his secret talks with Gerry Adams when Hume was under severe pressure to abandon them.

'I always felt very Irish, though my heritage as a Protestant is very dear to me. I always thought the Protestants had made a very big contribution to this country. Indeed, if the Catholic Church hadn't ruined Parnell, we might be in a better place today. We are all born innocent. We become victims of our tradition. My father had been land steward to a big house in Donegal. It had been strategically built so that the settlers could see all the roads. King James had stopped and had tea in the garden there on his way to the siege. On his way back, he burned all the settlers' houses but spared that one.'

His father was an Orangeman. For Protestants, it was a large family, with ten children. They moved to Derry, and his father started the business. Young's sister, Marlene Jefferson, had been Derry's first 'lady mayoress'. 'We have all done reasonably well, and if you earn your living from a town, you have to give something back.'

He almost left, though. He even went to South Africa, where one of his sisters lived, to see what his prospects might be there. The country was lovely, but he didn't care for apartheid. He decided to wait. Then tragedy hit his family. His teenage son, a promising rugby player, dropped dead in the middle of a schools game. 'It was just like him being shot. I started to think deeply about the young people in the Troubles.'

Hume asked him to join the board of the Derry–Boston venture, which was attempting to promote trade between the north-west and the United States. 'The political situation was stagnant and everyone was saying no to everything. We decided to get off our backsides and do something. I decided to try to use my position in business to influence politicians. They were looking at old ideas. They had to look at the economy.

'The economies of the North and the South should have merged. We could have got a good deal. We could have been part of the Celtic Tiger. I said on BBC radio three years ago, if a united Ireland or a new Ireland came about by agreement, I would have no trouble with it – it would be a great place to do business.'

Young said he invited Irish-American business people to Derry, 'to see the complexities'. 'They thought it was all chickens in the kitchen and Brits kicking the natives. There is a secret in portraying the city. You have to give out an air of confidence.' He boasted about the figures he'd met. President Clinton, Presidents Robinson and McAleese, successive taoisigh. 'Not many people know this,' he said.

'I was responsible for getting David Trimble a platform in the United States. I brought him out, and what did he do? He attacked Irish-Americans. Instead of presenting the good side of unionism, the shipyards, the work ethic, it was this little Dad's Army, keep-your-hands-off-Ulster attitude. The businessmen nearly choked. Now he's out there nearly every week trying to regain that ground.

'If only Protestants would be more confident, more outward-looking. The reason nationalists have pushed forwards is because they have an aspiration. Unionists don't. They have the status quo. It is like the branch that won't bend – it'll break. Faulkner gave crumbs and lost the loaf. The trouble with Unionists is, they won't give an inch and then it has to be taken away. They continually gain the high ground only to throw themselves off it.' He said that bigotry was spread across all classes. 'If any middle-class person tells you they are not bigoted, they are telling lies. It is bred into us. I've sat in rooms with moderate middle-class unionists and when something comes on the TV they say things like, "Oh, they always catch our side and never the others." We are all to blame and we all have the ability to change.'

Young saw his relationship with Hume as, in a way, emblematic of the political situation in the north-west. 'The failed policies of the past came from Stormont. There was no willingness to develop the north-west. The north-west was chosen for transatlantic flights – the British blocked it. We could have had the main airport. The little bit of shipbuilding was bought out by Shorts. The M2 should have joined the two main cities, Belfast and Londonderry. The university should have been sited here. When the Unionists were in power we were left out because this was perceived as a nationalist town. They alienated the working-class Protestants in the process. I remember when a Unionist politician would come to town you practically had to bow down before him.

'There was a massive spend on the east coast. I can accept that Belfast has the critical mass. But Belfast is bulging now. The Making Belfast Work programme gets £26 million. Making Derry Work gets about £3 million. But we have developed our own new economic policy now, City Vision. The east–west divide will have to be addressed.'

The Derry–Boston link has not been universally applauded. Community and voluntary groups, like the Northern Ireland Community Development Agency (NICDA), have argued that it was based on a US model which had signally failed to help people in areas of the greatest need. NICDA pushed for development of indigenous industry and the social economy alongside inward investment from big international companies. A decade on, NICDA pointed to the withdrawal of such investors, and noted with satisfaction that its earlier arguments had been incorporated in the new City Vision programme. There was also the issue of ethical investment – there were protests when Hume and Trimble stood together in Derry to welcome a multinational arms company to the city in the summer of 1999.

Protestants had held a high proportion of skilled jobs in Derry – industrial decline meant that their areas had been badly hit. A recent study of Irish Street, a Protestant estate on the Waterside, and Galliagh, a Catholic one on the cityside, found remarkably similar levels of social need.

Young pointed out that a certain solidarity had been created because of the history of geographical discrimination. 'The unionist people here are in a minority, so they have to work with their nationalist neighbour. When it comes to the good of the city, you get Sinn Féin, the SDLP, the DUP and the UUP all singing from the same hymn sheet. To give you an example, all the parties support the move to bring natural gas to the north-west. When they brought it to Belfast the whole talk was of linking with Kinsale in County Cork rather than with us. We brought in consultants and put the figures to the government. We showed after a long battle that it was economically viable.'

He had been one of those mediating between the Apprentice Boys and the Bogside Residents' Group. 'In 1997 we were nearly there but the BRG was holding out against the flying of the Union Jack. I said to him that it was flown for the same reason the tricolour was flown in the Bogside. I said to Alastair Simpson, "why not fly the crimson flag?" He said that in 1688, the Union flag *and* the crimson flag were flown to tell William all was well in the city. I had to tell him there was no Union flag till after the Act of Union in 1801. So I said I'd check out what sort of flag they'd have had, and I got the RUC to check the archives. They found one – it's a green flag with an Irish harp and King William's insignia. The Apprentice Boys fly it now. It's their official flag. A policeman told me that on the day of the parade, the Derry Apprentice Boys were having difficulty explaining it to the Belfast ones.'

It was easy to imagine the indignation of 'the Belfast ones'. Derry was not the militant loyalist city it had been. That mantle had passed to Portadown. One former UDA man in Derry told me that when Belfast UDA people came to the city, they couldn't understand why it was so quiet, and assumed that there must be some sort of pact between loyalists and republicans. There were many reasons. It was a small city, so people knew each other. It was on the border, and many Derry Protestants had strong Donegal connections. There was a Catholic majority. Segregation had made a barrier of the River Foyle. The UDA in recent times had concentrated on 'punishment' attacks on members of their own community, and on attempts to intimidate Catholics out of housing estates.

In 1998 the city had a DUP mayor and a Sinn Féin deputy mayor. Despite his party's hostility to John Hume, William Hay, the mayor, attended and took part in a ceremony in the Guildhall to honour Hume after the award of the Nobel Peace Prize. Young's admiration for Hume was boundless, and he spoke with far more enthusiasm about the SDLP's Seamus Mallon, deputy first minister at Stormont, than about any Unionist figure, including David Trimble. He said the party leader had qualities but also 'a personality problem'. 'I would count myself a unionist with a small u. We need to stop breaking it into unionists and nationalists. There is only one sort of democracy, and it is about the will of the people.' Young's children were business people like himself. He said, if there was no settlement, his son would leave.

'I am a little bit pessimistic,' he admitted. 'But I must read you something, a poem by Seamus Heaney that I quoted recently . . .' He knelt down to sift through a stack of speeches to find it. It was the extract from *The Cure at Troy* which had taken on an added power after Heaney dedicated it to the people of Omagh, after the Real IRA bomb in 1998. Young read: ' "Hope for a great sea change on the far side of revenge/ Believe that a further shore is reachable from here . . ."

Isn't that lovely?

'I love profound sayings and quotes. I've looked out a lot of them. Here's another one. 'Tomorrow comes into us at midnight very clean. It is perfect in every way. It puts itself into our hands and hopes we have learnt something from yesterday.' That's from the headstone of John Wayne, the great American cowboy actor.'

'STUCK UP IN THE FAR NORTH-WEST CORNER'

Derry's Low Pay Unit, set up in 1998, was run by Jim McCracken, a Belfast man married to a Derry woman. He was one of the sceptics about the value of bringing in big companies from abroad. 'We advise on low pay and give a thrust towards social inclusion. We are trying to show that it's not enough just to get inward investors, who just take up the grants and then go. We are stuck up in the far north-west corner here, and unemployment is higher than elsewhere.' Problems were not confined to multinationals. 'We did a survey recently and found that 40 per cent of employers were advertising jobs with pay at less than the new minimum wage of £3.60 an hour. A lot of hairdressers' and security officers' jobs were as low as £1.50 – pocket-money wages. We also look at ACE schemes and the New Deal.'

ACE was a government scheme which had provided training and employment, albeit low paid, largely in disadvantaged communities. Many community groups employed small numbers of ACE workers, but Derry had had two huge schemes, known to cynics as the ACE empires, one run by Paddy Doherty, the early civil rights activist who had become known as Paddy Bogside, and the other by Glenn Barr, a former UDA leader in the Waterside. New Deal was the scheme with which Tony Blair had replaced it.

McCracken was born on the Shankill, on a street which, like Dermot Seymour's, no longer exists. He was baptised into the Church of Ireland, but found it bland by comparison with the 'fundamentalist Bible bashing' he learned at the Presbyterian Sunday school to which he was sent because it was nearer his home. He was sixteen in 1969. 'Like everyone else, I was basically a hooligan. Rioting was the best thing ever. I never had just such a brilliant time.'

However, he said he had soon developed a leftist view. 'I'd have thought it was all right to attack the security forces, but sectarian to attack Catholics. As time went on I began to see things from a republican slant.' His first marriage was to a Catholic, and they moved to a Catholic area. 'It wouldn't have been on to stay on the Shankill. For nineteen years I was basically a Catholic, without the benefit of the spirituality.'

On the Lower Ormeau Road he got involved in Workers' Party politics, informed, essentially, by the Communist Party. 'The communists were very genuine, but they were caught in a difficult situation. A lot of abuses of rights had been exposed. Before the collapse of the communist states, they had said claims about such abuses were just a bourgeois plot. There is very little capacity for self-criticism on the left.' He said there was no point in seeing the class war as the only issue in politics. 'Class is very important and the working classes here have lost out by paying no attention to it. But there's no use just telling people they have been oppressed and hoping that then they'll twig on and all will be well. If you assume that all truth lies in one particular view, you are wrong.'

He had worked on building sites in Belfast at a time when Protestant workmen took their tea breaks in one hut, Catholics in another. 'I left a job once because I felt it was getting dodgy. A few weeks later, two Catholics were shot on their way to the site.' He did A levels and a degree, and he moved to Bangor, County Down, in 1989. 'I moved from a Catholic area to a middle-class area. Once you move up the social scale, you leave all that behind. I never saw a Union Jack. It wasn't done. I remember someone saying that Bangor was getting a bit rough. Someone had been stabbed a month previously. I thought, a month ago and they're still talking about it? I had seen houses in Belfast blitzed with machine-gun fire, people shot in the street. I used to keep a tally of people I knew who had been killed – I stopped at twenty-three.'

He got involved on the left of trade union politics, got divorced, remarried and moved to Derry. His second wife was a Protestant and they lived in a Protestant area. 'I suppose I would be an atheist. I put myself down on the census as agnostic because I couldn't spell atheist. Catholicism is too hierarchical. I think I prefer Protestantism because of its democratic tradition, though Northern Ireland Protestants have gone for a kind of Calvinism which is anti-popery. They have sold their birthright for this rather uninspiring bit of land. They have forgotten the free-thinking, democratic side of Protestantism, respect for civil liberties.

'They seem to have missed the bits in the Bible about love thy neighbour and love thine enemy. They have let that go, out of fear and the siege mentality. They have accepted things that Christians shouldn't. There has always been this ambiguity about the killing of Catholics – they tend to regard loyalists as like unruly children. And yet, probably among the most progressive thinkers are the former paramilitaries. That is very strange to me – for years these were the people who terrified me.'

He said Protestant fears for their safety were not as deep and insidious as the fears experienced by Catholics. 'My wife's father was shot by the IRA. He was a policeman. She always feels under threat, but she never had the same feeling of vulnerability that Catholics have. If the worst came to the worst, Protestants could phone the police. However, having said that, Catholics don't understand that Protestants do have real fears.' He paused and laughed. 'I always feel I have to make the balancing statement.'

He didn't care for racial theories about the differences between Catholics and Protestants. The work ethic was a myth. 'Protestants like to think Ireland was a bog until we brought along spades and showed the natives how to dig. But Protestants have a great deal of integrity and they don't take readily to being told what to do. Barricading themselves into the top corner of the country was a mistake. I'd say, if there hadn't been partition, they would have been the dominant force in the country by now. We have been dragged back by the UK connection. Though if we were united, we would have to fight for a place in the Celtic Tiger economy, which by no means benefits the low-paid and unemployed. On both sides of the border, we have to break down this idea that to make the rich work harder, you pay them more, to make the poor work harder, you pay them less.

'I'm not so sure that this edifice of Protestantism and the British way of life ever really obtained here. As for all this Ulster Scots sort of stuff it is just pathetic. Still, if people want to go around speaking with a Ballymena accent, I suppose, what harm? I know a lot of lower-middle-class Protestants and they are quite calm. The business types just want a slice of the Republic's wealth. Europe will unite Ireland. The border doesn't mean much. I think there will be liberation. The lunatic fringe like the DUP will be discredited eventually. We have not plunged into the pit of hell, despite their constant warnings.'

'OUR SIDE – WHICH IS NO SIDE'

Hazel McIntyre is the author of historical novels which have been praised on popular television shows. When we spoke, one of them was about to be serialised in *Woman's Way*, a homely magazine. She is a regular contributor to arts programmes at BBC Radio Foyle, where we met. An intent, vivacious woman in her fifties, Hazel was eager to talk about being a southern Protestant in the North – though as she pointed out, with a gay laugh, she came from the top of the Inishowen peninsula, much further north than the North, so called.

She'd been brought up on Inishowen, on a farm, had trained as a nurse in England, and had returned to Ireland with her English husband. They had bought a house in Derry because her husband and son both worked in the city. But Hazel hated it. She did not seem at home at all in the bungalow in the Waterside, though she had lit a big coal fire and bought in cream buns the morning I came to interview her. It was a medium-sized redbrick bungalow in an estate of medium-sized redbrick bungalows, with a view of a flat green area with more medium-sized redbrick bungalows on the far side. 'There is no sense of community spirit here,' she said. 'There is a sense of fear. Down home, when the doorbell rings, you are delighted. Here, it may be someone collecting for the flute bands. I don't want to give to them, but there is an aura about them, an "or else" feeling. So you pay up. I keep a jar of coins beside the door. My son was in a dilemma once – he had only an Irish punt coin in his pocket. He gave it to them anyway.

'I don't know anyone in the estate. I get the feeling that people are afraid of each other here. It is supposed to be a mixed community but they want to keep themselves to themselves. They don't want to divulge anything. When my first book came out, I called to a couple of neighbours and they opened the door just a chink, took the book and that was it.

'My parents were very forward-thinking people. My mother was from a French Canadian family and my father was from Culdaff. McIntyre is a Scottish Highland name. We came from Catholic to Church of Ireland. My parents in their wisdom sent us to the local school, where we were the only Protestants. We were integrated. Religious difference didn't matter. I find the hatred and bigotry here across the border hard to understand. I have little or no sympathy with the Protestant cause, even though I'm one of them. I have northern relations. I remember them spouting politics when I was a child. The bits I could understand frightened me.

'In the twenties some of them moved across the border to the North. They didn't have to, though they might tell you so. Some of my family stayed, and some moved. The things the ones who left said annoyed the people back home, a peace-loving people, because what was implied was that they were driven out, and that was lies. The Protestant people in Donegal have a different outlook to Protestants here, though people would be more inclined to be bigoted if they have northern relatives. The government in the Republic has been more than fair. Maybe they've even gone too far.'

This was a far cry from the dark implications from Paisleyites that what had happened to Protestants in the Republic only just fell short of a massacre, and amounted to ethnic cleansing. If that view was apocalyptic and false, Hazel's was perhaps excessively benign. Essayist Peter Hart wrote that 'between 1911 and 1926, the 26 counties lost 34% of their Protestant population ... this catastrophic loss was unique to the southern minority and unprecedented: it represents easily the single greatest measurable social change of the revolutionary era' (Hart, p. 81). The trigger for the exodus was the IRA's campaign.

Hart described southern Protestants during this period as politically inert and deeply afraid. In her novel *The Last September*, Elizabeth Bowen similarly describes the old Anglo-Irish ascendancy in the South. The Troubles are all around, guns in the plantation, reports of shootings and burnings, a Catholic neighbour arrested. But the people in the big houses seem disconnected and impotent. They seem almost to have bowed to the inevitability that they are a finished people. A snatch of dialogue:

'How far do you think this war is going to go? Will there ever be anything we can all do except not notice?'

'Don't ask *me*,' he said, but sighed sharply as though beneath the pressure of omniscience. 'A few more hundred deaths, I suppose, on our side – which is no side – rather scared, rather isolated, not expressing anything except tenacity to something that isn't there – that never was there' (Bowen, p. 82).

De Valera declared that Ireland was 'a Catholic nation', the moral authority of the Catholic Church was enshrined in the 1937 constitution, and divorce and contraception were banned. The *Ne Temere* decree, which predated partition, was vigorously applied. It required that Protestants who married Catholics had to agree to bring up their children as Catholics. In 1957 in the County Wexford village of Fethard on Sea the local priest organised a boycott of Protestant businesses after a young woman defied the rules on children of mixed marriages. She was taken up as a great prize by Paisley. Edna Longley said the South practised apartheid in the same way as the North.

In the early years of the new southern state Catholicism was undoubtedly a repressive force – and not just to Protestants. It had been authoritarian. The institutions it ran under the unconcerned eyes of the government were, in many cases, characterised by remarkable cruelty. The diminution of its power had been hard won through long, gruelling campaigns on social issues. Its decline has been hastened in recent years by its arrogant handling of scandals involving clerical child abuse. Although it lost its constitutional 'special position' in 1972, a referendum to change the constitution to allow divorce was passed by a fraction of a percentage only in 1996. This, despite the fact that one of the arguments of the pro-divorce lobby was that the ban was discriminatory against Protestants, whose Churches had no objection to divorce. In 1999 the Catholic Church attempted to use the abortion issue to reunite its scattered flock, and regain its moral authority.

However, as John Brewer concluded in his study of anti-Catholicism, echoing the findings of John Whyte in his survey of studies of Northern Ireland: 'Southern Protestants never were a downtrodden and disadvantaged minority. Economically they were privileged and secure, and research shows them to be overrepresented in the upper reaches of the class structure.' Brewer added that 'there is evidence of considerable cultural assimilation rather than isolation or ostracism', and described myths and overstatements about the oppression of Protestants in the South as a form of secular anti-Catholicism (Brewer, p. 163). Southern Protestants have protested in the letters pages of the *Irish Times* that they are quite happy, and have no wish to be championed by northern extremists.

Hazel felt that Protestants complained too much, said no as a reflex, and were altogether too hung-up with being long-suffering martyrs. 'What does it mean this constant cry, "We have given and given and given." What have they given?' She said Protestants were unforgiving. She remembered evangelical preachers who travelled around Donegal when she was growing up. 'The Anglican Church was bland. But the evangelicals were different. Fear was the word. The preachers were deep-south-of-the-USA mixed with south-of-the-Bann. There is this anti-Catholic thing in it too, a political agenda. It is all interlaced with guilt. As for the Orange Order, it frightens me. To say that it is Christian is poppycock.'

She was, nevertheless, a churchgoer, 'when I feel the need', and admired certain characteristics of her people. 'They are honest and hardworking. They don't want to be beholden to anyone. But they haven't got the charm of the native Irish people.' She went to ecumenical services in St Columb's Cathedral, and sometimes to Catholic services. 'There are aspects of Catholicism that I don't like. I don't like the idea that my passport to heaven is the number of masses I attend. But the vast majority of my friends are Catholics, though many don't practise.

'I hate to see the sectarian emblems in the churches – the flags of the Orange Order in the cathedral. I applaud the Church of Ireland ministers who were brave enough to stand up to the Order. I went to an ecumenical service once with some people I knew from Donegal. The DUP was protesting outside – all the usual slogans, shouting and ranting. It was kind of dark and I was alone going in. I was a little afraid. When we came out, it seemed to be floodlit. I was taking note of what was written on the placards, and I saw that one of the protesters was one of my old neighbours from Donegal. I said to him,

"Oh my God, is this what you've come to?" A sheepish look came into his face and the placard came down over it. He was ashamed. If you were so sure, you wouldn't be ashamed.'

She had spoken a lot about fear, although not a strong fear, not terror. Her fear of the knock at the door. Fear of the political opinions she'd heard. Fear of the protesters in the dark entrance to the church. But it was not enough to silence her. 'I have relations who say to me, "I don't know where you get your ideas from." Most Protestants who feel as I do would be afraid to speak out. I try to encourage those who do.'

'THE MOST IMPORTANT WORD IS RESPECT'

Derry, for Inez McCormack, represented 'the first time of freedom'. It was where, as a student in the sixties, she first became engaged in political struggle. She had not deviated from that path. In 1999 she was appointed to the North's new Human Rights Commission, and became president of the Irish Congress of Trade Unions, declaring that she would fight for the rights of the most excluded groups, and the poorest-paid workers. It was what she had always done. We spoke at the home she and her husband, academic Vincent McCormack, had bought on Inishowen. They would move there from their present home in north Belfast, she said, when she retired. It was a lovely house, with a view out over the Atlantic. The bookcases, made by a local carpenter, were full of books about human rights.

Born in east Belfast, McCormack was brought up in Holywood, County Down. Her father was a self-employed printer, her mother a nurse who gave up her job when she had her children. Her brother had left school early and started out selling advertising space for the *Belfast Telegraph*. He had moved to South Africa in the seventies and become a wealthy businessman. She remembered 'not fitting in' at primary school, and she didn't bother to do the eleven plus. Her parents, however, sent her to Glenola Grammar School. 'I was one of the first state primary school pupils to attend. It was an enormously snobbish atmosphere.' She didn't fit in.

'My father took me into the business when I was sixteen. After a year, I left, and left home. I got a clerical job in the civil service. They asked me at interview how I'd feel if my brother married a black.' That was in 1963, the year O'Neill became prime minister and said that his task would be to 'transform Ulster'. His civil service was not going to be much help to him. As former senior civil servant John Oliver noted in his memoirs, 'mediocre men were being encouraged, grey figures were beginning to predominate' (quoted in Bardon, p. 624). McCormack said it was an agreed thing within the service that no Catholic should get beyond the staff officer grade. 'They couldn't be trusted.' Another woman who worked in the service during this period told me that she had discovered that the woman who had been in her job before her had routinely sifted out and destroyed applications from Catholics.

McCormack did not fit in. She decided to study, got A levels and a place at Magee College in Derry. It was the time of the campaign to get the new university sited in the city, and the community seemed united. Afterwards, suspicions arose that there had been Unionists who, behind the scenes, had been working to undermine the campaign they claimed they supported. McCormack remembered that seven dummies had been hung from the cannons on the walls. 'They called them the seven faceless men. The people who betrayed Derry. I didn't understand the connotations.'

She hadn't really understood, either, that Magee was the Presbyterian theological college. 'The history teacher was the historian of the Orange Order. I remember meanness of spirit and of purse, repressed young men who'd arrange to meet you inside at the dance, so they wouldn't have to pay for you. A minister described dancing as "using your legs as the devil's drumsticks". I was picking up that things weren't right. You were warned not to go through the Bogside. You didn't know what would happen there. It was a place with no lights.' She finished her degree at Trinity in Dublin. She didn't fit in.

Back in Belfast, she did a secretarial course, and met Vincent, a Catholic from the Bogside. He was giving a lift to a man who had come to take her flatmate, a beauty queen, out on a date. It was 1967. 'He was in all the debates.' She was thrown out of the course, and she and Vincent set off to hitch around Europe. 'It was the summer of the Vietnam demos, a summer of complete joy. We were in London. It was Carnaby Street and one job after another. It was also taking part in demos and listening to Catholics talking about the North. I had

grown up in a world where there were no Catholics, so they hadn't
been mentioned.'

They were in a youth hostel in Portugal in October 1968 when
Derry came on the television. 'We hitched back immediately.' On the
way they met students who had been on the barricades in Paris. When
they got home they took part in the Burntollet march. 'It changed my
life fundamentally. I remember puzzlement and fear. Being hit.
Members of my family going on about "these IRA people and communists".' She was in Derry when the RUC 'invaded the Bogside and
beat up Sammy Devenney'. Mr Devenney died later of his injuries. An
inquiry by a British police officer found a 'conspiracy of silence'
among the RUC. McCormack reckoned that night had been 'written
out of history'.

She and Vincent got married. She had gone with her husband to
take statements from the Devenneys. 'I was struck by the terror, the
lack of law. I came from a background which saw the RUC and the B
Specials as defending a way of life against evil, upholding law and
order. A cousin of mine, a B Special, had been killed in what my
family called "the outrages". Now I was among people who referred
to that period as "the fifties campaign".

'My husband was writing a book unmasking the role of the B
Specials and the RUC at Burntollet. I remembered the pain in the
family when my cousin was killed. The not-very-bright boy who had
joined to get off the small farm and had been immensely proud when
he was accepted into the forces. You had to try and put these things
together. I felt an outsider in my own background, and an outsider in
this one. Although I was an actor, I felt like an observer.'

It wasn't about the IRA. It was the 'quiet knowledge' of people like
her husband's family. It was about people dressing up in their Sunday
best to go on civil rights marches. 'The fundamental thing was the
passionate anger about the daily humiliations – no jobs, kids with
asthma because the flat was damp. There was something wrong at the
core of Northern Ireland. The Protestants saw it as the IRA rising. It
was "them" trying to get in. I had crossed a line. I was therefore a
rebel.' She remembered being pushed down stairs by a big priest in
Belfast. 'I had extremely long legs and wore extremely short skirts. I
was a prostitute as far as he was concerned.' Within the civil rights

movement, she typed while men argued. 'Apart from Bernadette, women did the typing. Feminism hadn't hit yet.'

She did a diploma in social work and got a job in Ballymurphy, in west Belfast. Conditions were appalling. Her employers referred to it as 'bandit country'. The state started to take back the money Catholics had withheld during the campaign of civil disobedience in 1971 (in protest at the introduction of internment). 'I phoned the civil service and said, "Look, this woman needs her benefits. She is trying to feed her kids." They said, "She could always withdraw her conjugal rights and make her husband pay the rent."' She remembered gunfire and women keening. 'Also the bombs in the city centre, the killing of people from my background. Not believing it was the way to do it.' She lost a baby and became ill.

Then she started to work part-time for the trade union movement. She was five months pregnant when she was interviewed for her first full-time job. 'I went into a shop and asked for a dress that wouldn't show I was pregnant. All the women in the shop entered into the conspiracy. At the interview I was asked, "How would a young girl like you deal with a dockland meeting?"' She got the job, and plunged into feminism, largely through fighting for equality for women in the unions. 'I remember the brutality and excitement of those early years in the women's movement. There were no crèches. Married women with children weren't really acceptable. But women were part of other struggles which didn't acknowledge them. Within the unions, it was impermissible to raise issues of discrimination and women. They said it was divisive. It was male sectionalism.

'They put me on the Equal Opportunities Commission and the Fair Employment Commission to shut me up.' She withdrew from the EOC in 1978 in protest at its failure to enforce the law and rejoined it as deputy chair after it was restructured. She resigned from the FEC in 1981, claiming it was ineffective. Unemployment figures that year showed that the rate of Catholic male unemployment was still two and a half times higher than Protestant male unemployment. The differential for women was slightly less. 'We argued in the eighties that legislation wasn't enough. You had to have a statutory responsibility to test all policy to see that it promoted equality. This was resisted tooth and nail.' Along with John Robb, she was one of the signatories of the MacBride Principles.

In 1989 a new Fair Employment Act was introduced, with a tribunal to hear complaints. In 1992 the new commission reported that Catholics were still significantly underrepresented at senior levels in the public service, and a leaked civil service report indicated that substantial investment would have to be made in areas of high Catholic unemployment. McCormack was by this stage working for the National Union of Public Employees (NUPE). 'We started to build a coalition. Privatisation of the health services was affecting women's jobs. We applied the equality guidelines and got the Equal Opportunities Commission to investigate. What they called "efficiency" was only achieved by removing the rights of the poorest women in favour of giving more money to managers.'

The equality coalition fought a 'powerful battle,' she said. 'We frightened the employers, and the workers were proud.' McCormack saw in these struggles the beginnings of a process which would lead to the inclusion in the Belfast Agreement of the human rights for which the workers, through their unions, had campaigned. NUPE had become a branch of UNISON, with McCormack as regional secretary. 'We brought virtually all the political parties on side. The coalition brought workers and community activists from both communities together. It saw Protestant workers on the same side as groups which had criticised the RUC, together with ethnic groups, disability action groups and women's groups, and using tools whose background was in the struggle for black equality in South Africa and the United States, and Catholic equality in Northern Ireland. Our members had been seen as dirt, the bottom of the Thatcherite heap. The campaign was about the ability to participate, and not be humiliated by exclusion. The most important word is *respect*.'

She directed considerable anger at the civil service. 'The Northern Ireland Civil Service did much to destabilise things. They have a semi-racist mentality combined with an almost complete lack of accountability. They had loved administering Thatcherism. They believed the worst about people and they refused to change. But the ordinary people were changing. The dispossessed were arguing that money should go to where the greatest needs were. The civil service was saying that this was divisive. The Northern Ireland Office and the civil service have at various stages insisted that important and necessary change was impossible.'

In the end, the wording they fought for became the basis for the equality section in the Belfast Agreement. 'The way the agreement is written is spellbinding. We went through it page by page with our members – and they are from the tough areas. We didn't address the constitutional issues. The Catholics were very quiet. They understood the Protestants were struggling. It was so ... honourable. One Protestant woman said, "There's a lot in this I don't like, but I suppose that is what an agreement is about."' UNISON went on to campaign for a Yes vote in the 1998 referendum. 'For thirty years the stuff I was talking about was unacceptable. Now it's in the centre of the agreement.'

McCormack was one of those appointed to the new Human Rights Commission, chaired by Professor Brice Dickson, and set up under the terms of the agreement in 1999. There was an immediate storm of protest from unionists who claimed that nobody from a unionist background had been included. 'I have a track record of bringing people from both sides together. I would argue that I've fought for civil rights and values which are part of the Protestant tradition. Partnership, fairness and mutual respect – these are the values of conscience and therefore Presbyterianism. They are in the agreement, and a majority of Protestants voted for them.

'The challenge is to Protestants who are demoralised to recognise why relationships based on rights should make them feel bad. You don't have a right to a sense of identity which depends on dominating others. Middle-class people are going to have to realise that they can't live in a world without worries. The Protestant middle ground will always say there is a hidden agenda. But if you insist that to name an injustice and tackle it is divisive, then you are endorsing that injustice. That's the hard question for Protestants. It is not about *mea culpa*. It is about accepting responsibility. If believing in one's conscience in relation to human rights is not Protestant, what is?'

EPILOGUE

'Southern trees bear strange fruit,
Blood on the leaves and blood at the root.'

from 'Strange Fruit', ABEL MEEROPOL, sung by BILLIE HOLIDAY

'THE MOTE AND THE BEAM'

My grandfather was an Orangeman. I have a photo of him, a hard wee man in a bowler hat and sash, a determined look in his eye. As children, we used to be allowed to look at the sash, folded up in tissue paper in its box in the sideboard. He was a Black man and a Mason as well. The Granda Rodgers we loved, though, was also a teller of jokes, blower of smoke rings, presser of half-crown coins into small hands, and grower of roses and strawberries. I was twelve when he started shouting at the TV. It was 1969. 'There's one bad wee tinker,' he'd shout when Bernadette Devlin appeared.

He worked in the linen factory. He got a council house for his family in the new White City estate in Dungannon, after a word in the ear of a Unionist councillor. The next-door neighbours were Catholics. They got on fine. When my mother and her sister got scholarships to go to the high school, my granda was all for getting them into the factory instead. Grammar school! People would say they were getting above themselves. My granny, a Tipperary woman who'd come North as a house maid, put her foot down, and they continued their education. I have come to realise that my grandfather was a very typical, traditional working-class northern Protestant. He knew his place.

A friend of mine went on the Burntollet civil rights march in 1969. She was a student, from Dungiven, not far from Burntollet. When the march was ambushed at the bridge she ran into the river. She saw a man she knew, a neighbour, lashing into another student with a nail-studded stick. A couple of weeks later she was hitching home from college in Belfast. Her neighbour pulled up in his van, as friendly as could be, and brought her to her door, where she thanked him. Burntollet was not mentioned – nor would it have been even if neither of them had been there. Good neighbourliness in the North depends largely on a taboo on speaking of politics in 'mixed company'. Bizarrely, Protestants with anti-Catholic views may not want to express them in front of Catholics for fear of causing offence. After the murders of the Quinn brothers in Ballymoney, County Antrim, in July 1998, John Robb had described politeness as 'the ruination of this country'. In the *Belfast Telegraph* of 14 July 1998, he is quoted as saying that by avoiding the issues we had 'created a monster which has practically devoured us all'.

When I was researching this book I found that some people were very reluctant to talk without knowing which 'side' I was from. Some people asked directly. Others asked indirectly. Others said they'd talk to me, but made evasive polite conversation, waiting, I knew, for me to let them know. I said I was 'from a Protestant background'. Then a different story sometimes emerged. A woman who had said stiltedly that 'everyone gets on really well round here' told me she was sick and tired listening to nationalists whingeing, when she knew right well all they wanted was to put an end to Protestantism.

As far as faith is concerned, I went to church, irregularly, as a child, and was bored. I am thrilled by Patti Smith's song 'Gloria', with its opening line, 'Jesus died for somebody's sins – but not mine', but I also respond emotionally when I hear psalms like 'The Lord Is My Shepherd'. I do not go to any church now. I prefer Louis MacNeice's idea of 'God or whatever means the good', but feel the yearning in John Hewitt's lines: 'Yet like Lir's children banished to the waters/our hearts still listen for the landward bells' ('An Irishman in Coventry'

Collected Poems, 1991, p. 98). I suppose I am what the fine northern blues singer Henry McCullough calls a 'Failed Christian' – his magnificent song a sort of Protestant anti-hymn. An agnostic, then, but a Protestant agnostic. I had a Protestant upbringing in a largely segregated society. The voices I heard in my childhood were Protestant voices. By and large, there was a belief in the state and its institutions, though some of the voices were critical.

Later, as a feminist living in the Republic, I was involved in struggles against the oppressive influence of the Catholic Church on issues of social justice for women.

John Brewer called his excellent book *Anti-Catholicism in Northern Ireland, 1600–1998: The Mote and the Beam*. The biblical reference is to St Matthew: 'Why beholdest thou the mote that is in thy brother's eye, but considerest not the beam that is in thine own eye? ... Thou hypocrite, first cast out the beam out of thine own eye: and then thou shalt see clearly to cast out the mote out of thy brother's eye' (Matthew 7:3–5). It is not a passage which biblically minded northern Protestants often quote. I have not attempted, in this book, to balance Protestant views with a Catholic perspective, or to criticise things said or done by Catholics, nationalists or republicans. This is a study of the people I uneasily call my own.

Frank Wright wrote that it was impossible to understand conflict in the North without looking at relatively peaceful times. He quoted speeches made at a trade union march in Belfast in 1870, by a Liberal and by an Orange Unionist MP. The Liberal spoke about the march as the dawn of progress, a demonstration of 'unanimity and brotherhood' which proved 'how trifling, after all, are the differences' between Catholic and Protestant workers. The Orange MP said that 'there were times and circumstances when religious differences and party creeds must be forgotten' but at other times what was necessary was to be 'manfully asserting your beliefs and acting upon them' (quoted in Wright, 1996, p. 215). Wright described the Orange Order as a system of 'communal deterrence'. A constant warning. We haven't gone away, you know.

The Orange Order does not exist to provide a family day out once a year, though many Protestants do enjoy the Twelfth of July simply as a carnival. Increasingly, though, Drumcree has become the focus, not the Twelfth. People talk about 'Drumcree week' coming up. Drumcree turned nasty with the advent of the peace process, and has got nastier since the ceasefires. The threat was not violence, it was political compromise. As in the 1790s, Orange Protestants were lawabiding citizens until the law was used against their interests. The security forces were fine when they were 'ours'. The Order's depiction of the rulings of the Parades Commission as 'bad law' has a long historical lineage. Portadown has become the new Derry, the last bastion of No Surrender. A Protestant town for a Protestant people. 'If we're bate at Portadown, we're bate.'

In 1999 two women were murdered by loyalists there. One was Rosemary Nelson, a brave, intelligent and articulate lawyer who represented the Garvaghy Road Residents' Coalition in their battles with the Orange Order. She had become the voice of Portadown Catholics. A bomb under her car one ordinary Monday morning in March silenced her for ever. The other was Elizabeth O'Neill, a Protestant woman whose family said she had lived for her little grandchild. She had been living for more than twenty years with her Catholic husband in an estate which had become strongly loyalist in recent years. She was killed in June by a pipe bomb, thrown into her home in the early hours of the morning while she was watching television.

The Protestant North has its culture of dire warnings, biblical tracts in phone boxes, blowing in the wind. There is a liking for biblical desolation. A fatalism that revels in predicting the reaping of whirlwinds. Optimism does not come so easy. Derek Mahon writes of the lure of 'bleak afflatus', and in a recent poem described 'a glimmer of hope indefinitely postponed' ('Death in Bangor', *The Yellow Book*, 1997, p. 52). Paisley's apocalypse is a self-fulfilling prophecy.

It is easy to recognise Paisley's extremism. His opposition to the Catholic Church is explicit, and he has stated that Irish Catholics are united behind the 'beast of fascism', the IRA. But extreme statements from UUP politicians like John Taylor have attracted less attention. In 1979 he went so far as to suggest that if loyalist paramilitaries couldn't desist from violence, they should restrict it to the South (*Irish Times*, 31 August 1979). In 1991 he told young unionists that the 'harsh reality' was that 'one in three Catholics one meets is either a supporter of murder or worse still, a murderer' (quoted in *Fortnight*, October 1991). Other unionists have contributed to the general idea that the enemy is the Catholic population. A Derry UDP spokesman claimed in 1997 that Protestants could be forgiven for believing that all Catholics supported the IRA. Others claim that the paramilitary policy of 'terrorising the terrorist' by terrorising the Catholic community was what stopped the IRA in 1994. Some condemn the paramilitaries, but admit the effectiveness of their campaign. When DUP-type sources are quoted in the media, unionists who consider themselves progressive tend to distance themselves, while simultaneously attesting to some reality behind the material quoted. Among the middle classes there is much coasting, in the Hewitt sense, the rejection of the extremist, followed by the ambivalent 'there's something in what he says'. Similarly, while the Free Presbyterian Church is explicit about its politics, other Church leaders prevaricate, issue woolly statements, stop short of taking decisive action.

David Trimble led his people, hesitantly, to the Belfast Agreement. Afterwards, there was no celebration of the achievement, no affirmation of the Protestants who had backed him. It soon appeared that he was at least emotionally convinced by the arguments of the No bloc within his party. During the 1999 talks to 'save' the Belfast Agreement, Paisley was openly praying for failure. Trimble seemed merely to be waiting for it. At the UUP conference that year he reminded delegates that 17 per cent of the Catholic population voted for Sinn Féin, so they had to be part of a settlement. However, substantial numbers of Protestants believe that Catholics who vote for Sinn Féin are voting for an evil campaign of violence, and that therefore they are unable to regard them as having democratic rights. When, subsequently, the UUP went into government with Sinn Féin, Trimble said the party had jumped – but it became clear in early 2000 why it had kept its safety harness on, as it scrambled back to safety on the cliff top. To date, Trimble has yet to shake the hand of Gerry Adams.

One of the most commonly expressed ideas among Protestants is that 'the other side is better at propaganda than us'. Diane Greer's story about the Derry loyalist woman who said nobody was killed on Bloody Sunday is an extreme example. A variation is exemplified by the man in Portadown who said if the riots looked bad, it was 'because the TV cameras are against us'. When the UUP rejected the Way Forward proposals by the British and Irish governments in the summer of 1999, Chris McGimpsey said on an RTÉ television programme, 'We knew we'd be blamed.' Unionists revel in this ourselves-against-the-world stance. But just because everyone says you are wrong, does not mean you are right.

Many Protestants resist ideas of a shared history. They complain that Catholics have appropriated history and pushed them out. Community activist Michael Hall published a book which told the legends of the mythical Ulster hero Cú Chulain in cartoon form. He did so in an effort to show young loyalists that there were stories with which Protestants as well as Catholics could identify. He was exasperated when loyalists reacted by claiming that Cú Chulain had been seized back from the republican plunderers. They saw him as a sort of prototype UVF man, all muscle and primed for violence. Hewitt's great line about fables 'which gave us martyrs when we needed men' might equally apply if 'monsters' was substituted for 'martyrs'.

That Protestants are 'more sinned against than sinning' is debatable. But that idea can be used to avoid self-criticism. There is the 'what aboutery' syndrome, where people say, 'Of course that is wrong, but ...', and then move into a tirade against some worse atrocity by the 'other side'. It is allied with the romanticising of the past, when Catholics came to the Twelfth, or saved the Protestant hay, and all was well. Claims that anti-Catholic discrimination is a myth merge dangerously with this view of the past, and feed into the idea that what happened in 1968 was simply that the treacherous Catholics rebelled; the rebellion was against a good state, and therefore should simply have been crushed. At Drumcree, and in places where there is a large Protestant majority, there are plenty of voices advocating that there is still time to do just that. There is a constant sense of threat – ceasefires notwithstanding – an attachment to the legally held shotgun which has little to do with fear of the rabbit or the fox.

Brewer points out that the 1641 massacre is used by loyalists to endorse Covenantal theology: 'Protestants drew the obvious apocalyptic moral that their divine election was challenged by the idolaters and heathens, making them like the Israelites who needed to war with the Canaanites before the promised land could be theirs' (Brewer,

p. 28). The brutal violence of the IRA has similarly served Protestant ideas that what was going on was simply a war of good against evil. The good defend; the evil attack. The good have a right to their weapons; the evil must be disarmed. Those who consider themselves to be God's chosen people are inclined to be dangerous, wherever they turn up.

'FOR GOD AND ULSTER'

'Strange Fruit', Billie Holiday's brooding, chilling song, is about the lynching of black people in the southern states of America. The song captures the hideousness of lynching, but also the way white people in that society see themselves – 'Pastoral theme of the gallant south ...' Its mood seems apt to the murders of Bernadette Martin and James Morgan in the heady, drink-fuelled excitement of the loyalist summer of 1997. The Morgan murder was uncannily similar to another killing which occurred that year in the United States. It happened in the southern town of Jasper. A black man, James Byrd, was walking home when two local white men picked him up in their truck. The men talked about having picked up 'a nigger'. They beat him with a monkey wrench, kicked him, then tied him to the back bumper so that he was torn apart as the truck drove along, and his limbs were left strewn along the road.

James Morgan was on the Newcastle Road, not far from his home, when he was picked up by two local men who set upon him with a hammer. After they 'finished him off' they set fire to him and flung his body in a pit of decomposing animals. James Byrd was attacked because he was black. James Morgan was attacked because he was a Catholic. Both bodies were so hideously mutilated that they could only be identified by dental records. The killers of James Byrd had been drinking. One of them quickly confessed. Norman Coopey told the RUC he had been high on drink and drugs. He went to them the following morning. The other person who took part in the murder of James Morgan is still at large. The US killers hated blacks. David Ervine of the PUP said of those who killed Bernadette Martin and James Morgan that they simply hated Catholics.

The US killers were of the class which has been described as 'poor white trash'. They had come under the influence of the neo-Nazi Aryan Brotherhood while in prison. It is linked with the Christian Identity Church, founded in the 1940s by a member of the Ku Klux Klan on the belief that white Americans are the inheritors of the Israelites. Its pastors urge patriots to prepare for apocalyptic confrontations.

The Ku Klux Klan came to Jasper after the horrible murder had taken place. The Grand Wizard told a crowd that they should celebrate white pride: 'We will read about the guilt imposed on you by the Jewish-controlled media. It's time to quit apologising! Quit apologising for being white!' Ed Vulliamy reported that the Grand Wizard told the blacks that they were walking on diamonds in Africa, 'but none of you thought to pick one up till the white man told you' (quoted in *Guardian* magazine, 11 July 1998). There are those who hold similar ideas about Catholics in pre-Plantation Ireland. The aggressive self-pity is also familiar. The paranoia about government among these far-right groups is also replicated in the North. There are posters in Portadown which say: 'David Trimble – MI5 agent.' The US Anti-Defamation League produced a booklet warning that the line which separated the mainstream from the fringe was a porous one: 'When pernicious hate seeps into the mainstream dressed as political rhetoric, it threatens to legitimise intolerance and exclusion as an acceptable means for social change' (*Guardian* magazine, 11 July 1998).

In 1999, in the weeks before Rosemary Nelson was murdered, a leaflet was circulating in Portadown. It accused her of being part of a Jesuit conspiracy which also included Father Eamon Stack, formerly involved with the Garvaghy Road Residents' Coalition, and Breandán Mac Cionnaith. Residual fears, fanned up, turn to hatred. When David Trimble convened talks about Drumcree in May 1999, not long after Rosemary Nelson's murder, anti-Trimble loyalist protesters jeered at nationalists as they went in: 'Where's Rosemary?' Some people translate their hatred into a militaristic ethnic solidarity and into violence. Later in 1999 the neo-Nazi Combat 18 organisation held a meeting in Portadown.

Writing about Kosovo and the way Slobadon Milosevic used nationalist demagoguery as a strategy for electoral survival, Michael

Ignatieff described how the Serbs, who felt 'a combustible mixture of genuine grievance and self-pitying paranoia' were readily ignited (Ignatieff, p. 42). It is because differences are so minor that they must be expressed with such aggression, made absolute. He described the process whereby the individual in an ethnic conflict has to repress aspects of their own experience in order to dissolve their identity into that of the group.

One of the killers of James Byrd knew him, and had often given him lifts before. Norman Coopey lived in the same area as James Morgan. Trevor McKeown knew Bernadette Martin as the girlfriend of his friend, part of his social circle in the village of Aghalee. He had to wipe out that intimacy when he murdered her. She had to become just a 'taig'. As Ignatieff puts it, the foot soldier 'must do a certain violence to himself to make the mask of hatred fit' (Ignatieff, p. 51).

Protestants who want it to be clear that they do not hate Catholics sometimes describe themselves as 'not staunch', or 'not a strong Protestant'. It is as if the bigots had captured Protestantism, and 'proud to be Prod' was a status only available to those whose pride meant putting down Catholics. A majority of Protestants voted for an agreement which committed them to equality and democracy. In autumn 1999 the Confederation of Employers, along with the trade union movement, again urged the political parties to do a deal. At the inquest for a Catholic boy, Damien Walsh, who had been murdered by loyalists in 1993, an elderly Protestant man from the Shankill gave evidence. The gunmen had come to his house, and taken his car keys at gunpoint. They warned him not to leave the house, or he would be shot. As soon as they drove off, he rushed out to raise the alarm. He cried at the inquest, because his efforts to stop the murder had failed. But he had tried.

Former paramilitary Billy Mitchell said the loyalist sabre had been sheathed and so mainstream unionists could no longer rattle it. His efforts to keep it sheathed were strenuous. But it is obvious that others in the Protestant community need to do more to isolate dangerous ideas which intensify distrust and fear, and inexorably lead to anti-Catholic violence.

In February 2000, I wrote an article in the *Sunday Tribune* about the brutal knife murders in Tandragee, County Armagh, of two teenage

Protestants, Andrew Robb and David McIlwaine, by feuding loyalists. One man with a knowledge of the local paramilitary scene said he was shocked by the excessive violence used – the boys' throats had been slit. 'There's none of the local boys would be capable of doing that,' he said. 'Not to Protestants anyway.'

When Billy Wright was around he used to drive through Catholic areas – a glimpse of King Rat staring out of his car window was enough to terrorise. Billy Mitchell compared loyalist paramilitaries to Frankenstein's monster. One of Ian Knox's cartoons shows two crocodiles, one large and wearing a dog collar with a Bible in his hand, the other smaller, in a sash and bowler hat. Both hold the control leads of a little robot – Frankenstein's monster with a sledgehammer in one hand, a gun in the other, wearing a T-shirt with the initials of the loyalist paramilitary organisations on it. The crocodiles are weeping copiously. One of them says, 'So much hatred.' The other: 'Where does it all come from?' (Knox, p. 106).

The great American short story writer Eudora Welty's 'Where Is the Voice Coming From?' has as its narrator the poor white farmer who shoots dead a black civil rights leader. Loyalist killers have listened to voices too. In 1966, after one of the first sectarian murders, the *Belfast Telegraph*'s editorial said that Protestants should 'have nothing to do with those who have been sowing dragon's teeth, and can now see how terrible the harvest can be. Ulster is in danger of being thrown back into a dark past by sectarian forces which have too long been winked at by many who should know better' (quoted in McKittrick, *et al*, p. 29).

No one could have imagined then just how terrible the harvest would be. Protestants were the victims, but also the perpetrators. There are monsters which have to be faced down, but there is much to be proud of too. There is honest ground to stand on.

BIBLIOGRAPHY

Anderson, Don. *14 May Days: The Inside Story of the Loyalist Strike of 1974*, Gill and Macmillan, 1994

Bangor Grammar School, Report of the Independent Inquiry into the School's Handling of Complaints Made to It About Dr Lindsay Brown, DENI, July 1998

Bardon, Jonathan. *A History of Ulster*, Blackstaff Press, 1992

Bell, Desmond. *Acts of Union: Youth Culture and Sectarianism in Northern Ireland*, Macmillan, 1990

Bowen, Elizabeth. *The Last September*, Penguin, 1987

Brewer, J.D. *Anti-Catholicism in Northern Ireland, 1600–1998: The Mote and the Beam*, Macmillan, 1998

Bruce, Steve. *The Red Hand: Protestant Paramilitaries in Northern Ireland*, Oxford University Press, 1992

Coleman, Stephen. 'Public feedback in a divided space', *Public*, no. 2, vol. 5, 1998

Coulter, Colin. 'The culture of contentment: the political beliefs and practice of the Unionist middle classes', in Peter Shirlow and Mark McGovern (eds), *Who Are 'The People'? Unionism, Protestantism and Loyalism in Northern Ireland*, Pluto Press, 1997

Edwards, Ruth Dudley. *The Faithful Tribe: An Intimate Portrait of the Loyal Institutions*, Harper Collins, 1999

Farrell, Michael. *Northern Ireland: The Orange State*, Pluto Press, 1980

Farrell, Michael (ed.). *Twenty Years On*, Brandon, 1988

For God and Ulster, Pat Finucane Centre, 1997

Haddick-Flynn, Kevin. *Orangeism: The Making of a Tradition*, Wolfhound Press, 1999

Hall, Michael. *Ulster, The Hidden History*, Pretani Press, 1989

Harnden, Toby. *Bandit Country: The IRA and South Armagh*, Hodder and Stoughton, 1999

Hart, Peter. 'The Protestant Experience of Revolution in Southern Ireland', in Richard English and Graham Walker (eds), *Unionism in Modern Ireland*, Macmillan, 1996

Heaney, Seamus. *North*, Faber and Faber, 1992

Hepburn, A.C. *A Place Apart: Studies in the History of Catholic Belfast, 1850–*

1950, Ulster Historical Foundation, 1996

Hewitt, John. *The Collected Poems of John Hewitt* (ed. Frank Ormsby), Blackstaff Press, 1991

Hezlet, Arthur. *The 'B' Specials: A History of the Ulster Special Constabulary*, Mourne River Press, 1997

Ignatieff, Michael. *The Warrier's Honor: Ethnic War and the Modern Conscience*, Vintage, 1999

Jones, David, James Kane, Robert Wallace, Douglas Sloan and Brian Courtney. *The Orange Citadel: A History of Orangeism in Portadown District*, Portadown Cultural Heritage Committee, 1996

Kennedy, Billy (ed.). *A Celebration: 1690–1990. The Orange Institution*, Grand Orange Lodge of Ireland, 1990

Kingsley, Paul. *Londonderry Revisited*, Belfast Publications, 1989

Knox, Ian. *Culture Vultures: Political Cartoons 1990–99*, Blackstaff Press, 1999

Lacy, Brian. *Siege City: The Story of Derry and Londonderry*, Blackstaff Press, 1990

Longley, Edna. *Poetry in the Wars*, Bloodaxe, 1986

The Living Stream: Literature and Revisionism in Ireland, Bloodaxe, 1994

Longley, Michael. *Poems 1963–1983*, King Penguin, 1985

The Ghost Orchid, Cape Poetry, 1995

McCormack, Vincent and Joe O'Hara. *Enduring Inequality: Religious Discrimination in Employment in Northern Ireland*, National Council for Civil Liberties, 1990

McDonald, Henry and Jim Cusack. *UVF*, Poolbeg, 1997

McKittrick, David. *Through the Minefield*, Blackstaff Press, 1999A

McKittrick, David, Seamus Kelters, Brian Feeney and Chris Thornton. *Lost Lives: The Stories of the Men, Women, and Children who Died as a Result of the Northern Ireland Troubles*, Mainstream, 1999B

McMinn, J.B. 'Liberalism in North Antrim 1900–1914', *Irish Historical Studies*, no. 89, vol. 23 (May 1982)

McVeigh, Robbie. 'Symmetry and asymmetry in sectarian identity and division', *Journal for Community Relations Trainers and Practitioners* (summer 1997)

Mahon, Derek. *Night-Crossing*, Oxford University Press, 1968

Poems 1962–1978, Oxford University Press, 1979

Courtyards in Delft, Gallery Press, 1981

The Yellow Book, Gallery Press, 1997

Mitchell, Gary. *Tearing the Loom and In a Little World of Our Own*, Nick Hern, 1998

Moloney, Ed. 'Asking the right questions', in Michael Farrell (ed.), *Twenty*

Years On, Brandon, 1988

Morrow, Duncan. 'Suffering for righteousness' sake? Fundamentalist Protestantism and Ulster politics', in Peter Shirlow and Mark McGovern (eds), *Who Are 'The People'? Unionism, Protestantism and Loyalism in Northern Ireland*, Pluto Press, 1997

Murtagh, B. *A Study of Belfast's Peacelines*, University of Ulster, 1995
Community and Conflict in Rural Ulster, University of Ulster, 1996

O'Brien, Sean. *The De-regulated Muse*, Bloodaxe, 1998

O'Dowd, Liam, Tim Moore and James Corrigan. *The Irish Border Region – A Socio-economic Profile*, Queen's University Belfast, Department of Sociology, 1994

Oliver, Quintin. *Working for Yes: The Story of the May 1998 Referendum in Northern Ireland*, The Yes Campaign, 1998

O'Regan, John (ed.), *Dermot Seymour*, Gandon Editions, 1995

Paisley, Ian. *Northern Ireland – What is the Real Situation?*, Bob Jones University Press, 1970

Paulin, Tom. *Selected Poems 1972–1990*, Faber and Faber, 1993
Writing to the Moment, Faber and Faber, 1996
The Wind Dog, Faber and Faber, 1999

Richardson, Norman (ed.). *A Tapestry of Beliefs: Christian Traditions in Northern Ireland*, Blackstaff Press, 1998

Ryder, Chris. *The Ulster Defence Regiment – An Instrument of Peace?*, Methuen, 1991
The RUC 1922–1997: A Force Under Fire, Mandarin, 1997

Songs of Honour and Glory, UVF, n.d.

Stewart, A.T.Q. *The Narrow Ground – Aspects of Ulster, 1609–1969*, Faber and Faber, 1977; reissued by Blackstaff Press, 1997

Taylor, Peter. *Provos: The IRA and Sinn Féin*, Bloomsbury, 1997
Loyalists, Bloomsbury, 1999

Templegrove Action Project. *Hemmed in and Hacking it*, Guildhall Press, 1996

The True Story of South Armagh, FAIR, 1999

200 Years in the Orange Citadel – A Nationalist Perspective, submission to the Parades Commission, 1999

Wallace, Roy. *Goodbye Ballyhightown*, 1995

Whyte, John. *Interpreting Northern Ireland*, Clarendon Press, 1998

Wright, Frank. *Two Lands on One Soil: Ulster Politics Before Home Rule*, Gill and Macmillan, 1996
'Protestant ideology and politics in Ulster', *Journal of European Sociology*, vol. 14 (1973)

Wright, Max. *Told In Gath*, Blackstaff Press, 1990

INDEX